Monetary Policy

Studies in Business Cycles
Volume 29

National Bureau of Economic Research
Conference on Research in Business Cycles

Monetary Policy

Edited by   N. Gregory Mankiw

 The University of Chicago Press

Chicago and London

The University of Chicago Press, Chicago 60637
The University of Chicago Press, Ltd., London

Paperback edition 1997
Printed in the United States of America
03 02 01 00 99 98 97   2 3 4 5
ISBN: 0-226-50308-9 (cloth)
ISBN: 0-226-50309-7 (paperback)

Library of Congress Cataloging-in-Publication Data

Monetary policy / edited by N. Gregory Mankiw.
        p.   cm.—(Studies in business cycles; v. 29)
     Includes bibliographical references and index.
     1. Monetary policy—United States—Congresses.   I. Mankiw, N.
  Gregory.   II. Series: Studies in business cycles; no. 29.
  HG540.M653   1994   94-16029
  332.4'973—dc20   CIP

Relation of the Directors to the
Work and Publications of the
National Bureau of Economic Research

1. The object of the National Bureau of Economic Research is to ascertain and to present to the public important economic facts and their interpretation in a scientific and impartial manner. The Board of Directors is charged with the responsibility of ensuring that the work of the National Bureau is carried on in strict conformity with this object.

2. The President of the National Bureau shall submit to the Board of Directors, or to its Executive Committee, for their formal adoption all specific proposals for research to be instituted.

3. No research report shall be published by the National Bureau until the President has sent each member of the Board a notice that a manuscript is recommended for publication and that in the President's opinion it is suitable for publication in accordance with the principles of the National Bureau. Such notification will include an abstract or summary of the manuscript's content and a response form for use by those Directors who desire a copy of the manuscript for review. Each manuscript shall contain a summary drawing attention to the nature and treatment of the problem studied, the character of the data and their utilization in the report, and the main conclusions reached.

4. For each manuscript so submitted, a special committee of the Directors (including Directors Emeriti) shall be appointed by majority agreement of the President and Vice Presidents (or by the Executive Committee in case of inability to decide on the part of the President and Vice Presidents), consisting of three Directors selected as nearly as may be one from each general division of the Board. The names of the special manuscript committee shall be stated to each Director when notice of the proposed publication is submitted to him. It shall be the duty of each member of the special manuscript committee to read the manuscript. If each member of the manuscript committee signifies his approval within thirty days of the transmittal of the manuscript, the report may be published. If at the end of that period any member of the manuscript committee withholds his approval, the President shall then notify each member of the Board, requesting approval or disapproval of publication, and thirty days additional shall be granted for this purpose. The manuscript shall then not be published unless at least a majority of the entire Board who shall have voted on the proposal within the time fixed for the receipt of votes shall have approved.

5. No manuscript may be published, though approved by each member of the special manuscript committee, until forty-five days have elapsed from the transmittal of the report in manuscript form. The interval is allowed for the receipt of any memorandum of dissent or reservation, together with a brief statement of his reasons, that any member may wish to express; and such memorandum of dissent or reservation shall be published with the manuscript if he so desires. Publication does not, however, imply that each member of the Board has read the manuscript, or that either members of the Board in general or the special committee have passed on its validity in every detail.

6. Publications of the National Bureau issued for informational purposes concerning the work of the Bureau and its staff, or issued to inform the public of activities of Bureau staff, and volumes issued as a result of various conferences involving the National Bureau shall contain a specific disclaimer noting that such publication has not passed through the normal review procedures required in this resolution. The Executive Committee of the Board is charged with review of all such publications from time to time to ensure that they do not take on the character of formal research reports of the National Bureau, requiring formal Board approval.

7. Unless otherwise determined by the Board or exempted by the terms of paragraph 6, a copy of this resolution shall be printed in each National Bureau publication.

(Resolution adopted October 25, 1926, as revised through September 30, 1974)

Contents

Acknowledgments

This volume is the result of the efforts of many people beyond the authors and discussants. Staff members of the National Bureau of Economic Research helped in organizing the conference on monetary policy and putting together this collection of papers. I would like to mention in particular Geoffrey Carliner, Kirsten Foss Davis, Martin Feldstein, Deborah Kiernan, Mark Fitz-Patrick, and Lauren Lariviere. John Driscoll, a graduate student at Harvard, provided assistance in editing this volume, as did two anonymous reviewers. The Bradley Foundation provided financial support. To all these, I owe my gratitude.

Introduction

N. Gregory Mankiw

Monetary policy is not easy. Central bankers have multiple objectives and, over time, must confront a variety of economic circumstances. They know their actions have powerful effects on the economy, but the timing, magnitude, and channels of those effects are not fully understood. Their job is made all the more difficult by widespread disagreements among economists. Some economists view monetary policy as a potential cure for economic fluctuations. Others would be satisfied if monetary policy could avoid being a cause of fluctuations.

Just as there are many facets to the making of monetary policy, there are many facets to research on the topic. In January 1993, the National Bureau of Economic Research and I brought together a group of prominent macroeconomists in Islamorada, Florida, to present and discuss new research on monetary policy. This volume is the result.

Many topics are addressed in the papers that follow. As readers of this volume will learn, these authors do not always agree with one another. What binds these authors together is a conviction that monetary policy is important, and that it can be improved by serious, practical research. The papers collected here offer a sampling of that research.

The first three papers discuss alternative ways of conducting monetary policy. Martin Feldstein and James Stock study how the Fed could use the broad monetary aggregate M2. Robert Hall and I discuss the role of rules in the making of monetary policy, especially rules aimed at targeting nominal income. Michael Woodford examines the theoretical question of how one should judge alternative indicators for monetary policy.

A longstanding question in monetary economics is how much information is

N. Gregory Mankiw is professor of economics at Harvard University and director of the NBER Program in Monetary Economics.

contained in monetary aggregates and how the Fed might use that information. Feldstein and Stock argue that the Fed could use M2 to reduce both the average rate of inflation and the volatility of growth in nominal gross domestic product (GDP). They reach this conclusion by deriving an optimal M2 rule from a vector autoregression. This rule would, they conclude, reduce the standard deviation of annual GDP growth by over 20 percent. In addition, they consider a simpler policy based on a single equation linking M2 and GDP. They show that this policy is almost as successful in reducing nominal GDP volatility.

Feldstein and Stock also address the question of whether the link between monetary aggregates and economic activity is sufficiently reliable to form the basis of policy. They apply a battery of recently developed statistical tests for parameter stability. These tests do not detect any evidence of instability in the link between nominal GDP and M2. By contrast, the links between nominal GDP and more narrow monetary aggregates are found to be highly unstable. Feldstein and Stock interpret this evidence as contradicting those who have argued that the M2-GDP link is so unstable that it cannot be used to improve monetary policy.

Hall and I begin by discussing the desirability of a rule for monetary policy and the characteristics a good rule should have. We emphasize, in particular, three types of nominal income targets, which differ in how they respond to past shocks to prices and real economic activity. A key question is how any of these rules might be implemented in practice. We suggest that the consensus forecast of future nominal income could play a role in ensuring that the central bank does not deviate from its announced target. To show how economic performance might have differed historically if the Fed had been committed to some type of nominal income target, we offer simulations of a simple model of the economy. According to the simulations, the primary benefit of nominal income targeting would have been reduced volatility in the price level and the inflation rate. Whether real economic activity would have been less volatile is unclear.

Woodford's paper considers how one might judge the usefulness of various indicators for monetary policy, especially indicators other than measures of the money supply. Several policymakers and commentators have, in recent years, suggested that commodity prices, exchange rates, and interest-rate yield spreads could be useful in conducting monetary policy. Advocates of using such indicators often point to the historical forecasting performance of these indicators. In the spirit of Lucas's famous critique of econometric policy evaluation, Woodford argues that reduced-form forecasting regressions are of little value. Evaluating indicators for monetary policy, he argues, requires the use of structural econometric models.

The next three papers in the volume analyze the behavior of prices. Monetary policymakers monitor inflation closely, for inflation is a key measure of economic performance and, in the long run, is determined primarily by monetary policy. The short-run behavior of prices, however, is less well understood.

The papers by Alan Blinder, Laurence Ball, and Michael Bryan and Stephen Cecchetti take three quite different approaches to raise our understanding of prices and inflation.

Blinder's paper offers a new way of judging alternative theories of price adjustment. Blinder reports on a survey in which he asks firms about their behavior. He confirms that prices are indeed quite sticky: the typical price in the U.S. economy is changed once a year. Breaking with standard methodology in economics, Blinder also asks firms about which theories best describe their behavior. He finds, for example, that firms are highly concerned about coordination issues when considering price changes. This survey evidence should help us distinguish among alternative theories for the stickiness of prices.

Because prices are slow to adjust to changes in monetary policy, reducing inflation usually involves the temporary cost of high unemployment and low output. This cost is often summarized in a number called the sacrifice ratio: the ratio of the loss in output to the fall in inflation. Ball's paper investigates the determinants of the sacrifice ratio. He develops a method for estimating the sacrifice ratio in individual disinflation episodes, and applies it to sixty-five episodes in moderate-inflation countries in the Organization for Economic Cooperation and Development (OECD). Ball finds that the sacrifice ratio is usually smaller in more rapid disinflations. That is, when reducing inflation, cold turkey is less costly than gradualism. In addition, the sacrifice ratio is smaller in countries with more flexible wage-setting institutions, such as shorter labor contracts. Ball also examines whether the initial level of inflation, the openness of the economy, or incomes policies influence the sacrifice ratio, but the results are not decisive.

Inflation watchers, both inside and outside central banks, are always on the lookout for increases in inflation. Whenever a report on inflation is released, they face the difficult job of disentangling short-term noise from longer-term trends. Bryan and Cecchetti address this problem by considering alternative measures of core inflation, which they define as the persistent component of inflation. Although standard measures of inflation are the *average* over many goods, they suggest that the *median* rate of inflation may provide a superior measure of core inflation. They reach this conclusion using a model of asymmetric supply shocks with costly price adjustment. In this model, skewness in the cross-sectional distribution of inflation can cause short-term noise in the aggregate price index. This short-term noise affects median inflation less than it affects average inflation.

Bryan and Cecchetti document the statistical properties of core inflation as measured by the median. They find that median inflation is more correlated with past money growth and delivers better forecasts of future inflation than does average inflation. Moreover, unlike average inflation, median inflation does not forecast future money growth. Bryan and Cecchetti interpret this finding as suggesting that monetary policy has often accommodated supply shocks, which they measure as the difference between average and median inflation. They also compare alternative measures of core inflation: the consumer price index excluding food and energy, the 15 percent trimmed mean, and the median. They find that the median has the strongest relationship with past money growth and provides the best forecast of future inflation.

The next two papers examine the monetary transmission mechanism—the channel through which the central bank's actions affect spending on goods and services. The traditional view of the transmission mechanism, called the "money view," holds that contractionary monetary policy reduces spending by raising interest rates. Recently, attention has centered on an additional channel of monetary policy—the reduction in bank lending that must accompany a reduction in reserves. The papers by Anil Kashyap and Jeremy Stein and by Jeffrey Miron, Christina Romer, and David Weil offer alternative perspectives on the importance of this new "lending view."

Kashyap and Stein survey the recent literature—both theoretical and empirical—on the lending view of monetary policy. The traditional money view assumes that there is one important distinction among types of assets: assets used for transactions (money) and those held only as a store of value (bonds). By contrast, under the lending view, there are three types of assets: money, bonds, and bank loans. Like bonds, bank loans earn interest, but they are not perfectly substitutable with bonds. Banks make loans presumably because loans offer a higher return than bonds, while borrowers need these loans because they do not have access to bond markets. According to the lending view, when the central bank reduces reserves, it not only raises the interest rate on bonds, but it also reduces the supply of bank loans. Kashyap and Stein's paper offers a brief history of thought on the lending view, examines its theoretical foundations, and reviews the empirical evidence.

Miron, Romer, and Weil examine changes over time in the importance of the lending channel. They begin by using a simple theoretical model to isolate the observable factors that affect this channel's strength. They then show that several changes in the economy—the composition of bank assets, the composition of external firm finance, and reserve requirements—should have made the lending channel stronger before 1929 than during the period immediately after World War II. Yet, they show that conventional indicators of the importance of the lending channel, such as the spread between the loan rate and the bond rate and the correlation between loans and output, do not exhibit the predicted decline in the importance of the lending channel. They suggest two possible interpretations of these results. Either the traditional indicators are not good measures of the strength of the lending channel, or the lending channel has not been quantitatively important in any era.

The final paper in this volume, by Matthew Shapiro, builds on the pathbreaking work of Christina Romer and David Romer. Romer and Romer identified dates when the Fed appears to have shifted its policy toward reducing the rate of inflation. Shapiro's paper examines the causes and effects of this decision. He constructs variables measuring expected unemployment and inflation and then uses these variables in a model to explain the Fed's actions. He reports that the model does a good job of explaining the Fed's decisions to disinflate. Moreover, as one might have expected, the Fed appears to weigh the outlook for unemployment as well as that for inflation in making its decision about disinflation. Surprisingly, Shapiro finds little evidence that inflation in fact falls after the Romer dates. The Volcker disinflation is found to be the only disinflation to have reduced inflation permanently. The disinflation after the 1973 OPEC price increases was effective, but only temporarily. Other "disinflations" had negligible impacts on the rate of inflation.

The nine papers in this volume contain many intriguing results. Yet, surely, there is more work to be done. Many of the new empirical findings reported here deserve greater scrutiny using data from other time periods and other countries. I hope that readers will both learn from the papers in this volume and be inspired to undertake further work on these important and exciting topics.

1 The Use of a Monetary Aggregate to Target Nominal GDP

Martin Feldstein and James H. Stock

This paper examines the feasibility of using a monetary aggregate to influence the path of nominal gross domestic product (GDP) with the ultimate goal of reducing the average rate of inflation and the instability of real output. We measure the strength and stability of the link between the broad monetary aggregate (M2) and nominal GDP and we assess the likelihood that an active rule for modifying M2 growth from quarter to quarter would reduce the volatility of nominal GDP growth.

Our general conclusion is that the relation between M2 and nominal GDP is sufficiently strong and stable to warrant a further investigation into using M2 to influence nominal GDP in a predictable way. The correlation between nominal GDP and past values of M2 is, of course, relatively weak, so the ability to control nominal GDP is far from perfect. Nevertheless, the evidence suggests that a simple rule for varying M2 in response to observed changes in nominal GDP would reduce the volatility of nominal GDP relative to both the historic record and the likely effect of a passive constant-money-growth-rate rule. Our calculations indicate that the probability that this simple rule reduces the variance of annual nominal GDP growth over a typical decade is 85 percent.

The paper begins in section 1.1 with a discussion of the goals of monetary policy and of the specific form in which we shall assess the success of alternative monetary rules. Section 1.2 presents several alternative monetary policy rules that will be evaluated in the paper. Section 1.3 then discusses three issues

The authors thank Ben Friedman, Greg Mankiw, Ben McCallum, Steve McNees, John Taylor, Mark Watson, and an anonymous referee for helpful conversations and suggestions. They thank Graham Elliott for research assistance.

Martin Feldstein is the George F. Baker Professor of Economics at Harvard University and president of the National Bureau of Economic Research. James H. Stock is professor of political economy at the Kennedy School of Government, Harvard University, and a research associate of the National Bureau of Economic Research.

that must be resolved if a monetary aggregate is to be useful for targeting nominal GDP. These include not only the strength and stability of the link between nominal GDP and M2 but also the apparent inability of the Federal Reserve to control M2 in the short term and the risk that a more explicit use of a monetary aggregate to target nominal GDP would weaken the statistical relationship we have found in the historic evidence (that is, the so-called Goodhardt's Law problem).

In section 1.4 we present evidence about the strength of the link between M2 and nominal GDP and discuss Granger causality tests for the entire sample and for subsamples. Section 1.5 presents more explicit tests of the stability of the link between M2 and nominal GDP. Our focus on M2 reflects a belief that a broad monetary aggregate is likely to have a stronger and more stable relation with nominal GDP than a narrower aggregate. We test this assumption in section 1.6 by examining the strength and stability of the link from the monetary base and M1 to nominal GDP, and find strong evidence of instability in both the base/GDP and M1/GDP relations. There is much literature on the link from financial variables to output (recent contributions include Bernanke and Blinder 1992 and Friedman and Kuttner 1992, 1993a), and our results on the apparent usefulness and stability of the M2/GDP relation are at odds with some of it. As we explain, this is due to our focus on nominal rather than real output, to particulars of specification (we explicitly adopt an error-correction framework), and to our use of recently developed econometric tests for parameter stability.

Sections 1.7 and 1.8 then derive an optimal rule for targeting nominal GDP in a simple model and compare its performance with simpler alternative rules. Although a considerable amount has been written on the theory of nominal GDP targeting, fewer studies have examined the practical aspects of nominal GDP targeting; notable exceptions are Taylor (1985), McCallum (1988, 1990), Pecchenino and Rasche (1990), Judd and Motley (1991, 1992), and Hess, Small, and Brayton (1992). The investigation in sections 1.7 and 1.8 is in the spirit of these studies, except that we focus on probabilistic statements about the size and likelihood of improvements that result from using M2 to target nominal GDP. Section 1.9 examines the predictive validity of our M2-based time-series models by comparing them with private forecasts. Section 1.10 then returns to the question of the Federal Reserve's apparent inability to control the M2 money stock and discusses how that problem could be remedied by broader reserve requirements with interest paid on those reserves.

1.1   The Goals of Monetary Policy

It is widely agreed that the goals of monetary policy are a low rate of inflation ("price stability") and a small gap between actual real GDP and potential real GDP. There is general agreement that a low long-term rate of inflation can be achieved by sufficiently limiting the rate of growth of a broad monetary aggregate over a long enough period of time.

All the monetary policy rules that we consider in this paper are compatible with achieving any particular long-run average rate of inflation. Moreover, in the models that we consider, the short-term monetary policy rule that is selected does not affect the ability to achieve a low long-term average level of inflation. Technically, we are assuming that the Federal Reserve could set the long-run inflation rate by the identity that mean inflation equals mean money growth plus mean velocity growth less mean real output growth. Empirical evidence suggests that the long-run mean of the growth of M2 velocity is zero (a consequence of the long-run money demand functions reported in section 1.4). Although there is much interesting research on the relation between long-term real output and long-term money growth (a recent empirical contribution is King and Watson 1992), the problem of setting the means is separate from the problem of short-term stabilization considered here. In this sense, any gains achieved by short-run stabilization are gains in addition to those achieved by choosing the average money-growth rate which achieves low long-run inflation.

The general goal of reducing the gap between actual and potential GDP in the short and medium term can be made more precise in a variety of ways. This paper takes the approach of evaluating economic performance by the variance of the quarterly nominal GDP growth rate. This focus on the variance of nominal GDP implies giving equal weights to short-term variations of inflation and of real output. Alternative measures of short-term performance that might be used instead include the variance of real GDP growth and the mean shortfall of real GDP from potential GDP. Although such measures would ignore the short-term variation in inflation rates, the desired low long-run average rate of inflation would be assured by setting the appropriately low mean growth rate of the monetary aggregate.

Judging performance by the variance of the nominal GDP growth rate is equivalent to targeting the growth rate of nominal GDP rather than a path of nominal GDP levels. Although this distinction has no implication for the long-term inflation rate, it does affect the optimal response of policy to short-term shocks to the economy. In particular, the implicit desired future path of nominal GDP is always independent of the starting point.

This can be seen more clearly by contrasting the target of minimizing the variance of the nominal GDP growth rate (around its mean for the entire sample) with the alternative target of minimizing the variance of nominal GDP around a trend with an exponential rate of growth equal to the sum of the desired rate of inflation and the mean real GDP growth rate in the sample. If the economy starts on the trend line, the two criteria are the same for the first period. But any departure from the trend during the first period implies a different standard for the second period. The criterion of minimizing the variance of the nominal GDP growth rate ignores any "base drift" in nominal GDP. It can be thought of as minimizing the variance around the trend line with the starting point of the trend rebased in each period to the actual level achieved in the previous period.

Which of the two approaches is preferable depends on the types of shocks that are most likely to be encountered, the differential effects of money on real output and inflation, and the ultimate objective of monetary policy. For example, if in the extreme real output is a random walk unaffected by monetary policy, then a nominal GDP level target will result in the price level being a random walk, so that the future price level will deviate arbitrarily far from its desired fixed level. On the other hand, minimizing quarterly fluctuations in the growth of nominal GDP will result in constant (say, zero) inflation, thus stabilizing the future price level. Similarly, if the growth rate of potential real GDP varies significantly from quarter to quarter, minimizing the variance of the growth rate would be the better policy. The alternative of minimizing the variance from a prespecified nominal GDP path would require a contractionary policy after a positive productivity shock, even though there had been no increase in inflation, and an expansionary policy after a negative productivity shock, even though there had been no decrease in inflation. We have not explored this issue in the current research.

Our tests of the strength and stability of the link between M2 and nominal GDP are relevant, however, whether the criterion by which policy is judged is the variance of nominal GDP around its mean or the deviations of nominal GDP from a predetermined target path. The choice of criterion determines how the money stock should vary from quarter to quarter to minimize the relevant variance.

1.2   Alternative Approaches to Monetary Policy

Although the Federal Reserve is concerned with inflation and real economic activity, monetary policy must be made by adjusting some monetary variable—a monetary aggregate, an interest rate, or the exchange rate. In this section we discuss three possible approaches. This is far from an exhaustive set of alternatives, but rather provides a context for comparing an M2 approach to nominal GDP targeting with other commonly discussed options.

1.2.1   The Status Quo: Judgmental Eclecticism

In practice, the Federal Reserve controls the volume of bank reserves (a monetary aggregate) by open-market sales of Treasury securities. In recent years, the volume of such sales has been adjusted to target the value of the Federal funds interest rate. Thus, for time intervals up to several weeks, any disturbance in the statistical relation between the Federal funds rate and bank reserves (that is, in the banking system's bivariate demand function for reserves) induces the Federal Reserve to alter reserves in order to maintain the desired level of the Federal funds rate. In this context, the interest rate is the exogenous variable and the volume of reserves is endogenous. For longer periods of time, the relationship is more ambiguous because the Federal Reserve's Open Market Committee (FOMC) may revise the Fed funds-rate target in part in response to the magnitude of reserve growth and the corresponding movement of the narrow monetary aggregate M1 (as well as to other aspects of economic and financial performance).

It is significant that the FOMC now makes decisions and issues operating instructions to the New York Federal Reserve Bank in terms of the Federal funds interest rate and not in terms of M2 or some other monetary aggregate. Each member of the FOMC may vote to increase or decrease the Fed funds rate for his or her own reasons. Some see a reduction of the Federal funds rate as a way of increasing the rate of growth of M2 and therefore of subsequent nominal and real GDP. Others may ignore the potential impact on the money stock and choose an interest rate change because of what they regard to be the likely effect on inflation and real output.[1] At times, some FOMC members may consider the effect of changes in the Fed funds rate on the international value of the dollar. Still others may emphasize the psychological effect of changes in interest rates as an indication of the Fed's resolve to fight inflation or stimulate economic activity.

We do not try to model and test an explicit interest-rate rule for monetary policy or any other complex judgmental rule. Rather we take the historic record of economic performance as indicative of what the Federal Reserve can achieve by such an eclectic judgmental policy. Technically many of the statistics we report, in particular the regression R^2's and tests for predictive content in sections 1.4 and 1.6 and the performance measures in sections 1.7 and 1.8, should be interpreted as providing evidence on the ability of alternative policies to improve upon past performance. Indeed, were past performance optimal in the sense that money had been used to minimize the variance of quarterly nominal GDP, then we would expect to find no historical correlation between money and future GDP growth. In contrast, were the historical M2/GDP relationship strong and stable, this would open the door to an investigation of whether this link could be exploited to control GDP more effectively than has been done historically.

1.2.2   Passive Monetary Policy: A Constant Growth Rate of M2

A natural starting place among explicit quantitative monetary rules is Milton Friedman's proposal for a policy of constant growth of the money supply. Setting the constant growth rate of money equal to the expected growth of potential GDP minus the expected rate of increase of velocity implies a zero ex-

---

1. Twice a year the Federal Reserve Board staff presents to the FOMC simulations of a macro-economic model which emphasize the direct effect of alternative interest-rate levels on inflation and real economic activity (rather than through a monetary aggregate), and some members of the committee undoubtedly see their votes in these terms.

pected rate of inflation. Small errors in the estimated rate of growth of either potential GDP or velocity cause correspondingly small departures of inflation from price stability.

Friedman argues that a constant rate of money growth is actually likely to result in a more stable path of nominal GDP than a more active monetary policy aimed at achieving such stability (Friedman 1953). Friedman's argument can be summarized easily in the framework in which stability is defined as the variance of the growth rate of nominal GDP. Suppose that nominal GDP growth consists of two parts, one which would be achieved under a constant growth rule and one which reflects the impact of an activist rule. Then the variance of nominal GDP growth is the sum of the variances of these components, plus their covariance. Friedman's point is that activist policy reduces volatility only if the covariance is sufficiently negative to offset the additional variance contribution from activist control.

This decomposition provides a useful way to interpret the regression results elsewhere in the literature and in section 1.4. If M2 enters significantly, then an optimal or nearly optimal policy can reduce total volatility. However, if the regression R^2 is small, then the gains from such control will be modest. Moreover, following the "wrong" policy can increase rather than decrease output volatility.

1.2.3   Active Targeting Rules for Monetary Policy

McCallum (1988, 1990), Taylor (1985), and others have developed and simulated alternative rules for managing monetary policy with the aim of stabilizing nominal GDP growth. We build on this literature in sections 1.7 and 1.8 by proposing an optimal rule for using monetary policy to target nominal GDP and a simple partial-adjustment rule that approximates the effect of the optimal rule.

As part of our analysis of these rules, we calculate the probability that they would reduce the variance of nominal GDP growth. The specific calculation we perform addresses the following thought experiment: Suppose the Federal Reserve were to adopt a particular nominal GDP targeting rule and use it for a decade. Based on the data available to us from 1959 to 1992, what is the probability that the variance of quarterly nominal GDP growth would be less over this ten-year span than it would be under the status quo? What is the expected percent reduction in the ten-year standard deviation of quarterly GDP growth under the rule, and, more generally, what does the distribution of potential reductions look like? Our statistics answer these questions, and also qualify the distribution of ten-year variance reductions in two- and four-quarter growth of GDP. This calculation incorporates both the parameter uncertainty arising from working with a finite historical data set and the additional uncertainty introduced by different possible ten-year paths of future shocks to the economy. When the policy rule is designed to minimize quarterly GDP volatility, we refer to the performance measure applied to GDP as a performance bound, since by construction the monetary policy is designed to minimize the population (multiple decade, long data set) value of this ratio. Our calculations show that in principle the optimal M2 rule would have outperformed status-quo policy with a rather high probability.

The complexity of the optimal rule for varying M2, even in the simple model that we analyze, suggests that explicit optimization is more relevant as a benchmark than as an actual prescription for application by the Federal Reserve. We therefore examine simpler partial-adjustment rules, which are in the spirit of the rules examined by Taylor (1985) and McCallum (1988, 1990). In particular, the rule for which we tabulate results adjusts M2 40 percent toward closing the gap between realized and desired nominal GDP growth. Performance measures for this simplified rule show that it would have resulted in nominal GDP stabilization close to that of the optimal rule and better than the implicit status-quo policy. Moreover, long-run mean inflation would be reduced by choosing a lower mean money-growth rate. Thus this rule could result in both lower mean inflation and reduced volatility of GDP growth, relative to the status quo.

1.3   The Usefulness of a Monetary Targeting Rule: Three Issues

The research in this paper shows that an active monetary rule of the type described in section 1.2.3 and studied in sections 1.7 and 1.8 can in principle achieve a more satisfactory economic performance (as measured by the rate of inflation and the stability of nominal GDP growth) than that which has been achieved by the "eclectic judgmentalism" currently practiced by the Federal Reserve or would be achieved by the passive policy of constant M2 growth proposed by Milton Friedman. We show also that the professional forecasters do not appear to have an advantage relative to a simple M2-based vector autoregression (VAR) model at forecasting nominal GDP and therefore tentatively conclude that monetary activism based on professional forecasts may be no more satisfactory than policies based on simpler forecasting models.

The conclusion that a monetary rule can "in principle" be useful reflects our finding of a sufficiently stable link between money and nominal GDP. Two other issues must be resolved favorably in order to conclude that monetary targeting would be useful in practice as well as in principle. Briefly, a useful monetary targeting rule requires (*a*) a sufficiently stable link between money and nominal GDP; (*b*) satisfactory behavior of the Federal Reserve; and (*c*) a limited system response to the change in monetary policy.

1.3.1   A Stable Link between Money and Nominal GDP

The statistical tests presented in sections 1.4 and 1.5 show that M2 has predictive content for nominal GDP and that the relationship appears to have been stable over time. More precisely, section 1.4 shows that the link between money and nominal GDP exists for the entire thirty-year sample. It is strong enough that Milton Friedman's case against active policy cannot be based on the absence of an adequate link between short-run variations of M2 and nominal GDP. The evidence in section 1.5 suggests that the parameters have been stable in the sense that we cannot reject the null hypothesis of parameter constancy using several recently proposed tests for parameter stability.

1.3.2 Satisfactory Behavior of the Federal Reserve

Milton Friedman and others base their argument against an activist monetary policy in part on the claim that there is an inherent inflationary bias in central bank behavior: Even if the Federal Reserve could control M2 completely and knew an optimizing rule for setting M2, they would violate that rule because of political pressures or other reasons.

There is of course no way of fully answering that criticism. We do note however that the Federal Reserve and other central banks around the world have over the past decade been pursuing relatively tough anti-inflationary policies and that those central banks with greater independence have pursued that goal more aggressively. That is no guarantee about the future behavior of the Federal Reserve. Those who believe that any central bank that has discretion will eventually act incompetently or perversely may or may not be right, but they cannot be persuaded by evidence.

Nevertheless, if our evidence on the predictive link between money and nominal GDP is accepted, those who would still advocate a passive fixed-money-growth rule would have to argue that the gain in terms of reduced inflation that results from such a policy outweighs the potential benefit in terms of the output stability that can be achieved by an active rule-based monetary policy.

It seems likely, moreover, that any policy based on an explicitly quantitative rule is less subject to political and other pressures than the purely judgmental approach currently pursued by the Federal Reserve. Perhaps it would be a useful further discipline if the Federal Reserve were to state the rule publicly and to explain to the financial and policy community whenever monetary policy did not conform to the rule over a period of, for example, six months, just as the Federal Reserve now announces a target range for money growth and must explain to Congress whenever it fails to achieve money growth in that range.

In addition to the question of the Federal Reserve's willingness to use a monetary rule to target nominal GDP, there is the more technical aspect concerning the Federal Reserve's ability to act in compliance with a rule that requires managing quarterly changes in M2. Recent experience shows that conventional short-run money demand equations have broken down (Feinman and Porter 1992). Evidently the Fed has not been able to estimate the volume of open-market operations needed to achieve its desired changes in M2. For example, the increase of M2 at a rate of only 2.2 percent from the fourth quarter of 1991 to the fourth quarter of 1992 was below the lower end of the Fed's target range (2.5 percent to 6.5 percent) at a time when most Fed officials acknowledged that faster M2 growth would have been desirable. We return to this problem in section 1.10 and explain that the Federal Reserve could control M2 by expanding reserve requirements to include all of the components of M2. Until then, we will ignore the difference between controlling reserves and controlling M2 and will assume that the Federal Reserve can control the growth of money from quarter to quarter.

1.3.3   A Limited System Response to the Change in Monetary Policy

Even if the relation between money and nominal GDP has been stable in the past, an attempt to exploit that relation in an optimizing mode could cause a change in these reduced-form parameters. Continuing to assume the old parameter values would lead to suboptimal results that could, in principle, be worse than those implied by the existing judgmental policies.

There are two sources of this possible instability. First, as discussed in section 1.10, to control M2 effectively would entail placing reserve requirements on its components. To the extent that this changes the M2/nominal GDP relation, the historical correlations upon which our analysis is based would become less useful. While this effect might take some time to detect, in principle these relations could be updated using new data and the policy rule could be modified to account for the effect of consistent reserve requirements.

The second source is more problematic, and concerns the empirical relevance of the Lucas critique of all policy analysis. One extreme form of this concern (suggested in a British context by Charles Goodhardt and known as Goodhardt's Law) is that trying to use M2 (or any other aggregate) to target nominal GDP would break the causal link with nominal GDP and make controlling M2 irrelevant. Because we use an explicitly reduced-form model, our calculations are an obvious target for this critique. However, all extant empirical macro models are approximations—there is no compelling reason to think that any empirical macroeconomic model incorporates the "deep parameters" stable to policy interventions—so this criticism is equally applicable to all exercises in this area. The empirical relevance of the Lucas critique has been the topic of considerable debate (see, for example, Sims 1981, 1986), and we have little to add on this topic. Yet we note that the tests of sections 1.5 and 1.6 suggest that the M2/GDP relation—unlike the M1/GDP relation, the monetary base/GDP, and the relation between various interest rates and output—has been stable over the past thirty years, a period which has experienced several shifts in Fed operating procedures. More generally, the research of Friedman and Schwartz (1963) that originally established the existence of a link between money and nominal GDP covered a much longer period of time with even more substantial changes in monetary policy and economic institutions. This gives us reason to hope that further changes in monetary policy would have limited effects on this relationship. These concerns do, however, imply that the relation between nominal GDP and M2 should be closely monitored were the Fed to change its approach to monetary policy.

1.4   Strength of the Link from M2 to Nominal GDP

The question taken up in this section is whether M2 has predictive content for future nominal GDP growth. We address this by considering quarterly historical time-series data on money, output, interest rates, and prices over the period 1959:1–1992:2. (Data sources and transformations are detailed in appendix A.) Visual inspection of the time-series data from 1959:1 to 1992:2, presented in figure 1.1, indicates a link between the four-quarter growth in M2 and nominal GDP over the business cycle and indeed over longer periods. However, there appears to be less correlation between M2 and either inflation or real GDP growth.

Econometric evidence on the predictive content of various monetary aggregates for nominal GDP is presented in table 1.1. Each row of the table corresponds to a regression of nominal GDP growth on a constant and three lags of the indicated variable. As discussed in appendix A, in these regressions nominal GDP, real GDP, the GDP deflator, and M2 appear in growth rates; individual interest rates appear in first differences; and spreads appear in levels. The first numeric column of table 1.1 provides the $\bar{R}^2$ of the regression of the quarterly growth of nominal GDP against the first through third lag of the indicated regressors. The second and third columns report the $\bar{R}^2$'s from regressions of two- and four-quarter growth (current quarter growth plus growth over the next, or the next three, quarters), respectively, against the same set of regressors. The final columns report the results of F-tests for predictive content (Granger causality tests) for M2 and other financial variables entering the regressions.

The results in table 1.1 suggest that there has been a systematic relationship between M2 and nominal GDP over the 1959–92 sample: M2 is a statistically significant predictor of nominal GDP growth at the 1 percent level in those regressions which include M2 or M2 in conjunction with inflation and interest rates. M2 is capable of predicting a statistically significant yet quantitatively modest amount of the movements in output at the one-quarter horizon; for example, the regressions in equations 7 and 8 indicate that M2 improves the one-quarter $\bar{R}^2$, relative to using lagged real GDP growth and lagged GDP inflation, by 0.127. However, at the four-quarter horizon the improvement from using M2 is more substantial, increasing the $\bar{R}^2$ of that regression from 0.092 to 0.326. In contrast, while the regressions with interest rates alone (equations 9 and 10) have comparable if somewhat smaller $\bar{R}^2$'s at the one-quarter horizon, their $\bar{R}^2$'s at the four-quarter horizon are less than 0.18.

A conventional question in the literature on the money-output relationship is whether the inclusion of interest rates eliminates the predictive content of M2 (e.g., Sims 1972, 1980). If it does, this would suggest for our purposes that interest rates would make a more appropriate control variable than M2. The results in table 1.1 indicate that for nominal GDP this is not the case. For example, when the ninety-day T-bill rate or the Fed funds rate is added to the

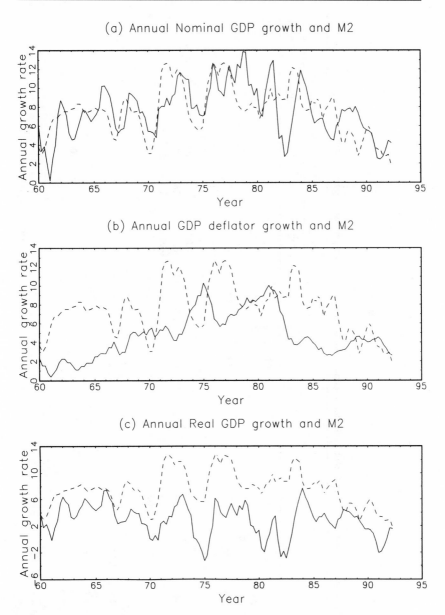

Fig. 1.1   Four-quarter growth of (a) nominal GDP (solid line) and M2 (dashed line); (b) GDP inflation and M2; and (c) real GDP and M2, 1960–92

Table 1.1   Predictive Content of M2 Dependent Variable: Nominal GDP Growth (estimation period: quarterly, 1960:2 to 1992:2)

Eq.	Regressors	R^2	$\bar{R}^2(2)$	$\bar{R}^2(4)$	F-tests (p-values) on Lags of: M2	R-90	R-FF	G10_G1	CP6_G6
1	NGDP	0.101	0.105	0.073					
2	NGDP M2	0.228	0.293	0.295	7.88 (0.000)				
3	NGDP M2 R-90	0.272	0.284	0.279	6.67 (0.000)	3.43 (0.019)			
4	NGDP M2 R-FF	0.277	0.294	0.288	5.11 (0.002)		3.77 (0.013)		
5	NGDP M2 R-90 R-FF	0.302	0.318	0.282	6.12 (0.001)	2.38 (0.074)	2.70 (0.049)		
6	NGDP M2 R-90 ZMD	0.317	0.344	0.328	7.57 (0.000)	2.90 (0.038)			
7	NGDP PGDP	0.094	0.113	0.092					
8	NGDP PGDP M2	0.221	0.295	0.326	7.60 (0.000)				
9	NGDP PGDP R-FF	0.199	0.195	0.174			6.30 (0.001)		
10	NGDP PGDP R-90	0.166	0.151	0.161		4.48 (0.005)			
11	NGDP PGDP M2 R-90	0.271	0.286	0.310	6.76 (0.000)	3.77 (0.013)			

#							$\bar{R}^2$	$\bar{R}^2(2)$	$\bar{R}^2(4)$			
12	NGDP	PGDP	M2	R-FF			0.277	0.294	0.316	5.31 (0.002)		4.10 (0.008)
13	NGDP	PGDP	M2	R-90	ZMD		0.334	0.375	0.388	8.54 (0.000)	3.20 (0.026)	
14	NGDP	PGDP	M2	R-90	POIL	ZMD	0.324	0.371	0.378	8.61 (0.000)	2.88 (0.039)	
15	NGDP	PGDP	R-90	CP6_G6			0.224	0.249	0.176		3.00 (0.034)	3.99 (0.010)
16	NGDP	PGDP	M2	R-90	CP6_G6	ZMD	0.356	0.413	0.378	6.92 (0.000)	3.09 (0.030)	2.27 (0.084)
17	NGDP	PGDP	R-90	G10_G1			0.195	0.194	0.192	2.09 (0.106)	2.43 (0.069)	
18	NGDP	PGDP	M2	R-90	G10_G1	ZMD	0.355	0.400	0.386	8.23 (0.000)	3.64 (0.015)	2.25 (0.086)

Note: $\bar{R}^2$, $\bar{R}^2(2)$, and $\bar{R}^2(4)$ are, respectively, the $\bar{R}^2$'s from regressions of one-, two-, and four-quarter growth of the dependent variable onto a constant and three lags of the listed regressors. Data sources and transformations are given in appendix A. The F-statistics (p-values in parentheses) test the restriction that coefficients on the indicated regressors are zero. In the regressions including the money demand cointegrating residual ZMD, the F-statistics on M2 include the test of this restriction.

regression in equation 8, M2 remains statistically significant; in fact, the $\bar{R}^2$ for the four-quarter regression declines because of the inclusion of these additional interest rates, which evidently have no additional predictive content at this horizon.

The specifications discussed thus far only incorporate short-run relationships, in the sense that they relate growth rates to growth rates or changes. However, there is substantial evidence that there is a long-run relationship between the levels of money and output (both in logs) and interest rates, which can be thought of as a long-run money demand relation. Unit root tests suggest that velocity and interest rates can be treated as being integrated of order one, and cointegration tests suggest that these two variables are cointegrated (see, for example, Hafer and Jansen 1991; Hoffman and Rasche 1991; and Stock and Watson 1993); thus long-run money demand can be thought of as a cointegrating relation among these vectors. If so, then a candidate for inclusion in these output regressions is the "error correction" term, which is the residual from the long-run money demand relation. Previous investigations suggest that a unit income elasticity is appropriate (see Stock and Watson 1993 for results and a discussion), so the money demand cointegrating vector is specified here as $ZMD_t = \ln(X_t/M_t) - \beta_r R_t$, where X_t is log nominal GDP, M_t is log nominal money, and R_t is the level of the interest rate, here taken to be the ninety-day Treasury-bill rate. The interest semielasticity of money demand, β_r, was estimated by asymptotic maximum likelihood using the Philips-Loretan (1991)/Saikkonen (1991)/Stock-Watson (1993) procedure, and one lag of the resulting estimate of ZMD_t was entered as an additional regressor in the specifications in table 1.1.[2] Thus these regressions correspond to a single-equation error correction model (see, for example, Hendry and Ericsson 1991). Although this motivation for including ZMD stems from the theory of cointegration, this term has a natural interpretation in a regression of nominal output growth on money: it controls for deviations in velocity from its long-run value as determined by the interest rate.

The results in table 1.1 indicate that the long-run money demand residual has noticeable predictive power; for example, adding ZMD to regression 11 improves the one-quarter $\bar{R}^2$ by 0.061 and improves the four-quarter $\bar{R}^2$ by 0.078. When the money demand residual is included in the regression, the hypothesis that money does not enter implies that the lagged first differences *and* the money demand residual do not enter; thus in the regressions with ZMD the Granger causality tests for M2 in table 1.1 test both sets of exclusions (on all lags of M2 growth and on lagged ZMD). The hypothesis that M2 is statisti-

2. Specifically, the long-run interest semielasticities were estimated using the Dynamic OLS (DOLS) procedure in Stock and Watson (1993) with a four leads and lags, with standard errors computed using an AR(2) model for the regression error. The estimated long-run interest semielasticity of M2 demand is .0061 (standard error .0020), based on the ninety-day Treasury-bill rate. The DOLS regression was run over 60:2–91:2, with the remaining observations used for initial and terminal conditions.

cally insignificant in the one-quarter horizon continues to be rejected in these regressions.

Despite this statistical significance of M2 in these regressions, it should be emphasized that the $\bar{R}^2$'s for these regressions are all rather low. For example, an $\bar{R}^2$ for a four-quarter horizon of 39 percent (equation 13) indicates that the ratio of the root mean square error (RMSE) from using this regression, relative to using a constant forecast, is only 0.78. Looking ahead to the question of whether M2 can be used to further reduce the fluctuations in GDP, this inherent relative unpredictability of nominal GDP growth over the past three decades places a limit on any gains from modifying the control of M2 relative to the Fed's historical behavior.

Most of the recent research has focused on the relation between money growth and real, rather than nominal, output (e.g., Bernanke and Blinder 1992; Friedman and Kuttner 1992, 1993b; Stock and Watson 1989a). As a basis of comparison, we therefore present in table 1.2 econometric evidence on the predictive content of M2 for real GDP growth. In the case of real GDP growth, money has substantial predictive content and continues to enter each of the regressions with ZMD at the 1 percent level.

It is interesting to note that M2 is significant even in the regression with the commercial paper–Treasury-bill spread. Other authors, in particular Friedman and Kuttner (1992, 1993a) (see also Bernanke 1993), have found that the inclusion of this spread in similar regressions has eliminated the predictive content of money. The main difference between those results and the results in table 1.2 is that the F-tests in table 1.2 include the lagged money demand cointegrating residual, as well as lags of money growth; the F-statistic on the three lags of money growth alone in the table 1.2 regression with the paper-bill spread is 1.68, which, with a p-value of 0.175, is not significant at the 10 percent level. However, the t-statistic on the cointegrating residual in this regression is 3.23, and the joint F-test is significant. This phenomenon is present in the corresponding nominal GDP regression with the paper-bill spread, in which the F-test on the lags of money alone is 1.76 (p-value 0.16) and the t-statistic on ZMD is 3.71. In all other regressions in table 1.1, however, the F-test on just the lags of M2 growth is significant at the 5 percent level.[3] This statistical significance of the money demand residual agrees with recent independent results obtained by Konishi, Ramey, and Granger (1992), who find that the logarithm of M2 velocity is a significant predictor of real GDP growth; however,

---

3. The in-sample $\bar{R}^2$'s are typically larger for the real GDP and inflation regressions (not reported here) than they are for the nominal GDP regressions. This might appear puzzling at first, since nominal GDP growth is the sum of real GDP growth and GDP inflation. However, over this period real GDP growth and inflation growth, and especially their predictable components, have been negatively correlated; that is, predictably high inflation has been associated with predictably slow real growth. For example, in a VAR(3) with real GDP, GDP inflation, M2, and R-90, the in-sample forecasts of one-quarter inflation and real GDP growth from 1960:2 to 1992:2 have a cross-correlation of $-.50$ while their forecast errors have a correlation of .07.

Table 1.2   Predictive Content of M2. Dependent Variable: Real GDP Growth (estimation period: quarterly, 1960:2 to 1992:2)

Eq.	Regressors	R^2	$\bar{R}^2(2)$	$\bar{R}^2(4)$	F-tests (p-values) on Lags of: M2	R-90	R-FF	G10_G1	CP6_G6
1	RGDP	0.093	0.091	0.039					
2	RGDP M2	0.181	0.206	0.145	5.47 (0.001)				
3	RGDP M2 R-90	0.222	0.280	0.328	2.38 (0.073)	3.16 (0.027)			
4	RGDP M2 R-FF	0.262	0.335	0.357	2.16 (0.096)		5.46 (0.002)		
5	RGDP M2 R-90 R-FF	0.265	0.340	0.351	1.98 (0.121)	1.16 (0.327)	3.30 (0.023)		
6	RGDP M2 R-90 ZMD	0.293	0.361	0.379	5.19 (0.001)	2.21 (0.091)			
7	NGDP PGDP	0.118	0.162	0.196					
8	NGDP PGDP M2	0.265	0.359	0.426	9.15 (0.000)				
9	NGDP PGDP R-FF	0.235	0.316	0.382			7.22 (0.000)		

10	NGDP	PGDP	R-90				0.193	0.246	0.339		4.77 (0.004)			
11	NGDP	PGDP	M2	R-90			0.290	0.352	0.437	6.46 (0.000)	2.40 (0.071)			
12	NGDP	PGDP	M2	R-FF			0.304	0.384	0.463	4.97 (0.003)		3.24 (0.025)		
13	NGDP	PGDP	M2	R-90	ZMD		0.329	0.400	0.457	7.03 (0.000)	1.97 (0.122)			
14	NGDP	PGDP	M2	R-90	POIL	ZMD	0.313	0.391	0.444	6.97 (0.000)	1.90 (0.134)			
15	NGDP	PGDP	R-90	CP6_G6			0.290	0.396	0.383		2.29 (0.082)			6.42 (0.000)
16	NGDP	PGDP	M2	R-90	CP6_G6	ZMD	0.383	0.486	0.468	5.37 (0.001)	1.70 (0.171)			4.35 (0.006)
17	NGDP	PGDP	R-90	G10_G1			0.235	0.304	0.384		1.64 (0.184)		3.21 (0.026)	
18	NGDP	PGDP	M2	R-90	G10_G1	ZMD	0.359	0.438	0.469	6.60 (0.000)	2.58 (0.057)		2.82 (0.042)	

Note: See the note to table 1.1.

Konishi, Ramey, and Granger use M2 velocity and thus impose a long-run interest semielasticity of money demand of zero rather than estimating it as we do here.

The generally low predictive content of interest rates for nominal GDP contrasts with the findings for real GDP. For example, the regression of real output growth on lags of NGDP, PGDP, R-90, and G10_G1 (the Treasury yield spread) has a four-quarter $\bar{R}^2$ of 0.384, while its four-quarter $\bar{R}^2$ for nominal GDP is only 0.192. This is consistent with previous results in the literature that emphasize the value of the slope of the yield term curve as a forecaster of real output (Estrella and Hardouvelis 1991; Stock and Watson 1989b, 1990).

1.5   Stability of the Link from M2 to Nominal GDP

This section examines the stability of the direct link from M2 to nominal GDP. In their investigation of the M2/output relation Friedman and Kuttner (1992) concluded that much of the full-sample predictive content of money for both nominal and real income was attributable to the 1960s, a finding they attributed to disintermediation during the 1970s and 1980s. As a starting point, we therefore consider whether the main findings of section 1.4 are robust to using the shorter sample with Friedman and Kuttner's (1992) starting date of 1970:3.

Table 1.3 presents the summary statistics of table 1.1, evaluated over the more recent sample. In general, M2 has somewhat less predictive content in the later sample, although the deterioration in forecasting performance is modest. For example, the four-quarter $\bar{R}^2$ for the regression with lagged nominal GDP growth and lagged M2 growth is 0.30 in the full sample and 0.25 in the later sample. The Granger causality test statistics indicate that M2 continues to be significant, albeit only at the 5 percent level in most regressions rather than at the 1 percent level found in table 1.1. Because this sample period is only two-thirds the length of the full sample, one would not expect to find the statistical significance of the monetary variables to be as strong as that which could be found over the full sample, even if the relationship is stable. For this reason, a more useful statistic is the marginal $\bar{R}^2$'s from adding money to the regressions. While the increases remain economically significant, they drop in the later sample: at the four-quarter horizon, in the regression with nominal GDP, inflation, and the ninety-day Treasury-bill rate, over the full sample M2 alone has a marginal $\bar{R}^2$ of 0.149 and, in conjunction with ZMD, of 0.227; over the later subsample, these marginal $\bar{R}^2$'s are, respectively, 0.073 and 0.185. In the later sample, when interest rates, M2, and ZMD are included, interest rates are never significant at the 5 percent level, while M2 and ZMD are jointly significant at the 5 percent level in all regressions.

The results in table 1.3 contrast with the findings of Friedman and Kuttner (1992). Although the primary focus of their investigation was real output, their table 1 presents results on forecasts of nominal GDP. One of their conclusions

Table 1.3   Predictive Content of M2. Dependent Variable: Nominal GDP Growth (estimation period: quarterly, 1970:3 to 1992:2)

Eq.	Regressors	$\bar{R}^2$	$\bar{R}^2(2)$	$\bar{R}^2(4)$	M2	R-90	R-FF	G10_G1	CP6_G6
						_F_-tests (_p_-values) on Lags of:			
1	NGDP	0.075	0.088	0.082					
2	NGDP, M2	0.186	0.247	0.250	4.80 (0.004)				
3	NGDP, M2, R-90	0.229	0.226	0.231	3.60 (0.017)	2.51 (0.065)			
4	NGDP, M2, R-FF	0.232	0.238	0.239	2.86 (0.042)		2.61 (0.057)		
5	NGDP, M2, R-90, R-FF	0.238	0.229	0.223	3.48 (0.020)	1.21 (0.312)	1.30 (0.280)		
6	NGDP, M2, R-90, ZMD	0.246	0.256	0.251	3.46 (0.012)	1.98 (0.124)			
7	NGDP, PGDP	0.057	0.091	0.079					
8	NGDP, PGDP, M2	0.159	0.233	0.271	4.25 (0.008)				
9	NGDP, PGDP, R-FF	0.156	0.179	0.171			4.17 (0.000)		
10	NGDP, PGDP, R-90	0.135	0.156	0.183		3.42 (0.021)			
11	NGDP, PGDP, M2, R-90	0.206	0.213	0.256	3.31 (0.024)	2.54 (0.063)			

(_continued_)

Table 1.3 (continued)

Eq.	Regressors						$\bar{R}^2$	$\bar{R}^2(2)$	$\bar{R}^2(4)$	F-tests (p-values) on Lags of:				
										M2	R-90	R-FF	G10_G1	CP6_G6
12	NGDP	PGDP	M2	R-FF			0.209	0.224	0.261	2.75 (0.049)		2.68 (0.053)		
13	NGDP	PGDP	M2	R-90	ZMD		0.246	0.311	0.368	3.87 (0.007)	1.74 (0.167)			
14	NGDP	PGDP	M2	R-90	POIL	ZMD	0.224	0.298	0.342	3.89 (0.007)	1.60 (0.196)			
15	NGDP	PGDP	R-90	CP6_G6			0.171	0.205	0.169		2.17 (0.099)			2.12 (0.105)
16	NGDP	PGDP	M2	R-90	CP6_G6	ZMD	0.269	0.346	0.347	3.51 (0.011)	1.36 (0.263)			1.77 (0.161)
17	NGDP	PGDP	R-90	G10_G1			0.172	0.233	0.248		1.65 (0.185)		2.18 (0.097)	
18	NGDP	PGDP	M2	R-90	G10_G1	ZMD	0.286	0.359	0.365	3.98 (0.006)	2.43 (0.072)		2.38 (0.077)	

Note: ZMD was computed using the full-sample estimated cointegrating vector. See the note to table 1.1.

was that, over the 1970:3–1990:4 sample, M2 ceased to be a significant fore-caster of nominal GDP. In a mechanical sense, the difference between their findings and ours is explained, in order of importance, by (*a*) our inclusion of the error correction term ZMD; (*b*) the choice of lag length; and (*c*) the slight difference in sample periods.[4] If, as argued in section 1.4, the cointegrated model applies, then the error correction term should be included in the regression, and because ZMD includes M2, a test of whether M2 Granger causes output should test both lags of M2 growth and the error correction term. Concerning lag length, in the regression on GDP and M2 growth, the first lag of M2 is significant, but the others, considered one at a time, are not; moreover, a joint test of the significance of the fourth lags in the regression suggests choosing the shorter specification. The effect of including the final six quarters in the sample suggests that the recent slow growth of nominal output and M2 in the face of low and declining interest rates and a sharply positive yield curve has tilted the results somewhat toward M2 as a predictor. While we therefore prefer the specifications in table 1.3, those results and Friedman and Kuttner's (1992) findings suggest investigating further the question of whether the M2/nominal-output relation is stable. The differences between our findings and Friedman and Kuttner's ultimately point to the limitations of simple regression statistics, and suggest that information of a different type is needed on the stability of this relationship.

We therefore subject these relations to a series of formal tests for parameter stability. The overall purpose of these tests is to detect parameter instability when the type of instability is unknown a priori. If it were presumed that a break had occurred at some known date, then the simplest test for such a break would be a Chow-type test for a shift in the parameters. However, in practice the date at which the break occurred is typically unknown a priori and the candidate break date is based upon knowledge of the historical data. In this case, the subsequent test statistic does not have its classical sampling distribution, and the precise sampling distribution will depend on the preliminary method used to select the break date. (Christiano 1992 provides an empirical example of this point; for the associated econometric theory, see the July 1992 special issue of the *Journal of Business and Economic Statistics* on unit root

---

4. Friedman and Kuttner's (1992) regression 3 in their table 1b and regression 2 in our table 1.3 are the most directly comparable. Both regress quarterly nominal output growth on lagged growth of nominal output and M2. Friedman and Kuttner use four lags over 1970:3–1990:4 and nominal gross national product (GNP), and report an F-statistic of 2.37. Using nominal GDP rather than nominal GNP, over 1970:3–1990:4 with four lags this F-statistic is 2.85 (p-value .030). The p-value of the test of the hypothesis that three lags of both M2 and GDP are adequate is 0.64. Using three lags and nominal GDP, 1970:3–1990:4, the Granger causality statistic is 3.89 (p-value .012). Using the 1970:3–1992:2 sample, with four lags it is 3.39 (p-value .013; the test of three versus four lags for M2 and GDP has a p-value of .69), and with three lags it is 4.80 (p-value .004), the value in our table 1.3, regression 2. The remaining differences presumably are accounted for by their use of GNP rather than GDP and by data revisions.

and break-point tests.) The test statistics considered here handle this difficulty by explicitly treating the break data as unknown.

Three classes of tests are considered. These tests are described in appendix B and are briefly summarized here. Tests in the first class look for a single structural break which occurred at an unknown date during the sample. These tests are based on the sequence of likelihood ratio statistics testing the hypothesis that the break occurred in quarter k. The most familiar of these tests is the Quandt likelihood ratio statistic (the QLR statistic), which is the maximum over k of these likelihood ratio statistics; the other two tests are the average of the likelihood ratio statistics (mean-Chow) and an exponential average of these proposed by Andrews and Ploberger (1991) (AP Exp-W). As discussed by Andrews and Ploberger (1991), these tests are designed to have good power properties against a single break in one or more of the regression coefficients. These tests are implemented with trimming parameter $\lambda = 0.15$ (see appendix B). For comparison purposes, we also report the value of the conventional Chow test, testing for a single break occurring in 1979:3 (Chow). However, this date is conventional in the literature precisely because it is associated with the Fed's change in operating procedures *and* the double recessions of 1979–82. Because this break date is at least in part data-dependent, conventional critical values are inappropriate and proper p-values are not readily ascertained.

Tests in the second class are similar in spirit to the Brown-Durbin-Evans CUSUM statistic, except that the statistics here are computed using the full-sample residuals as suggested by Ploberger and Kramer (1992a, 1992b). These tests are the maximum of the squared scaled partial sum process of the residuals (P-K max) and its average (P-K meansq). These tests mainly have power against breaks in the intercept in the regression in question.

Unlike the previous tests, the final class of statistics is derived to have power against continuously shifting parameters. These tests, due to Nyblom (1989), are derived as LM tests of the null of constant coefficients against the alternative that the regression coefficients follow a random walk, although they also have power against single-break alternatives. Two versions of these tests are considered: the "L-all" statistic tests the hypothesis that all the regression coefficients are constant against the random walk alternative, while the "L-fin" statistic tests only the constancy of the coefficients on the financial variables (money, interest rates, spreads, and the money demand cointegrating residual). In practice, these tests often yield different inferences. Because the various tests were derived to have power against different alternatives, when used together they can provide insights into which types of instabilities, if any, are present in these regressions.

The results of these tests are presented in table 1.4 for the nominal GDP forecasting regressions in table 1.1. In all the M2 regressions, the only tests which reject at the 5 percent level are the Ploberger-Kramer tests (ignoring the fixed-Chow test, for which we cannot compute proper critical values because

Table 1.4 Tests for Structural Breaks and Time-Varying Parameters with M2. Dependent Variable: Nominal GDP Growth (estimation period: quarterly, 1960:2 to 1992:2)

Eq.	Regressors	QLR	mean-Chow	AP Exp-W	$\hat{k}$	Chow	P-K max	P-K meansq	L-all	L-fin
1	NGDP	6.32	3.28	1.77	79:2	4.71	0.96	0.25	0.58	
2	NGDP M2	12.47	6.06	3.81	64:2	7.49	0.75	0.09	0.82	0.42
3	NGDP M2 R-90	20.13	7.85	6.16	79:2	18.37*	0.77	0.14	0.99	0.58
4	NGDP M2 R-FF	14.52	7.09	4.82	64:2	13.79	0.67	0.10	0.84	0.47
5	NGDP M2 R-90 R-FF	28.31	10.61	9.80	79:2	21.85*	0.78	0.13	1.28	0.85
6	NGDP M2 R-90 ZMD	25.22	9.70	8.50	79:2	22.84**	0.95	0.14	1.20	0.78
7	NGDP PGDP	17.71	7.11	5.31	74:1	9.58	0.98	0.20	1.08	
8	NGDP PGDP M2	20.82	9.78	7.16	79:4	16.20	0.73	0.05	1.31	0.42
9	NGDP PGDP R-FF	15.98	7.65	4.84	80:2	12.30	0.99	0.19	1.04	0.12
10	NGDP PGDP R-90	14.88	8.21	5.29	74:1	12.33	0.93	0.19	1.11	0.16
11	NGDP PGDP M2 R-90	24.49	10.97	8.87	79:3	24.49**	0.55	0.06	1.43	0.60
12	NGDP PGDP M2 R-FF	20.87	10.44	7.46	80:2	20.69	0.62	0.05	1.27	0.46
13	NGDP PGDP M2 R-90 ZMD	24.98	12.29	9.50	79:3	24.98*	1.03	0.15	1.52	0.64
14	NGDP PGDP M2 R-90 POIL ZMD	28.55	13.79	10.77	79:2	27.91*	0.97	0.12	1.55	0.44
15	NGDP PGDP R-90 CP6_G6	26.21	13.45	10.34	72:1	22.13*	0.94	0.26	1.79	0.65
16	NGDP PGDP M2 R-90 CP6_G6 ZMD	34.02	17.82	14.10*	72:1	29.15*	1.15	0.27	1.91	0.77
17	NGDP PGDP R-90 G10_G1	23.31	15.77	9.77	73:4	21.27*	1.34**	0.52**	2.18	0.82
18	NGDP PGDP M2 R-90 G10_G1 ZMD	27.98	15.85	10.82	73:4	22.30	1.22*	0.28	1.78	0.82

Note: The fixed-date Chow test ("Chow") has a break date of 1979:3. Because this break date is arguably data-dependent, as discussed in the text the critical values for this statistic are difficult to ascertain and the reported significance levels for this statistic (based on the standard F distribution) are at best a rough guide.

*Significant at the 10 percent level.

**Significant at the 5 percent level.

***Significant at the 1 percent level.

of the partly endogenous break date). This suggests that the constant term in some of these regressions is unstable, but that the coefficients on the stochastic regressors do not exhibit statistically significant shifts. The only case in which another test rejects at the 10 percent level is for regression 16, which includes both the spread CP6_GM6 and the ninety-day Treasury-bill rate FYGM3: the AP test rejects with an estimated break in 72:1. Since no other regression rejects using this statistic, this suggests that there might be some instability in the relationship between the commercial paper–Treasury bill spread and nominal output. This spread moves with other private-public spreads (Stock and Watson 1990); in this light, its instability is consistent with the 5 percent rejection of the P-K max statistic in regression 17, which includes the Treasury yield curve spread. Aside from these two regressions with the interest rate spreads, the results suggest stable regression coefficients on the stochastic variables.[5]

Overall, the results of this section suggest that the predictive content of M2 (as well as other financial variables) for nominal GDP is somewhat less over the 1970–92 subsample than over the full period. However, formal tests for parameter instability fail to reject the hypothesis that the M2-GDP regressions have stable coefficients over the thirty-year sample.

1.6   Links from Other Monetary Aggregates to Nominal GDP

At various times, the Federal Reserve has considered employing alternative financial instruments as control variables, such as the monetary base, M1, and interest rates. In this section, we examine the predictive content of these other instruments for nominal GDP growth and the stability of these forecasting relationships.

Casual evidence suggests that the link from other monetary aggregates to output is less stable. The Federal Reserve is required by law to announce target ranges for monetary aggregates. In recent years, the Federal Reserve has provided target ranges for M2 and M3 as well as for a broader debt aggregate, but it no longer provides a target range for M1. Federal Reserve officials argue that the payment of interest on most checking accounts (a component of M1) has increased the substitutability between M1 accounts and the components of M2 and has therefore greatly increased the volatility of M1 velocity. In the first two quarters of 1992, for example, M1 grew at 13.4 percent at annual rates while nominal GDP increased only 5 percent. Annual growth rates of the monetary base and of nominal GDP, real GDP, and GDP inflation are plotted in

---

5. In contrast to the general lack of rejections in table 1.4, there is more evidence of instability in comparable equations which forecast real GDP. The evidence of instability is quite strong when GDP inflation is the dependent variable: at least one test rejects at the 5 percent level in ten of the twelve regressions involving M2. The estimated break dates occur early in the sample, most commonly 67:2 and 71:1.

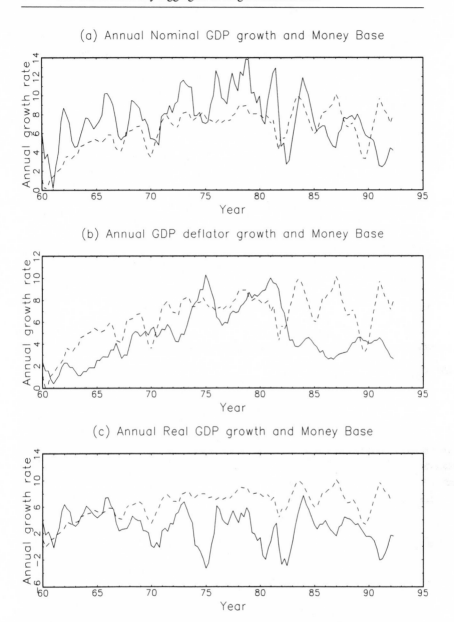

Fig. 1.2   Four-quarter growth of (a) nominal GDP (solid line) and the monetary base (dashed line); (b) GDP inflation and monetary base; and (c) real GDP and the monetary base, 1960–92

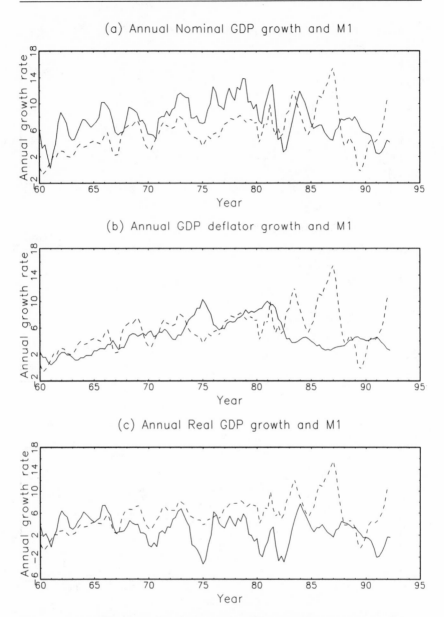

Fig. 1.3   Four-quarter growth of (a) nominal GDP (solid line) and M1 (dashed line); (b) GDP inflation and M1; and (c) real GDP and M1, 1960–92

figure 1.2. In figure 1.3, the monetary base is replaced by M1. In contrast to figure 1.1, no clear cyclical link is evident between either the base or M1 and nominal output.

To investigate these links more formally, we apply the statistics described in section 1.4 and 1.5 to regressions involving base money and M1. Evidence on the predictive content of base money and M1 is presented in tables 1.5 and 1.6.[6] The most striking feature of these results is that the predictive content of these regressions is substantially less than the corresponding regressions with M2, with four-quarter $\bar{R}^2$'s in the range of 0.09–0.20, compared with $\bar{R}^2$'s in table 1.1 of almost 0.40. In the regressions with interest rates, the monetary base fails to be statistically significant at the 5 percent level, and M1 is no longer significant at the 10 percent level.

The stability of the base, M1, and interest rate regressions is examined in table 1.7 and 1.8 using the tests for parameter constancy described in section 1.5. The hypothesis of parameter constancy is rejected overwhelmingly for base money, with every regression having at least one statistic which rejects stability at the 5 percent level. The evidence against stability for M1 is equally strong. Interestingly, all the rejections for M1 result from the break-point tests rather than from Nyblom's (1989) tests for time-varying parameters, suggesting a regime-shift in the parameters rather than a slow evolution. In both the base and M1 regressions, the break date is estimated to be in the late 1970s, perhaps reflecting the widespread introduction of interest-bearing checkable deposits during this period. In contrast, the regressions with only interest rates in table 1.4 suggest that the interest-rate relations are relatively stable. The instability of the base and M1 regressions provides some insight as to why the base and M1 are insignificant when interest rates are also included in the regressions: even if these variables have predictive content, the nature of that predictive content varies over time, and the more stable interest-rate relations "drive out" the two narrow monetary aggregates.

Several conclusions emerge from these results. Neither M1 nor the monetary base has substantial predictive content for GDP over the full 1959–92 sample, and both aggregates are no longer significant once interest rates are included in the regressions. Moreover, the link between these two aggregates on the one hand and nominal GDP growth on the other is unstable, with the stability tests rejecting in most specifications at the 1 percent level. While the link between interest rates and GDP growth appears to be more stable (with the exception

6. The cointegrating residuals ZMD in the regressions in tables 1.6 and 1.7 are based on long-run monetary-base and M1-demand relations, respectively, estimated using the ninety-day Treasury-bill rate, using the same estimation procedure applied to the M2 cointegrating vector discussed in section 1.4. The interest semielasticities are .0503 (.0172) for base money and .0737 (.0304) for M1. The evidence is weak, however, that the monetary base system is cointegrated, so the F-statistics involving ZMD for the base should be interpreted with caution; this term for the base is included for comparison with the results for M1 and M2. We suspect that these F-statistics overstate the predictive content of the base; see Ljungqvist, Park, Stock, and Watson (1988).

Table 1.5   Predictive Content of Monetary Base. Dependent Variable: Nominal GDP Growth (estimation period: quarterly, 1960:2 to 1992:2)

Eq.	Regressors	$\bar{R}^2$	$\bar{R}^2(2)$	$\bar{R}^2(4)$	F-tests (p-values) on Lags of: BASE	R-90	R-FF	G10_G1	CP6_G6
1	NGDP BASE	0.169	0.188	0.167	4.45 (0.005)				
2	NGDP BASE R-90	0.199	0.192	0.189	2.46 (0.066)	2.49 (0.064)			
3	NGDP BASE R-FF	0.222	0.233	0.208	1.94 (0.126)		3.76 (0.013)		
4	NGDP BASE R-90 R-FF	0.244	0.250	0.198	2.69 (0.050)	2.12 (0.101)	3.35 (0.021)		
5	NGDP PGDP BASE	0.153	0.180	0.159	3.85 (0.011)				
6	NGDP PGDP BASE R-90	0.185	0.181	0.182	1.93 (0.129)	2.52 (0.062)			
7	NGDP PGDP BASE R-FF	0.208	0.219	0.198	1.45 (0.233)		3.70 (0.014)		
8	NGDP PGDP BASE R-90 ZMD	0.178	0.175	0.175	1.44 (0.226)	2.50 (0.063)			
9	NGDP PGDP BASE R-90 POIL ZMD	0.160	0.162	0.155	1.45 (0.222)	2.43 (0.069)			
10	NGDP PGDP BASE R-90 CP6_G6 ZMD	0.227	0.267	0.187	1.12 (0.352)	2.34 (0.077)			3.46 (0.019)
11	NGDP PGDP BASE R-90 G10_G1 ZMD	0.191	0.195	0.183	0.86 (0.492)	1.85 (0.142)		1.61 (0.190)	

Note: See the note to table 1.1.

Table 1.6   Predictive Content of M1. Dependent Variable: Nominal GDP Growth (estimation period: quarterly, 1960:2 to 1992:2)

Eq.	Regressors						$\bar{R}^2$	$\bar{R}^2(2)$	$\bar{R}^2(4)$	F-tests (p-values) on Lags of:				
										M1	R-90	R-FF	G10_G1	CP6_G6
1	NGDP	M1					0.152	0.166	0.098	3.50 (0.018)				
2	NGDP	M1	R-90				0.185	0.167	0.132	1.75 (0.161)	2.67 (0.051)			
3	NGDP	M1	R-FF				0.204	0.208	0.154	1.00 (0.397)		3.68 (0.014)		
4	NGDP	M1	R-90	R-FF			0.229	0.230	0.144	1.91 (0.131)	2.29 (0.082)	3.27 (0.024)		
5	NGDP	M1	R-90	ZMD			0.185	0.172	0.138	1.55 (0.191)	2.73 (0.047)			
6	NGDP	PGDP	M1				0.140	0.164	0.111	3.17 (0.027)				
7	NGDP	PGDP	M1	R-90			0.176	0.161	0.145	1.49 (0.220)	2.73 (0.047)			
8	NGDP	PGDP	M1	R-FF			0.194	0.199	0.161	0.78 (0.507)		3.66 (0.014)		
9	NGDP	PGDP	M1	R-90	ZMD		0.181	0.177	0.166	1.57 (0.188)	2.90 (0.038)			
10	NGDP	PGDP	M1	R-90	POIL		0.170	0.174	0.148	1.80 (0.134)	2.49 (0.064)			
11	NGDP	PGDP	M1	R-90	CP6_G6	ZMD	0.219	0.252	0.173	0.80 (0.525)	2.82 (0.042)			2.85 (0.041)
12	NGDP	PGDP	M1	R-90	G10_G1	ZMD	0.194	0.199	0.169	0.98 (0.421)	2.39 (0.073)		1.61 (0.191)	

Note: See the note to table 1.1.

Table 1.7   Tests for Structural Breaks and Time-Varying Parameters with Monetary Base. Dependent Variable: Nominal GDP Growth
(estimation period: quarterly, 1960:2 to 1992:2)

Eq.	Regressors						QLR	mean-Chow	AP Exp-W	$\hat{k}$	Chow	P-K max	P-K meansq	L-all	L-fin
1	NDGP	BASE					31.33***	17.68***	12.76***	80:1	29.09***	1.45**	0.53**	2.42***	1.11**
2	NGDP	BASE	R-90				32.19**	17.31**	12.99***	79:3	32.19***	1.41**	0.53**	2.37*	1.16
3	NGDP	BASE	R-FF				31.09**	16.91**	12.66***	79:3	31.09***	1.46**	0.52**	2.19	0.96
4	NGDP	BASE	R-90	R-FF			38.34***	18.39*	15.71***	79:2	33.35***	1.46**	0.57**	2.48	1.34
5	NGDP	PGDP	BASE				40.23***	23.20***	16.23***	74:1	32.45***	1.43**	0.54**	2.83**	0.95*
6	NGDP	PGDP	BASE	R-90			36.44**	21.86**	15.12***	79:3	36.44***	1.37**	0.52**	2.66	1.02
7	NGDP	PGDP	BASE	R-FF			33.51**	21.05**	14.04**	79:4	33.36***	1.41**	0.50**	2.44	0.86
8	NGDP	PGDP	BASE	R-90		ZMD	54.82***	29.53***	23.38***	79:3	54.82***	1.38**	0.54**	2.86	1.20
9	NGDP	PGDP	BASE	R-90	POIL	ZMD	53.51***	29.57***	22.84***	79:3	53.51***	1.34**	0.53**	2.91	0.53
10	NGDP	PGDP	BASE	R-90	CP6_G6	ZMD	56.92***	30.02***	24.26***	79:3	56.92***	1.28**	0.49**	3.09	1.53
11	NGDP	PGDP	BASE	R-90	G10_G1	ZMD	48.31***	30.44***	20.84***	79:3	48.31***	1.44**	0.58**	3.17	1.63

Note: See the note to table 1.4.

*Significant at the 10 percent level.

**Significant at the 5 percent level.

***Significant at the 1 percent level.

Table 1.8   Tests for Structural Breaks and Time-Varying Parameters with M1. Dependent Variable: Nominal GDP Growth (estimation period: quarterly, 1960:2 to 1992:2)

Eq.	Regressors						QLR	mean-Chow	AP Exp-W	$\hat{k}$	Chow	P-K max	P-K meansq	L-all	L-fin
1	NDGP	M1					33.52***	15.00***	12.71***	80:3	27.36***	1.23*	0.31	1.53	0.74
2	NGDP	M1	R-90				33.54***	16.42**	13.83***	79:2	33.39****	1.20*	0.30	1.62	0.89
3	NGDP	M1	R-FF				35.41***	15.02**	13.80***	80:3	32.04****	1.26*	0.30	1.41	0.68
4	NGDP	M1	R-90	R-FF			42.19***	17.53*	16.94***	79:2	35.83****	1.30**	0.34	1.91	1.22
5	NGDP	M1	R-90	ZMD			54.30***	26.27***	22.93***	79:2	51.08****	1.34**	0.44*	2.31	1.34
6	NGDP	PGDP	M1				32.57***	18.14**	13.33***	74:1	29.82****	1.22*	0.32	1.90	0.54
7	NGDP	PGDP	M1	R-90			36.46**	18.47*	14.38**	80:2	32.70****	1.18*	0.32	1.89	0.65
8	NGDP	PGDP	M1	R-FF			37.12**	17.07	14.52**	80:2	31.21**	1.21*	0.31	1.68	0.51
9	NGDP	PGDP	M1	R-90		ZMD	50.76***	30.50***	22.38***	79:2	50.72***	1.35**	0.57**	2.90	1.21
10	NGDP	PGDP	M1	R-90	POIL	ZMD	50.23***	30.24***	21.54***	79:3	50.23****	1.32**	0.56**	2.99	1.01
11	NGDP	PGDP	M1	R-90	CP6_G6	ZMD	47.97***	29.51***	21.04***	80:2	45.45****	1.23*	0.48**	2.88	1.38
12	NGDP	PGDP	M1	R-90	G10_G1	ZMD	47.18***	30.94***	21.34***	83:1	44.98****	1.43**	0.61**	3.04	1.45

Note: See the note to table 1.4.

*Significant at the 10 percent level.

**Significant at the 5 percent level.

***Significant at the 1 percent level.

of the term structure spread), the predictive content of interest rates for nominal GDP growth is substantially less than that of M2.

1.7   Optimal Nominal GDP Growth-Rate Targeting: Performance Bounds

1.7.1   Methodology

We now turn to the task of estimating what the volatility of key economic variables would be were the Federal Reserve to follow a nominal GDP targeting rule. Answering hypothetical questions such as this is central to the empirical analysis of macroeconomic policies. A standard approach to answering such questions, which we employ, is to adopt an empirical macroeconomic model, to change one of its equations to reflect the policy rule in question, to solve the model with this new equation, and then to compute summary statistics and counterfactual historical simulations which illustrate the effects of the change. In the context of evaluating the effect of nominal GDP targeting, this strategy was used by Taylor (1985), McCallum (1988), and Pecchenino and Rasche (1990) to evaluate various targeting rules, although the rules and/or empirical models used in these studies differed.

The empirical models we consider are a series of VAR models of the form (1), (2), and (3) below. The focus is on constructing performance bounds which measure the best outcome the Fed could achieve were it to adopt a nominal GDP targeting strategy, relative to the performance of its historical monetary policy. As we discussed in section 1.3, we therefore make three admittedly extreme assumptions: that the monetary instrument in question is perfectly controllable; that the Fed could adopt the GDP targeting rule which was optimal over the 1959–92 period; and that changing the rule by which money growth is set does not change the dynamics of the rest of the system and, in particular, does not change the relationship between money and output, inflation, and interest rates. In reality, these assumptions could not be completely satisfied, nor in practice could one expect to achieve the performance bound. Nonetheless, the computation of such a bound is a useful step: were the performance bound to indicate little room for improvement beyond historical Fed policy, there would be little reason to switch to a nominal GDP targeting regime.

To determine the optimal GDP targeting policy, we adopt the objective of minimizing the variance of GDP growth. It should be emphasized that this differs from the performance criterion used by McCallum (1988), who examined the deviation of the level of nominal GDP from a constant growth path of 3 percent per year. The key difference is that, by attempting to stabilize the growth rate rather than the level around a constant growth path, we are permitting base drift in the target. As discussed in section 1.1, not permitting base drift has the feature—which to us seems undesirable—of leading to a policy of inflating when nominal GDP is below its target path but is growing stably at 3 percent per year, and of tightening when GDP growth is stable at 3 percent but GDP is above its target path.

Because of lags in data availability, the Fed is unable to measure all shocks to the economy as they occur. The money control rules considered here therefore set the money-growth rate in the current quarter as a function of economic data through the previous quarter.[7]

The Optimal Control Rule

The class of models we work with are VARs of the form

(1) $x_t = \beta_x + A_{xx}(L)x_{t-1} + A_{xY}(L)Y_{t-1} + A_{xm}(L)m_{t-1} + \varepsilon_{xt}$

(2) $Y_t = \beta_Y + A_{Yx}(L)x_{t-1} + A_{YY}(L)Y_{t-1} + A_{Ym}(L)m_{t-1} + \varepsilon_{Yt}$

(3) $m_t = \beta_m + A_{mx}(L)x_{t-1} + A_{mY}(L)Y_{t-1} + A_{mm}(L)m_{t-1} + \varepsilon_{mt}$,

where x_t is the growth rate of nominal GDP, Y_t denotes additional variables, such as inflation as measured by the GDP deflator, and m_t denotes the monetary variable of interest, for example, the growth rate of M2. The model dynamics are summarized by the lag polynomials $A(L)$ and the error covariance matrix, $\Sigma = E\varepsilon_t\varepsilon_t{}'$. To implement the optimal control algorithms we assume that the VAR is stable, that is, the roots of $I-A(L)L$ all fall outside the unit circle. To simplify exposition we henceforth assume that variables enter as deviations from their means so that the intercepts can be omitted.

The rules considered in this paper are specified in terms of growth rates of money and output. These rules automatically adjust for historical shifts in the level of velocity because target money-growth rates are computed from past growth rates rather than levels. These rules do, however, assume a constant mean growth of velocity. Although M2 velocity growth has had a mean of approximately zero over the 1959–92 period, in principle it is desirable to permit the mean growth rate of velocity to change with interest rates, and to consider rules which adjust for persistent nonzero growth in velocity. Including a levels relation between velocity and the interest rate in (1), (2), and (3) is a natural way to do this, and the result would be a vector error correction model. The empirical results of section 1.4 suggest that this error correction term (the long-run money demand residual) should enter this specification. Although

---

7. The choice of a one-quarter lag in the money-growth rules represents an attempt to incorporate realistic lags in data availability. Many important series are available monthly with no lag or lags of at most eight weeks; these include interest rates, employment and unemployment, industrial production, and personal income. However, other key series are available with lags exceeding one quarter. In particular, advance GDP estimates are not available until four weeks after the end of the quarter, and revised estimates are available later still, so that the availability lag for GDP is at least one quarter plus four weeks, arguably longer. The one-quarter availability lag used here represents a compromise among these various true availability lags.

the general nature of the calculations for a vector error correction model are the same as for the VAR model analyzed here, the details differ, and the analysis of the vector error correction model is beyond the scope of the investigation and is left to future research.

Let $Z_t = (x_t, Y_t)'$, $\varepsilon_{zt} = (\varepsilon_{xt}, \varepsilon'_{Yt})'$, $A_{Zm}(L) = [A_{xm}(L) \, A_{YM}(L)']'$, and let $A_{ZZ}(L)$ be the matrix with (1,1) block $A_{xx}(L)$, (1,2) block $A_{xY}(L)$, (2,1) block $A_{Yx}(L)$, and (2,2) block $A_{YY}(L)$. Then (1), (2), and (3) can be rewritten

$$(4) \qquad\qquad Z_t = A_{ZZ}(L)Z_{t-1} + A_{Zm}(L)m_{t-1} + \varepsilon_{Zt}$$

$$(5) \qquad\qquad m_t = A_{mZ}(L)Z_{t-1} + A_{mm}(L)m_{t-1} + \varepsilon_{mt}.$$

The roots of $A_{ZZ}(L)$ are assumed to lie outside the unit circle, so that $C_{ZZ}(L) = (I - LA_{ZZ}(L))^{-1}$ exists. Then (4) can be written

$$(6) \qquad\qquad Z_t = \Gamma(L)m_t + C_{ZZ}(L)\varepsilon_{Zt},$$

where $\Gamma(L) = C_{ZZ}(L)A_{Zm}(L)$. Let $\Gamma_{xm}(L)$ denote the (1,1) element of $\Gamma(L)$ and let $C_{xZ}(L)$ denote the first row of $C_{ZZ}(L)$.

The optimal control problem is to choose the money growth rule which solves

$$(7) \qquad\qquad \min \mathrm{var}(x_t) = \mathrm{var}[\Gamma_{xm}(L)m_{t-1} + C_{xZ}(L)\varepsilon_{Zt}].$$

Because m_t is assumed to be a function of data only through the previous quarter, the solution to this problem has the form $m_t = d(L)\varepsilon_{Zt-1}$, where $d(L)$ solves (7). The solution sets

$$(8) \qquad\qquad \Gamma_{xm}(L)m_{t-1} + C^+_{xZ}(L)\varepsilon_{Zt-2} = 0,$$

where $C^+_{xZ}(L) = \sum_{j=2}^{\infty} C_{xZj}L^{j-2}$, so $m_t = \Gamma_{xm}(L)^{-1}C^+_{xZ}(L)\varepsilon_{zt-1}$ and $d(L) = \Gamma_{xm}(L)^{-1}C^+_{xZ}(L)$.

The rule $m_t = d(L)\varepsilon_{Zt-1}$ is expressed in terms of the shocks to the x_t equations (4). In terms of implementation, it is more natural to express the rule in terms of actual historical data. This mathematically equivalent form of the rule is obtained by expressing ε_{Zt-1} in terms of the data using (4). The optimal control rule thus is

$$(9) \qquad\qquad m_{t-1} = h^*_{mZ}(L)Z_{t-1},$$

where $h^*_{mZ}(L) = [1 + d(L)A_{Zm}(L)L]^{-1}d(L)[I - A_{ZZ}(L)L]$. The controlled system is thus given by (4) and (9).

A primary measure of the performance of the optimal rule (9) considered here is the ratio of the standard deviations of the variables when the system is controlled relative to the standard deviation of the variables when the system is uncontrolled. To make this precise, let r_i denote the ratio of the standard deviation of the ith variable in (1), (2), and (3) under the optimal control rule to its standard deviation in the uncontrolled case. Let $F(L)$ denote the moving average lag polynomial matrix of the uncontrolled system, that is, $F(L) =$

$(I - LA(L))^{-1}$, where $A(L)$ is the matrix lag operator with elements $A_{xx}(L)$, etc., in (1), (2), and (3). Let $F^*(L)$ denote this matrix when the system is controlled using the optimal feedback rule (9), so that $F^*(L) = [(F^*_{ZZ}(L)\ 0)'\ (F^*_{mZ}(L)\ 0)']'$, where $F^*_{ZZ}(L) = C_{ZZ}(L) + \Gamma(L)d(L)L$ and $F^*_{mZ}(L) = d(L)L$. Let Z^*_t denote the ith variable in Z_t when the system is controlled (so that $Z^*_t = F^*_{ZZ}(L)\varepsilon_{Zt}$). Finally, let e_i denote the ith unit vector. Then the performance measure r_i is

$$(10) \qquad r_i = \{\text{var}(Z^*_{it})/\text{var}(Z_{it})\}^{\frac{1}{2}}$$

$$(11) \qquad = \{e_i{'}\sum_{j=1}^{\infty} F^*_j \Sigma_\varepsilon F^{*'}_j\, e_i \big/ e_i{'} \sum_{j=1}^{\infty} F_j \Sigma_\varepsilon F'_j\, e_i\}^{\frac{1}{2}}.$$

Econometric Inference

Because the coefficients of the VAR (1), (2), and (3) are unknown, r_i must be estimated. A natural estimator of r_i, $\hat{r}_i$ is obtained by substituting the empirical estimates of $F(L)$, $F^*(L)$, and Σ into (11). However, in evaluating the distribution of r_i, two sources of uncertainty need to be addressed. The first is the conventional sampling uncertainty which arises because only estimates of the VAR parameters are available. The second source of uncertainty arises because for any set of fixed VAR parameters, different shocks to the system will result in different realizations of Z_{it} and Z^*_{it}, so that the ratios of the sample variances computed using these shocks will differ from the population variances in (10). Both sources of uncertainty need to be addressed in estimating the distribution of the performance measures. For example, one might wish to know the probability of realizing a decade-long sequence of shocks which have the perverse effect of making the optimal policy destabilizing relative to maintaining the status quo, that is, the probability of realizing r_i as greater than one simply as a result of adverse shocks.

The statistics reported below estimate the distribution of variance reductions which would be realized over a ten-year span were the Fed to adopt the optimal policy (9). The first source of uncertainty, parameter uncertainty, can be handled by conventional means. Because r_i is a continuous function of the unknown VAR parameters and because those parameters have a joint asymptotic normal distribution, the estimator $\hat{r}_i$ has an asymptotic normal distribution. In principle, this asymptotic distribution can be computed using the "delta" method, although we employ a numerically more convenient technique (discussed below).

The second source of uncertainty, shock uncertainty, can be handled by considering the distribution of the sample estimator $\tilde{r}_{i|A,\Sigma,h^*}$,

$$(12) \qquad \tilde{r}_{i|A,\Sigma,h^*} = [\tilde{\text{var}}(Z^*_{it}|A,\ \Sigma,\ h^*)/\tilde{\text{var}}(Z_{it}|A,\ \Sigma)]^{\frac{1}{2}},$$

where $\tilde{\text{var}}(Z_{it}|A,\ \Sigma))$ denotes the sample variance of a realization of Z_{it} of length N (say) generated from the VAR (1), (2), and (3) with parameters A and Σ, and where $\tilde{\text{var}}(Z^*_{it}|A,\ \Sigma,\ h^*)$ denotes the corresponding sample variance when Z^*_{it} is generated from the controlled system (4) and (9) with the parameters $A_{zz}(L)$, $A_{Zm}(L)$, $\Sigma_{ZZ} = \varepsilon_{Zt}\varepsilon_{Zt}'$, and $h^*_{Zm}(L)$. With the additional assumption that ε_t is normally distributed $N(0, \Sigma)$, these parameters completely describe the uncontrolled system (1), (2), and (3) and the controlled system (4) and (9). Conditional on these parameters, the statistic (12) is a ratio of quadratic forms of normal random variables, and a variety of techniques are available for computing this conditional distribution. For example, this can be computed by stochastic simulation, which is the approach used by Judd and Motley (1991) to estimate ranges of inflation and output growth produced under McCallum's (1988) monetary base rule (holding constant the model parameters and the control rule), and by Judd and Motley (1992) in their investigation of using interest rates as intermediate targets.

The measures of uncertainty reported in this and the next section combine the parameter and shock uncertainty arising from using the optimal rule (9). This was done using Monte Carlo methods. Specifically, in each Monte Carlo draw a pseudorandom realization of (A, Σ) was drawn from its joint asymptotic distribution; $F^*(L)$ was computed using the submatrices $A_{zz}(L)$ and $A_{Zm}(L)$, using the estimate of $h_{mZ}(L)$ obtained from U.S. historical data; pseudorandom realizations of length N were drawn from stochastic steady states of the controlled and uncontrolled system; and the sample variance (12) was computed. The distribution of these sample variances estimates the distribution of r_i given $h^*_{mZ}(L)$.[8] Throughout, $N = 40$ was used, corresponding to a ten-year span.

In general the distribution of $\tilde{r}_i$ is asymmetric ($\tilde{r}_i$ by construction is nonnegative but can be arbitrarily large). The distribution of r_i is therefore summarized by its mean, median, and 10 percent and 90 percent percentiles. In addition, the fraction of realizations of r_i which would be expected to fall below one—that is, to indicate reduced volatility under the control rule—is also reported.

1.7.2 Empirical Results

The optimal control algorithm was applied to two VARs using quarterly data over the 1959–92 period. In both models, the optimal rule minimizes the variance of quarterly nominal GDP growth, with M2 as the instrument. Both modes include quarterly growth in GDP, quarterly inflation as measured by the GDP deflator, the quarterly growth of interest rates, and the quarterly growth of M2. This use of growth rates of interest rates, rather than their changes, differs from the specifications of sections 1.4 and 1.5. While this modification has a negligible effect on the estimated distributions of the performance measures, it prevents interest rates from taking on negative values in the simulations used to compute the performance measures.

---

8. Technically, to compute the conditional distribution we would need to draw $A(L)$ from the conditional distribution of $A(L)$ given $h^*_{mZ}(L)$, where $h^*_{mZ}(L)$ is given by the expression following (9). Instead, $A(L)$ was drawn from its unconditional distribution. Sampling from the conditional distribution with these nonlinear restrictions would be computationally prohibitive and is beyond the scope of this investigation.

Estimated performance measures and their distributions are reported in table 1.9 for two systems. Because the objective is to minimize the variance of nominal GDP growth, these ratios represent performance bounds for nominal GDP growth.

First consider the system in panel A. The point estimate of r_{GDP} is 0.840, but the mean and median of the distribution of ten-year realizations of r_{GDP} is somewhat larger, approximately 0.88. The mean ratio for four-quarter growth in GDP drops to 0.76. While the spread of the distribution also increases, the 90 percent point remains approximately constant, and the fraction of realizations of r_{GDP} under one is approximately 90 percent. In short, over a ten-year span the expected effect of the optimal GDP rule would be to reduce the standard deviation of annual GDP growth by one-fourth; in nine out of ten decade-long spans the optimal rule would result in at least some reduction in the variance of nominal GDP.

The reductions in the volatility of real GDP and GDP inflation (not shown in the table) are less than for nominal GDP. At the four-quarter horizon, the GDP targeting rule results in a mean improvement of only 6.6 percent for inflation and 12.6 percent for real GDP. However, in two-thirds of the simulated decades the volatility of inflation is reduced, while in three-fourths of the decades the volatility of real GDP growth is reduced.

The main findings from this exercise are robust to using the funds rate rather than the ninety-day Treasury-bill rate as the financial variable. In this system,

Table 1.9   **Estimated Performance under Optimal GDP Targeting Rule (ratio of standard deviations of quarterly, semiannual, and annual growth rates, controlled versus uncontrolled system, over a ten-year span)**

Variable	Aggregation	$\hat{r}$	Mean	Standard Deviation	Median	10% Point	90% Point	Fraction
		A. Y = (GDP, PGDP, R-90); control = M2						
GDP	1	0.840	0.881	0.109	0.887	0.752	1.010	0.88
	2	0.762	0.824	0.147	0.824	0.644	1.001	0.90
	4	0.668	0.761	0.202	0.748	0.519	1.019	0.89
		B. Y = (NGDP, PGDP, R-FF); control = M2						
GDP	1	0.851	0.900	0.115	0.903	0.762	1.034	0.83
	2	0.788	0.855	0.151	0.852	0.677	1.041	0.84
	4	0.699	0.788	0.205	0.774	0.542	1.039	0.87

Note: The entry in the third column is the estimated reduction in the standard deviation of the variable given in the first column, temporally aggregated over the number of quarters given in the second column, for the system controlled using the optimal controller derived for the indicated control variable. The remaining columns summarize the distribution of the sample realizations of r_i over a ten-year span were the optimal rule, computed using the 1960–92 data, implemented in the future; these distributions incorporate both parameter and shock uncertainty, as discussed in the text. Data transformations are as given in the appendix. Estimation period: 1960:2–1992:2. Based on 2000 Monte Carlo replications.

the optimal monetary policy still reduces nominal GDP volatility in 83 percent to 87 percent of the decades, depending on the horizon. The mean reductions for inflation volatility and real GDP volatility are again more modest than those of nominal GDP. However, the optimal policy results in reductions of the volatility of annual inflation and real output in, respectively, three-fifths and three-fourths of the simulated decades.

1.7.3 Counterfactual Historical Simulations and Interpretation

Supposing the Fed had optimally used M2 to reduce GDP volatility, how might the economy have performed over the 1959–92 period? Answering this question both is of interest in its own right and provides a vehicle for illustrating the dynamic interactions in the model. Because the VAR captures the historical correlations between lagged money and future output, it is a useful framework for computing the performance bounds reported in the previous section. It is, however, arguably less well suited for performing counterfactual simulations, for several reasons. The model does not impose any restrictions implied by economic theory and thus is at a minimum inefficiently estimated; because structural shocks are not identified (in the sense of structural VAR

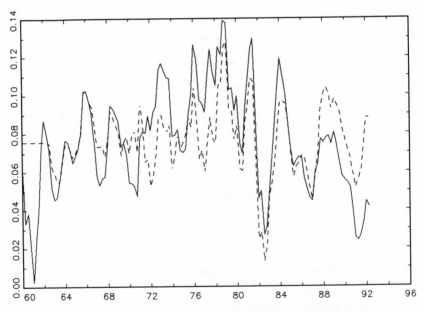

Fig. 1.4   Actual and simulated historical values of four-quarter growth of nominal GDP: Optimal nominal GDP targeting rule, 1960–92
Note: Actual: solid line; simulation: dashed line.

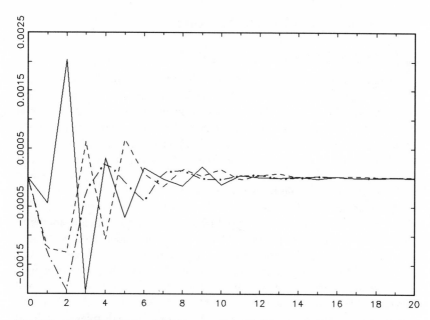

Fig. 1.5   Impulse response functions: optimal GDP targeting rule
Note: Response of money growth after *k* quarters, relative to its mean, to a one-standard-deviation shock in the equations for nominal GDP (solid line); GDP inflation (dashed line); the interest rate (dotted-dashed line).

analysis), simulated responses to shocks are difficult to interpret. Nonetheless, the computation of counterfactual simulations sheds light on the dynamic properties of the model.

With these caveats in mind, we therefore simulate the path of nominal GDP under the optimal policy rule. The simulated path is computed using the historical shocks to the first three equations in the system, with M2 determined using the ex post optimal control rule. This simulated path, computed from the system in panel A of table 1.9, is plotted in figure 1.4 along with the actual path of GDP. The optimal policy rule would have produced markedly different paths of money and interest rates, but only somewhat different paths of nominal GDP, real GDP, and inflation, relative to the actual data.

A convenient way to summarize the optimal control rule is in terms of its impulse response function to shocks to GDP, inflation, and interest rate; this impulse response function is $d(L)$ given following (8). The change in the log of money in response to a one-standard deviation error in each of the three equations for the other system variables is plotted in figure 1.5. These shocks have not been orthogonalized so the impulse responses have no ready structural interpretation. However, for a given system this impulse response facilitates the comparison of the optimal rule to the simpler rule examined in the next section.

1.8   Performance of Alternative M2 Growth Rules

1.8.1   Simpler Nominal GDP Targeting Rules

The optimal rule provides a bound by which to gauge the potential performance of alternative nominal GDP targeting schemes. As practical advice, however, the rule has some shortcomings. It involves multiple lags of several variables and thus would be rather complicated to follow. More important, the optimal rule depends on the specified model; because all empirical models are best thought of as approximations, as long as these approximations "fit" (for example, forecast out-of-sample) equally well, there is no compelling reason to choose the optimal rule from any one model. Thus, it is natural to wonder whether there are simpler money-growth rules which would result in a performance nearly as good as that achieved by the optimal rule, but are simpler to explain and to implement and do not hinge on any one model specification.

In this section we therefore consider alternative, simpler models for targeting nominal GDP. In doing so, we parallel the investigations of simple money-growth rules by Taylor (1985), McCallum (1988), Hess, Small, and Brayton (1992), and Judd and Motley (1991) and extend this work to the distribution of the performance measures r_i. The money-growth rules considered here have the partial adjustment form

$$(13) \qquad (m_t - \mu_m) = \lambda(\mu_x - x_{t-1}) + (1 - \lambda)(m_{t-1} - \mu_m),$$

where μ_x is the target growth rate of nominal GDP, μ_m is the mean money-growth rate, and $0 < \lambda < 1$. Thus money growth adjusts by a fraction λ when realized GDP growth in the previous quarter deviates from its target value by the amount $\mu_x - x_{t-1}$.

It was suggested in section 1.4 that long-run money demand is well characterized as a cointegrating relationship between money, nominal GDP, and interest rates, with a unit income elasticity. If interest rates are I(1) with no drift (an empirically and economically plausible specification), velocity growth has mean zero. Thus μ_m is set to equal μ_x, and the rule (13) simplifies to $m_t = -\lambda x_{t-1} + (1 - \lambda)m_{t-1}$. As in section 1.7, the rule (13) is implemented in its deviations-from-means form, so that m_t and x_t are taken to be deviations from their 1960 to 1992 averages.

The effect of the partial adjustment money-growth rule (13) can be evaluated using the techniques of section 1.7.1. For example, the formulas (10) and (11) for the performance measure r_i are as described in section 1.7.1, except that the rule (13) replaces the optimal rule (9). Econometric inference concerning the performance measure can also be performed using the procedure described in section 1.7.1.

1.8.2   Empirical Results

The partial adjustment rule (13) was examined on a coarse grid of values of λ between .1 and .5. In general, the performance measures r_i were insensitive to the choice of λ for $.2 \leq \lambda \leq .4$; within this range, no value of λ dominated in terms of variance reduction at all horizons. The results for $\lambda = .4$ are shown in table 1.10 for the two systems analyzed in table 1.9.

The striking conclusion from table 1.10 is that this simple partial adjustment rule produces nearly the same distributions of performance measures as does the optimal rule. The partial adjustment rule results in a somewhat lower fraction of simulated decades of improved performance for nominal GDP at the quarterly horizon—only 70 percent, compared with 88 percent under the optimal rule—but 85 percent of the simulated decades have reduced annual nominal GDP volatility. As is the case under the optimal rule, under the partial adjustment rule the improvements in inflation and real output variability are less than for nominal GDP. However, the partial adjustment rule still results in improvements in inflation and output in two-thirds of the simulated decades.

The results in panel B of table 1.10 indicate that these findings are robust to replacing the ninety-day Treasury-bill rate with the funds rate. Overall, according to these performance measures the simple rule comes close to achieving the reduction in nominal GDP volatility of the optimal rule and is robust to changing the interest rate used in the specification.

1.8.3   Counterfactual Historical Simulations and Interpretation

The fact that the simple rule approximates the optimal rule suggests that the counterfactual historical values simulated using the partial adjustment rule will

Table 1.10   **Estimated Performance under Partial Adjustment GDP Targeting Rule (ratio of standard deviations of quarterly, semiannual, and annual growth rates, controlled versus uncontrolled system, over a ten-year span)**

Variable	Aggregation	$\hat{r}$	Mean	Standard Deviation	Median	10% Point	90% Point	Fraction < 1
			A. $Y = $ (GDP, PGDP, R-90); control = M2					
GDP	1	0.882	0.932	0.124	0.933	0.780	1.083	0.70
	2	0.818	0.901	0.173	0.899	0.686	1.122	0.73
	4	0.659	0.779	0.213	0.762	0.527	1.060	0.85
			B. $Y = $ (NGDP, PGDP, R-FF); control = M2					
GDP	1	0.881	0.923	0.112	0.928	0.789	1.051	0.77
	2	0.818	0.890	0.156	0.889	0.698	1.079	0.77
	4	0.683	0.790	0.199	0.777	0.549	1.043	0.87

Note: Ratios of standard deviations were computed using the partial adjustment nominal GDP targeting rule, $m_t = -\lambda x_{t-1} + (1 - \lambda)m_{t-1}$, where $\lambda = .4$, as discussed in the text. See the note to table 1.9.

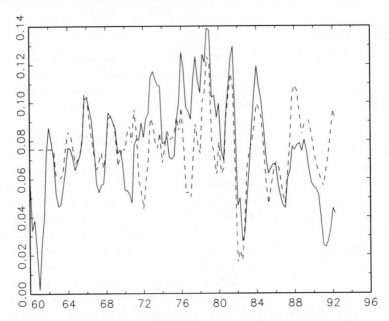

Fig. 1.6   Actual and simulated historical values of four-quarter growth of nominal GDP: Partial-adjustment GDP targeting rule, 1960–92

Note: Actual: solid line; simulation: dashed line.

be close to the counterfactual values based on the optimal rule. This is in fact the case. The actual and simulated values of annual GDP growth for the system with the ninety-day Treasury-bill rate are plotted in figure 1.6. A comparison of figures 1.4 and 1.6 reveals only slight differences between the historical values of output growth under the two rules; perhaps the largest difference is the decline in output in 1972 under the partial adjustment rule.

The impulse responses of the partial adjustment rule are plotted in figure 1.7. (These impulse responses are the lag polynomial $d[L]$ in the representation $m_t = d[L]\varepsilon_{z_t}$, which is obtained by solving [4] and [13]; the plotted impulse responses are scaled by the standard deviation of ε_{z_t}, and so represent responses to one-standard-deviation changes in ε_{z_t}.) Although the simulated output and inflation paths are quite similar under the two rules, the impulse responses of the rules are quite different. Clearly the partial adjustment rule is not an approximation of the optimal rule, in the sense that its impulse response function approximates the impulse response function of the optimal rule. However, its effect on nominal output (and also on inflation and real output) is close to that of the optimal rule. A partial explanation for this is that, as was emphasized in section 1.4, the estimates of the short-run effect of money on output, while statistically significant, are still rather small, small enough that

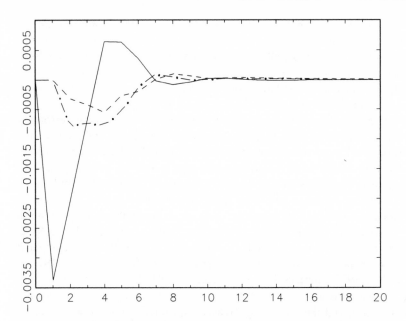

Fig. 1.7 Impulse response functions: partial-adjustment GDP targeting rule
Note: Response of money growth after k quarters, relative to its mean, to a one-standard-deviation shock in the equations for nominal GDP (solid line); GDP inflation (dashed line); the interest rate (dotted-dashed line).

rather different money-growth paths can have similar, modest effects on nominal output and inflation. More generally, these results indicate that the objective function of the variance of nominal GDP is rather flat with respect to various money-growth rules.[9]

1.9 Adjusting Monetary Policy to Consensus Forecasts

The empirical analysis in sections 1.7 and 1.8 uses a simple VAR model to derive and to evaluate policy rules. This analysis assumes that these low-dimensional models adequately capture stable historical correlations and that the remaining predictable structure in GDP is limited. If the VARs have performed worse than alternative forecasting systems, then one would be reluctant to place much weight on them in designing or evaluating monetary policy. This section assesses the predictive performance of our simple VAR model by comparing it to professional economic forecasts: had our simple VAR models been run historically, would they have produced forecasts of nominal GDP as

9. It does not follow that *any* money-growth rule results in modest improvements. For example, letting $m_t = .4x_t + .6m_{t-1}$ (so that money growth *increases* when nominal output is above its target) is destabilizing and results in a point estimate of four-quarter r_{GDP} of 1.70.

good as the historical professional record? McNees's (1986) comparison of ex ante forecasts indicates that, at least for some economic variables, VARs are capable of performing as well as or better than conventional professional forecasting models. The VARs examined in McNees's study, however, are structured differently from and have more variables than our models, so his work does not directly address ours.

We therefore provide evidence on how our models would have performed over this period, relative to those of private forecasters. Of course, the main problem with such an exercise is that our models have been estimated on the full sample while the forecasters were operating in real time with all the difficulties that entails. Thus a comparison of our full-sample VAR with real-time forecasts would be quite unfair. Consequently, we examine pseudo out-of-sample forecasts from recursive regressions with the variables in our VARs, with the initial forecast quarter ranging from 1971:1 to 1991:2. For example, the forecast of GDP growth from 1971:1 to 1972:1 is computed on the basis of a regression estimated for the period from 1960:2 to 1971:1; the 1971:2–1972:2 forecast is based on data for 1960:2—1971:2; and so forth. The systems used are those in the previous two sections, with nominal income, inflation, M2, and the ninety-day Treasury-bill rate; systems where M2 and then the interest rate are dropped; and a system in which oil prices are included.

The professional forecasts considered are the DRI (Data Resources, Inc.) and the ASA-NBER forecasts. The DRI forecasts are "early in quarter forecasts" released approximately four weeks into the first quarter of the year being forecasted. The survey date of the ASA-NBER survey has varied historically but is typically between four and six weeks into the first quarter being forecasted. (The DRI and ASA-NBER professional forecasts are of four-quarter GNP and are evaluated relative to four-quarter GNP growth.) For comparison we also present the "constant" forecast, in which the forecast is simply the average four-quarter growth rate of nominal GDP over the 1971:1–1992:2 interval.

The RMSEs of the recursive VAR forecasts and of the professional forecasters are given in table 1.11. The RMSE for the DRI and ASA-NBER forecasts are very similar at 2.26. A comparison with the "constant" forecast shows that the forecasts reduce the mean square error (the square of RMSE) by approximately one-third. The simple three-lag recursive regression that includes lagged values of M2, real GDP, and the GDP deflator (line 3 of table 1.11) has an RMSE of 2.37. Adding lagged three-month interest rates reduces the RMSE to 2.26, the same as the DRI and ASA-NBER forecasts. With the addition of oil prices, the RMSE of the VAR forecasts is actually slightly lower than the RMSE of the DRI and ASA-NBER forecasts.

The conclusion from table 1.11 is that the variables used in sections 1.7 and 1.8 in fact predict nominal GDP with the same accuracy as either the median of private forecasters in the ASA-NBER survey or the forecasts issued by the

Table 1.11   **RMSEs of Forecast of Four-Quarter Growth in Nominal Output, 1971:1 to 1991:2**

Forecasting System	RMSE
Constant only: 71:2–91:2 sample	2.76
Recursive time-series forecasts	
1. Constant	2.89
2. VAR(3): RGDP, PGDP	2.68
3. VAR(3): RGDP, PGDP, FM2	2.37
4. VAR(3): RGDP, PGDP, FM2, FYGM3	2.26
5. VAR(3): RGDP, PGDP, FM2, FYGM3, POIL	2.20
Professional forecasts	
6. DRI, 4-quarter	2.27
7. ASA-NBER, 4-quarter	2.26

Note: All RMSEs refer to annual forecasts made from 1971:1 to 1991:2. For the time-series models, the forecasts are of nominal GDP growth, computed using recursive regression with three lags of the indicated variable. For example, the forecast of GDP growth from 71:1 to 72:1 in model 2 was computed by regressing $ln(GDP/GDP_{t-4})$ onto $(1, z_{t-4}, z_{t-5}, z_{t-6})$, where z_t is quarterly real GDP growth and quarterly inflation in quarter t, with a regression period of 1960:2–1971:1 with earlier observations for initial conditions; for the 71:2 forecast, the regressions were reestimated using data through 71:2, etc. The DRI and ASA-NBER forecasts are of four-quarter GNP and are evaluated relative to four-quarter GNP growth. The entry in the first line uses as the forecast the average four-quarter growth rate of nominal GDP over 71:1–91:2, so this RMSE is $\sqrt{(n-1)/n}$ times the standard deviation of four-quarter output growth over 71:1–91:2.

DRI. Of course, despite the use of recursive forecasts this is not a true comparison of ex ante forecasts: we have the advantage of using the final rather than the preliminary values of the data and have drawn on the past decade of experience with VARs to specify our model. Also, our models are silent on one main feature of most professionally used models, the forecasting of the detailed components of real output. Still, the results are sufficiently encouraging to lead us to conclude that the systems simulated in sections 1.7 and 1.8 provide a plausible empirical framework for the discussion of alternative monetary policy rules.

1.10   The Federal Reserve's Ability to Control M2

Although the Federal Reserve announces broad annual target ranges for M2 growth, the actual growth of M2 in 1992 was below the bottom of the target range and in 1991 was at the very bottom of the range. In both years the target range was 2.5 percent to 6.5 percent; actual M2 growth was 2.7 percent in 1991 and 2.2 percent in 1992. Both years had substantial periods of zero or negative growth of M2.

Federal Reserve officials emphasize that they do not control M2 directly. To the extent that the Fed wants to alter M2, it proceeds indirectly based on an estimated statistical relationship between M2 and the federal funds rate. If the level of M2 projected by that relationship lies below the desired level, open-market purchases could be used to lower the federal funds rate until the projected level of M2 is satisfactory. This might of course cause a conflict between those who focus on the M2 targets and those who focus on how changes in the federal funds rate affect inflation and real economic activity and thus regard M2 as only a coincident indicator of nominal GDP rather than as a policy instrument that causes future changes in nominal GDP.

Such a conflict did not arise during 1991 and 1992, however, because the Federal Reserve's statistical relation consistently overestimated the level of M2 that would result from the existing federal funds rate. Many Federal Reserve officials who wanted to see a higher level of M2 believed that M2 was about to increase more rapidly without the need for the future stimulus of a lower federal funds rate (and the associated increase in reserves).

The Fed's indirect and inaccurate approach to controlling M2 is currently necessary because the link between Federal Reserve policy and the M2 money stock has become very different from the standard textbook picture.[10] In the textbook world, banks must keep reserves in proportion to their liabilities, that is, in proportion to the noncurrency portion of the stock of money. When Federal Reserve open-market purchases of Treasury bills increase bank reserves, banks are automatically induced to increase the noncurrency component of the money stock in proportion to the increase in reserves.

In reality, however, banks are now required to hold reserves against only a small fraction of their liabilities. Since reserves are no longer required for time deposits and certain other liabilities, reserve requirements apply to only about 20 percent of total M2. An open-market purchase of securities by the Fed automatically leads to a rise in M1 (since reserves are required for almost all of the noncurrency components of M1) but does not necessarily cause a rise in M2. In practice, the banks have responded to increases in reserves by substituting low-cost M1 funds (checkable deposits) for the more expensive M2 funds (time deposits). As a result, M1 grew very rapidly during 1991 and 1992 while M2 grew at less than the targeted level.

It is possible that a more aggressive trial and error procedure for adjusting reserves (or the Federal funds rate) might allow the Fed to achieve its desired level of M2 within each quarter. Fed officials doubt this, however, asserting that the lag between changes in the Federal funds rate and the subsequent change in M2 is much longer than a quarter. The Fed could eventually achieve the desired M2 level by trial and error changes in reserves but could not do so in each quarter.

This problem could be avoided and the Federal Reserve could reassert control over the quarterly level of M2 if reserve requirements were expanded to all the components of M2. Throughout most of the history of the Federal Reserve System, banks were required to maintain reserves against both demand depos-

---

10. For an earlier discussion of this subject, see Feldstein (1991, 1992).

its and time deposits. But the ratio of reserves to deposits has been reduced since the 1970s, with the reserve requirements on personal time deposits eliminated in 1980 and on nonpersonal time deposits in 1990.

The Federal Reserve has reduced reserve-requirement ratios and eliminated the reserve requirements on time deposits to eliminate the implicit tax that is otherwise levied on the banks. Because the Federal Reserve pays no interest on the funds that the banks deposit as required reserves, the reserve requirements act as a tax on bank deposits. This tax was particularly heavy in the 1970s and early 1980s, when inflation caused short-term interest rates to be very high. The "reserve requirement tax" made it particularly difficult for banks to attract deposits after the creation of money market mutual funds, since such funds are not subject to reserve requirements at all. More recently, the Federal Reserve reduced the reserve requirement tax as a way of temporarily increasing bank profitability at a time when banks are under pressure to increase capital.

Because the Federal Reserve is precluded by law from paying interest on reserves, it has chosen to reduce and eliminate reserve requirements as the only way of reducing the reserve requirement tax. If Congress had responded to the higher short-term interest environment of the 1970s and 1980s by permitting the Federal Reserve to pay interest on required reserves and by extending reserve requirements to personal deposits, the Fed would have been able to maintain reserve requirements on all the types of bank deposits in M2 and would therefore be better able to control M2 directly.

Extending reserve requirements to time deposits so that all of M2 is subject to the same reserve requirement, while paying interest on those additional required reserves, would have no economic or financial impact as such but would give the Federal Reserve the ability to control M2 from quarter to quarter.[11] Since the banks would obtain the needed additional reserves by selling Treasury bills to the Federal Reserve, this open-market operation would neutralize the otherwise contractionary macroeconomic effect of the increase in reserve requirements. If the interest rate paid on the additional reserves were the same as the Treasury-bill rate, the interest the banks would receive on the additional required reserves would just balance the interest they would otherwise have collected on the Treasury bills that they sell to obtain those additional reserves; the banks would thus be neither better nor worse off financially as a result of the increased reserve requirements. Similarly, since the Federal Reserve would pay in interest on the additional reserves the same amount it receives on the Treasury bills acquired through the associated open-market operations, there would be no effect on the budget of the Federal Reserve and therefore no effect on the budget of the federal government. The only effect would be to increase the ability of the Federal Reserve to control M2.

Achieving accurate control of M2 requires that the same reserve require-

11. This point is developed in Feldstein (1991).

ment apply to all of the components of M2. The Federal Reserve has historically imposed substantially lower reserve requirements on time deposits than on demand deposits on the theory that the time deposits were less liquid and that banks therefore required fewer reserves for prudential and liquidity purposes. It is important to emphasize that such considerations are irrelevant in the current context. The reserve requirements must be set uniformly in order to give the Federal Reserve control over the M2 money stock, not to assure that the banks have adequate liquid reserves. Since paying interest on time deposits would mean that this increase in the reserve requirements on such accounts would have no impact on the profitability of the banks or on the budget of the government, there is no problem with having reserve requirements on time deposits that are high by historic standards. Failure to do so is likely to mean Federal Reserve inability to control quarterly changes in M2.

1.11   Conclusion

This paper has studied the possibility of using M2 to target the quarterly rate of growth of nominal GDP. The evidence we present indicates that the Federal Reserve could probably guide M2 in a way that reduces not only the long-term average rate of inflation but also the variance of the annual GDP growth rate.

The statistical tests we present show that M2 is a useful predictor of nominal GDP. We cannot reject the assumption of parameter stability over time using a variety of tests that permit the data to determine a point at which parameter changes occur.

A simple optimizing model based on a VAR reduces the mean ten-year standard deviation of annual GDP growth by over 20 percent. Although there is uncertainty about this value because of both parameter uncertainty and stochastic shocks to the economy, we estimate a probability of more than 85 percent that the annual variance would be reduced over a ten-year period. A much simpler policy based on a single equation linking M2 and nominal GDP is shown to be almost as successful in reducing this annual GDP variance. The evidence thus contradicts those who assert that there is no stable relation between nominal GDP and M2 and those who, like Milton Friedman, have argued that the relation is so unstable in the short run that it cannot be used to reduce the variance of nominal GDP. Our empirical models are too simplified for us to recommend either of the rules considered as a normative and quantitative prescription for monetary policy; at a minimum the analysis would need to be extended to handle data revisions, frequency of data availability, and additional predictive variables. We have argued, however, that our main conclusion—that controlling M2 growth can result in substantial reductions in the volatility of GDP growth—is robust to the details of our empirical model and policy rule.

Despite the evidence of a potentially useful link between nominal GDP and

M2, there are two possible problems in implementing this strategy. First, the Federal Reserve does not currently control M2 directly. We show that the link between the monetary base, which the Fed now controls, and nominal GDP is too weak and erratic to provide a reliable instrument for targeting nominal GDP. We explain, however, that the Federal Reserve could control quarterly M2 growth completely by extending reserve requirements to all of the components of M2.

Second, we cannot be certain that a shift of Fed policy to control M2 in this way would not change the basic reduced-form parameters linking M2 and nominal GDP. We take some comfort from the fact that the many changes in financial institutions and Federal Reserve procedures during our thirty-year sample period did not cause significant parameter instability. These two issues cannot be resolved by empirical research. The reader will have to decide whether either is likely to be an insuperable problem. We hope not.

This research has encouraged us to extend our investigation in several ways. On a technical level, the simulations do not allow for a slowly changing mean growth of velocity which would be linked to long-run trends in interest rates. The Granger causality tests suggested that introducing this additional error-correction term (the long-run money demand residual) was empirically warranted. This leads us to speculate that replacing the VARs in sections 1.7 and 1.8 with vector error correction models will improve the estimated performance of the money rules and will produce more meaningful simulations by tying together velocity and interest rate movements.

The objective analyzed here has been to reduce the variance of quarterly nominal GDP growth. An alternative rule with considerable appeal is one in which the objective is to minimize the expected square of the GDP gap, that is, the deviation of GDP from potential GDP. An example of this is the "hybrid" rule studied in Hall and Mankiw's contribution to this volume (chap. 2). An alternative objective would be to minimize the one-sided shortfall of real GDP from the estimated level of potential GDP. In either case, these alternative objectives would result in monetary policies which are more aggressive when the GDP gap is larger, in particular producing relatively more expansionary monetary policy at a cyclical trough.

Central bankers object to strict rules for controlling M2 because they do not like the increased variability of short-term interest rates which would result. An idea worth investigating would therefore be a monetary policy rule that includes short-term interest-rate changes as part of the criterion function, for example, a weighted average of the change in the nominal or real GDP growth rate and in the level of the short-term interest rate.

International experience shows that central banks prefer to define their goal as price stability rather than the control of nominal GDP. It would be interesting to examine the effects on nominal and real GDP stability of alternative monetary policy rules that sought to adjust M2 growth in a way that achieved a desired level of inflation in the medium term.

We expect to return to these important issues in a future paper.

Appendix A
Data: Definitions and Transformations

Series Definitions

NGDP	Gross domestic product (seasonally adjusted, current-year dollars)
PGDP	Gross domestic product: implicit price deflator
RGDP	Real gross domestic product (NGDP/PGDP)
M2	Money stock: M2 (Citibase series FM2)
MBASE	Monetary base, adjusted for changes in required reserves (constructed by the Federal Reserve Bank of St. Louis; seasonally adjusted) (Citibase series FMBASE)
R-90	Interest rate: U.S. Treasury bills, secondary market, three month (percent per annum) (Citibase series FYGM3)
R-FF	Interest rate: Federal funds (percent per annum) (Citibase series FYFF)
R-1YR	Interest rate: U.S. Treasury bonds with constant one-year maturity (percent per annum) (Citibase series FYGT1)
R-10YR	Interest rate: U.S. Treasury bonds with constant ten-year maturity (percent per annum) (Citibase series FYGT10)
G10_G1	R-10YR minus R-1YR
CP6_G6	Six-month commercial paper rate minus six-month U.S. Treasury-bill rate (using Citibase definitions, CP6 _GM6 = FYCP-FYGM6)
POIL	Producer price index: crude petroleum (value is set to 100 in 1982) (Citibase series PW561)
ZMD	Residual from M2 money demand cointegrating relation (unit income elasticity) as discussed in the text

All data are taken from Citibase. All data are quarterly. Monthly data (interest rates and money supply data) were aggregated to the quarterly level by averaging the data for the months within the quarter.

Data Transformations

Unless explicitly stated otherwise the data are used after the following transformations: NGDP, PGDP, RGDP, and POIL enter in first differences of logarithms, and interest rates (R-90, R-FF) enter in first differences. There are three exceptions to this general rule. The long-run money demand cointegrating relations discussed in section 1.4 are specified between log velocity and the level of interest rates. Error correction terms (the money demand error ZMD and the interest rate spreads CP6 _GM6 and G10 _G1) enter the regressions and tests in sections 1.4, 1.5, and 1.6 in levels. In the VARs in sections 1.7 and 1.8, interest rates appear in growth rates (first log differences) rather than first differences.

Appendix B
Tests for Parameter Stability

This appendix summarizes the construction and asymptotic distribution theory of the tests for parameter stability employed in sections 1.5 and 1.6. The tests apply to the standard time-series regression model, modified to incorporate the possibility of nonconstant parameters:

$$(B1) \qquad y_t = \alpha_t + \beta_t' x_t + \varepsilon_t, t = 1, \ldots, T,$$

where ε_t is a homoskedastic martingale difference sequence with variance σ^2. The k-1 stochastic regressors x_t are assumed to be mean zero and integrated of order zero (I(0)). Under the assumption that the regressors are I(0), the assumption that they have mean zero is made without loss of generality under the null, since a constant is included in the regression. (Under the alternative of changing coefficients, the transformation to mean zero regressors can always be done, but it changes the time-variation process of the intercept so the power of the tests discussed below is not invariant to demeaning the data although the asymptotic size is.) Additional technical conditions are needed to obtain formal distribution theory for these tests. These conditions are typically weak: for example, that the sample x_t covariance matrix is consistent for a positive definite matrix; that x_t has at least four moments; and that the partial sum process constructed from ε_t obeys a functional central limit theorem. Note that x_t may include lagged y_t, assuming there are no unit roots in the y_t process.

The stability tests employed in sections 1.5 and 1.6 examine the hypothesis that the parameters α and β are constant, against the alternative that they change one more times during the sample. The tests fall into three classes: Chow-type tests for a break at a single, unknown date; CUSUM-type tests; and Nyblom's (1989) tests of time-varying parameters. These three classes of tests are described in turn.

Chow-Type Break-Point Tests

These statistics test the null hypothesis, H_0: $(\alpha_t, \beta_t) = (\alpha, \beta)$, against the alternative,

(B2) $H_1: (\alpha_t, \beta_t) = (\alpha, \beta), t \leq k; = (\bar{\alpha}, \bar{\beta}), t > k,$

where k is an unknown date, $1 \leq k \leq T$. Were k known a priori, then the appropriate test statistic would be the Wald test of parameter constancy, that is, the Chow test, say $F_T(k)$. Because k is unknown, a natural modification would be the maximum of these, say $\max_{k \in [t_0, T-t_0]} F_T(k)$, where t_0 reflects initial and terminal values for which the test is not evaluated. This modification was proposed by Quandt (1960) and is termed the Quandt likelihood ratio (QLR) statistic (we return to QLR terminology although the test is implemented here as a maximal Wald, not LR, statistic). Optimal tests against the alternative (B2) were studied by Andrews and Ploberger (1991). No uniformly most powerful test exists in this problem, even asymptotically and with normal errors, so different tests are powerful against different alternatives. Two alternative statistics they propose are the mean of the F-statistics (in general a weighted mean, which has an interpretation as an LM statistic) and an exponential average of the F-statistics, the so-called exponential Wald statistics (which are most powerful against distant local alternatives in a sense made precise in Andrews and Ploberger 1991). The three Chow-type statistics thus considered here are

(B3) $$QLR = \max_{k \in [t_0, T-t_0]} F_T(k)$$

(B4) $$\text{mean-Chow} = (T - 2t_0)^{-1} \sum_{k=t_0}^{T-t_0} F_T(k)$$

(B5) $$AP \text{ exp-W} = \ln\{(T - 2t_0)^{-1} \sum_{k=t_0}^{T-t_0} \exp((F_T(k)/2))\}.$$

Because these tests involve increasingly many single-break F-statistics, conventional distribution theory cannot be used to obtain their limiting distribution. However, their limiting distribution is readily obtained by applying the functional central limit theorem and the continuous mapping theory. To obtain these limits, suppose that $t_0/T \to \lambda$ as $T \to \infty$. Let $=>$ denote weak convergence on the space $D[0,1]$. Then (e.g., Andrews and Ploberger 1991), under the null hypothesis,

(B6) $$QLR => \sup_{s \in [\lambda, 1-\lambda]} F^*(s)$$

(B7) $$\text{mean-Chow} => \int_{\lambda}^{1-\lambda} F^*(s)ds$$

(B8) $$AP \text{ exp-W} => \ln\{ \int_{\lambda}^{1-\lambda} \exp(F^*(s)/2)ds\},$$

where $F^*(s) = B_k(s)'B_k(s)/(s(1-s))$, where $B_k(s)$ is a k-dimensional Brownian bridge; that is, $B_k(s) = W_k(s) - W_k(1)$, where $W_k(s)$ is a standard k-dimensional Brownian motion on the unit interval. For extensions of these results to the case that some regressors are I(1), see Banerjee, Lumsdaine, and Stock (1992) and Hansen (1992). The limiting representations in (B6), (B7), and (B8) facilitate the computation of the limiting distributions under the null and thus of the critical values for the tests.

CUSUM-Type Tests

An intuitively appealing test for structural breaks is the CUSUM statistic proposed by Brown, Durbin, and Evans (1975). This test rejects if the time-series models systematically over- or under-forecast y_t, more precisely, if the cumulated one-step-ahead forecast errors, computed recursively, tend to be either too positive or negative. Ploberger and Kramer (1992a, 1992b) proposed a modification of this statistic which is computationally simpler because it is based on full-sample residuals rather than recursive residuals. Let e_t be the residuals from the OLS fit of (B1), and let $S_T(k)$ denote the standardized partial sum process of these residuals, that is, $S_T(k) = (\hat{\sigma}^2 T)^{-\frac{1}{2}} \sum_{s=1}^{k} e_s$, where $\hat{\sigma}^2$ is the usual OLS estimator of σ^2. The two statistics considered here are

(B9) $$\text{P-K max} = \max_{k \in [1, T]} |S_T(k)|$$

(B10) $$\text{P-K meansq} = T^{-1} \sum_{k=1}^{T} (S_T(k))^2.$$

The P-K meansq statistic was previously proposed by MacNeill (1978) as a test for parameter stability.

The limiting distribution of these statistics is readily obtained using the functional central limit theorem and the continuous mapping theorem. Because the regressors are I(0) by assumption, under the null hypothesis the residual partial sum process has the limit $S_T(\cdot/T) => B_1(\cdot)$, where B_1 is a one-dimensional Brownian bridge on the unit interval. By the continuous mapping theorem, we have

(B11) $$\text{P-K max} => \sup_{s \in [0, 1]} B_1(s)$$

(B12) $$\text{P-K meansq} => \int_0^1 (B_1(s))^2 ds,$$

which can be used to obtain limiting distributions under the null.

These tests have nontrivial local asymptotic power only against shifts in the intercept term, assuming the regressors are mean zero and stationary: a shift in the coefficient β in a $T^{-1/2}$ neighborhood will remain asymptotically undetected, since the sample mean of x_t is consistent for zero (formal results proceed following Ploberger and Kramer 1990).

Nyblom's (1989) Test for Time-Varying Parameters

A different alternative hypothesis is that the parameters of the process are stochastic and follow a random walk. Nyblom (1989) considered the more general alternative that the parameters follow a martingale, a special case of which is the single-break model (B2), and LM tests against the random-walk alternative. He considered the case that all the parameters are time varying, but in our application we are interested as well in testing the hypothesis that a subset of the parameters are time varying. Let R be a $q \times k$ matrix of known constants, so that the null hypothesis is that $R[\alpha_t \beta_t']' = R[\alpha \beta']'$, and the alternative is that

(B13) $H_1: R[\alpha \beta_t']' = \zeta_t, \zeta_t = \zeta_{t-1} + v_t, v_t$ i.i.d. $(0, \sigma^2)$,

where $(v_1, \ldots, v_T)$ and $(\varepsilon_1, \ldots, \varepsilon_T)$ are independent. It is maintained that $R^\dagger[\alpha_t \beta_t']' - R^\dagger[\alpha \beta']' = O_p(T^{-1/2})$, where $R^\dagger$ is the complement of R in $\Re^k$. In the linear regression model (B1) for the alternative hypothesis (B13) with jointly normal i.i.d. errors, Nyblom's (1989) test is

(B14) $$L = T^{-1} \sum_{\ell=1}^{T} V_T(\ell)'(R \Sigma R')^{-1} V_T(\ell),$$

where Σ is the OLS variance-covariance matrix of (α, β) and V_T is the partial sum process $V_T(\ell) = T^{-1/2} \sum_{s=1}^{\ell} e_s[1\ x_s']'$.

In the special case that R tests only the constancy of the intercept, because the regressors have mean zero this test is asymptotically equivalent to the P-K meansq statistic. In general, however, these tests differ. Under the null hypothesis, $\varepsilon_t x_t$ is a martingale difference sequence. Thus the asymptotic null representation of the statistic is

(B15) $$L => \int_0^1 B_k(s)'B_k(s)ds.$$

For Monte Carlo results comparing these tests in the linear regression model, see Andrews, Lee, and Ploberger (1992).

References

Andrews, D. W. K., I. Lee, and W. Ploberger. 1992. Optimal changepoint tests for normal linear regression. Discussion Paper no. 1016. New Haven, Conn.: Cowles Foundation.

Andrews, D. W. K., and W. Ploberger. 1991. Optimal tests of parameter constancy. Yale University. Manuscript.

Banerjee, A., R. L. Lumsdaine, and J. H. Stock. 1992. Recursive and sequential tests of the unit root and trend break hypotheses: Theory and international evidence. *Journal of Business and Economic Statistics* 10: 271–88.

Bernanke, B. S. 1993. Comment on Friedman and Kuttner: Why does the paper-bill spread predict real economic activity. In *Business cycles, indicators and forecasting*, eds. J. H. Stock and M. W. Watson, 249–53. University of Chicago Press.

Bernanke, B. S., and A. S. Blinder. 1992. The federal funds rate and the channels of monetary transmission. *American Economic Review* 82: 901–21.

Brown, R. L., J. Durbin, and J. M. Evans. 1975. Techniques for testing the constancy of regression relationships over time with comments. *Journal of the Royal Statistical Society,* ser. B, 37: 149–92.

Christiano, L. J. 1992. Searching for a break in GNP. *Journal of Business and Economic Statistics* 10 (3):237–50.

Estrella, A., and G. Hardouvelis. 1991. The term structure as a predictor of real economic activity. *Journal of Finance* 46 (2): 555–76.

Feinman, J. N., and R. D. Porter. 1992. The continuing weakness in M2. FEDS Discussion Paper no. 209. Board of Governors of the Federal Reserve System.

Feldstein, M. 1991. Reasserting monetary control at the Fed. *Wall Street Journal,* 10 June.

———. 1992. The recent failure of U.S. monetary policy. 1992 Jan Tinbergen Lecture of the Royal Netherlands Economics Association.

Friedman, B. M., and K. N. Kuttner. 1992. Money, income, prices and interest rates. *American Economic Review* 82: 472–92.

———. 1993a. Why does the paper-bill spread predict real economic activity? In *Business cycles, indicators and forecasting,* eds. J. H. Stock and M. W. Watson, 213–49. University of Chicago Press.

———. 1993b. Another look at the evidence on money-income causality. *Journal of Econometrics* 57: 189–203.

Friedman, M. 1953. The effects of a full-employment policy on economic stabilization: A formal analysis. In *Essays in positive economics.* Chicago: University of Chicago Press.

Friedman, M., and A. Schwartz. 1963. *A monetary history of the United States, 1867–1960.* Princeton, N.J.: Princeton University Press.

Hafer, R. W., and D. W. Jansen. 1991. The demand for money in the United States: Evidence from cointegration tests. *Journal of Money, Credit and Banking* 23: 155–68.

Hansen, B. E. 1992. Tests for parameter instability in regressions with I(1) processes. *Journal of Business and Economic Statistics* 10: 321–36.

Hendry, D. F., and N. R. Ericsson. 1991. Modeling the demand for narrow money in the United Kingdom and the United States. *European Economic Review* 35: 833–86.

Hess, G. D., D. H. Small, and F. Brayton. 1992. Nominal income targeting with the monetary base as instrument: An evaluation of McCallum's rule. Board of Governors of the Federal Reserve System. Manuscript.

Hoffman, D., and R. H. Rasche. 1991. Long-run income and interest elasticities of money demand in the United States. *Review of Economics and Statistics* 73: 665–74.

Judd, J. P., and B. Motley. 1991. Nominal feedback rules for monetary policy. *Economic Review, Federal Reserve Bank of San Francisco,* no. 3 (summer): 3–17.

———. 1992. Controlling inflation with an interest rate instrument. Research Department, Federal Reserve Bank of San Francisco. Manuscript.

King, R. G., and M. W. Watson. 1992. Testing long-run neutrality. Northwestern University. Manuscript.

Konishi, T., V. A. Ramey, and C. W. J. Granger. 1992. Stochastic trends and short-run relationships between financial variables and real activity. University of California, San Diego, Department of Economics. Manuscript.

Ljungqvist, L., M. Park, J. H. Stock, and M. W. Watson. 1988. The convergence of multivariate "unit root" distributions to their asymptotic limits: The case of money-income causality. *Journal of Economic Dynamics and Control* 12 (2/3): 489–502.

MacNeill, I. B. 1978. Properties of sequences of partial sums of polynomial regression residuals with applications to tests for change of regression at unknown times. *Annals of Statistics* 6: 422–33.

McCallum, B. T. 1988. *Robustness properties of a rule for monetary policy.* Carnegie-Rochester Conference Series on Public Policy, vol. 29: 175–203. Amsterdam: North-Holland.

———. 1990. Targets, indicators, and instruments of monetary policy. In *Monetary policy for a changing financial environment,* eds. W. S. Haraf and P. Cagan, 44–70. Washington, D.C.: AEI Press.

McNees, S. 1986. Forecasting accuracy of alternative techniques: A comparison of U.S. macroeconomic forecasts. *Journal of Business and Economic Statistics* 4: 5–24.

Nyblom, J. 1989. Testing for the constancy of parameters over time. *Journal of the American Statistical Association* 84: 223–30.

Pecchinino, R. A., and R. H. Rasche. 1990. P*-type models: Evaluation and forecasts. NBER Working Paper no. 3406. Cambridge, Mass.: National Bureau of Economic Research.

Phillips, P. C. B., and M. Loretan. 1991. Estimating long run economic equilibria. *Review of Economic Studies* 58: 407–36.

Ploberger, W., and W. Kramer. 1990. The local power of the CUSUM and CUSUM of squares tests. *Econometric Theory* 6: 335–47.

———. 1992a. The CUSUM test with OLS residuals. *Econometrica* 60: 271–86.

———. 1992b. A trend-resistant test for structural change based on OLS-residuals. University of Dortmund, Department of Statistics. Manuscript.

Quandt, R. E. 1960. Tests of the hypothesis that a linear regression system obeys two separate regimes. *Journal of the American Statistical Association* 55: 324–30.

Saikkonen, P. 1991. Asymptotically efficient estimation of cointegrating regressions. *Econometric Theory* 7: 1–21.

Sims, C. A. 1972. Money, income and causality. *American Economic Review* 62: 540–52.

———. 1980. Macroeconomics and reality. *Econometrica* 48: 1–48.

———. 1982. Policy analysis with econometric models. *Brookings Papers on Economic Activity* 1: 107–64.

———. 1986. Are forecasting models usable for policy analysis? *Quarterly Review, Federal Reserve Bank of Minneapolis,* winter, 2–16.

Stock, J. H., and M. W. Watson. 1989a. Interpreting the evidence on money-income causality. *Journal of Econometrics* 40 (1): 161–82.

———. 1989b. New indexes of leading and coincident economic indicators. *NBER Macroeconomics Annual,* 351–94.

———. 1990. Business cycle properties of selected U.S. economic time series, 1959–1988. NBER Working Paper no. 3376. Cambridge, Mass.: National Bureau of Economic Research.

———. 1993. A simple estimator of cointegrating vectors in higher-order integrated systems. *Econometrica* 61 (4): 783–820.

Taylor, J. B. 1985. *What would nominal GNP targeting do to the business cycle?* Carnegie-Rochester Conference Series on Public Policy, vol. 22: 61–84. Amsterdam: North-Holland.

Comment   John B. Taylor

My comments focus mainly on the policy aspects of this paper by Martin Feldstein and James Stock. The authors provide us with a thorough analysis of nominal GDP targeting culminating in a specific policy rule for the Federal Open Market Committee (FOMC) to follow when conducting monetary policy. Actually there are two alternative policy rules discussed in the paper. One rule is extraordinarily complicated. It would have the FOMC respond to several lagged values of every variable the authors bring into the analysis. This rule is computed using linear quadratic control methods based on an estimated vector autoregression.

The second policy rule is a very simple feedback rule in which the growth rate of M2 is adjusted in response to the deviations of nominal GDP growth from a stated target. When nominal GDP growth exceeds the target, the growth of M2 is slowed by the FOMC. When nominal GDP growth falls below target, the growth of M2 speeds up. The authors favor the second simple rule over the more complicated rule. For example, they do not even write down the more complicated rule in the paper. Hence, most of my comments are directed to this simple rule.

I find several features of the Feldstein/Stock policy analysis and their proposals for monetary policy to be very attractive. First, monetary policy actions are discussed entirely within a modern policy rule framework. The paper shows how sophisticated econometric analysis can be brought into the policy evaluation process and at the same time incorporate the advantages of policy rules, including credibility and greater certainty about policy.

Second, the policy rule they propose is an example of a responsive rule that contrasts with constant growth rate rules for the money supply, as proposed by Milton Friedman. The authors provide considerable evidence that this responsiveness would improve economic performance. This more general notion of a policy rule is a common feature of modern macro research.

Third, the rule implicitly entails a flexible exchange-rate system. Monetary policy—as described by their policy rule—is not guided directly by exchange rates or events abroad. That this is likely to be preferred to a policy rule that incorporates exchange rates is a finding which appears to be emerging from several research efforts, including my own.

Fourth, in analyzing the performance properties of their proposed rule—that is, how the policy rule would affect macroeconomic performance—the authors do not stop with a point estimate of the reduction in volatility of this target variable (nominal GDP). They also report statistical confidence measures. For example, they estimate that there is an 85 percent chance that the

John B. Taylor is professor of economics at Stanford University and a research associate of the National Bureau of Economic Research.

This research was supported by a grant from the National Science Foundation at the National Bureau of Economic Research and by the Stanford Center for Economic Policy Research.

simple rule would improve performance by reducing the variance of nominal GDP. This is a welcome innovation in policy evaluation research.

Fifth, the authors' method of looking for a simple rule that approximates a more complicated rule derived from optimal control is a good one. It is certainly essential that a rule be fairly simple if it is to be used in practice. While the authors' simulations indicate that their simple rule would work well in reducing the volatility of nominal GDP, it would be useful to formalize the approximation method. It might be possible to improve on the approximation and show how analogous approximation methods could be used in other applications. For example, in Taylor (1981) I used results from David Livesey (1980) to approximate the more complex rules I had computed in an earlier paper (Taylor 1979).

Despite these valuable features of the Feldstein/Stock paper, I have several concerns about the results, especially when viewed as something for the FOMC to use in practice. I have some suggestions for future research based on these concerns.

One concern is methodological. In evaluating the effects of policy, Feldstein and Stock do not use a structural model. For example, they neither take a position on a credit or money view of monetary policy, nor do they say whether a sticky-price or sticky-transactions view underlies the monetary transmission mechanism; further, they state no assumptions about international capital mobility, which in many countries figures as a key issue in exchange-rate policy. Perhaps it is asking too much to provide a policy model in areas where there is still so much controversy, but in my view, depending entirely on reduced-form correlations is worse than using some structural model, or certainly worse than using several alternative structural models. Instead, the authors use an estimated vector autoregression (VAR). They simply replace the equation for M2 in the VAR and see how the stochastic-dynamic properties of the VAR change through stochastic simulation.

An alternative approach is to develop a structural econometric framework. Technically speaking, my concern is with the Lucas critique—that the parameters of the VAR will change with policy. I do not mean this criticism to be destructive, for I think using *structural* models is an alternative approach that deals with the Lucas critique. The framework I use includes staggered contracts, perfect capital mobility, and an interest-rate view of the monetary transmission mechanism. Even if you do not like this particular model, there are many structural models with which to do the analysis. For example, Ralph Bryant, Peter Hooper, and Catherine Mann (1993) have used a number of econometric models to comparatively evaluate the performance of policy rules like the one suggested by the authors.

Are these technical concerns quantitatively important to the analysis? Consider two examples. First, the authors' simulations seem to show that with their optimal policy rule, inflation would have gone into double digits in the 1970s, and the 1982 recession would have been worse than it was. See figure 1.4 of their paper. But would not a money rule such as that which the authors suggest have been able to avoid the great inflation and the subsequent great disinflation of the early 1980s? Perhaps the use of a reduced-form correlation explains this finding. Second, using the reduced forms may explain why the performance improvement is so small; the volatility of inflation is reduced by only 6.6 percent during the past twenty years.

I am also concerned with the authors' stated goal of policy. I found that the paper focused too much on *nominal* GDP growth rather than its two components. Should not the criterion of performance relate more directly to how the economy performs in the two dimensions we care about: inflation and real GDP? What are the implications of the policy rule for the fluctuations in inflation and real GDP? I am also concerned about not using the *level* of nominal GDP in the evaluation. Feldstein and Stock discuss this, but it seems to me that a good policy allows a speedup in growth (above potential GDP growth) after a recession. In my view, the faster growth in the United States compared with that in Europe just after the 1982 recession is an example of a better policy.

My preference is to examine policy in terms of (1) the deviations of real GDP from an estimate of potential GDP and (2) the fluctuations in inflation. Robert Hall and Greg Mankiw in their paper in this volume (chap. 2) call such a rule a *hybrid* nominal-income rule. I proposed such a rule in my 1985 paper (Taylor 1985) and called it a *modified* nominal-income rule. It might even be better to consider a rule that looks at the deviation of the price level from a target as well. But the point is that if we are concerned about inflation and economic fluctuations, then it would be useful to examine these features directly.

Another concern is the complete focus on M2 as the policy instrument. One of the appealing features of nominal GDP targeting is that it automatically controls for velocity shifts. If you use M2 as an instrument, you bring velocity shocks right back in. One could have considered a rule with the federal funds rate as the instrument. In fact, one rule I have found attractive has the federal funds rate adjusted up if GDP goes above target or if inflation goes above target, and vice versa. This rule comes fairly close to the type of decision the Fed actually makes, so it may be a more plausible place to begin. It also appears as a preferred instrument in the Bryant, Hooper, and Mann (1993) review of policy evaluation using structural models.

The paper addresses the *design* of a policy rule, not its *operation*. However, it raises some operational questions. How would such a rule operate in the context of the FOMC as currently constructed? Should the Fed publicly state the rule and give an explanation to Congress whenever policy does not conform to the policy rule? To get things started, one possibility, at least in the short term, would be for the FOMC to have the Fed staff put in their briefing books the M2 growth forecasts implied by the rule. Then the FOMC could at least discuss policy in the context of the rule. However, with our current state of knowledge, some alternative rules—including an interest rate rule—would probably need to be placed alongside the Feldstein/Stock rule.

References

Bryant, Ralph C., Peter Hooper, and Catherine L. Mann, eds. 1993. *Evaluating policy regimes: New research in empirical macroeconomics.* Washington, D.C.: Brookings Institution.
Livesey, D. A. 1980. Stabilization policy: A view from the complex plane. CARESS Working Paper no. 80–09. University of Pennsylvania.
Taylor, John B. 1979. Estimation and control of a macroeconomic model with rational expectations. *Econometrica* 47:1267–86.
———. 1981. Stabilization, accommodation, and monetary rules. *American Economic Review, Papers and Proceedings* 71:145–49.
———. 1985. *What would nominal GNP targeting do to the business cycle?* Carnegie-Rochester Conference Series on Public Policy, vol. 22:61–84. Amsterdam: North-Holland.

Comment   Bennett T. McCallum

The Feldstein and Stock paper is a stimulating and constructive addition to the growing literature on nominal income targeting. It includes some nice technical innovations, such as the derivation of the distribution of $\hat{r}_j$, the estimator of a variance-reduction performance measure. And from a substantive policy perspective, the spirit of Feldstein and Stock's paper is in many ways similar to that of my own work,[1] so there is much in it that I would applaud. But there are also some important differences which deserve to be pointed out.

In discussing these differences I will focus on Feldstein and Stock's simplified policy rule (13) rather than their "optimal" rule of form (9). Because of its comparative simplicity, the former is considerably more attractive from a practical policy perspective, given that it performs nearly as well as the "optimal" rule in the one particular model in which the latter is (by construction) optimal. Since there is no professional agreement on the "true" model, the

Bennett T. McCallum is the H. J. Heinz Professor of Economics at Carnegie Mellon University and a research associate of the National Bureau of Economic Research.

1. The main items are McCallum (1988, 1990a). The first of these proposes four "principles" to be kept in mind when specifying a monetary rule: (i) neither theory nor evidence points convincingly to any one of the many competing models of the dynamic interaction between nominal and real variables; (ii) output and growth levels will be essentially independent, over long spans of time, of the average rate of growth of nominal variables; (iii) a rule should specify settings of an instrument variable that the monetary authority can control directly and/or accurately; and (iv) a rule should not rely upon the absence of regulatory change and technical innovation in the payments and financial industries.

sensible way to proceed—as I have argued—is to look for a simple rule that will perform reasonably well in a variety of models.

This simplified rule (13) is fairly similar to the one emphasized in my work,[2] but differs in three significant ways. One, which Feldstein and Stock mention, is that their targets are set in terms of GDP growth rates rather than levels along a prespecified growth path. Thus their rule (13) treats past target misses as *bygones,* matters not requiring corrective action. With regard to this difference, I am quite sympathetic to their position. In fact, my most recent working paper on the subject (McCallum 1990b) provides some support for that position, that is, for targets of the form $x_t^{**} = x_{t-1} + 0.00739$ rather than $x_t^* = x_{t-1}^* + 0.00739$.[3] Of course a weighted average of x_t^{**} and x_t^* would be another possibility worth considering.

A second difference, not explicitly mentioned, is that my rule is specified in terms of settings for the monetary base rather than M2.[4] One of my tenets for the analysis of policy rules has been that a rule should be specified in operational form, relying on available data and with an instrument that the Fed can actually control. Feldstein and Stock recognize that M2 is not such a variable, and that as matters stand their rule would not be operational. Their response is to propose some rather major regulatory changes that would make M2 more controllable—basically, uniform reserve requirements on all components of M2 (with the payment of interest on reserves). But even with such changes, M2 would still not be a fully controllable instrument—it would not be a quantity that appears on the Fed's own balance sheet or an instantly observable interest rate. So a complete statement of their rule would still require specification of the link between M2 and a genuine instrument. And regarding the suitability of the base as an instrument, I would argue that their results in section 1.6 are not compelling. What they show is that there has not been a stable relationship between the base and nominal GDP over the period 1960–92. But my rule was designed to be applicable despite changing relationships (see principle [iv] in note 1) and therefore embodies two semiactivist adjustment mechanisms, one intended for cyclical fluctuations and one for longer-lasting institutional changes.

The third difference in rule specification is less obvious. It is that their rule

---

2. That rule specifies quarterly adjustments in growth of the monetary base according to the formula $\Delta b_t = 0.00739 - (1/16)(x_{t-1} - b_{t-1} - x_{t-17} + b_{t-17}) + \lambda(x_{t-1}^* - x_{t-1})$ where b_t and x_t are logs of the monetary base and nominal GNP averaged over quarter t. The target variable x_t^* grows at a constant pace, $x_t^* = x_{t-1}^* + 0.00739$, chosen to reflect an assumed 3 percent annual growth rate of output and zero inflation. These values could of course be specified differently without affecting the form of the rule. Various values of the adjustment coefficient λ have been considered, with good performance obtained for the range of values 0.1–0.25.

3. For notation, see note 2.

4. McCallum (1990a) also considers the use of a short-term interest-rate instrument. In his recent work on nominal income targeting, John Taylor (1988, 1993) has used an interest-rate instrument. This is, of course, the instrument actually used at present by almost all central banks. For an attempt to explain this practice, see Goodfriend (1990).

(13) relies upon an assumption about the average growth rate of velocity that will prevail in the future. Whereas my rule constantly updates its implicit forecasts of this magnitude on the basis of past velocity changes, theirs incorporates the assumption that M2 velocity growth will be fixed at the value zero. It is of course true that M2 velocity has shown neither upward nor downward trends since 1960, but I believe it would be a mistake to rely upon this pattern to continue in the future. After all, M2 velocity behavior was drastically different before 1960, as chart 57 of Friedman and Schwartz (1963, 640) quite clearly shows.

Therefore, from a methodological perspective, I would fault the Feldstein and Stock study for building this constant-velocity assumption into their rule when studying its performance over the period 1960–92. Had they proposed their rule (13) in 1960, they would have had no basis for setting μ_m equal to μ_x, so the specification studied in table 1.10 is one that relies on ex post knowledge gained from the experience of the 1960–92 period. The rule used in my studies, by contrast, relies on no such ex post knowledge but instead incorporates the velocity-adjustment term mentioned above.

I would also suggest, in conclusion, that their presumption about velocity growth is one manifestation of a somewhat excessive emphasis on a rule's ability to smooth fluctuations, with inadequate concern given to its "trend" properties—to its ability to generate the desired amount of inflation on average (be it 0 or 2 percent per annum, or whatever). Feldstein and Stock conduct their study as if it were trivial to design a rule that would accomplish this objective. But it is not, I would suggest, in analytical studies that are realistic about operationality and about our lack of knowledge of the economy's structure.[5]

References

Friedman, Milton, and Anna J. Schwartz. 1963. *A monetary history of the United States, 1867–1960.* Princeton: Princeton University Press.

Goodfriend, Marvin. 1991. *Interest rates and the conduct of monetary Policy.* Carnegie-Rochester Conference Series on Public Policy, vol. 34 (spring): 7–30. Amsterdam: North-Holland.

McCallum, Bennett T. 1988. *Robustness properties of a rule for monetary policy.* Carnegie-Rochester Conference Series on Public Policy, vol. 29, (autumn): 173–204. Amsterdam: North-Holland.

———. 1990a. Targets, indicators, and instruments of monetary policy. In *Monetary policy for a changing financial environment,* eds. William S. Haraf and Phillip Cagan. Washington, D.C.: American Enterprise Institute.

———. 1990b. Recent developments in monetarist thought. Unpublished working paper, November.

Taylor, John B. 1988. The treatment of expectations in large multicountry econometric

5. See principles (i), (iii), and (iv) in note 1.

models. In *Empirical macroeconomics for interdependent economies,* eds. Ralph C. Bryant, Dale W. Henderson, Gerald Holtham, Peter Hooper, and Steven A. Symansky. Washington, D.C.: Brookings Institution.

————. 1993. *Macroeconomic policy in world economy: From econometric design to practical operation.* New York: W. W. Norton.

2   Nominal Income Targeting

Robert E. Hall and N. Gregory Mankiw

There is increasing agreement among economists on two broad principles of monetary policy. The first principle is that monetary policy should aim to stabilize some nominal quantity. Monetarists have sought to make monetary policy stabilize the growth of the nominal money stock. In some periods of history, policy has been committed to pegging the nominal price of gold. Some economists have proposed stabilizing a bundle of commodity prices or even the consumer price index (CPI).

The second principle, which was taken for granted up until the past fifty years, is the desirability of a credible commitment to a fixed rule for monetary policy. It is now apparent that there are substantial gains if the central bank commits in advance to a set policy, rather than leaving itself free to exercise unconstrained discretion. Traditionally, policy rules took the form of a committed value for the monetary unit in terms of gold or silver. Today, the focus is on rules that promise to deliver better performance as measured by stability in output and prices. One frequently advocated rule is targeting nominal income. Some advocates of such rules advocate the complete suppression of discretion in monetary policy-making; others view the rules as more general guides and would give policymakers discretion to depart occasionally from targets.

This paper explores some of the issues raised by rules for monetary policy. We proceed as follows. Section 2.1 discusses the desirable properties of commitment and the characteristics of a good policy rule. We emphasize, in particular, rules aimed at stabilizing nominal income. Section 2.2 considers how a government could implement a nominal income rule. We discuss the role that

Robert E. Hall is professor of economics at Stanford University and the director of the NBER Program in Economic Fluctuations. N. Gregory Mankiw is professor of economics at Harvard University and director of the NBER Program in Monetary Economics.

The authors are grateful to John Driscoll and Stefan Oppers for research assistance, to Kenneth West for comments, and to the National Science Foundation for financial support.

the consensus forecast of nominal income could play in ensuring that the central bank not deviate from an announced target. Section 2.3 examines the time-series properties of nominal income and its consensus forecast in order to evaluate how actual policy has differed from nominal income targeting. Section 2.4 presents simulations using a simple model of the economy in order to consider how economic performance might have differed historically if the Fed had been committed to some type of a nominal income target.

2.1   Rules for Monetary Policy

We begin by discussing some general issues regarding rules for monetary policy.

2.1.1   The Benefits of Rules

The principal economic argument for policy rules comes from the analysis of strategic behavior. It is a general proposition that a player in a game has much to gain from the ability to commit in advance (Fudenberg and Tirole, 1991, 74–77). Absent that ability, a player cannot make a credible threat to take a later action that will not be in the player's interest when the time comes to take the action. The most cosmic example is the doomsday bomb, wired in advance to destroy the world upon nuclear attack. Similarly, it can be advantageous to commit *not* to take an action that would be rational on the spot. For example, as Fischer (1980) pointed out, it is desirable that the government be able to commit not to impose one-time capital levies. Commitment in advance is essential, because an unexpected one-time capital levy is the ideal nondistorting tax once capital is in place.

Kydland and Prescott (1977), Barro and Gordon (1983), and others applied this principle to monetary policy, pursuing Lucas's (1972) hypothesis that surprising monetary expansions raise output. If other distortions in the economy make it desirable to raise output, then the government will, rationally, try to create a new surprise each year. But the public will be able to see what the government is doing. The result of these attempted monetary surprises, therefore, will be higher expected inflation and higher actual inflation, but not higher output. By committing in advance not to try to create monetary surprises, the government can lower expected inflation and achieve better performance.

The monetary history of the United States and many other countries seems to support this view. After the gradual departure from the commitments implicit in the Bretton Woods system, there was a worldwide episode of inflation in the 1970s. It appears that most major governments are now committed to reasonably stable prices. Yet the form of the commitment is vague. One of our purposes in this paper is to discuss ways that the commitment could be made more precise and therefore more credible. Because any reasonable government will abandon a policy rule that is unworkable, there must be a strong practical case in favor of any particular form of commitment.

There is also a political argument for policy rules. If the central bank is under the control of elected politicians, or is closely allied with their interests, it may be tempted to make opportunistic policy changes before elections. A rule for monetary policy would largely suppress these political influences. Moreover, to the extent that a monetary rule induces the central bank to offset the macroeconomic effects of fiscal policy, as a nominal income target would, a monetary rule can suppress the political business cycle resulting from fiscal policy as well.

2.1.2 Characteristics of a Good Rule for Monetary Policy

The generic monetary policy rule requires the central bank to keep a designated indicator within a prescribed band. A rule is defined by the choice of indicator and the location and width of the band. In evaluating the desirability of a particular rule, there are four principal characteristics to consider.

The first characteristic is *efficiency*. A good policy should deliver the minimum amount of price variability for a given level of employment variability. To put it differently, one should restrict attention to those policies that are on the frontier in the price variability-employment variability space. In the past, economists have derived optimal policy rules within fully developed macro models. By contrast, we would recommend a different approach. A policy rule should deliver satisfactory performance across a wide spectrum of macro models. On the one hand, the policy should give reasonable price stability in a model of full monetary neutrality, where monetary policy has no important influence over real activity. On the other hand, the policy should yield a reasonable compromise between price and employment stability in a model where money is not neutral.

A second characteristic of a good rule is *simplicity*. A rule that is simple has a better chance of adoption in the first place and a better chance of continuing to be enforced. Closely related is *precision*. Under a precise rule, such as "Keep the price of gold at $300 per ounce," there can be no doubt whether the central bank is adhering to the rule. A rule such as "Keep employment stable in the short run but prevent inflation in the long run" has proven to be hopelessly vague; a central bank can rationalize almost any policy position within that rule.

A fourth characteristic, closely related to simplicity and precision, is *accountability*. A monetary policy is more credible if the citizens of a country can make the agency responsible for monetary policy—typically the central bank—accountable for achieving the policy. Therefore, a policy rule should have the property that there is no doubt whether the central bank is performing its role properly. Under the relatively vague definition of the Federal Reserve's responsibilities currently in force, the Fed can justify a range of actions as being consistent with achieving price and output stability. When policy turns too expansionary, as it probably did in the early 1970s, or too contractionary, as it probably did in the early 1980s, there is no immediate breach of the rule for which the Fed can be disciplined. By contrast, these policy deviations would have been unambiguous under the type of policy we consider below.

Policy rules—even those with these four desirable characteristics—have side effects. Keeping one variable under tight control may bring high volatility to other variables. Rules that make an intelligent choice between price and employment stability may require tolerance of large swings in interest rates and exchange rates, for example, especially if policy in other major countries is volatile. Yet if a policy rule is on the frontier of price and employment stability, such side effects should probably be ignored.

2.1.3 Rules Based on Nominal Income

Recent advocates of rules for monetary policy have called for the close pegging of a variety of nominal indicators—monetary aggregates, commodity price indexes, the consumer price index, exchange rates, and the price of gold. But it seems fair to say that the consensus today favors nominal income as the most suitable object of monetary policy.

Keeping nominal income on a smooth path is a monetary policy that receives support from all branches of modern macroeconomics. In equilibrium macroeconomics, with full monetary neutrality, smooth growth of nominal income implies a path for the price level which is simply the ratio of the nominal income target to the equilibrium level of real income. Absent erratic behavior of equilibrium output, price stability will be the result of the policy. In views of macroeconomics admitting monetary nonneutrality, the nominal income standard amounts to an intermediate position on the hard question of how monetary policy should respond to a shock to the price level. Under a nominal income target, real output falls 1 percent for each percentage point by which the price level is too high. By contrast, under a price standard, monetary policy would be called upon to deliver unlimited contraction until it eliminated all of a price shock. Later, we will illustrate the operation of a nominal income target in a simple aggregate model with a Phillips curve. But the desirability of this policy comes from its robustness with respect to the characteristics of the economy in general and to the sources of monetary nonneutrality in particular.

Nominal income targeting is one policy in a broader class which Hall (1985) dubbed "elastic price targets." Policies in this class set a fundamental price target, but permit deviations from the target to the extent that the unemployment rate deviates from its equilibrium level. A more elastic policy permits a larger price deviation per point of unemployment deviation. Within a Phillips curve economy, an elastic price policy is efficient in the sense we defined earlier: it puts the economy on the frontier of best achievable combinations of price and employment variability.

The policy of targeting nominal income has long been discussed among economists. Early contributions to the contemporary literature are Meade (1978), von Weizsäcker (1978), and Tobin (1980). Bean (1983) developed a formal analysis of the implications of nominal income stabilization in a general equilibrium macro model. In his model, there is an "aggregate demand" shock whose effects are the same as those of a random component of the money stock. All reasonable policies offset the part of this shock that is known when monetary policy is determined. In addition, the model considers a random shift of the production function. With inelastic labor supply, nominal income targeting minimizes the variance of the deviation of real output from its equilibrium value; otherwise, the minimum variance policy targets a combination of real income and the price level with different weights on the two variables.

West (1986) pointed out that Bean's conclusions were specific to his particular model of monetary nonneutrality. Moreover, Bean used a criterion to evaluate the performance of policy that gives no weight to stability of the price level. Finally, Bean did not consider the source of disturbances that seem to have generated the most acute problems of monetary policy in the last few decades—random disturbances in the price level itself. Asako and Wagner (1992) further investigated issues raised by the Bean and West papers.

Taylor (1985) concentrated on dynamic aspects of nominal income targeting. He considered three policy rules. The first calls upon the central bank to keep the *growth* of nominal income as close to a constant as possible. Past deviations from the policy are not considered in setting the policy for a new year. The second policy is an empirical summary of actual postwar policy. The third sets the nominal income growth target equal to a prescribed constant plus the deviation of real income from equilibrium at the beginning of the year; this rule has the central bank raise nominal income growth when the economy is in recession.

According to Taylor's calculations, the effects of stabilizing the growth rate of nominal income are quite unfavorable: because the rule does not concern itself with the level of real activity, it lets random shocks build into large movements of output, with overshooting relative to equilibrium. The postwar actual policy rule does better on this account. The third rule seems to deliver the best performance, when the volatilities of output and inflation are the criteria.

Taylor called attention to the importance of stabilizing the *level* of real output and not its rate of change, if the level is what really matters. The same point applies to the price level, though Taylor does not explore this area. If the ultimate goal is to stabilize the price level, then the logic developed in Taylor's paper with respect to the level of output applies equally to the price level. Policy should make up for deviations of the level of output from equilibrium and the price level from target. The best policy rule will be one that keeps the *level* of nominal income on a target path.

McCallum (1988) made two important contributions to the recent literature on stabilization. First, he stressed the need for robustness in policy rules: given our ignorance of the true structural model of the economy, a good policy will be one that performs reasonably well across a wide variety of models, rather than one that is optimal for one model. Second, McCallum focused on a policy rule to which the central bank could be held precisely accountable. Rather than prescribe a nominal income target, McCallum would prescribe changes in the bank's own portfolio based on the most recent observation of nominal income and on various lagged variables. In McCallum's view, the central bank could be held to a much tighter standard for the monetary base than for nominal income.

Interestingly, none of the theoretical papers on stabilization has tackled the questions of the fundamental motivation for stabilizing either output or the price level. Two questions seem central: Should policy try to stabilize the growth rate or the level of real activity? Should policy try to stabilize the inflation rate or the price level? These questions have remained largely outside the professional commentary on stabilization. For real activity, if there is an increasing marginal cost of departures of real output from equilibrium, then a simple convexity argument establishes that volatility is socially undesirable. In this case, Taylor is right that stabilization efforts should be directed at the level, not the rate of growth. Alternatively, if fluctuations are costly in part because there are costs associated with adjusting to different levels of economic activity, then the volatility of the growth rate may be of independent interest.

For prices, the issue is even less clear. As Hall (1985) observed, an important source of the social cost of unstable prices is in personal financial planning. It would appear to be desirable to run the economy so that the probability distribution of the price level thirty years in the future has a mean close to the current level (no chronic inflation) and with only a moderate amount of dispersion. In this respect, it would be better to stabilize the price level rather than the rate of inflation. By contrast, under inflation stabilization, there will be a random-walk element to the price level, representing the accumulation of random influences not deliberately canceled by stabilization policy. The variance of the conditional distribution of the future price level will grow in proportion to the time horizon. By thirty years out, the dispersion will inevitably be large, even though the incremental randomness from each year may be small.

Other costs of price instability point toward the desirability of inflation stabilization. For example, a traditional argument holds that inflation is socially costly because it enlarges the wedge between the private cost of holding currency and the social cost of producing it. By this argument, it would only add to the social cost of a burst of inflation for it to be followed by a compensatory period of deflation, as a policy to stabilize the price level would mandate.

A related question is the measure of the price level that is most suited for stabilization. Again, the answer should flow from a theory of the social benefits of price stability. If the benefits are mainly in the area of personal financial planning, the object of stabilization should be prices relevant for consumers. Monetary policy could promise to remove almost all macroeconomic uncertainty from the CPI, so families could plan without having to consider variations in the purchasing power of their earnings. Alternatively, the promise could apply to a wage index, so plans could be made without macro uncertainty about earnings. A compromise between the two would be the gross domestic product implicit deflator. In the past few decades, the primary source of differences between the CPI and the implicit deflator has been the world oil price. Because the United States consumes more oil than it produces, the CPI gives more weight to oil than does the implicit deflator. Stabilizing the implicit deflator or the nominal wage means that monetary policy does not have to erase all of the effect of changing oil prices on the cost of living. By contrast, under CPI stabilization, changes in oil prices would necessitate changes (in the opposite direction) in the implicit deflator and nominal wages.

2.1.4   Conclusions on the Form of the Monetary Policy Rule

We find a reasonable professional consensus on the proposition that a good, if not precisely optimal, rule for monetary policy is to target nominal income. The exact form of a nominal income target depends on one's view of the relative importance of stabilizing the level or growth of output, and of stabilizing the price level or inflation rate. The literature suggests a consideration of three types of nominal income policies:

- *Growth-rate targeting.* Keep the growth of nominal income as close to a constant as possible.
- *Level targeting.* Keep the level of nominal income as close as possible to a path that is prescribed, once and for all, at the time the policy is first put into effect.
- *Hybrid targeting.* Keep the growth of nominal income over the coming year as close as possible to a constant plus the current percentage gap between real income and its equilibrium level.

Below we perform some simulations to estimate the economic performance that might result from each of these policies. Our next topic, however, is how the central bank should implement a nominal income policy rule.

2.2   Implementation of the Policy Rule

The feedback from monetary change—purchases or sales of securities in exchange for reserves—to nominal income is notoriously slow. Proposals to stabilize nominal income through optimal control rules based on estimated causal relations between money growth and nominal income growth may lack robustness. Control rules must be biased strongly toward inaction in order to avoid the possibility of unstable feedback.

Control is most effective and least likely to result in instability when the variable under control responds quickly to the inputs. Steering a car comes naturally to most people because the effects of moving the steering wheel are almost instantaneous. Steering a large ship is a highly specialized task because there are long lags between changing the rudder and the actual movement of the ship. And once the ship starts to turn, it continues long after the rudder is returned to normal. A novice is likely to oversteer in the first place and then make larger and larger unstable corrections. A central bank faces a similar problem if it uses its portfolio to keep nominal income on target.

As Gordon (1985) and Hall (1985) observed, forecasts can help deal with the problem of long lags and unstable feedback. The spirit of such a rule is that policy is too expansionary when today's forecast of nominal income a year or two hence is above the target for that time. It is reasonable to expect the central bank to make the forecast of a serious independent forecaster exactly on target, even though it could never be expected to put actual income on target. The feedback loop from current monetary policy to current forecasts of nominal income a year or two in the future is quick and powerful. It takes many months for monetary policy to affect actual income, but the consensus forecast that far in the future is quite responsive to current monetary policy. Within a few days of a change in monetary policy, the consensus forecast changes to reflect expert opinions about the effects on all macro variables, including nominal income.

In the United States, the Federal Reserve Board already is a close follower of outside forecasts. Moreover, the Fed has a large and respected forecasting group of its own. Forecasts are already an important part of the process of executing policy. Just as the experienced pilot of a large ship can predict the movements of the ship well into the future, based on observations of tide, wind, engine speed, and rudder settings, the Fed already takes advantage of the contribution that forecasts make to the control process. Were the Fed to be fully committed to the nominal income target, it would probably be unnecessary to tell it to use forecasts to improve the feedback control process.

The most important role of forecasts is to enforce the monetary policy rule upon the central bank. Because there are random unpredictable determinants of nominal income, the central bank cannot be expected to keep nominal income itself exactly on target. A band of a few percentage points in either direction would have to be part of a statement of a policy rule formulated in terms of nominal income itself. In this case, the public could not know whether any given deviation from the policy rule was the result of recent random events or the result of the central bank having decided to depart from the rule.

By contrast, there is no need for any band if the policy is stated in terms of a forecast for one to two years in the future. If the consensus of outside forecasters says that nominal income will come in below target, the public and the legislature will know that the central bank has failed to adhere to the policy. A policy to peg the consensus forecast is on much the same footing as a policy to peg the exchange rate; it is subject to immediate and almost indisputable verification.

We say "almost indisputable" because there is an issue of defining the consensus. In the United States, there is a published consensus of respected private forecasters (*Blue Chip Economic Indicators*), but the definition of the consensus is potentially open to argument. Compared to the current debates about the conduct of monetary policy, however, this issue seems minor.

The argument for tying the Fed to outside forecasts rests in part on a principal-agent argument. A principal (in this case, the citizens) needs to set up incentives for the agent (the Fed) to deliver the result that the principal wants. The agent's own incentives can lead to behavior quite undesirable for the principal. Certainly the chronic inflation experienced in much of the postwar era supports this style of analysis. Even if there is some reduction in policy effectiveness associated with tying monetary policy to outside forecasts, this may be a reasonable price to pay to solve the principal-agent problem.

Once the Fed is committed to pegging the consensus forecast of nominal income, we see no need to tell it how to go about achieving the peg. The Fed's bond traders should simply buy or sell securities as needed to keep the forecast at the peg. In practice, this would be similar to the way in which many central banks today achieve exchange-rate pegs. There is a difference in response time, of course. The exchange rate reacts to portfolio changes in a few seconds, whereas the consensus forecast reacts to portfolio changes in a few days or a week. Just as a supertanker needs a more qualified pilot than a small ship, a central bank pegging a nominal income forecast needs a better technician than one pegging an exchange rate. But the peg is still just a technical issue.

2.2.1 The Lead Time

So far, we have discussed the idea of targeting nominal income forecasts made today for a year or two in the future. How should the lead time be chosen? If the forecast lead time is short, pegging the forecast will come close to achieving the nominal income target itself. That is, the error in a forecast for nominal income next quarter is smaller on average than the error in a forecast for four or eight quarters in the future. Thus a short lead time yields a policy with little slippage relative to the target. On the other hand, a short lead time means that the target—the forecast for the near future—is not very responsive to monetary policy. Large swings in interest rates, exchange rates, and related variables may be needed to keep the forecast on target.

Moreover, it is not entirely clear whether closer achievement of the nominal income target is desirable. Nominal income targeting puts a large implicit weight on price stability. Using a forecast for nominal income well into the future to guide monetary policy is more tolerant of short-term disturbances in the price level. It may therefore result in an economy that performs better than one that is held to a tight short-term nominal income target.

2.3 The Time-Series Behavior of Nominal Income and Its Forecasts

In this section we examine the time-series behavior of actual nominal income and forecasts of nominal income. First, we examine the predictive power of the consensus forecast; we show that the power is substantial, so that the forecast makes sense as a target. Second, we comment on what type of nominal income rule comes closest to describing the Fed's actual policies over the past two decades.

2.3.1 The Predictive Power of the Consensus Forecast

How predictable is growth in nominal income over the next year? In tables 2.1 and 2.2 we present regressions of the change in the log of nominal gross national product (GNP), denoted x, over four quarters on variables one might use to forecast this variable, including the consensus forecast. The residual

Table 2.1   **The Efficiency of Nominal Income Forecasts, Part I**

	Dependent Variable $x_{+4} - x$				
	(0)	(1)	(2)	(3)	(4)
Constant	.011	.009	.007	.003	.002
	(.014)	(.018)	(.013)	(.015)	(.014)
Forecast	.825	.790	1.108	.870	1.180
	(.178)	(.170)	(.189)	(.184)	(.207)
$x - x_{-1}$		.139			
		(.333)			
$x_{-1} - x_{-2}$		.039			
		(.284)			
$x_{-2} - x_{-3}$		.019			
		(.226)			
$x_{-3} - x_{-4}$		.067			
		(.285)			
$p - p_{-1}$			1.198		1.216
			(.516)		(.536)
$p_{-1} - p_{-2}$			−.311		−.382
			(.505)		(.516)
$p_{-2} - p_{-3}$			−.953		−1.152
			(.539)		(.609)
$p_{-3} - p_{-4}$			−1.308		−1.232
			(.714)		(.795)
$y - y_{-1}$				.109	−.192
				(.391)	(.307)
$y_{-1} - y_{-2}$				.131	−.095
				(.273)	(.279)
$y_{-2} - y_{-3}$				.177	.181
				(.205)	(.216)
$y_{-3} - y_{-4}$				.311	.225
				(.279)	(.290)
$\bar{R}^2$	.38	.35	.43	.38	.42
p-value		.95	.16	.56	.12
S.E.E.	.023	.023	.022	.023	.022

Note: Standard errors are in parentheses. These are computed allowing for heteroskedasticity and an MA(3) error term.

Table 2.2   **The Efficiency of Nominal Income Forecasts, Part II**

	Dependent Variable $x_{+4} - x$			
	(0)	(1)	(2)	(3)
Constant	.011	.0006	.0067	.044
	(.014)	(.016)	(.014)	(.016)
Forecast	.825	.845	.668	.880
	(.178)	(.177)	(.217)	(.137)
$M1 - M1_{-1}$		.193		
		(.216)		
$M1_{-1} - M1_{-2}$		−.086		
		(.255)		
$M1_{-2} - M1_{-3}$		−.069		
		(.247)		
$M1_{-3} - M1_{-4}$		.489		
		(.333)		
$M2 - M2_{-1}$			.561	
			(.289)	
$M2_{-1} - M2_{-2}$			−.132	
			(.248)	
$M2_{-2} - M2_{-3}$			−.126	
			(.282)	
$M2_{-3} - M2_{-4}$			.559	
			(.348)	
r				−2.15
				(1.32)
r_{-1}				−1.01
				(2.07)
r_{-2}				1.41
				(2.54)
r_{-3}				−2.74
				(1.98)
$\bar{R}^2$	.38	.38	.39	.57
p-value		.25	.15	.00
S.E.E.	.023	.023	.022	.019

Note: Standard errors are in parentheses. These are computed allowing for heteroskedasticity and an MA(3) error term.

from such a regression should follow a moving average process, so we report robust standard errors. We examine the period 1971:2–1992:4, for which we have data on the consensus forecast. We obtained the consensus forecast from Steven McNees of the Federal Reserve Bank of Boston. These consensus forecasts are the median of the forecasts of several large forecasting firms.

The regression in the first column of table 2.1 indicates that the consensus forecast by itself is a good indicator for the future path of nominal income. The R^2 of the regression with only the consensus forecast is 0.38. Other forecasting variables contribute little beyond the consensus forecast. The other columns of table 2.1 try lags of nominal GNP, prices (p), real GNP (y), and prices and real

GNP together. The regressions in table 2.2 try traditional indicators of monetary policy: the growth in monetary aggregates and the federal funds rate (r).

If the consensus forecast were fully rational, it would aggregate all available information, so that none of the other variables would help forecast nominal GNP growth. The evidence on this point is almost, but not quite, decisive. In all these regressions, the coefficient on the forecast is close to the theoretically predicted value of one. In most cases, the hypothesis that the coefficients on the other lagged variables are zero cannot be rejected at conventional significance levels. The only exception is regression (3) in table 2.2: lagged interest rates appear to help predict growth in nominal income. This apparent rejection of forecast rationality may be the result of the small sample bias discussed in Mankiw and Shapiro (1986).

Overall, the results in tables 2.1 and 2.2 suggest that substantial information is contained in the consensus forecast of nominal income. This finding is broadly supportive of the plan of using the consensus as the target for monetary policy. That is, the consensus is a reasonable indicator of future values of a key nominal quantity.

2.3.2   The Fed's Historical Policy

Although the Fed has never adopted any formal nominal income target, it is interesting to see to what extent the actual behavior of nominal income and its forecast have corresponded to any form of nominal income targeting. The line marked with squares in figure 2.1 shows the data for the four-quarter ahead consensus forecast of nominal GNP growth. Data on forecasted growth are useful to examine because they eliminate noise coming from short-run surprises.

The data show no sign of any policy of stabilizing the forecasted *level* of nominal GNP. Under a level policy, forecasted growth in nominal income would be low when nominal income was above the target path and *vice versa*. The line in figure 2.1 marked with circles shows the deviation of the level of nominal GNP from its trend path over the period from 1969 through 1991. For the decade from 1971 to 1981, nominal GNP rose further and further above trend, but there was no systematic decline in forecasted nominal growth. Toward the end of the period, when nominal income was much closer to trend, forecasted nominal GNP growth was actually lower than at almost any earlier time.

Another approach to determining if policy has followed a level target is to look at the serial correlation of nominal income growth itself. Under level targeting, the serial correlation would be negative, as policy would depress growth in later quarters if nominal GNP grew excessively in one quarter. But the actual autocorrelations of nominal income growth are somewhat positive.

There is also little evidence that the Fed has followed a policy of keeping nominal GNP *growth* constant. In contrast to what would occur under growth-rate targeting, forecasted nominal income growth fluctuated substantially

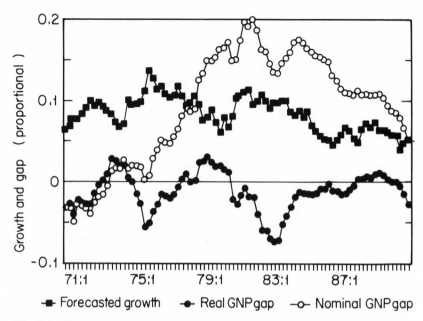

Fig. 2.1   Forecasted nominal GNP growth

through 1980. Starting in 1980, however, the data are roughly consistent with the idea that policy adopted the rule of gradually slowing nominal income growth through 1985, and then holding it at a constant level of about 6 percent per year.

The data show some support for the idea that the Fed pursued a policy similar to hybrid targeting. The lower line shows the real GNP gap at the time of the forecast. The hybrid policy would call for higher forecasted nominal growth when the output gap was negative and lower forecasted growth when the output gap was positive. There are signs of high forecasted growth at the troughs of 1971 and 1975. Yet in late 1982 and early 1983 there is no support for the hybrid policy's strategy of raising forecasted nominal income growth when the economy is far below potential.

As a general matter, one might interpret figure 2.1 as suggesting that the Fed pursued hybrid targeting in the 1970s, and growth-rate targeting in the 1980s. Yet, throughout this period, the mean level of nominal income growth was too high to prevent chronic inflation.

2.4   A Historical Counterfactual

Our goal in this section is to examine how economic performance might have differed historically if the Fed had pursued a policy of targeting nominal income. We specify a simple model of the economy, calibrate it to U.S. data, and then use it to examine this historical counterfactual. The model allows for monetary nonneutrality because of short-run price stickiness, and it can be described in the familiar terms of aggregate demand and aggregate supply. The behavior of aggregate supply is summarized by a backward-looking Phillips curve. Aggregate demand is summarized by the behavior of nominal income. Expressing all variables in logarithms, we can write nominal income as the sum of the price level and real income:

$$(1) \qquad\qquad x = p + y.$$

We do not look into the details of aggregate demand, but rather assume that the Fed can expand or contract as needed to keep the nominal income forecast exactly on target. We are interested in comparing historical performance with three policies for the rule governing growth in nominal income.

The first policy is *growth-rate targeting*. Under this policy, the Fed tries to keep nominal income growth stable, but it allows base drift. That is, past shocks to nominal income, whether reflected in output or prices, do not influence future nominal income growth. Therefore, growth in nominal income is white noise around a constant mean:

$$(2) \qquad\qquad \Delta x = \mu + \varepsilon.$$

We interpret this equation as the aggregate demand schedule, with the policy rule treated as an endogenous element of aggregate demand. The disturbance, ε, represents the influence of factors that cause policy to miss the nominal income growth target. With policy based on pegging the consensus forecast exactly, the disturbance is precisely the error in the consensus forecast.

The second policy is *level targeting*. Under this policy, no base drift is allowed. Shocks to nominal income, whether reflected in output or prices, are reversed in the following year, as the Fed takes action to return nominal income to the target level. Therefore, nominal income obeys

$$(3) \qquad\qquad x = \mu t + \varepsilon.$$

Again, ε is the forecast error in the consensus forecast.

The third rule is *hybrid targeting*. In contrast to the previous two policies, this policy treats output and prices differently. Under hybrid targeting, the Fed raises nominal income growth when output falls below the natural rate, but it does not adjust nominal income growth when the price level deviates from target. We express this policy as

$$(4) \qquad\qquad \Delta x = \mu + \varepsilon + (y^N - y)_{-1}.$$

The last term is the difference between potential and actual real output observed at the time the forecast is made (four or eight quarters in advance).

For all three of these policies we set the mean level of nominal income growth μ to be 2.5 percent per year.

2.4.1   The Model

We use a traditional expectations-augmented Phillips curve. In particular, inflation depends on past inflation, the deviation of output from its natural rate, and supply shocks. That is,

$$(5) \qquad \Delta p = \pi + \lambda\,(\Delta p_{-1} - \pi) + \alpha\,(y - y^N)_{-1} + v,$$

where π is the mean rate of inflation for the monetary regime, λ measures the persistence of inflation, and α governs the short-run trade-off between prices and output. To determine the natural rate of output, we use smoothed actual real GNP.[1]

To calibrate the model, we need to choose the key parameters α and λ. We apply the model to quarterly data and use λ of 0.9 and α of 0.05. These parameter estimates imply that a shock to nominal income falls about three-fourths on output and one-fourth on prices at the end of the first year. This estimate is broadly consistent with studies of U.S. data, such as Ball, Mankiw, and Romer (1988).

Next, we find the time series of shocks (ε and v). The time series for v is chosen to make the Phillips curve fit history exactly (the series has mean zero as a result of estimating the mean rate of inflation for the monetary regime as the average over the period). As an estimate of ε, we use the actual forecasting errors over four- and eight-quarter horizons, as provided by McNees.

These estimates of the forecasting errors surely overstate what would have occurred under a policy of nominal income targeting. One element of the actual forecasting errors comes from instability in monetary policy itself. For example, actual nominal GNP growth for the four quarters ending in the first quarter of 1973 was 12.4 percent, whereas the forecast made four quarters earlier was 10.1 percent. Much of this error is probably attributable to expansionary monetary policy in 1972. Similarly, unexpectedly contractionary policy was partly responsible for the huge overprediction of nominal GNP in the period ending in the first quarter of 1982, when actual nominal income fell short of forecast by 6.5 percent. These spontaneous changes in policy would not have occurred under a monetary policy rule. To take into account the increase in forecasting accuracy that would result from such a rule, we also carry out simulations with zero forecasting errors. The actual magnitude of the forecasting errors under nominal income targets probably lies somewhere between the two cases we calculate.

---

1. To be more specific, potential output is .98 times its own lagged value plus .02 times current real GNP, all multiplied by a constant so that the average level of potential is the same as the average of actual real GNP.

2.4.2   Results

Table 2.3 shows the simulation results. The first line describes the historical performance of three key macroeconomic variables from 1972 to 1991. Because of chronic inflation, the price level had a huge standard deviation of 34 percent. The rate of inflation had a relatively modest standard deviation of 2.5 percent at annual rates, but with a mean of almost 6 percent per year. The root mean squared deviation, which includes both the random deviations from the mean and the mean itself, was over 6 percent. The standard deviation of the gap between actual output and equilibrium was about 2.5 percent, and the standard deviation of the annual rate of growth of output was almost 4 percent.

The next major block presents the results under the three alternative policies discussed above, based on targeting the forecast of nominal income four quarters ahead. The lower block of table 2.3 has the same format, except that the policy execution errors, ε, are taken as zero rather than historical actuals (the price disturbances are taken as historical actuals, however). Note that, with perfect achievement of the target, the level and growth policies are the same.

Table 2.3 yields several conclusions. First, the volatility of the price level would have been much lower under any of these policies than it has been historically. This result is not surprising, of course; it follows directly from the lower mean growth of nominal income. The differences among the three alternative policies are substantial. Level targeting is the policy that would have yielded the most stable price level. The growth and hybrid policies both introduce an integrated (random-walk) element into the price level. Over a long enough period, the standard deviation of the price level would become large

Table 2.3   Performance under Alternative Four-Quarter Ahead Targets

	Price Level	Inflation (annual rate)	Output Gap	Output Growth (annual rate)
Actual				
Standard deviation	34.09	2.51	2.49	3.97
Mean		5.74		
Root mean squared deviation		6.27		
		Standard Deviations		
Simulated, actual forecast errors				
Growth	4.43	3.26	5.15	18.60
Level	1.92	2.14	3.20	6.64
Hybrid	2.34	1.74	2.26	6.28
Simulated, perfect achievement of target				
Growth and level	1.82	1.89	1.72	1.91
Hybrid	1.86	1.62	1.12	2.22

without limit. It is only good luck that causes the growth and hybrid policies to deliver reasonably low volatility of the price level. Only the level policy guarantees low volatility of the price level over long periods.[2]

Second, these policies would have yielded a more stable inflation rate than has been experienced historically. The magnitude of this result is significant: any of the nominal income targets would have reduced the average deviation of the inflation rate from zero by at least half. (Remember that much of the penalty associated with actual policy arises from the chronic inflation it produced.) The growth-rate target is less successful in stabilizing inflation than are the two other policies.

Third, the volatility of real income around its equilibrium level depends crucially on which nominal income target one considers. Growth-rate targeting scores badly by this standard, with about double the actual historical volatility, and level targeting is also above the actual. Hybrid targeting would have delivered a slightly lower volatility of real output.

The lower block of table 2.3 shows what a perfect nominal income target would achieve. The volatility in all four measures that comes from price shocks alone is around 2 percent, substantially below the volatility when forecast errors are included. Forecast errors are a major source of volatility for policies that peg forecasted future levels. The magnitude of the improvement in economic performance that would result from one of these policies depends crucially on how much forecasting would improve.

Table 2.3 shows that actual policy has been *inefficient*. A hybrid policy would have delivered better output stability and better price stability, even if the forecast errors with the policy in operation had been as large as those that had actually occurred. And the improvement in both dimensions would be even greater in the likely case that the forecast errors were smaller in the presence of a stable policy. Alternatively, a level policy could have delivered more stable prices with somewhat more output volatility, in the conservative case of historical forecast errors, and considerably lower output volatility with smaller forecast errors.

Although our explorations in this paper do not go outside the territory of policies based on nominal income, table 2.3 contains a strong hint (confirmed by calculations not presented here) that a policy that combined features of the hybrid and level policies would dominate all others. The hybrid policy gives better output performance because of its response to the level of output relative to potential. But it suffers from paying no attention to the price level. A policy that pegs the consensus forecast of a weighted average of the price level and real output, with most of the weight on output, can produce the low output

2. If there is a random-walk element in real output (a property that cannot be refuted by the existing data), targeting the level of nominal income introduces a complementary random-walk element into the price level. By contrast, a growth-rate targeting introduces a random-walk component into the price level even if real output is stationary around a deterministic trend.

volatility of the hybrid policy without incurring the cost of the integrated component of the price level.

Figures 2.2 through 2.5 illustrate the findings of table 2.3. Figure 2.2 shows the historical deviations of real GNP from potential, for comparison with the simulated deviations in the later figures. We cannot present any meaningful version of price deviations because the price level rose so much during the period.

Figure 2.3 shows our simulations for the four-quarter ahead growth policy. There are two reasons visible in the figure for the high volatility of output. First, the policy permits a collapse of output in early 1983. Under growth-rate targeting, unlike the other two policies we consider, the Fed would not alter future nominal income growth in response to the low growth in nominal and real income during the recession in 1981–82. Second, there is a sawtooth pattern to the level of output, especially after 1983. A growth-based policy propagates any such pattern into the future once it gets started. In a quarter when nominal GNP is high, a growth policy requires that the target for that quarter in the following year be correspondingly higher. The figure also shows the random walk that a growth-based policy introduces into the price level. All told, figure 2.3 amply illustrates the defects of the strict policy that considers only the rate of growth of nominal income.

Figure 2.4 shows the simulated performance of a four-quarter level policy.

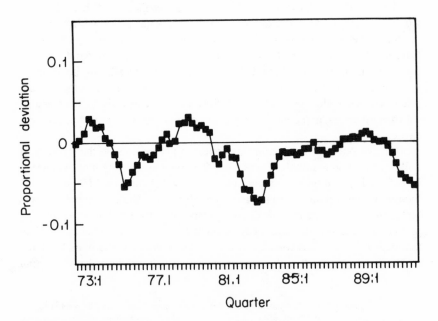

Fig. 2.2   Output deviation
Note: Actual.

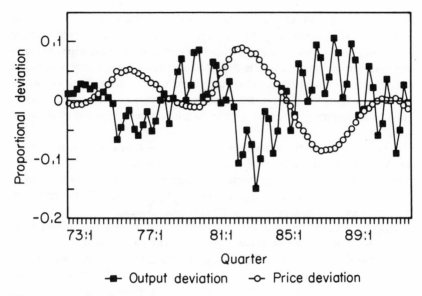

Fig. 2.3   Price level and output
Note: Four-quarter ahead growth policy.

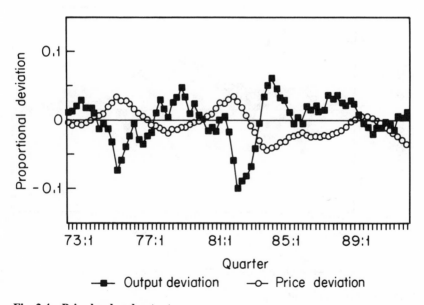

Fig. 2.4   Price level and output
Note: Four-quarter ahead level policy.

Output volatility is lower than for the growth policy, but is higher than actual. A deep recession occurs in 1981–82, based on the conservative view that the forecasting errors actually made during that period would have happened anyway and were not the result of unexpected instability in monetary policy. The price shocks around 1980 are also partly responsible for the depth of this recession. Under a level target, any short-run accommodation of price shocks must be subsequently reversed in order to return nominal income to its target path.

Figure 2.5 shows the simulation record of the hybrid policy. Its single-minded attention to keeping real output at potential makes it deliver much less output volatility than the other policies. The recession in late 1981 is about as deep as actual, but is reversed much more quickly than actually occurred. On the other hand, the drift of the price level is quite evident.

Table 2.4 provides information about the issue of the lead time for the forecasts used as policy targets. It compares four- and eight-quarter ahead targets for the three types of policy. The results in table 2.4 indicate that longer lead times may be desirable. For growth-rate targeting, the volatilities of all four measures of performance are substantially lower in the eight-quarter case. For the level and hybrid policies, price stability is comparable for both lead times, and output volatility is lower for the eight-quarter lead time.

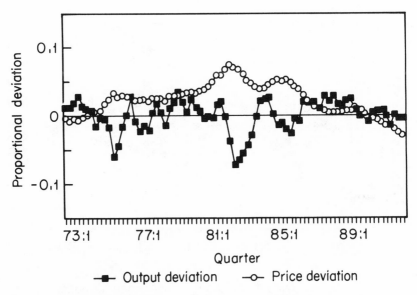

Fig. 2.5 Price level and output
Note: Four-quarter ahead hybrid policy.

Table 2.4   Comparison of Four-Quarter and Eight-Quarter Ahead Targets

	Price Level	Inflation (annual rate)	Output Gap	Output Growth (annual rate)
Simulated, actual forecast errors				
Target		Standard Deviations		
Growth				
Four-quarter ahead	4.43	3.26	5.15	18.60
Eight-quarter ahead	3.21	2.00	2.58	6.33
Level				
Four-quarter ahead	1.92	2.14	3.20	6.64
Eight-quarter ahead	1.99	2.20	2.72	4.53
Hybrid				
Four-quarter ahead	2.34	1.74	2.26	6.28
Eight-quarter ahead	2.26	1.58	1.90	3.56

2.5   Conclusion

Although nominal income targeting is not a panacea, it is a reasonably good rule for the conduct of monetary policy. Simulations of a simple macro model suggest that, compared to historical policy, the primary benefit of nominal income targeting is reduced volatility in the price level and the inflation rate. Under conservative assumptions, real economic activity would be about as volatile as it has been over the past forty years. If the elimination of spontaneous shifts in monetary policy improves forecasts markedly, real activity could be much less volatile.

We have discussed various ways in which a central bank might formulate a nominal income target. We have emphasized three in particular, which we call growth-rate targeting, level targeting, and hybrid targeting. Our calculations indicate that none of these policies clearly dominates all the others, although growth-rate targeting seems to yield the least desirable outcomes. Which targeting scheme a central bank should adopt depends on the relative costs of volatility in price levels, inflation rates, real income levels, and real income growth rates. These are topics on which more research is needed.

Our discussion has stayed within the domain of nominal income targets, guided by the principle of simplicity. But our results suggest that, if the monetary authorities will consider a slightly more complicated policy, one that looks primarily at the level of real activity and secondarily at the level of prices, they can achieve a considerably more appealing combination of output and price stability.

We have avoided discussion of the place of monetary policy rules in the world economy. In effect, we give a prescription for the activities of the central bank of a nation or monetary union which does not look beyond its own geographical boundaries. We have not considered the possible merits of making the rule of one monetary authority depend on outcomes beyond its borders. There is no question that each major central bank influences other economic units. But there is no consensus on the way in which monetary policies should be coordinated. Just as important, any attempt to impose coordination by policy formula would plainly violate the principle of simplicity.

References

Asako, Kazumi, and Helmut Wagner. 1992. Nominal income targeting versus money supply targeting. *Scottish Journal of Political Economy* 39 (May): 167–87.

Ball, Laurence, N. Gregory Mankiw, and David Romer. 1988. The new Keynesian economics and the output-inflation trade-off. *Brookings Papers on Economic Activity,* no. 1: 1–65.

Barro, Robert J., and David B. Gordon. 1983. A positive theory of monetary policy in a natural rate model. *Journal of Political Economy* 91 (August): 589–610.

Bean, Charles R. 1983. Targeting nominal income: An appraisal. *The Economic Journal* 93 (December): 806–19.

Fischer, Stanley. 1980. Dynamic inconsistency, cooperation, and the benevolent dissembling government. *Journal of Economic Dynamics and Control* 2 (February): 93–107.

Fudenberg, Drew, and Jean Tirole. 1991. *Game theory.* Cambridge: MIT Press.

Gordon, Robert J. 1985. The conduct of domestic monetary policy. In *Monetary policy in our times,* eds. Albert Ando, Hidekazu Eguchi, Roger Farmer, and Yoshio Suzuki, 45–81. Cambridge: MIT Press.

Hall, Robert E. 1985. Monetary strategy with an elastic price standard. In *Price stability and public policy: A symposium sponsored by the Federal Reserve Bank of Kansas City.* Federal Reserve Bank of Kansas City.

Kydland, Finn, and Edward Prescott. 1977. Rules rather than discretion: The inconsistency of optimal plans. *Journal of Political Economy* 85: 473–91.

Lucas, Robert E., Jr. 1972. Expectations and the neutrality of money. *Journal of Economic Theory* 4 (April): 103–24.

Mankiw, N. Gregory, and Matthew Shapiro. 1986. Do we reject too often? Small sample properties of tests of rational expectations models. *Economics Letters* 20: 139–45.

McCallum, Bennett T. 1988. Robustness properties of a rule for monetary policy. *Carnegie-Rochester Conference Series on Public Policy,* vol. 29: 173–204. Amsterdam: North-Holland.

Meade, J. E. 1978. The meaning of internal balance. *The Economic Journal* 91: 423–35.

Taylor, John B. 1985. *What would nominal GNP targeting do to the business cycle?* Carnegie-Rochester Conference Series on Public Policy, vol. 22: 61–84. Amsterdam: North-Holland.

Tobin, James. 1980. Stabilization policy ten years after. *Brookings Papers on Economic Activity,* no. 1: 19–72.

von Weizsäcker, Carl Christian. 1978. Das Problem der Vollbeschaftigung Heute. *Zeitschrift fur Wirstschafts und Sozialwissenshaften* 98: 33–51.

West, Kenneth D. 1986. Targeting nominal income: A note. *The Economic Journal* 96 (December): 1077–83.

Comment   Kenneth D. West

This is a thoughtful and sensible paper. It makes an important, and policy relevant, contribution to our understanding of how nominal income targeting might affect the U.S. economy. But its conclusion in section 2.5 that "nominal income targeting is . . . a reasonably good rule for the conduct of monetary policy" is, in my view, premature.

Let me begin by reviewing what Hall and Mankiw have done. They have a two-equation model. Let p_t be the price level, y_t output, y_t^N the natural rate of output, $x_t = p_t + y_t$ nominal income. One equation is a Phillips curve,

$$\Delta p_t - \pi = \lambda(\Delta p_{t-1} - \pi) + \alpha(y_t - y_t^N) + v_t.$$

The second equation is a nominal income rule:

$$\text{level rule: } x_t = \mu t + (x_t - E_{t-4}x_t)$$
$$= \mu t + \varepsilon_t,$$
$$\varepsilon_t = \text{MA}(3) \text{ error in consensus forecast;}$$
$$\text{growth rule: } x_t - x_{t-4} = \mu + \varepsilon_t;$$
$$\text{hybrid rule: } x_t - x_{t-4} = \mu + \varepsilon_t + (y_{t-4} - y_{t-4}^N).$$

Hall and Mankiw also experiment with eight- instead of four-quarter rules.

Given time series for y_t^N, v_t, and ε_t (computed from the actual data, and assumed not to change from simulation to simulation), the Phillips curve and the nominal income rule are two equations in the two unknowns p_t and y_t. In each simulation, the constant π in the Phillips curve is adjusted so that the average value of $y_t - y_t^N$ is zero.

It seems to me that the hypothetical nominal income policies do not fare particularly well relative to actual policy. Tables 2.3 and 2.4 indicate that when actual forecast errors are used, the growth and level policies invariably yield higher standard deviations for the output gap and output growth rates than the actual policy did. While the hybrid policy generally does better than the actual on these measures of output volatility, it exploits information that would not be available if the Fed were trying to follow such a rule, in that it uses the final, revised, and rebenchmarked figures for y_t and y_t^N. Whether use of data actually

Kenneth D. West is professor of economics and director of the Social Systems Research Institute at the University of Wisconsin and a research associate of the National Bureau of Economic Research.

available would make much difference I do not know; the fact that it might make a difference suggests caution.

All the hypothetical policies tend to do better on volatility of inflation and remarkably better on price-level volatility. For the latter, it is important to note that this is true essentially by assumption. In all the simulations, the mean rate of nominal income growth is fixed at 2.5 percent, the mean rate of output growth to that actually observed in the sample. This fixes the mean rate of inflation; one can see from figures 2.3 to 2.5 that this implied rate is such that there is essentially zero (in fact, slightly negative) inflation over the period. Since prices have a marked trend in the actual data, and essentially no trend in the simulations, the standard deviation is much larger in the actual than in the simulated data.

Of course, a basic advantage of a nominal income rule is that it may yield stable prices; as the authors note, there are well-known reasons why discretion tends to lead to inflation. But this is not necessarily an argument for a nominal income rule rather than a price or inflation or money-growth rule, or, for that matter, an old-fashioned textbook rule that aims to minimize a weighted sum of inflation and/or price and/or output volatilities. Indeed, the class of nominal income rules considered seems to me to be inefficient in the sense defined by Hall and Mankiw in section 2.1. Suppose for concreteness that one cares about the variability of inflation and of output growth, and considers the nominal income growth rule. This rule minimizes the variance of the sum of inflation and output growth, a variance that depends in part on the covariance between inflation and output growth. In conventional models, one can get lower variability of both inflation *and* output growth by ignoring the covariance term.

It is possible that rules that yield substantial efficiency gains relative to nominal income rules will be so complicated that holding the Fed accountable to the theoretically preferable rules will be difficult in practice. But an analysis of the trade-off between efficiency and accountability remains to be done. To take just one example, why not target not the consensus forecast of nominal income, but a weighted sum of the consensus forecasts of real output and the price level, the weight reflecting the relative cost of output and price variability?

This is the sort of question I would like to see answered before I conclude that nominal income targeting is a reasonably good rule.

3   Nonstandard Indicators for Monetary Policy: Can Their Usefulness Be Judged from Forecasting Regressions?

Michael Woodford

In recent years there has been a great deal of interest in proposals to use non-standard indicator variables as a guide to the conduct of monetary policy. By nonstandard indicators I mean indicators other than the various measures of the money supply that the Federal Reserve System computes, and to which academic economists in the monetarist tradition have long directed their attention, and other than the variables that can be more or less directly controlled by the Fed, such as borrowed and nonborrowed reserves or the federal funds rate, and measures of the Fed's success at achieving its ultimate objectives, such as measures of inflation and economic activity in the recent past.

Some of the new indicators that have been discussed include commodity price indexes, nominal exchange rates, and spreads between the interest yields on longer- and shorter-maturity Treasury securities. Interest in the new indicators seems mainly to have been a response to the perceived instability in the 1980s of the relations between traditional monetary aggregates and nominal aggregate demand. The various new proposals just mentioned all represent variations upon the idea that a desirable monetary policy, that would be able to respond to, and counteract, incipient inflationary pressures before much inflation had developed, could be conducted by monitoring various indicators that are known to be valuable as *forecasts of future inflation,* rather than by giving one's sole attention to the evolution of variables such as the money supply that are thought to be *proximate causes of inflation.*

I do not attempt here to evaluate the likely consequences of any of these specific proposals. Instead, the present note addresses a general issue raised by proposals of this general type, that of how to determine which variables, of all

Michael Woodford is professor of economics at the University of Chicago and a faculty research fellow of the National Bureau of Economic Research.

The author thanks Bob Barsky and Anil Kashyap for helpful discussions, Michael Bordo for helpful comments on an earlier draft, and the National Science Foundation for research support.

the many types of data available to the Fed, are reasonable indicators to use as the basis for a feedback rule for one or another instrument of monetary policy. The discussion of the new indicators has tended to assume that one should simply look for any or all available variables that have proved to be useful in forecasting inflation over some relevant horizon. The advocates of the new variables within the Federal Reserve System have stressed their usefulness as leading indicators of inflation, and much of the academic commentary has addressed itself to formal econometric evaluation of their forecasting ability, typically within a completely atheoretical vector autoregression (VAR) framework.

The question I consider here is whether analysis of this sort is a sufficient ground for choosing variables to be used in making monetary policy. I will argue that such investigations are no substitute for an analysis of the consequences of making policy on the basis of one indicator or another in the context of a specific structural model of the economy, which models both the determination of the indicator in question and the effects of possible monetary policy interventions. Before developing this point further, however, I first review from a purely statistical point of view the literature that has addressed the issue.

3.1   Econometric Evaluations of the Usefulness of Commodity Prices as an Indicator

The type of nonstandard indicator most often discussed has been one index or another of commodity prices. The recent interest in commodities prices began with the revival of interest among "supply-side economists," during the first Reagan administration, in the stabilization of commodities prices (including, perhaps, a return to a gold standard) as a goal of monetary policy, as an alternative to the monetarist program of controlling the growth rate of a monetary aggregate. For example, Reynolds (1982) advocated stabilizing spot commodity prices, especially the price of gold. Miles (1984) discussed a variety of possible types of "price rules," including the stabilization of the spot prices of gold or other commodities, eventually coming down in favor of a rule that would involve stabilization of commodity futures prices, as well as stabilization of long-term bond yields. Others argued for the use of commodity prices as an indicator if not as a target variable; for example, Genetski (1982) argued for making the range of permissible growth rates for the monetary base change automatically in response to movements of a commodity price index. These proposals received some attention among policymakers, especially in 1982, when the United States suffered from a severe recession that was widely attributed to the Fed's attempt to bring money growth under control. At that time, Representatives Jack Kemp and Trent Lott introduced into Congress the Balanced Monetary Policy and Price Stability Act, which would have required the Fed to pursue "price stability" over all other objectives, with price stability to be measured by one of two possible indexes of commodity prices. While the primary goal of such measures was obviously stability of the general price level, some proponents also argued that basing monetary policy on commodities prices would stabilize interest rates and economic activity as well; Genetski (1982) argued that such a rule would have enabled the United States to avoid all major recessions since 1915.

Proposals to actually stabilize commodities prices soon fell out of favor, in the face of skepticism about the feasibility of commodity price stabilization by the Fed (see, e.g., Hafer 1983), and about whether stabilization of commodities prices would in fact imply stability of prices more generally. Because of the high volatility of gold and other commodity prices, relative to the volatility of general price indexes like the consumer price index (CPI), many argued that commodities prices evidently move in response to many factors other than the true current stance of monetary policy—not only factors affecting the supply of and demand for individual commodities, which ought to affect their relative prices, but incorrect perceptions perhaps on the part of market participants about what the current policy stance is—so that the concern with stabilizing these particular prices might actually make monetary policy, and prices generally, more volatile. (See, e.g., Bordo testimony in U.S. House 1987 and DeFina 1988.)

Nonetheless, in the late 1980s commodity prices were again widely discussed as a desirable basis for monetary policy, this time within the Federal Reserve itself, and this time with an emphasis on their usefulness as indicators of inflationary pressures, rather than as a target variable. Federal Reserve governor Wayne D. Angell (1987) proposed that a commodity price guide be used to adjust short-run money-growth target ranges, and Governor H. Robert Heller (1987) endorsed such a rule as a way of bringing about not only domestic price stability, but greater exchange-rate stability as well. Vice Chairman Manuel H. Johnson (1988) suggested that not only commodity prices, but interest-rate spreads and nominal exchange rates, should serve as information variables to evaluate the current stance of monetary policy. The general idea behind these proposals is clearly expressed by Johnson: "Changes in monetary policy should be reflected in these financial auction market prices well before they affect the broader price measures. Thus, there is reason to believe that they may give advance warning of impending change for important concerns such as inflation." A similar idea lies behind the more recent proposal by Robert Hetzel (1990, 1992) that the Fed create a market for a new type of financial instrument, an indexed bond, so that the spread between the yield on this bond and the yield on a nominal bond of similar maturity can be used as an indicator of inflationary expectations, and hence as a guide to monetary policy.[1]

This second generation of proposals for the use of nonstandard indicators is

---

1. Goodfriend (1993), in an account of the actual conduct of Fed policy during the 1980s, argues that the term structure has in fact been an important source of information about inflationary expectations and an important determinant of changes in the stance of monetary policy.

explicitly based upon the statistical claim that these variables serve as leading indicators of inflation; for example, Angell (1987) presented evidence that over a long historical period peaks and troughs in indexes of commodity prices have preceded peaks and troughs in consumer price inflation. As a result, a considerable scholarly literature evaluating these proposals has given particular attention to econometric tests of the extent to which the proposed indicator variables do in fact forecast inflation—generally in a completely atheoretical way.[2]

Several types of econometric analyses of the relation between commodity prices and inflation have been undertaken.[3] One popular test examines the cointegration of commodity price indexes with general price indexes such as the CPI. For example, Garner (1989) tests for cointegration between several commodity price indexes and the CPI, and concludes that none are cointegrated with it. That is, not only is the real price of commodities (the commodity price index deflated by the CPI) a nonstationary variable, but no linear combination of the logarithms of the two price indexes is found to be a stationary variable, so that independent factors evidently determine the long-run behavior of the two series. He argues on this ground that commodity prices are not useful as an intermediate target for monetary policy, as stabilization of commodity prices would not imply stabilization of consumer prices. Sephton (1991) extends the cointegration analysis and confirms Garner's conclusions. Baillie (1989) reports similar results and draws a similar conclusion. Boughton and Branson (1991) test for cointegration between various commodity price indexes and an aggregate of consumer prices in seven industrial countries, and also find no cointegration.

On the other hand, a number of authors have pointed out that the fact that commodity prices and consumer prices do not move together in the long run does not exclude commodity prices from playing a useful role in improving forecasts of consumer price inflation. Garner tests for Granger causality of CPI inflation by several commodity price indexes, and finds that a null hypothesis of no causality can be statistically rejected; that is, that future CPI inflation can be somewhat better forecasted when the commodity price series is included in one's vector autoregression, than when that variable is excluded. He also uses his (nonstructural) VAR model to decompose the variance in CPI inflation into

2. An exception is the study of Cody and Mills (1990), which uses a "structural" vector autoregression approach. I do not discuss this study here, as an evaluation of the particular identifying assumptions proposed by Cody and Mills is beyond the scope of this note. A number of authors have also sought to evaluate the usefulness of nonstandard indicators through policy simulations in the context of structural models, as I advocate here. See, e.g., Fuhrer and Moore (1992), Porter (1990), and Brayton and Tinsley (1991).

3. I emphasize the literature on commodity prices here, because this literature is explicitly motivated by the monetary policy proposals just mentioned. A considerable literature has also examined the relation between the term structure and inflation, for example, but this literature is not primarily motivated by the suggestion that the term structure should be a guide to monetary policy; on the whole, it seeks rather to test particular theories of the term structure that emphasize variations in inflationary expectations as a source of changes in the term structure.

fractions attributable to innovations in each of the several variables included in the regression, and concludes that innovations in a commodity price index "explain about 25% of the prediction error variance for the CPI after 48 months," even when the monetary base is included in the VAR as another of the forecasting variables. As a result, he concludes that "the empirical evidence suggests that an index of commodity prices may be a useful information variable for policymakers," though he argues that it is not a suitable intermediate target because of the absence of cointegration. Sephton confirms the results of Garner with respect to Granger causality as well. Whitt (1988) similarly finds that commodity prices significantly improve forecasts of inflation.

On the other hand, a number of authors have criticized the conclusion from a finding of Granger causality alone that commodity prices are useful indicators for monetary policy. Webb (1988) finds that a commodity price index enters *significantly* in forecasting regressions for inflation, but that the *magnitude* of the improvement in forecastability is very small. He therefore concludes: "That commodity prices added a *small* amount of predictive power suggests that a *small* improvement in anti-inflation policy could be achieved by using them as an indicator variable." Aguais, DeAngelis, and Wyss (1988) find that commodity prices provide little additional information about future inflation, once wages and measures of supply conditions are also included as regressors, and Baillie (1989) and Barsky (1993) report similar results. Boughton and Branson (1991), in their study of the relation between commodity prices and industrial-country inflation, also report a finding of Granger causality. However, they find that while including the commodity price index in their VAR substantially improves the *within-sample* fit of their model of inflation, it results in no improvement in *post-sample* inflation forecasts. They thus conclude that "the quantitative linkages between commodity and consumer prices are significant, but are not stable enough to permit one to draw quantitative inferences about the extent to which consumer prices might respond to a given change in commodity prices."

I do not propose here to settle the issue of the nature of the statistical relationship between commodity prices and inflation, but rather to address an issue of method raised by this literature, and by studies such as that of Barsky (1993) that appraise other proposed indicator variables using similar methods. This is the question of whether a simple measurement of the extent to which an indicator has been associated in the past with subsequent inflation—even supposing that purely statistical issues such as the stability of the relationship over time can be satisfactorily addressed—suffices to determine the appropriate use that should be made of such an indicator in the formulation of monetary policy.

To be sure, careful econometric analysis of the extent to which a given indicator does in fact forecast inflation provides a better basis for policy discussions than mere impressions gleaned from the financial press. Some of the early enthusiasts of a monetary policy rule based on commodity prices seemed to think that the mere fact that commodity prices are observed to be *volatile* suggests their importance as a source of information,[4] and certainly regression analysis quickly exposes the fallacy in such reasoning. Still, the econometric literature often seems to regard as obvious the fact that policy rules can be directly formulated on the basis of the kinds of nonstructural regression relationships that are estimated. Even when the authors are critical of the proposed policy rules, they write as if it *would* make sense to stabilize commodity prices if they *were* found to be cointegrated with the CPI, or to adjust the stance of monetary policy in response to a commodity price index if its marginal forecasting power were found to be larger than it happens to be in the data examined. This is what I wish to challenge.

It might seem that shifting the terms of the discussion of desirable indicators for monetary policy, from consideration of what causes inflation to a simple consideration of how to forecast it, would have great advantages. One might argue that the monetarist case for tracking the money supply was based upon an assertion that money growth forecasts future inflation; however appealing the theoretical case for such a link, one can test econometrically whether other variables might not allow inflation to be forecasted even more accurately, and if so, it might seem that one should base monetary policy upon those other variables instead. Furthermore, it is a more straightforward matter to settle which variables have had what degree of forecasting power than to show conclusively that certain causal mechanisms have been operative.

I wish to argue that these advantages are more illusory than real. Despite the greater difficulty of deciding what a correctly specified structural model for the analysis of the effects of monetary policy should look like, we have no alternative but to undertake such an inquiry. In particular, supposing that one finds that a particular indicator *has* been reliably associated with subsequent inflation, I wish to argue that it matters a great deal whether the association exists because (*a*) the indicator is itself a measure of, or is directly influenced by, the underlying *causes* of inflation, and will indicate those inflationary pressures regardless of whether market participants understand them and regardless of whether the inflation is in fact allowed to develop; or (*b*) the indicator is influenced by market participants' *expectations* of inflation, and so responds to the underlying causes of inflation, but only insofar as market participants are aware of them and actually expect inflation to result. The basic idea behind the interest in nonstandard indicators has been a suggestion that indicators that work for the second reason are actually the *better* guides for monetary policy; but I wish to argue exactly the opposite.

There are several reasons why a conclusion about the right type of feedback rule for monetary policy on the basis of atheoretical forecasting regressions alone can be highly misleading. I take them up in sequence.

---

4. For example, Reynolds (1982) stresses the importance of controlling a "sensitive measure of price," and writes: "Since broader price indexes are too insensitive, what about narrowing the list to only one commodity—namely, gold—that is notoriously sensitive to every whiff of inflation or deflation?"

3.2   Low Forecasting Power May Not Justify Ignoring an Indicator

First, the mere fact that an indicator is found not to enter significantly in an inflation forecasting regression does not necessarily mean that the Fed should be advised not to pay any attention to that variable. For the absence of forecasting power might simply mean that the variable is already being used by the Fed in making policy, and in approximately the right way, from the point of view of minimizing the variability of inflation.

The point can be illustrated by the following extremely stylized model. Suppose that inflation over the relevant horizon is determined by a relation of the form

$$(1) \qquad \pi_{t+1} = s_t + u_t + \varepsilon_{t+1},$$

where π_t is inflation between dates t and $t + 1$, s_t is an indicator observed at date t, u_t is a control variable of the monetary authority chosen at date t, and ε_{t+1} is a mean-zero random variable not forecastable at date t. Equation (1) is intended to represent a causal effect of u_t on the probability distribution of possible values for π_{t+1} which is understood by the monetary authority; for simplicity, this effect is assumed to be a simple shift in the conditional mean, and the size of the effect is assumed to be independent of the value of s_t that is observed. The appearance of s_t on the right-hand side of (1) need not have a causal interpretation; s_t may simply be correlated with factors that influence inflation independently of the control variable. The realizations of s_t and ε_{t+1} are assumed to be independent of the choice of u_t, and the realization of ε_{t+1} likewise independent of s_t.

It follows that the variance of π_{t+1} is minimized by a policy feedback rule of the form $u_t = -s_t$. If such a rule is followed, $\pi_{t+1} = \varepsilon_{t+1}$, and a regression of π_{t+1} on s_t will yield (asymptotically) a zero coefficient. But it would be incorrect in such a case to tell the monetary authority to stop monitoring the value of s_t before choosing the value of u_t. Since many of the indicators the recent literature is concerned with have been argued to be useful by officers of the Fed, one can hardly be certain that the Fed's policy actions during the period from which one's data are drawn did not respond to these variables; and in fact Goodfriend (1993) argues that Fed policy for at least the last decade has been guided to a great extent by the movements of an interest-rate spread. Hence the finding of low incremental forecasting power for some of these variables might be due to the way in which they are already being used. Without an attempt to understand the data in terms of a structural model (which would include a model of the Fed's policy rule), it is hard to reach a conclusion about this.

One might argue that in any event a finding of insignificant forecasting power for a given indicator allows one to make the recommendation that policy should respond to that variable to exactly the extent that it already does— neither more nor less. But this is not a particularly useful sort of recommendation. In the absence of a determination of what the Fed's current policy rule is (or has been in the period under study), it would not be clear what sort of response had been shown to be desirable. (The Fed itself might not know what it would mean to "maintain the status quo"; would a new Board member be required to adopt the opinions of whatever member he or she had just replaced in order to maintain some balance of forces?) Also, if one were recommending that *some* indicators could be used to reduce inflation variability relative to past policies, it would not be clear that the optimal response to the other variable (that is believed to have been used optimally in the past) would be unchanged if the use of the former variables were changed.

3.3   Pitfalls in Basing Policy upon Indicators That Have Forecasted Inflation in the Past

On the other hand, the mere fact that an indicator is found to be useful in forecasting inflation does not tell much about the desirability of a policy that involves feedback from that indicator. There are several reasons why such an inference requires caution. One is that the ability of the indicator to signal the underlying sources of inflationary pressures that one wants to respond to may be impaired *by the very fact that the monetary authority responds to it.*

This point is, of course, simply a variant of the by now familiar Lucas (1976) critique of econometric policy evaluation. The Lucas critique is perhaps sometimes invoked in too sweeping a way, to discredit all attempts at econometric policy evaluation as such (an issue to which I return below). However, the point seems particularly likely to be an important one in the present context. This is because the nontraditional indicators with which the recent literature is concerned are clearly *not* believed to be useful for forecasting inflation because of being causal determinants of inflation. In fact, they are not even believed to be proxies for such causal determinants (because, say, of a direct causal effect of the underlying sources of inflationary pressure on the indicators); instead, they are believed to be of interest because of being strongly affected by (and hence signaling) the state of inflationary expectations. But if the connection between the underlying sources of inflationary pressure (that one wishes to respond to) and the indicator is mediated primarily by expectations, one is in the situation where it is most plausible that the relation should radically change in the case of a policy intervention that modifies the relation between the underlying states and the inflation that eventually occurs.

The point may be illustrated by a simple example. (This admittedly has not been proposed by any of the advocates of nonstandard indicators, but is in the spirit of some of those proposals.) If the best indicator for monetary policy is simply the variable that best forecasts future inflation, why not simply use published inflation forecasts as the basis for policy? I expect that if one were to include among the regressors some kind of consensus forecast of inflation in forecasting regressions like those in Barsky (1993), one would find not only that it had marginal significance, but that there was little marginal significance for the other variables once the forecast was included in the regression.

But should the Fed then be advised to simply respond to the current consensus forecast of inflation, to the exclusion of all other available information? Such a proposal could have paradoxical effects. The use of the forecasts in setting policy would change the relation between the forecasters' information variables and inflation, and so would lead them to change the way they form their forecasts. But once they did, the relation between their forecasts and the underlying sources of inflationary pressure would change, so that the Fed's optimal response to the forecast would change. And if the Fed changes its response, as it ought to, this again changes the way in which forecasters ought to form their forecasts. This process of adjustment between the two sides need not admit any equilibrium.

A simple example shows why. Let (1) again describe the determination of inflation, but now suppose that the variable s_t is not observed by the monetary authority. Instead, suppose that s_t is observed by a private forecaster, and that the authority observes the forecast f_t. Finally, suppose that the forecaster seeks to minimize the expected squared forecast error $(\pi_{t+1} - f_t)^2$. It follows that f_t will equal the conditional expectation of π_{t+1}, given the forecaster's observation of s_t. If the monetary authority uses a feedback rule of the form

$$(2) \qquad\qquad u_t = -\lambda f_t,$$

then optimal use of the forecaster's information requires that the forecast be

$$(3) \qquad\qquad f_t = \alpha s_t,$$

where $\alpha = \alpha(\lambda) \equiv (1 + \lambda)^{-1}$. On the other hand, if the forecaster uses any rule of the form (3), the monetary authority's optimal feedback rule (in order to minimize the variance of π_{t+1}, given its observation of f_t but not of s_t) is of the form (2), where $\lambda = \lambda(\alpha) \equiv \alpha^{-1}$. However, the curves $\alpha = \alpha(\lambda)$ and $\lambda = \lambda(\alpha)$ never intersect, for any values of α and λ.[5]

This result is reminiscent, of course, of the celebrated Grossman-Stiglitz paradox, according to which traders in financial markets cannot use private information about the future value of assets being traded to earn higher returns, because their trade on the basis of the information should cause the market price to reflect the information, so that they should have no informational advantage over other traders. This result is often viewed as posing an analytical challenge for theorists (to explain why the result is not true despite its appeal-

5. Bob Hall and Greg Mankiw (chap. 2 in this volume) suggest, in the context of a different assumed objective of monetary policy, that the minimization of the variance of a variable should be achieved by eliminating variation in the consensus forecast of that variable. Furthermore, they argue that it should be possible for the Fed to eliminate variation in the consensus forecast by an appropriate choice of policy, given timely information about the forecast. But in the present model, this is not possible. "Pegging the forecast" would mean choosing a policy rule that induces forecasters to choose $\alpha = 0$, but there is no choice of λ that achieves this. Thus the possibility of such an objective for the Fed depends upon details of the economy's information structure.

ing logic) rather than a problem for traders who expend effort in learning about companies whose shares are publicly traded; for it seems obvious that traders with superior information can make money from it (some who trade on the basis of "inside information" are sent to jail for it), whether our models can explain it or not. I do not think the result just presented is of the same kind. In the case of the Grossman-Stiglitz analysis, it is a rather subtle consequence of a specific model of market equilibrium that the market price should fully reveal the private information of the informed traders; and one can avoid this conclusion in various ways, for example, by assuming the presence of "liquidity traders." One may well suppose that in reality there is not full revelation, and this resolves the paradoxical features of their analysis. In the present case, there is no similar reason to doubt the assumption that the informed agents' forecasts are fully revealed to the monetary authority. First of all, the forecasters can make use of their superior information only insofar as they make their forecasts public—they have no motive to allow only a "noisy" report of their forecasts to become known. But more important, the policy proposal above is premised upon the authority's ability to observe the private forecasts; there is plainly no possibility of following such a rule if the private forecasters seek to and are able to keep their forecasts confidential.

Of course it is still possible, under the circumstances described above, for the monetary authority to reduce the variability of inflation to a great degree by choosing a very large value for λ. But this is hardly an attractive method. (It gives the forecaster extreme power over the economy, on the understanding that it will not be rational for him to use it.) If the monetary authority could observe s_t as well as f_t, it is plainly more desirable for the authority to choose a rule involving feedback from s_t (ideally, $u_t = -s_t$) than any rule of the form (2). Yet this fact would not be revealed by a simple consideration of the relative forecasting power of the variables s_t and f_t for inflation; for the two variables would be perfectly correlated (as long as forecasters use a rule of the form [3]), and neither would enter a forecasting regression with a more significant coefficient than the other.

A second pitfall in basing policy upon an indicator variable simply because it is found to enter significantly in forecasting regressions is that monetary policy interventions may affect the determination of the indicator, in such a way as to create a feedback loop from policy to the indicator back to policy that results in policy instability (and hence inflation instability as well). An absurd policy proposal serves to illustrate this. One variable that has been shown to forecast inflation is the return on Treasury bills (Fama 1975). A control variable that the Fed frequently uses to respond to changes in the perceived threat of inflation is the Federal funds rate. Would it then be a reasonable policy proposal to direct the Fed to raise the funds rate whenever higher than average T-bill yields are observed? Of course no one would propose this. But this is because of additional structural information that we have about the determination of these variables; specifically, we know that when the Fed raises the funds rate, T-bill yields rise as a result. It is because of this that we would expect the proposed rule to create instability. This illustrates the general point that an evaluation of policy rules must be based upon a structural model, both of the determination of the indicator variables and of the effects of monetary policy.

This example, while drawn as a caricature to make the point simply, is not without relevance to recent proposals for the use of nonstandard indicators. One proposal is to raise short-term interest rates whenever a long-term bond rate rises.[6] Now the connection between the funds rate and long-term rates is not as transparent as in the case of the previous absurd proposal. But still, according to the expectations theory of the term structure, the expectation that short rates will remain high makes long-term rates high. This raises the possibility that a disturbance to the long-term bond rate could trigger a policy shift whose effects on long-term rates would justify continuation of the policy, keeping long-term rates high, and so on.[7]

3.4   Feedback from Inflation Indicators Can Create Instability due to Self-Fulfilling Expectations

A further pitfall is the possibility of creating, through the monetary policy rule, a feedback loop that allows arbitrary changes in expectations to become self-fulfilling. This possibility again is one that can be evaluated only in the context of a structural model. It seems, however, particularly likely to be a problem in the case of rules that create feedback to policy from indicators that are themselves very sensitive to expectations. Thus an approach to the selection of policy rules that simply emphasizes the use of indicators with good forecasting power may direct attention to precisely the kind of policy rules that are most likely to create feedback loops that allow expectations to become self-fulfilling.

The following provides a simple example of a policy rule that might appear desirable, based upon the correlations that would be observed prior to the introduction of feedback from the indicator, but that would make possible "sunspot equilibria" (in some of which the variability of inflation would be higher than in the equilibrium that exists in the absence of feedback). The analysis is based upon an IS-LM model with rational expectations. Let output and nominal interest rates be determined by log-linear equations of the familiar sort:

(4) $$m_t - p_t = y_t - \gamma i_t + \varepsilon_{mt}$$

(5) $$y_t = -\delta[i_t - (E_t p_{t+1} - p_t)].$$

Here m_t is the log of the money supply, p_t the log of the price level, y_t the log of output, and i_t the nominal interest rate; I assume that $\gamma > 0$ and that $0 < \delta$

---

6. This is the policy that Goodfriend (1993) describes the Fed as having actually followed.

7. This is, I believe, essentially the reason for the negative conclusion of Fuhrer and Moore (1992) regarding the consequences of feedback rules of this type.

$< 1.$[8] To eliminate constants from the equations, units are chosen so that in the steady state equilibrium with a constant money supply and no disturbance, $y = 0$, $i = 0$, and $m = p$. (Thus y_t should be interpreted as the percentage deviation of output from its "natural" level.) The price level p_t is assumed to be chosen at date $t - 1$, in such a way that[9]

$$(6) \qquad\qquad E_{t-1}(y_t) = 0.$$

The disturbance term in (4) represents stochastic variation in money demand. I assume that ε_{mt} follows a random walk (independent of monetary policy), whose increments $\Delta\varepsilon_{mt}$ are bounded mean-zero random variables, and that it is not observed by the monetary authority. It is this source of inflationary pressure for which the authority would like to find an indicator. I consider this particular type of disturbance because the recent discussion of nonstandard indicators seems to have been largely a response to the perceived instability of the demand for familiar monetary aggregates during the 1980s.

Consider first a policy regime in which the money supply is constant. (We may without loss of generality suppose that $m_t = 0$ for all t.) In this case, there is a unique rational expectations equilibrium (REE) in which the variables $z_t = (y_t, i_t, m_t - p_t, \Delta p_t)$ are forever bounded.[10] In this equilibrium,

$$p_t = -\varepsilon_{mt-1}$$

$$y_t = -\frac{(1 + \gamma)\delta}{\delta + \gamma} \Delta\varepsilon_{mt}$$

$$i_t = \frac{(1 - \delta)}{\delta + \gamma} \Delta\varepsilon_{mt}.$$

8. The assumption that $\delta < 1$ in this model is needed in order for an unexpected permanent increase in the money supply to result in a temporary decrease in the nominal interest rate.

9. In the specification of aggregate supply, I follow McCallum (1989).

10. One might wonder why I consider only bounded solutions when I wish to suggest that the existence of multiple equilibria indicates a real source of economic instability. I regard equations (4) and (5) as log-linear approximations to some exact structural relations, whose approximation is accurate only as long as the variables z_t remain sufficiently close to their steady-state values. Hence explosive solutions to (4) and (5) need not even approximate solutions to the exact structural relations. Furthermore, there may be additional requirements for equilibrium besides the relations that (4) and (5) approximate that are satisfied by all solutions in which the values of the variables z_t do not leave a certain region, but need not be satisfied more generally. For example, when the liquidity-preference relation (approximated by [4]) is derived from a Sidrauski-Brock model of money demand, there is also a transversality condition that must be satisfied in equilibrium. Discussion of whether additional solutions have any economic meaning in the present case would thus require that more explicit foundations for equations (4)–(6) be provided. Nonetheless, consideration of the nonexplosive solutions alone should suffice to show that alternative policy rules can have very different consequences for the determinacy of equilibrium.

For examples of analyses of how the uniqueness of rational expectations equilibrium depends upon the monetary policy rule, in the context of explicit general equilibrium models and with consideration of the complete set of equilibria, see Smith (1994) and Woodford (1994).

Note that an innovation $\Delta\varepsilon_{mt} < 0$ results in a temporary increase in output (one period only), a temporary decline in the nominal interest rate (also one period only), and a permanent increase in the price level (after a one-period lag). Thus the shocks to money demand, not accommodated by any change in money supply, produce fluctuations in both economic activity and in the price level. Hence a policy of targeting the money supply might be judged undesirable.

Now suppose that the monetary authority, observing the fluctuations that occur under the constant money supply policy, seeks an indicator of the shocks that can be used to reduce the volatility of both output and inflation. The price level itself is not the best indicator, for it responds to the shock with only a one-period lag. (Of course the monetary authority does not know this unless it knows the structural model set out above; but it can observe that using other variables price-level variations can be forecasted earlier than they can be using only the price level itself.) If output is not observed immediately (and this is probably realistic) it also may not be the best indicator. The nominal interest rate reflects the shock immediately, and this variable is easy to monitor in practice, so that it would seem to be the most promising indicator.

This might suggest a policy of expanding the money supply whenever the nominal interest rate rises above its steady-state level, to offset the increase in money demand that one infers to have occurred. A well-known problem with this proposal, of course, is that nominal interest rates can also be high because of expected inflation; so there is the danger of expectations of inflation being self-fulfilling because they raise nominal interest rates and so bring about the money growth that in turn brings about the inflation. This is the reason for an interest instead in interest-rate spreads of various sorts. Let there be observed as well a two-period nominal interest rate, that I denote i_{2t}, and let it be related to the single-period rate in the way indicated by the expectations theory of the term structure, that is,

$$i_{2t} = \frac{1}{2}i_t + \frac{1}{2}E_t i_{t+1}.$$

If we define the spread as $s_t = i_t - i_{2t}$, we obtain

(7)
$$s_t = -\frac{1}{2}E_t(\Delta i_{t+1})$$

to complete our model. Note that in the equilibrium for the case of a constant money supply,

$$s_t = \frac{(1 - \delta)}{2(\delta + \gamma)}\Delta\varepsilon_{mt},$$

so that the spread is also an indicator of the current money demand shock, and like the single-period interest rate it should be observed by the monetary authority almost immediately.

This may suggest the desirability of a feedback rule for monetary policy of the form

(8) $$\Delta m_t = \lambda s_t,$$

for some $\lambda > 0$, so that the money supply is permanently increased whenever the term structure spread indicates that an increase in money demand has occurred. Note that according to our model, if a permanent increase in the money supply of the right size can be arranged each time such a shock occurs, there will never be any variations in either output or in the price level. Furthermore, the monetary authority might be led to consider such a response, even in the absence of knowledge of the structural model, based upon a comparison of the observed consequences of a temporary increase in the spread (in the absence of any change in the money supply) with the consequences of an increase in the money supply (assuming that independent stochastic variations in the money supply have also been observed).

In fact, *one* nonexplosive REE that always exists in the case of a policy of the form (8) is an equilibrium similar to the one described above, but one in which the amplitude of the fluctuations in prices and in output is reduced. In this equilibrium,

$$p_t = -\alpha\varepsilon_{mt-1}$$

$$m_t = (1 - \alpha)\varepsilon_{mt}$$

$$y_t = -\frac{(1 + \gamma)\delta}{\delta + \gamma}\alpha\Delta\varepsilon_{mt}$$

$$i_t = \frac{(1 - \delta)}{\delta + \gamma}\alpha\Delta\varepsilon_{mt}$$

$$s_t = \frac{(1 - \delta)}{2(\delta + \gamma)}\alpha\Delta\varepsilon_{mt},$$

where now

$$\alpha = \frac{2(\delta + \gamma)}{2(\delta + \gamma) + \lambda(1 - \delta)}.$$

Note that this implies that $0 < \alpha < 1$ for any $\lambda > 0$. Hence the fluctuations in both output and prices are reduced in amplitude. But one should also note that for *no* value of λ are they completely eliminated. This is another example of the problem discussed earlier, in which the use of the indicator to stabilize reduces its information content. (Note that the response of s_t to $\Delta\varepsilon_{mt}$ is proportional to α as well.)

The fluctuations can nonetheless be very greatly reduced in amplitude (in this particular equilibrium) by choosing λ to be sufficiently large. But this creates another problem. As long as $\lambda < 2(1 + \gamma)$, one can show that the above solution is the unique REE in which the variables z_t are forever bounded. But if the monetary authority chooses a value $\lambda > 2(1 + \gamma)$, there exists a very large multiplicity of nonexplosive REE. These include both "sunspot" equilibria, in which prices and output fluctuate in response to random events that do not affect any of the equilibrium conditions (4)–(7), and equilibria in which there is no effect of such events, but the response to money demand shocks is different from that described above. The fluctuations in output and inflation associated with these other equilibria can be arbitrarily large (whether they involve "sunspot" effects or not). Hence the choice of a large value of λ need not succeed in stabilizing either output or prices.[11]

I will not describe in detail the additional equilibria, but I wish to at least indicate why the multiplicity arises only in the case of large values of λ. Taking the expectations of (4) and (5) conditional upon information at date $t - 1$, and using (6) and the fact that ε_{mt} is a random walk, yields

$$(9) \qquad E_{t-1}(m_t - p_t) = -\gamma E_{t-1}i_t + \varepsilon_{mt}$$

$$(10) \qquad E_{t-1}i_t = E_{t-1}(p_{t+1} - p_t).$$

If we consider the equation corresponding to (4) at date $t + 1$, similarly take its expectation condition upon date $t - 1$ information, and subtract this from (9), we obtain

$$E_{t-1}(\Delta m_{t+1} - \Delta p_{t+1} + \gamma \Delta i_{t+1}) = 0.$$

Using (10), this becomes

$$E_{t-1}(\Delta m_{t+1} - i_t + \gamma \Delta i_{t+1}) = 0.$$

Then substituting (8) and using (7), we obtain

$$(11) \qquad E_{t-1}(A(L)i_{t+2}) = 0,$$

where

$$A(L) = \lambda - (\lambda + 2\gamma)L + 2(1 + \gamma)L^2.$$

The uniqueness of bounded equilibrium then depends upon the roots of $A(L)$, for reasons of the sort developed in Blanchard and Kahn (1980). If $\lambda < 2(1 + \gamma)$, $A(L)$ has both roots inside the unit circle, and so (11) is satisfied only if $E_{t-1}i_t = 0$. In this case, it follows from (10) that $E_{t-1} \Delta p_{t+1} = 0$. Furthermore, (7) then implies that $E_{t-1}s_t = 0$, and (8) that $E_{t-1} \Delta m_t = 0$. From these results one then easily shows that the equilibrium described above is the only one. On the other hand, if $\lambda > 2(1 + \gamma)$, $A(L)$ has both roots outside the unit circle, and

---

11. Because the equilibrium conditions (4)–(7) are linear, a linear combination of any two solutions (with weights summing to one, but not necessarily both positive) is also a solution. So once we know that there exist at least two distinct solutions, we know that there exist solutions in which the amplitude of fluctuations is arbitrarily large.

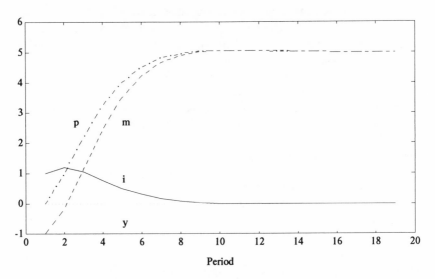

Fig. 3.1   An example of self-fulfilling expectations of inflation

there are many bounded solutions to (11). To these there then correspond a multiplicity of equilibria for the model.

Figure 3.1 gives an example of how expectations of inflation can be self-fulfilling when λ is sufficiently large. The plots represent a possible perfect foresight equilibrium in the case of no shocks to money demand, and given a predetermined initial price level $p_1 = 0$, for parameter values $\gamma = 1$, $\delta = 0.5$, $\lambda = 10$. In the absence of money demand shocks, one possible equilibrium is for m_t, p_t, y_t, and i_t to equal zero forever; this is the equilibrium described previously. In the equilibrium shown in the figure, instead, the price level steadily rises after date 1, asymptotically approaching a higher level. This expected inflation causes nominal interest rates to rise above their steady-state level at date 2 and thereafter, falling back to the steady-state level as inflation returns to zero asymptotically. (Note that [10] implies that there cannot be any deviation of ex ante real rates from the steady-state level that is anticipated a period or more in advance.) During these periods, there is an inverted yield curve (as interest rates are expected to decline), and this positive spread triggers money growth, bringing about the inflation as expected. The fact that this is expected to occur beginning at date 2, in turn, makes the two-period interest rate already high at date 1. This results in a negative spread at date 1, leading to contraction of the money supply for one period only, as a result of which single-period interest rates are also above their steady-state level at date 1. Expectations may switch from the zero-inflation path to this one at date 1 (after p_1 has already been fixed) as a result of an arbitrary random event; and a stationary "sunspot equilibrium" may be constructed as a stochastic process in which events of this kind occur each period, in each case triggering a dynamic response of the kind shown in the figure.[12]

It is also worthwhile to consider briefly the policy rules that become possible if aggregate output y_t is also observed at date t. Note that, under the constant money supply policy, y_t and s_t would be observed to always move together, so that the two variables would have *identical* power in inflation forecasting regressions. Thus it might seem that a policy of the form

(12) $$\Delta m_t = -\lambda y_t$$

for some $\lambda > 0$ should have no advantages over one of the form (8). And in fact, a policy of the form (12) can support the equilibrium previously described for policy (8), although α is now given by

$$\alpha = \frac{\delta + \gamma}{\delta + \gamma + \delta(1 + \gamma)\lambda}.$$

But with the policy rule (12), this is the *unique* nonexplosive REE, no matter how large λ is. Hence it is possible (by choosing $\lambda > 0$ large) to reduce the fluctuations in output and inflation to any desired degree, without creating the possibility of self-fulfilling expectations.

The advantage of real activity y_t as an indicator is that it indicates the occurrence of a money demand shock for a different reason than do financial variables such as s_t. When output deviates from its "natural" level, this indicates that current aggregate demand has deviated from the level it was expected to have when prices were set. The change in the indicator thus represents a relatively direct effect of the shock itself, rather than an indication of the existence of expectations of future inflation. Indeed, an "output gap" can be taken to directly indicate a condition that *will cause* inflation in the future if a change in demand conditions does not occur in the meantime, insofar as it indicates an existing discrepancy between current prices and/or wages and those that the contracting parties would have wished to choose ex post. Because the indicator is not valuable solely due to its sensitivity to expectations, policy can be based upon it without creating the sort of feedback loop that allows expectations to be self-fulfilling. (For the same reason, policy can be based upon it without the use of the variable as a basis for policy rendering it useless as an indicator of inflationary pressures.) But this sort of difference between the two possible indicators cannot be revealed by a consideration of inflation forecasting regressions alone.

---

12. In a sunspot equilibrium made up of repeated fluctuations of this particular kind, there are no deviations of output from its "natural" level. But this is only because of the particular example of self-fulfilling expectations that I have chosen to exhibit. There also exist sunspot equilibria in which arbitrary changes in expectations cause fluctuations in output, and these can be of arbitrarily large magnitude.

3.5 Conclusions

All of these considerations point in the same direction: one cannot conclude too much about the desirability of alternative indicators without analyzing the effects of proposed operating procedures for monetary policy in the context of a structural model. I have not attempted here to provide an evaluation of specific proposed rules for monetary policy, or even of the usefulness of specific proposed indicators. This would require an analysis of the effects of candidate policies in the context of a structural model, which I have not undertaken in anything more than an illustrative way.

I have suggested, however, that there are general grounds for skepticism about a general approach to monetary policy that would advocate responding to variables because they have served in the past to forecast inflation, without regard to whether they forecast inflation because they represent (or are directly affected by) *proximate causes* of inflation, or because they indicate the *inflationary expectations* of other economic agents. The analysis above suggests important advantages to finding indicators of the causes of inflation rather than of inflationary expectations. What these variables would be depends upon one's model of the inflationary process. Various measures of the money supply can certainly be argued for on these grounds, but one cannot say on the basis of economic theory that these are the only such indicators or even the best ones. The evidence for recent instability of money demand certainly suggests the desirability of finding other indicators as well. In the simple model analyzed in section 3.3, the "output gap" can be a more useful indicator of inflationary pressure than the money supply. Whether it is in practice depends upon the details of an empirically adequate structural model of the sources of aggregate fluctuations and of the nature of aggregate supply and price-setting.

At this point it might be asked what sort of "structural model" I have in mind. Presumably one of the main reasons that policy evaluation on the basis of dynamic simulations of complete macroeconomic models is not practiced as much now as twenty years ago is that nowadays there is little agreement about the type of model that should be used for such a purpose. Fischer (1991) attributes this paralysis to the Lucas (1976) critique of econometric policy evaluation.

But the evaluation of policy is still one of our most important tasks. This volume shows that interest in that task is far from extinct, even among academic economists. The impression I get from some of the papers in this volume, however, is that it is hoped that the evaluation of policy in the context of econometric models that do not even pretend to be structural can somehow sidestep the difficult business of justifying a structural model. This is an odd response to Lucas's article. His point, after all, was that when a model is used to predict the consequences of adopting a new policy rule, it is important that one believe the model's equations to be structural (in the sense of continuing to hold if a policy change of the kind being considered were made). It is hard to see why the potential pitfalls in reasoning that he warns of should be avoided by resorting to econometric specifications that make even less claim to representing structural relations than did the consumption function or the Phillips curve that Lucas discusses. Perhaps the implicit argument is that, as virtue has been shown to be impossible, vice no longer requires an apology.

I do not see any reason to accept such a nihilistic view. Of course, certainty is impossible as to the true structural relations, and the claims we can make about the consequences of adopting one policy or another must be qualified on this account. But this is no reason not to attempt an analysis. Criticisms of analyses as being based upon relations that may not truly be structural need not be answered unless the critic proposes an alternative specification that is argued to be more accurate and the critic furthermore can show that under the alternative specification the answer reached would be quite different. Lucas provides examples of criticisms of that sort, but these are not criticisms that lead to nihilism; one has a specific alternative to consider, and the justification for the change and its quantitative significance can be discussed in the light of available evidence. Agreement may be difficult to reach (for the facts seldom speak unambiguously), but productive discussion is possible once there are clearly posed alternative models to confront.

There is also some wisdom in the method followed by Bennett McCallum (1990), in which the effects of a proposed rule are simulated under several different specifications of the basic structural relations. The point of this, I think, is not that one can often hope that different specifications will make no important difference for the effects of a proposed policy change. But it is surely important to know *which* differences in specification make a crucial difference for the predicted outcome of a particular policy experiment, so that one can then search for evidence that bears upon the adequacy of one or another model in this particular respect.

References

Aguais, Scott D., Robert A. DeAngelis, and David A. Wyss. 1988. Commodity prices and inflation. *Data Resources U.S. Review,* June, 11–18.

Angell, Wayne D. 1987. A commodity price guide to monetary aggregate targeting. Paper presented to the Lehrman Institute, New York City, 10 December.

Baillie, Richard T. 1989. *Commodity prices and aggregate inflation: Would a commodity price rule be worthwhile?* Carnegie-Rochester Conference Series on Public Policy, vol. 31:185–240. Amsterdam: North-Holland.

Barsky, Robert B. 1993. Commodities and some other novel indicators in an anti-inflation policy: A synthesis and evaluation. Paper presented at the NBER Conference on Monetary Policy. 21–24 January.

Blanchard, Olivier J., and Charles M. Kahn. 1980. The solution of linear difference models under rational expectations. *Econometrica* 48:1305–11.

Boughton, James M., and William H. Branson. 1991. Commodity prices as a leading indicator of inflation. In *Leading economic indicators: New approaches and forecasting records,* eds. K. Lahiri and G. H. Moore. Cambridge: Cambridge University Press.

Brayton, Flint, and Peter A. Tinsley. 1991. Interest rate feedback policies for price level targeting. Division of Research and Statistics, Federal Reserve Board, October. Mimeo.

Cody, Brian J., and Leonard O. Mills. 1990. The role of commodity prices in formulating monetary policy. Working Paper no. 90–2. Federal Reserve Bank of Philadelphia, February.

DeFina, Robert H. 1988. Commodity prices: Useful intermediate targets for monetary policy? *Business Review, Federal Reserve Bank of Philadelphia,* May/June, 3–12.

Fama, Eugene F. 1975. Short-term interest rates as predictors of inflation. *American Economic Review* 65:269–82.

Fischer, Stanley. 1991. Rules versus discretion in monetary policy. In *Handbook of monetary economics,* eds. B. M. Friedman and F. H. Hahn, vol. 2. Amsterdam: North-Holland.

Fuhrer, Jeff, and George Moore. 1992. Monetary policy rules and the indicator properties of asset prices. *Journal of Monetary Economics* 29:303–38.

Garner, C. Alan. 1989. Commodity prices: Policy target or information variable? *Journal of Money, Credit and Banking* 21:508–14.

Genetski, Robert J. 1982. The benefits of a price rule. *Wall Street Journal,* 10 December, 30.

Goodfriend, Marvin. 1993. Interest rate policy and the inflation scare problem: 1979–1992. *Economic Quarterly, Federal Reserve Bank of Richmond* 79, no. 1 (winter): 1–24.

Hafer, R. W. 1983. Monetary policy and the price rule: The newest odd couple. *Review, Federal Reserve Bank of St. Louis,* February, 5–13.

Heller, H. Robert. 1987. Anchoring the international monetary system. Paper presented to the Heritage Foundation, Washington, D.C., 24 March.

Hetzel, Robert L. 1990. Maintaining price stability: A proposal. *Economic Review, Federal Reserve Bank of Richmond,* March/April, 53–55.

———. 1992. Indexed bonds as an aid to monetary policy. *Economic Review, Federal Reserve Bank of Richmond,* January/February, 13–23.

Johnson, Manuel. 1988. Current perspectives on monetary policy. *Cato Journal* 8:253–60.

Lucas, Robert E., Jr. 1976. Econometric policy evaluation: A critique. In *The phillips curve and labor markets,* eds. K. Brunner and A. Meltzer. Carnegie-Rochester Conference Series on Public Policy, no. 1. Amsterdam: North-Holland.

McCallum, Bennett T. 1989. *Monetary economics: Theory and policy.* New York: Macmillan.

———. 1990. Targets, indicators, and instruments of monetary policy. In *Monetary policy for a changing financial environment,* eds. W. Haraf and P. Cagan. Washington, D.C.: AEI Press.

Miles, Marc A. 1984. *Beyond monetarism: Finding the road to stable money.* New York: Basic Books.

Porter, Richard D., ed. 1990. *Proceedings of the monetary affairs workshop on asset prices and the conduct of monetary policy.* Finance and Economics Discussion Series, no. 125. Federal Reserve Board, April.

Reynolds, Alan. 1982. The trouble with monetarism. *Policy Review* 21 (summer): 19–42.

Sephton, Peter S. 1991. Comment on Garner: Commodity prices: Policy target or information variable? *Journal of Money, Credit and Banking* 23:260–66.

Smith, Bruce D. 1994. Efficiency and determinacy of equilibrium under inflation targeting. *Economic Theory.* Forthcoming.

U.S. House. 1987. Committee on Banking, Finance, and Urban Affairs. Subcommittee on Domestic Monetary Policy. Subcommittee on International Finance, Trade, and Monetary Policy. *Role of commodity prices in the international coordination of economic policies and in the conduct of monetary policy.* 100th Cong., 1st sess. 17 November, 108–21.

Webb, Roy H. 1988. Commodity prices as predictors of aggregate price change. *Economic Review, Federal Reserve Bank of Richmond,* November/December, 3–11.

Whitt, Joseph A. 1988. Commodity prices and monetary policy. Working Paper no. 88–8. Federal Reserve Bank of Atlanta, December.

Woodford, Michael. 1994. Monetary policy and price level determinacy in a cash-in-advance economy. *Economic Theory.* Forthcoming.

4   On Sticky Prices: Academic Theories Meet the Real World

Alan S. Blinder

Any theory of how nominal money affects the real economy must face up to the following conundrum: Demand or supply functions derived—whether precisely or heuristically—from basic micro principles have money, M, as an argument only in ratio to P, the general price level. Hence, if monetary policy is to have real effects, there must be some reason why changes in M are *not* followed promptly by equiproportionate changes in P. This is the sense in which some kind of "price stickiness" is essential to virtually any story of how monetary policy works.[1]

Keynes (1936) offered one of the first intellectually coherent (or was it?) explanations for price stickiness by positing that money *wages* are sticky, and perhaps even rigid—at least in the downward direction. In that case, what Keynes called "the money supply in wage units," M/W, moves in the same direction as nominal money, thereby stimulating the economy. In the basic Keynesian model,[2] prices are not sticky *relative to wages*. It is wage rigidity that makes P respond less than one-for-one to M.

In recent years, macroeconomists have focused more on *price* rigidity than on *wage* rigidity. This shift of emphasis appears to have two roots. The first is the well-known fact that real wages do not display the pronounced counter-cyclical pattern that is implied by rigid nominal wages and flexible (and pre-sumably procyclical) prices. Hence *price* rigidity must be part of the story.

Alan S. Blinder is the Gordon S. Rentschler Memorial Professor of Economics at Princeton University and a research associate of the National Bureau of Economic Research. He is currently serving on President Clinton's Council of Economic Advisers.

1. There are some exceptions. For example, changes in the money-growth rate can affect real interest rates via their effects on inflationary expectations. However, no one seems to think such effects are quantitatively large. And in some models these effects are absent entirely.

2. By this I mean an IS-LM system with an aggregate supply side consisting of a standard marginal productivity condition for labor demand and a labor supply function with money illusion. As a limiting case, the latter could simply be a fixed money wage.

The second is the suggestion, made by Barro (1977) and Hall (1980), that the observed market wage rate might not be allocative—that is, it might equal neither the marginal product of labor nor the marginal utility of leisure. Instead, they suggested, the current real wage might simply be an installment payment on a long-term contract. In this view of the labor market, which derives from Azariadis (1975), Baily (1974), and Gordon (1974), labor and management enter into long-term agreements under which the firm offers stable real wages but variable employment. In present-value (or expected-value) terms, the wage matches both the marginal product of labor and the marginal utility of leisure. But these equalities need not hold period by period.

It is unclear how important this view of the labor market is in practice.[3] But the idea has nonetheless helped shift theorists' attention from wage rigidity to price rigidity. After all, it seems clear that however important long-term implicit contracts are in the labor market, they must be vastly *less* important in the product market. The research reported on here follows this recent tradition by focusing exclusively on theories of sticky *prices,* not sticky wages.[4]

There is no shortage of theories of either price or wage rigidity. The supply is limited only by the imagination of economic theorists; and since theorists can be produced at roughly constant cost, the supply of theories is quite elastic. In fact, it appears that new theories are generated far more frequently than old ones are rejected. Worse yet, the ebb and flow of competing theories seems to have more in common with hemlines than with science—based more on fad and fashion than on fact. Try to think of even a single case in which a theory of sticky prices has been rejected econometrically.

What is the reason for this sorry state of affairs? I believe it is that many, if not most, of the theories are epistemologically empty in the following concrete sense: (*a*) they predict that prices adjust less rapidly than some unmeasured Walrasian benchmark, (*b*) many of the theories predict nothing other than this, and (*c*) often the theories rely on variables which are either unmeasurable in principle or unmeasured in practice. Under such conditions, it is no wonder that conventional econometric methods get us nowhere.

Is there a better way? The research project reported on here is based on the notion that there is. Specifically, almost all of the theories share one aspect in common: each traces a chain of reasoning that allegedly leads the decision maker to conclude that rapid price changes are against the firm's best interests. It struck me that if a particular price setter actually follows such a chain of reasoning, *he just might know it!*[5] He might not be able to give an intellectually coherent explanation of his behavior, just as a pool player cannot explain mechanics. But if the idea is explained to him in plain English, he should recognize and agree with it. At least that was the belief that motivated this research.

---

3. See, for example, Brown and Ashenfelter (1986).
4. For some related work on theories of sticky wages, see Blinder and Choi (1990).
5. Pardon the chauvinistic use of the male pronoun throughout, but it turned out that virtually 100 percent of the respondents were men.

With a team of graduate students, I interviewed two hundred randomly selected firms about their pricing behavior. The results are now being written up in a book, and full details on the survey methodology will be found there. But a few points need to be mentioned:

- The sampling frame represented the private, nonfarm, for-profit, unregulated gross domestic product (GDP)—about 85 percent of the total. Since sample selection probabilities were proportional to value added, further weighting of responses is neither necessary nor appropriate.
- At 61 percent, the response rate was gratifyingly high—which eases, but does not entirely eliminate, worries that the sample might be unrepresentative.
- The interviews were conducted in waves between April 1990 and March 1992, and most of the interviewers were Princeton graduate students trained by me. The interviews were done face-to-face, almost always in the respondent's place of business.
- Questions were usually read verbatim from the questionnaire, but were sometimes paraphrased. Respondents always answered in their own words, and interviewers coded the responses on prescribed scales.

This paper focuses on a small but interesting subset of the results: what we learned about the nature and validity of five theories of sticky prices that were prominent in the academic discussions of the 1980s. The five theories were selected by me on a purely subjective basis. But my intent was to pick the theories that were most discussed, say, at NBER conferences and in graduate classrooms during the decade.

On average, as we shall see, these five theories get lower marks than the seven theories that were not "hot" in the 1980s. But the point of this paper is not to argue that economic theorists have been barking up the wrong trees, but to see what we can learn about the trees up which they have been barking. For example, the following question is often thought to be a showstopper in discussions of the "menu cost" theory: Aren't there even bigger fixed costs of adjusting quantities? Or another example: How common is judging quality by price? Answers to questions like these are available from the survey data—and apparently nowhere else.

The paper is organized into eight sections. Section 4.1 offers evidence that prices are indeed sticky. Section 4.2 looks briefly at some of the reasons why, including a list of the twelve theories "tested" by the survey. Then sections 4.3–4.7 examine in turn the evidence on each of the five recently popular theories. Section 4.8 is a brief summary.

4.1 Evidence That Prices Are Sticky

I suggested earlier that there is no such thing as definitive evidence that prices are "sticky" because (*a*) the Walrasian adjustment norm is unmeasured, and (*b*) the prices that actually clear markets might be long-run contract prices

Table 4.1   Frequency of Price Adjustment (number of times per year)

Frequency	Percentage of Firms
Less than once	10.2%
Once	39.3%
1.01 to 2	15.6%
2.10 to 4	12.9%
4.01 to 12	7.5%
12.01 to 52	4.3%
52.01 to 365	8.6%
More than 365	1.6%

and (*b*) the prices that actually clear markets might be long-run contract prices rather than spot prices. Nonetheless, empirical evidence on the frequency of price adjustment makes it hard for many economists—including me—to believe that the macroeconomy is an auction hall writ large.

Our survey collected what may be the first evidence on price stickiness ever derived from a random sample of the whole economy. To begin with, we asked:

A10.[6] How often do the prices of your most important products change in a typical year?

Of our 200 firms, 186 answered this question, giving a median response of 1.3 times per year. As table 4.1 shows, there is a strong mode at 1.0, meaning that *annual* price changes are most typical. Perhaps more pertinent for macro models, fully 78 percent of GDP is apparently repriced quarterly or less often. That certainly seems like enough price stickiness to matter.

The most fascinating numbers in the table may be in the tails of the distribution, however. About 10 percent of GDP is apparently repriced less frequently than once a year; and an equal amount is repriced more than once a week. Indeed, 1.6 percent is repriced more than once a day. Yes, Virginia, there is an auction-market sector. But it is pretty small.

From a theoretical point of view, table 4.1 does not really offer the right measure of price stickiness. For example, if cost and demand shocks occur infrequently, Walrasian prices might change only once or twice a year. We would not want to call that price rigidity. Therefore, another series of questions inquired about what seem to me the conceptually correct measures of price stickiness: how much time elapses between a shock to either demand or cost and the corresponding price adjustment?

There were actually four such questions, corresponding to positive and negative shocks to both demand and cost. For example:

A13(a). Firms and industries differ in how rapidly their prices respond to changes in demand and costs. How much time normally elapses after a significant increase in demand before you raise your prices?

---

6. Numbers like this throughout the paper correspond to question numbers on the questionnaire.

The other three questions were similar, with "decrease" replacing "increase" and/or "cost" replacing "demand." Respondents were left to decide for themselves the meaning of the adjective "significant." Table 4.2 summarizes the results.

Much detail lies behind this small table. (The meaning of the last column will be explained below). But the main observations seem to be the following:

1. Lags in price adjustment are long. In round numbers, about three months typically elapses between the shock that would change prices in a Walrasian world and the firms' price response. This is good news for simple macro models that assume a "one period" lag in adjusting prices.

2. There is essentially no evidence for the common belief that prices adjust more rapidly upward than downward. For demand shocks, the data suggest equal response times. For cost shocks, price increases do appear to come about a half-month faster than price decreases—a difference which is highly significant in a statistical sense but not very large economically.

3. There is no evidence for the commonly held view that firms respond more rapidly to cost shocks than to demand shocks. Rather, the data suggest strikingly similar response times.

4. The cross-sectional variances in adjustment lags are huge—larger than the mean itself in all four cases. It would be a mistake, I believe, to interpret these large standard deviations as reflecting mostly sampling variance, though some is surely present. Rather, these numbers testify to the enormous heterogeneity across firms in the speed of adjusting prices.

An important technical point about item nonresponse must be made at this point. The response rates to the four variants of this question were among the lowest in the survey. Thus the bad news is that we got fewer responses to the more appropriate (but harder) question about price stickiness. About three quarters of the nonresponse stems from the fact that the question was inappropriate for some firms. (See the final column in table 4.2) For example, when we inquired about delays in cutting prices following a decline in cost, seventy-one firms told us that they never experience cost reductions. As you can see in the table, many more firms experience positive than negative cost shocks.

In sum, looking at a random sample of GDP, rather than a selected corner of the economy, reveals a substantial degree of price stickiness—certainly enough to give monetary policy a handle on real activity. But this stickiness does not appear to be asymmetric in the two ways commonly assumed by econ-

Table 4.2   **Lags in Price Adjustments (in months)**

Type of Shock	Mean Lag	Standard Deviation	Number of Responses	Number of "Never Happens"
Increase in demand	2.88	3.21	128	52
Increase in cost	2.76	3.00	163	23
Decrease in demand	2.90	3.70	132	50
Decrease in cost	3.27	3.92	101	71

Table 4.3   The Twelve Theories

Theory Number and Name	Brief Description
B1 Nominal contracts	Prices are fixed by contracts
B2 Implicit contracts	Firms tacitly agree to stabilize prices, perhaps out of "fairness" to customers (Okun 1981)
*B3 Judging quality by price	Firms fear customers will mistake price cuts for reductions in quality (Allen 1988)
B4 Pricing points	Certain prices (like $9.99) have special psychological significance (Kashyap 1992)
*B5 Procyclical elasticity	Demand curves become less elastic as they shift in (Bils 1989; Shapiro 1988)
B6 Cost-based pricing with lags	Price rises are delayed until costs rise (Gordon 1981; Blanchard 1983)
*B7 Constant marginal cost	Marginal cost is flat and markups are constant (Hall 1986)
*B8 Costs of price adjustment	Firms incur costs of changing prices (Rotemberg 1982; Mankiw 1985)
B9 Hierarchical delays	Bureaucratic delays slow down decisions
*B10 Coordination failure	Firms hold back on price changes, waiting for other firms to go first (Ball and Romer 1991)
B11 Inventories	Firms vary inventory stocks instead of prices (Blinder 1982)
B12 Delivery lags, service, etc.	Firms prefer to vary other elements of the "vector," such as delivery lags, service, or product quality (Carlton 1990)

omists. Firms tell us that they do not typically respond faster to demand shocks than to cost shocks; nor do they raise prices faster than they lower them. It pays to ask![7]

4.2   Reasons for Price Stickiness

This survey sought to find out which theories of sticky prices hold most appeal for real-world decision makers. Table 4.3 names the twelve theories that were evaluated in the survey and offers brief explanations (and citations) for each. Asterisks indicate the five that I subjectively selected for attention in this paper on the grounds that they received the most academic attention in the 1980s.

Most of the entries in table 4.3 are self-explanatory, but a few are not. The procyclical elasticity theory represents a class of models of *countercyclical markups*. If new customers are more price-elastic than old ones, then the price elasticity of demand will be procyclical, making the optimal markup count-

7. In this case, asking bolsters the answers given by the paltry econometric evidence that exists. As early as 1981, Okun (1981, 165) noted that empirical Phillips curves do *not* offer evidence of asymmetry.

ercyclical. No one doubts that prices depend on costs. What makes cost-based pricing with lags a macroeconomic theory of price stickiness, rather than a tautology, is the recognition that most goods and services pass through several stages of processing (each with its own lag) on their way to ultimate users. Hierarchical delays is the one theory on the list that did *not* come from the academic literature; it was suggested, instead, by a top executive of a large manufacturing company during pretesting of the questionnaire. Some (including me) may prefer to think of it as a particular kind of menu cost.

The popularity poll among the twelve contending theories was run as follows. I translated the basic idea of each theory into plain English, and then asked price setters how important it was in affecting the speed of price adjustment *in their own company*. For example, the question about nominal contracting was

B1. One idea is that many goods are sold under explicit contractual agreements that set prices in advance, so firms are not free to raise prices while contracts remain in force.

How important is this idea in slowing down price adjustments in your company?

And there was a similar question for each of the twelve theories. Respondents answered in their own words, and interviewers coded the responses on the following four-point scale:

1 = totally unimportant
2 = of minor importance
3 = moderately important
4 = very important

It is straightforward to compare the average ratings given to each of the twelve theories, as I shall do shortly. But first a few important caveats.

First, the reader should be cautioned against identifying the above mentioned scale with the standard four-point scale used to grade college students. For example, an average grade of 4.0 would not connote anything as mundane as a straight-A average. Rather, it would mean that *every single respondent* considered the theory "very important," that is, we had stumbled upon God's truth! Plainly, this is not going to happen. A more plausible standard of excellence would be an average rating of, say, 3.0. On the low end, an average score of 1.0 would mean that *every single respondent* totally rejected the theory— which is more like brain death than a D. So it is perhaps more useful to think of the likely range of survey results as going from a top score of 3.0 for a wonderful theory to, say, 1.5 for a disastrous one.

Second, with very few exceptions, the theories are not mutually exclusive. Firms can, and often did, agree with several.

Third, the survey appraises *microeconomic* importance, not *macroeconomic*

Table 4.4   **Ratings of the Twelve Theories**

(1)	(2)	(3)	(4)	(5)	(6)	(7)
Rank	Theory Number[a]	Mean Score	Standard Deviation	t-statistic[b]	Accept Rate	Premise?
1	*B10	2.77	1.25	1.0	60.6%	100.0%
2	B6	2.66	1.26	0.6	55.5	100.0
3	B12	2.58	1.20	1.6	54.8	77.0
4	B2	2.40	1.26	2.1**	50.5	68.3
5	B1	2.11	1.25	1.8*	35.7	62.2
6	*B8	1.89	1.18	0.4	30.0	64.3
7	*B5	1.85	1.07	0.8	29.7	58.5
8	B4	1.76	1.04	1.8*	24.0	50.8
9	*B7	1.57	1.03	0.1	19.7	48.4
10	B11	1.56	0.97	1.9*	20.9	85.6[c]
11	B9	1.41	0.87	1.2	13.6	100.0
12	*B3	1.33	0.77	—	10.0	21.0

[a]Refer to table 4.3 for descriptions of the theories.

[b]For the hypothesis that the mean score is significantly above that in the next row.

[c]The question was not asked of firms producing services. Thus 85.6 percent is the percentage of these firms that report holding inventories of finished goods.

*Significant at the 10 percent level.

**Significant at the 5 percent level.

importance; and the aggregation process is complex. To illustrate, imagine that ten firms selling intermediate goods followed the menu-cost theory while thirty firms selling final goods simply marked up costs *immediately,* with no lags. Then menu costs would be *the* macroeconomic source of price stickiness even though three-quarters of all firms reject the theory entirely.

   With this understood, I turn to the results of the beauty contest. Table 4.4 ranks the theories by mean scores (column 3) and also shows the standard deviation across firms (column 4).[8] Asterisks in column 2 once again indicate the five recently popular theories. The other columns require some explanation.

• The t-statistic in column 5 is the test statistic for the hypothesis that the theory's mean score significantly exceeds that of the theory ranked *just below it.* As you can see, a single-rank difference is statistically significant in only four cases. However, eight of the ten two-rank differences are significant at the 10 percent level, and all nine three-rank differences are significant at the

   8. To put the estimated standard errors into perspective, some benchmarks may be useful. The standard deviation of a multinomial distribution with four equally likely outcomes—1, 2, 3, and 4—is 1.12. If the four probabilities are (1/8, 3/8, 3/8, 1/8) instead, the standard deviation drops to 0.87; if they are (3/8, 1/8, 1/8, 3/8), the standard deviation rises to 1.32.

5 percent level. Thus the rankings shown in table 4.4 are sharper than they may seem.

- The Accept Rate in column 6 offers an alternative way to rank the theories, offered because our numerical scale does not really have the *cardinal* significance that the rankings in column 1 pretend it has. Column 6 therefore reports a simple measure of how many firms accept each theory—the fraction of respondents rating the theory as "moderately important" or higher. As you can see, the two rankings hardly differ.
- I come now to the puzzling column 7. Nine of the twelve theories apply only to firms that have some particular characteristic. For example, inventories cannot explain price stickiness in firms that have no inventories. In each of these nine cases, we first pose a preliminary factual question (for example, "Does your firm hold inventories?"), and proceed to inquire about the theory only if the factual question is answered in the affirmative. If not, we skip over the theory and score it as "totally unimportant" by definition. The column marked Premise? shows the percentage of the sample to which the theory applies *in principle*—that is, for which the factual premise is true. For example, 68.3 percent of the firms in our sample say they enter into implicit contracts with their customers (as assumed by theory B2).

The theories naturally group themselves into three tiers, each with four members.

The top group scores well—if we are not too fussy about grading standards! If these results are believed, economists interested in the microfoundations of sticky prices should be focusing their attention on these four theories. Three of them are part of the modern Keynesian tradition: implicit contracts a la Okun (B2), cost-based pricing (B6), and coordination failure (B10). And nominal contracts (B1) finishes in fifth place. It is worth noting that two of the theories in the top group (implicit contracts and delivery lags) have especially high acceptance rates within their spheres of applicability: 74 percent (that is, .505/.683 = .74) and 71 percent, respectively. Thus, while there are sectors of the economy to which these theories do not apply, they appear to offer quite good explanations of price stickiness for the majority of firms.

The bottom tier of four theories scores amazingly poorly. Remember, a mean score of 1.5 is equivalent to half the firms rejecting the theory outright and the other half attaching only "minor importance" to it. That two theories (judging quality by price [B3] and hierarchical delays [B9]) actually rate lower than this minimum score is remarkable.[9] Unless my results are way off the mark, these theories deserve to be eliminated from further consideration. The inventory-based theory (B11) is the only one on the list of twelve in which I had a proprietary interest; I offer this as evidence that the election was not

9. Remember, there was some preselection: I rejected theories that in my judgment seemed fanciful.

rigged. Two of the four theories in the bottom group (constant marginal cost [B7] and judging quality by price [B3]) are among the five I selected as having garnered the most scholarly attention in the past decade, and so merit more extensive discussion.

About half of the private for-profit economy apparently has the cost structure assumed by Hall (1986): marginal cost curves that are flat within the relevant range. Obviously, the theory does not apply to the other half. But even within the half of GDP produced under constant marginal cost (MC), the theory's acceptance rate is a mere 41 percent. Thus it seems most unlikely that constant marginal cost is a major factor behind *aggregate* price stickiness.[10] The adverse selection theory fares much worse. The premise that customers judge quality by price apparently applies to just one-fifth of GDP; and only half of these firms rate it an important cause of price rigidity. Apparently, adverse selection is an important source of price rigidity in only a corner of the economy.

In the middle comes a group of four theories that earn "average" grades:[11] nominal contracts (B1), costs of price adjustment (B8), procyclical elasticity (B5), and pricing points (B4). These theoretical bottles are either half full or half empty, depending on your tastes. The survey results for these four theories will neither persuade a skeptic nor dissuade a believer. In each case, roughly half of the firms to which the theory applies rate it as "moderately important" or higher. The differences in mean scores stem from the 51 percent who report the existence of psychological pricing points to the 69 percent who have a meaningful volume of nominal contracts.

The way we posed the questions underlying table 4.4 has two virtues:

1. It asks each price setter to describe only *his own* firm's *actual* behavior, rather than deal in hypotheticals.

2. It does not ask respondents to think or talk abstractly about the reasons for sticky prices, but only to react to concrete suggestions. While I consider this second virtue extremely important, it does have one drawback: in outlining the theories, we may have put ideas into people's heads. Based on my experience in the field, I doubt that this was a major problem. But for those who are worried about it, the survey offers an alternative.

Prior to mentioning any of the twelve theories, we asked each respondent the factual question given earlier:

A10. How often do the prices of your most important products change in a typical year?

---

10. Even ignoring the difference between *real* marginal costs (to which the theory applies) and *nominal* marginal costs.

11. The average ranking across all theories and all respondents is exactly 2.0. Economists have a way to go! On the positive side, however, 89 percent of all firms rated at least one theory a 4 and every firm rated at least one theory a 3.

Immediately after, we followed up with the question

A10(a). Why don't you change prices more frequently than that?

This is not the sort of question I like to ask, for it is too abstract and requires a great deal of introspection. It is a bit like asking the proverbial pool player, "Why didn't you shoot that shot differently?" Nonetheless, the question did give respondents a chance to choose their favorite explanation for price stickiness before their minds were contaminated by our suggestions.

Because the question is open-ended, the answers defy neat categorization. One hundred seventy-one firms answered; but some gave us two or three replies, and others answered with some variant of "We change prices as often as we please"—suggesting that they should not have been asked the question in the first place. This left 217 usable responses, and table 4.5 is my heroic attempt to tabulate them in some coherent, albeit admittedly subjective, way.

The explanation that tops the list, antagonizing customers, is open to various interpretations and does not obviously correspond to any of our theories—though it does evoke implicit contracts. Much the same can be said of the catch-all "competitive pressures," which reminds one of coordination failure but is also open to other interpretations. After that, however, we can clearly recognize several of the theories listed in table 4.3. Twenty-eight firms cite costs of price adjustment. The twenty-seven firms that said they change prices infrequently because their costs change infrequently are implicitly agreeing with cost-based pricing. An additional fifteen firms gave answers that evoked coordination failure. And nineteen companies mentioned either explicit or implicit contracts.

The remainder of the paper looks in more detail at the five theories of greatest recent interest.

Table 4.5	Why Don't You Change Prices More Frequently Than That? (n = 217 responses from 171 firms)	
Response		Number of Firms
It would antagonize or cause difficulties for our customers		41
Competitive pressures		28
Costs of changing prices (**B8**)		28
Our costs do not change more often (**B6**)		27
Coordination failure, price followership (**B10**)		15
Explicit contracts fix prices (**B1**)		14
Custom or habit		11
Regulations		7
Implicit contracts with regular customers (**B2**)		5
Miscellaneous other reasons		20

Note: Bold-faced numbers in the table refer to the theories listed in table 4.3.

4.3   What Price Setters Think about Coordination Failure

Coordination failure, the top-rated idea in table 4.4, is old wine in new bottles. The notion that some industries consist of a "price leader" and several "price followers" is ancient, and has long been used to explain sticky oligopoly prices. But it requires a characteristic skewness in the industrial structure and/or begs the question of who becomes the price leader and why.

Ball and Romer (1991) developed a modern version of this old idea—one that is applicable to symmetric and *competitive* market structures—by combining menu costs with some theoretical ideas set forth by Cooper and John (1988). The basic notion is that firm i's optimal degree of nominal price flexibility depends positively on firm j's.[12] So, if other firms select high price flexibility, then firm i will, too. Conversely, firm i will choose sticky prices if other firms do so. There are, in a word, multiple equilibria with varying degrees of price rigidity.

We enquired about this theory by posing the following question:

B10. The next idea is that firms would often like to raise their prices, but are afraid to get out of line with what they expect competitors to charge. They do not want to be the first ones to raise prices. But when competing goods rise in price, firms raise their own prices promptly.

How important is this idea in explaining the speed of price adjustment in your company?

Notice that the question is phrased to sound like Ball and Romer's symmetric version of coordination failure, not the classic asymmetric leader/follower pattern. Nonetheless, a number of firms answered with the latter in mind. The distribution of responses in the full sample is shown in table 4.6. If we divide the sample into five major industrial sectors, the theory ranks first in trade and services, second in manufacturing and the transportation-communications-utilities composite, and third in construction. If we divide the sample according to (self-reported) cyclical sensitivity, the coordination failure theory again ranks first in each subsample. It seems clear that this is the theory that practitioners regard most highly.[13]

When we asked those respondents who agreed at least somewhat with the theory *why* they did not want to go first, the overwhelmingly most frequent reply was fear of a large loss of sales if rivals did not match the price increase. This fear, by the way, mainly deters price *increases,* not price *decreases,* as the following question in table 4.7 attests. There is thus strong evidence of asymmetry in this theory, but it is in the direction opposite from that usually assumed: prices are more rigid upward than downward!

One thing we would like to understand is the cross-sectional variation in

---

12. This is what Cooper and John (1988) call "strategic complementarity."
13. One caveat: table 4.4 shows that its overall rating is not significantly higher than the second-ranked theory, cost-based pricing with lags.

Table 4.6   **Distribution of Ratings of the Coordination Failure Theory (n = 198)**

Code	Response	Percentage of Firms
1	Totally unimportant	27.5%
2	Of minor importance	10.6%
3	Moderately important	19.4%
4	Very important	42.4%

Note: Mean response = 2.77. Mean response among those not answering 1 = 3.41.

Table 4.7   **B10(b). Do You Also Delay Price Cuts Because You Do Not Want to Be among the First Firms in the Industry to Cut Prices? (n = 183)[a]**

Code	Response	Percentage of Firms
1	Rarely or never	61.3%
2	Sometimes	13.8%
3	Usually or always	24.8%

Note: Mean response = 1.63.

[a]Twenty firms answered, "We never cut prices"; hence we have only 163 *numerical* responses.

how firms rate the various theories. This can be done by looking at cross tabulations. But, in a data set with twelve theories and more than 125 variables, the number of possible cross tabulations is enormous. A more efficient way of summarizing the correlations is by estimating regression models with the rating of each theory on the left and a variety of explanatory variables on the right. The reader should understand that, in doing so, I am not testing any hypotheses. The estimate models are intended merely as convenient summaries of the *partial* correlations found in the data.

What is the most appropriate statistical model? In this paper, I estimate an *ordered probit* model for each theory. So, before presenting any results, I ought to explain what that model is.

Suppose we have a categorical variable (like the scores respondents give to some theory) which can take on one of k discrete values: $1, 2, 3, \ldots, k$. These responses are *ordinal* rather than cardinal—that is, 4 is bigger than 3, which is bigger than 2; but there is no sense in which 4 is twice as big as 2. the ordered probit or logit model postulates the existence of a continuous latent variable, call it z, which indicates the firm's evaluation of the theory. The value of variable z for firm i is assumed to be linearly related to a set of regressors, X_i:

(1) $$z_i = X_i b + c + u_i,$$

and the respondent is presumed to give response j ($j = 1, \ldots, k$) if

(2) $$a_{j-1} < z_i < a_j.$$

In most applications, the lowest bound, a_0, is taken to be zero and the highest bound, a_k, is taken to be infinity.

The model is completed by the assumption that the cumulative distribution function (cdf) of the random error, u, is either normal (the ordered *probit* model) or logistic (the ordered *logit* model). I chose the former for no other reason than that it makes it easier to think of (1) as a linear regression. But nothing hinges on this decision; ordered *logit* models yielded substantially identical results.

The probability of observing response j from firm i is the probability that

$$a_{j-1} - X_i b - c < u_i < a_j - X_i b - c,$$

evaluated according to the normal cdf. In what follows, I adopt the notation $OP(B1) = Xb$ to connote the ordered probit model explaining the scores of theory B1 by regressors X with coefficients b.[14]

Estimation is by maximum likelihood, as described in Greene (1990, chap. 20).[15] If there are m regressors, the model has $m + k$ parameters: c, the m-vector b, and the $(k - 1)$-vector a. In most of my applications, k can be as large as seven—allowing for intermediate responses like 3.5. The algorithm usually converged rapidly if m was no larger than, say, ten or twelve. But with larger numbers of regressors and smaller numbers of observations,[16] we began pushing the limits of computability.

The best fitting ordered probit model for the coordination-failure theory (B10) was (with asymptotic standard errors in parentheses):[17]

$$OP(B10) = .0074 \text{ REGULARS} + 1.01 \text{ REG} - .28 \text{ INFL} + .13 \text{ MC}$$
$$(n = 169) \quad (.0043) \qquad\qquad (0.25) \qquad (.11) \qquad (.07)$$

$$-.15 \text{ INTERVAL} - .35 \text{ ACCURACY} - 1.18 \text{ UNION} - .63 \text{ IMPLICIT}$$
$$(.11) \qquad\qquad (.14) \qquad\qquad (0.61) \qquad (.21)$$

$$\log L = -210.7, \text{ pseudo-}R^2 = .122, \text{ linear } R^2 = .353.$$

The variables will be defined momentarily. In addition to the log likelihood, two measures of goodness of fit are offered:[18]

1. The pseudo-R^2 is McFadden's statistic, defined as $1 - L_1/L_0$; where

L_1 = the log likelihood for the estimated model, and
L_0 = the log likelihood for a model with only a constant.

14. Again, see table 4.3 for brief descriptions of the theories.

15. The precise model fit is known as the proportional odds model. It is programmed into the STATA package.

16. Owing to missing data, the sample size often shrinks when a new independent variable is added.

17. Several interviewer dummies were also included in this and subsequent regressions, but their coefficients are not shown separately.

18. Here, and in what follows, I do not bother to report p-values for the chi-squared tests of the overall significance of the models; they are always below .0001.

2. The linear R^2 is a concept I invented as a more intuitive measure. It is interpreted simply as the R^2 we would get if the latent variable z were actually measured and we ran the linear regression (1). It is a transformation of the McFadden measure calibrated by Monte Carlo methods.

The variables found "significant" in regression (3) are:

REGULARS = the fraction of sales going to regular customers. Apparently, coordination failure is a less important source of price stickiness when you have off-the-street customers. One interpretation is that it is the regular customers who are angered by unmatched price increases.

REG = a dummy equal to 1 if the firm has any regulatory restrictions on pricing.[19] The coefficient means that such firms are much more likely to deem coordination failure important.

INFL = a categorical variable indicating how often the firm uses economy wide inflation forecasts in setting prices. I interpret this as an indicator of economic rationality, since *any* price setter concerned about his desired *relative* price must take forecasts of future inflation into account. The negative coefficient means that "smarter" firms are less constrained by coordination failure.

MC = a categorical variable indicating the shape of the firm's marginal cost function (higher values of MC connote more increasing marginal cost). Apparently, the coordination failure theory rates better with firms that have rising MC curves.

INTERVAL = a dummy variable indicating that the firm follows a time-dependent (rather than state-dependent) policy for price reviews. It seems natural that firms with regular periodic price reviews should be less concerned about coordination problems; but the statistical association is weak.

ACCURACY = a categorical variable indicating how accurately the firm can estimate its marginal costs. Those that can do this well apparently worry less about coordination.

UNION = the unionization rate in the firm's three-digit industry. Thus firms in more unionized industries view the coordination theory less favorably.

IMPLICIT = a dummy variable indicating the presence of implicit contracts of the Okun variety. An Okunesque interpretation of the negative coefficient would probably say that implicit contracts permit price increases when (and only when) costs increase—regardless of whether other firms are raising their prices at the same time.

4.4   What Price Setters Think about Adjustment Costs

Perhaps the simplest explanation for price stickiness is that firms face explicit costs of changing prices. This theory comes in two variants. In the first (e.g., Rotemberg 1982), adjustment costs are convex and, where explicit solu-

---

19. Truly regulated firms were excluded from the sample. But, for example, firms in the sample might sell some regulated products or face restrictions such as prenotification.

Table 4.8	A10(b). When You Do Raise or Lower Prices, Do You Normally Do It All at Once or in a Series of Smaller Changes? (n = 198)		
Code	Response	Percentage of Firms	
1	Normally all at once	74.0%	
2	It varies	9.6%	
3	Normally in small steps	16.4%	

tions are needed, quadratic. More recent theoretical efforts (e.g., Mankiw 1985) focus on models in which a lump sum ("menu cost") must be paid any time the price is changed.

The two different types of adjustment costs carry starkly different implications at the micro level. If adjustment costs are convex, a firm wishing to raise its price will do so gradually, in a series of small steps, rather than all at once. But if the costs of price adjustment are lump sum, we should observe infrequent price changes of sizable magnitude. At the macro level, aggregation smooths the adjustment, thereby blurring the distinction between the two models. But firm-level micro data offer a rare opportunity for a sharp test.

We have several such tests in the survey, and they all point strongly toward menu costs. First—before even mentioning adjustment costs—we asked all two hundred firms about their pricing practices. Do they normally adjust prices all at once or in a series of small steps? The answers are shown in table 4.8. The vote points overwhelmingly toward menu costs—*if* adjustment cost is the reason behind these responses.

Later in the interview we turned to adjustment costs explicitly, asking respondents if their firms really have such costs. Specifically:

B8(a). Another idea is that the act of changing prices entails special costs in itself, so firms hesitate to change prices too frequently or by too much. The costs we have in mind are not production costs, but costs like printing new catalogs, price lists, etc., or hidden costs like loss of future sales by antagonizing customers, decision-making time of executives, problems with salespeople, and so on.
Does your firm incur such costs when it changes prices?

Notice that there is at least one item on this list that economists would not normally classify as an adjustment cost: the notion that *today's* price change might affect *tomorrow's* demand curve by "antagonizing customers." There is certainly a danger that respondents might have confused the idea that q_{t+1} depends on $p_{t+1} - p_t$ given p_{t+1}—which *would* constitute a genuine adjustment cost—with the simpler idea that higher p_t probably means higher p_{t+1} and therefore lower q_{t+1}. Unfortunately, there seemed to be no way around this problem in the context of an interview.[20]

20. One reader asked why we included "antagonizing customers" on the list at all. The answer is simple: in pretesting, respondents kept bringing it up.

Table 4.9   **B8(a). Does Your Company Have Explicit Costs of Price Adjustment? (n = 200)**

Code	Response	Percentage of Firms
1	No	35.8%
2	Yes, but trivial	21.3%
3	Yes	43.0%

Note: Mean response = 2.07.

With this caveat in mind, I proceed to the answers to the question, which are shown in table 4.9. What you make of these results depends on how you interpret the intermediate response, "yes, but trivial." If it is viewed as affirming the existence of adjustment costs, then firms representing almost two-thirds of GDP report having such costs. If, on the other hand, we treat trivial adjustment costs as, well, trivial, then the adjustment-cost theory applies to only 43 percent of the economy.

The impression that menu costs are the dominant form of adjustment costs was strongly confirmed by a follow-up question, asked only of firms that reported having adjustment costs (see table 4.10). By a margin of more than five to one, respondents gave the answer associated with menu costs rather than the one suggested by convex costs.

Note, by the way, that the evidence presented by Carlton (1986) and Kashyap (1992) in no way contradicts my finding that menu costs are dominant. Tables 4.8 and 4.10 suggest that convex adjustment costs apply to around 20 percent of GDP. Thus it should not be hard to find examples of very small price changes. But they are the exception, not the rule.

I come now to the main question about the importance of the adjustment-cost theory. The answers are shown in table 4.11. The theory scores fairly well (an average rating of 2.97) among the eighty-five firms that report nontrivial adjustment cost. But, since so many companies have either zero or trivial adjustment costs, its overall rating is quite low. The average score of 1.89 (a bit below "of minor importance") places it sixth among the twelve theories tested.

4.4.1 Adjustment Costs for Quantities?

Proponents of the adjustment-cost theory of price rigidity are often confronted with the following theoretical question. While there may be adjustment costs for changing *prices,* there surely are adjustment costs for changing *quantities.* Why should we believe that the former are greater than the latter? In some quarters, this question is thought to be a showstopper: adjustment costs for quantities are *assumed* to be greater than adjustment costs for prices, and so the theory is dismissed as an implausible explanation of sticky prices.[21]

While the relative size of the two types of adjustment costs is surely an

---

21. For an example, see Gordon (1990, 1146).

Table 4.10   **B8(c). Do These Costs of Changing Prices Come Mainly from Changing Prices Often or Mainly from Changing Them by Large Amounts? (n = 81)**

Code	Response	Percentage of Firms
1	Mainly from often	69.1%
2	Mainly from large amounts	13.6%
3	Both	17.3%

Table 4.11   **B8. How Important Are Costs of Changing Prices in Slowing Down Price Adjustments in Your Company? (n = 200)**

Code	Response	Percentage of Firms
1	Totally unimportant	59.3%*
2	Of minor importance	9.8%
3	Moderately important	14.3%
4	Very important	16.8%

Note: Mean response = 1.89. Mean among those reporting nontrivial costs = 2.97. Rank = sixth.
*This includes seventy-one firms that said they have no adjustment costs.

empirical issue, it cannot be resolved with standard data since we have no direct measurements of these costs. The survey offered a unique way of approaching this issue, and we did so through a series of questions. First, we asked firms whether they prefer to adjust price or output when demand changes. Most prefer output adjustments, as table 4.12 shows. Notice once again the indication that prices are more sticky upward than downward: the vast majority prefer to raise production rather than price when demand rises, but only a slim majority prefer to cut volume rather than price when demand falls.

We followed each of these questions with the simple query "Why is that?" Since the inquiry was open-ended, the answers are not easy to summarize, and doing so would take far too long. Suffice it to say that relatively few firms cited costs of price adjustment as the reason for their preference.

Finally, we asked directly whether the firm also has explicit costs of changing *output:*

B8(j). Do you incur special costs from the act of changing your production—analogous to the special costs you incur when you change prices? We have in mind things like temporary halts in production, expenses in recruiting new workers, etc. (*n* = 77)

The answers were as follows: no—34.4 percent; yes, but minor—23.4 percent; yes—42.2 percent.

It is surprising, I think, that about one-third of all firms deny having *any* adjustment costs for changing production. While the sample distributes itself somewhat evenly across the three categories, one should remember that this question was asked *only* of firms that reported meaningful costs of adjusting prices. Thus I read the responses as suggesting that, contrary to intuition, adjustment costs for *quantities* may well be *smaller* than adjustment costs for *prices*.

4.4.2   Correlates of Adjustment Costs

What kinds of firms believe that costs of changing prices are a significant factor behind price stickiness? I approach this question by estimating *two* ordered probit models. The first explains ADJ, a categorical variable indicating the presence or absence of adjustment costs, that is, the response to question B8(a) above, coded as follows:

$$1 = \text{no}$$
$$2 = \text{yes, but trivial}$$
$$3 = \text{yes}$$

Then, *only* for firms that answer either 2 or 3 to this question, I estimate an ordered probit model for the answer to question B8—the firm's evaluation of the adjustment-cost theory.

The best-fitting equations are

(4)   OP(ADJ) = -1.47 RET -1.03 WHOLE -1.51 CON
        ($n = 169$)   (.47)   (.36)   (.38)

+.010 CONSUMER $-$.29 CYCLICAL $+$ .36 INFL $-$.13 CONTRACTS
  (.004)   (.12)   (.12)   (.07)

  $+$ .17 INTERVAL $-$.34 LOYAL $-$.17 MC $+$ .23 INVENTORY;
    (.11)   (.21)   (.08)   (.13)

    $\log L = -154.1$; pseudo-$R^2 = .198$; linear $R^2 = .508$.

(5)   OP(B8) = 0.76 MFG $+$ 1.41 SERV $+$ .91 TCU
        ($n = 112$) (.33)   (.45)   (.54)

Table 4.12   **Reactions to Changes in Demand (B8(f), [h]. When your demand rises [falls], do you normally prefer to raise [decrease] your production, increase [cut] your prices, or both? [n = 78 (76)])**

		Percentage of Firms when	
Code	Response	Demand Rises	Demand Falls
1	Level of production	61.5%	36.8%
2	Prices	4.5%	27.0%
3	Both	34.0%	36.2%

$$-.44 \text{ CYCLICAL } -.15 \text{ CONTRACTS}$$
$$(.13) \qquad\qquad (.08)$$

$$-.64 \text{ LOYAL } +.28 \text{ MC } + .37 \text{ INVENTORY;}$$
$$(.23) \qquad (.09) \qquad (.17)$$

$$\log L = -151.9; \text{ pseudo-}R^2 = .143; \text{ linear } R^2 = .401.$$

As earlier, asymptotic standard errors are in parentheses.

The fit of these regressions is good. Indeed, the first is extraordinary for a model with categorical data—equivalent to an R^2 of .51 in a linear regression of the latent variable on the regressors. The significant righthand variables are

RET, WHOLE, CON, MFG, SERV, TCU = a set of dummy variables for retailing, wholesaling, construction, manufacturing, service industries, and a composite of transportation, communications, and utilities.

Thus the coefficients in the two equations mean that the trade (especially retail trade) and construction sectors are considerably less likely than the others (a) to have significant adjustment costs, and (b) to view such costs as an important source of sticky prices, even if they have them. In the case of construction, this is to be expected: for the most part, each sale has its own unique price. In the case of retail trade, however, this may be a bit surprising. After all, the phrase "menu costs" derives from a retailing application. However, what made Mankiw's (1985) paper so interesting was his demonstration that *presumably small* adjustment costs could account for sizable rigidities.

CONSUMER = the fraction of output sold to consumers. The strong positive coefficient in equation (4) is as expected; it means that adjustment costs are larger when you sell to consumers rather than to businesses. However, this does not carry over to equation (5). The importance of adjustment costs as a cause of price rigidity is apparently independent of whether the firm sells mainly to consumers or businesses.

CYCLICAL = a categorical variable indicating whether the firm is cyclically sensitive or insensitive (self-reported). The strongly negative coefficients in both regressions mean that cyclically sensitive firms both report smaller adjustment costs and see them as a less important source of sticky prices. Perhaps this is because firms with volatile demand curves arrange their affairs this way.

CONTRACTS = a categorical variable indicating the fraction of sales made under written contracts. The negative coefficients in both equations mean that firms that sell more under written contracts worry less about adjustment costs, as is to be expected.

INTERVAL, defined earlier, gets a weak positive coefficient in equation (4), which is puzzling; but it is not significant in equation (5). Perhaps regular periodic price reviews are costly even though they do not rigidify prices.

LOYAL = a dummy variable equal to 1 for firms that lose their less loyal customers (and retain their most loyal ones) when demand falls (see the next theory). The source of the correlation here is far from obvious, but it is quite strong. Firms that accept this premise are much less likely to see adjustment costs as important.

MC was defined earlier: higher values connote more steeply sloped MC curves. Curiously, the coefficients are of opposite signs in the two equations. The negative coefficient in equation (4) and positive coefficient in equation (5) mean that firms with more upward-sloping MC curves report *smaller* adjustment costs for changing prices but nonetheless attribute *more* importance to the theory.

INVENTORY = a dummy variable indicating whether the firm holds inventories of finished goods.[22] Such firms apparently have larger costs of price adjustment and view these costs as a more important source of price rigidity. This finding may reflect conscious decisions in firms' choices of pricing and inventory technologies. A flexible inventory policy makes it easier to vary *sales* instead of *prices* when demand fluctuates—which is just what you would want to do if it was costly to adjust prices but not very costly to adjust sales.

4.5   What Price Setters Think about Countercyclical Markups

There are many theories of countercyclical markups, but some are uniquely unsuited to this type of investigation. For example, we cannot very well ask firms whether oligopolistic collusion is more effective at cyclical peaks or troughs. The version we did try to test assumes that countercyclical markups derive from procyclical elasticity of demand. This is an old idea, dating back at least to Pigou (1927) and recently revived by Bils (1989) and Shapiro (1988).

The specific version tested in the survey posits that firms have different classes of customers who vary systematically in their price and income elasticities of demand. More loyal customers have lower elasticities and less loyal customers have higher ones. Thus, as the firm's demand curve shifts inward during a recession, its customer base becomes less price-elastic.

For purposes of the questionnaire, the idea was translated as follows:

B5(a). It has been suggested that, when business turns down, a company loses its least loyal customers first and retains its most loyal ones. Since the remaining customers are not very sensitive to price, reducing markups will not stimulate sales very much.

Is this idea true in your company?

The sample divided roughly 60/40 on this question, with 114 firms answering "yes" and 81 answering "no."

Notice an ambiguity in the way the question is worded—one which I deliberately let stand. The change in a firm's customer base when its sales decline

---

22. This question is not asked of service firms; instead they are automatically coded as holding zero inventory.

presumably depends on whether the drop in sales is economywide, industrywide, or specific to the firm. In addition, a firm's elasticity of demand should depend on how its competitors react when it changes its price. Rightly or wrongly, I judged these matters too complex—and too wordy—to be embodied in the question, and so left it to each firm to answer under whatever blend of ceteris paribus and mutatis mutandis conditions seemed most relevant. That, of course, leaves significant ambiguity over what respondents were assuming.

We followed this question by asking the 114 firms that accepted the theoretical premise what they thought of it as an explanation for sticky prices:

B5. How important is it in explaining the speed of price adjustment in your company?

The answers, which are displayed in table 4.13, fall somewhat short of a ringing endorsement of the theory. Taken at face value, they imply that the notion that cyclical shifts in customer loyalty account for price stickiness has no empirical relevance at all for 56 percent of American industry and substantial relevance for only 31 percent.

When we disaggregate the responses by industry, manufacturing and retailing stand out as the two sectors of the economy in which this theory has the most validity.

4.5.1   Correlates of Agreement with the Theory

It is of interest to know, first, what kinds of firms believe they can distinguish among customer groups identified by loyalty, for only such firms can possibly find this theory of any importance. One way to summarize these cross-sectional differences is in the following ordered probit regression (all variable names but one have been previously defined):

$$(6)\quad \text{OP(LOYAL)} = .54 \text{ IMPLICIT} - .33 \text{ CYCLICAL} - .26 \text{ ADJ}$$
$$(n = 179)\quad (.22)\qquad\qquad (.12)\qquad\qquad\quad (.13)$$

$$- .90 \text{ CON} - .00002 \text{ SIZE};$$
$$(.39)\qquad (.00001)$$

$$\log L = -101.6, \text{ pseudo-}R^2 = .163, \text{ linear } R^2 = .443.$$

Table 4.13   **B5. How Important is Procyclical Elasticity in Slowing Down Price Adjustments in Your Company? (n = 195)**

Code	Response	Percentage of Firms
1	Totally unimportant*	55.9%
2	Of minor importance	12.8%
3	Moderately important	21.5%
4	Very important	9.7%

Note: Mean response = 1.85. Mean among those accepting the premise: 2.46 (n = 114). Rank = seventh.

*This category includes firms that denied the premise by answering "no" to question B5(a).

The fit of the model is excellent as these things go. It makes sense that firms with implicit contracts draw a clear distinction between "loyal" and other customers, and *perhaps* it makes sense that larger firms do not (the variable SIZE measures annual sales). But I see no obvious intuitive explanations for the other three coefficients.

I turn now to the evaluation of the theory. What kinds of firms find the procyclical elasticity theory an important factor behind sticky prices? The best ordered-probit model explaining the answers to the main theory question was[23]

(7)   OP(B5) = .44 CYCLICAL + 1.15 NONPRICE − .12 MC
        (n = 100) (.14)   (.34)   (.09)

        + .018 FIXED + .50 RATION + 1.37 RETAIL + .47 MFG
        (.006)   (.14)   (.53)   (.32)

    + .27 ACCURACY − .016 GOVT − .56 POINTS − .24 INVENTORY
    (.19)   (.009)   (.29)   (.18)

$\log L = -108.4$, pseudo-R^2 = .221, linear R^2 = .548.

These results seem very erratic and hard to explain.[24] The only regressor common to both equations—CYCLICAL—has opposite signs in each.[25] Firms with rising marginal costs are actually *less* likely to agree with the procyclical elasticity theory, which is unfortunate since the idea is meant to explain constant price in the face of rising MC. But the coefficient is not significant at conventional standards. The new variables appearing in (7) are

NONPRICE = a dummy for competing on nonprice elements instead of price. The highly significant positive coefficient may indicate that these firms elect not to compete on price because of elasticity pessimism.

FIXED = the percentage of costs that are fixed. Since relatively high fixed costs mean relatively low marginal costs, these two cost variables (MC and FIXED) may be picking out firms that base prices more on costs and less on demand. However, the positive coefficient on ACCURACY—a categorical variable indicating how well firms think they know their marginal costs—argues against this interpretation.

RATION = a categorical variable indicating the frequency with which customers are rationed in what they may buy. Firms that do so frequently apparently place less faith in procyclical elasticity.

POINTS = a categorical variable indicating the presence or absence of psychological pricing points—as suggested by Kashyap (1992). For some reason, firms with such pricing points are less likely to attribute importance to procyclical elasticity.

23. This equation was estimated *only* for firms that answered 2 ("yes") to equation B5(a).
24. The small sample size for equation (7) may be playing a role here.
25. However, the industry results are consistent in that CON gets a negative coefficient in (6) and (implicitly) a negative one in (7). Similarly for MFG and RETAIL.

The dummy variables RETAIL and MFG show that retailers are much more likely, and manufacturers slightly more likely, to see their customer base as divided into loyal and disloyal segments. I had no particular priors on these industry dummies.

Finally, firms that hold inventories (INVENTORY) or sell more to the government (GOVT) are less likely to believe in procyclical elasticity.

4.6   What Price Setters Think about Constant Marginal Cost

Go back to thinking of the elasticity of demand as a constant. If marginal cost is also constant, then price should be, too. That simple idea is *almost* a theory of price rigidity over the business cycle, but it leaves one important loose end. The demand and cost functions of micro theory implicitly apply to *relative* prices and *real* marginal costs. The theory therefore really says that *markups* are constant over the business cycle. Nominal prices are sticky only if nominal input costs are.

Although neither price stickiness nor constancy of MC was his primary concern, Robert Hall (1986) revived interest in this very old idea. Hall's goal was to explain procyclical productivity by appealing to market power—markups of price over marginal cost. Constant MC entered the picture to resolve a paradox that Hall pointed out: the high degree of market power that he estimated on U.S. data is hard to reconcile with the comparatively low level of business profits.

Hall's explanation was that fixed costs ("excess capacity") are substantial. Thus he envisions a world in which the typical marginal cost curve is flat up to capacity and then nearly vertical. A competitive firm producing on the flat portion of its MC curve with $P = $ MC is not making any contribution to its fixed costs. Therefore, to cover fixed costs in the long run, it must spend a reasonable amount of time on the vertical portion of its MC curve—with high prices in periods of peak demand. Hence prices should be cyclically sensitive. But a firm with substantial market power need do no such thing. Since it maintains P above MC all the time, it is constantly earning a contribution toward its fixed costs. That is why, in Hall's (1986, 315) words, "a finding of market power points in the direction of constant marginal cost."

Notice the highly qualified phrase "points in the direction of." High fixed costs do not imply that marginal cost must be flat, and Hall makes no such claim. Instead, he uses a kind of "menu cost" argument to suggest that MC curves are flat: if they are, then the cost of price rigidity is small because profits drop only slightly when output deviates from its profit-maximizing level.

To believe in constant marginal cost as a theory of price rigidity, you must accept two premises: first, that marginal costs are constant, and second, that this constancy is an important source of sticky prices. Hence, I again evaluate the theory in two stages.

First, how are firms' marginal cost curves really shaped? This turned out to be a tricky question because the term *marginal cost* is not in the lexicons of most businesspeople; the concept itself may not even be a natural one. For purposes of the survey, we translated "marginal cost" into "variable costs of producing additional units," and posed the following question:

B7(a). Some companies find that their variable costs per unit are roughly constant when production rises. Others incur either higher or lower variable costs of producing additional units when they raise production.

How would you characterize the behavior of your own variable costs of producing additional units as production rises?

This proved a difficult question. It often had to be repeated, rephrased, or explained. Even so, 10 of our 200 respondents were unable to answer it. The other 190 executives answered in their own words, sometimes at great length, and interviewers classified the responses into one of five categories offered on the questionnaire. The simplest way of summarizing the answers is graphically. Figure 4.1 depicts five possible shapes for the MC curve and the fraction of firms selecting each. The spikes in panels b and d indicate cases in which costs jump discretely when output crosses certain critical thresholds—as when a bank opens a new branch office or a railroad adds an additional car.

When juxtaposed against the standard neoclassical assumption that panel e is the rule, the answers are stunning. Only 11 percent of firms report that their MC curves are rising (panel e). By contrast, 40.5 percent claim that their MC curves are falling, presumably *globally* (panels a and b).[26] The good news for the constant-marginal-cost theory is that approximate constancy of MC (panels c and d) is the modal case—encompassing 48.4 percent of GDP. The bad news is that this group accounts for less than half of GDP and that almost as many firms say they have *falling* MC. If anything, it appears that Hall did not go far enough in arguing against the standard neoclassical view that the MC curve is upward sloping.

My own experience as an interviewer leads me to discount these results somewhat because many executives had difficulty understanding the question. Some may have confused marginal cost with average cost (AC), and it is surely not surprising that many firms have falling AC curves. Nonetheless, the discount would have to be pretty severe before we read figure 4.1 as saying that rising MC is the norm. In any case, we certainly could not ask firms that denied having constant MC whether constant MC is an important source of sticky prices. So the main question about the theory was posed only to firms that classified themselves in panels c or d of figure 4.1—a total of ninety-two companies. The others were automatically coded as answering "totally unimportant" to the following question:

26. Ramey (1991) offers econometric evidence for declining MC in seven industries, six of them in manufacturing.

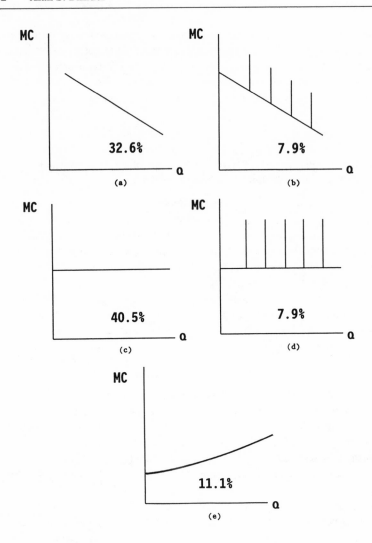

Fig. 4.1   Possible shapes of marginal cost curves

B7. It has been suggested that many firms base prices on costs. Hence firms with constant variable costs per unit have no reason to change prices when production changes.

How important is this idea in explaining the speed of price adjustment in your company? (n = 90)

Table 4.14 summarizes the answers; they give the theory a pretty poor rating. Firms representing almost three-quarters of GDP reject the theory outright, either because their MC curves are not flat (52 percent) or because they do not see constant MC as an important cause of price rigidity (21 percent). Only about 20 percent of respondents accept the theory in the sense that they give it a rating of 3 or higher. The average score of 1.57 on the four-point scale is low in an absolute sense and ranks the theory ninth of the twelve evaluated in the survey. Even within the population of firms that report flat MC curves, the theory's average rating is only 2.19. Simply put, it seems most unlikely that constant marginal cost is an important factor behind macroeconomic price rigidity.

4.6.1 Correlates of the Theory

Few variables carry any predictive power for the shape of the firm's marginal cost curve, that is, for the appropriate panel in figure 4.1. Even the ordered probit models that best predict the answers have exceedingly modest fits:

(8) $\text{OP(MC)} = .40 \text{ POINTS} - .24 \text{ ADJ} - .23 \text{ MFG}$
         $(n = 190)\ (.17) \qquad\qquad (.10) \qquad (.18)$

         $\log L = -248.5,\ \text{pseudo-}R^2 = .049,\ \text{linear } R^2 = .17,$

(9) $\text{OP(MC)} = .40 \text{ POINTS} - .25 \text{ ADJ} - .39 \text{ MFG}$
         $(n = 154)\ (.19) \qquad\qquad (.11) \qquad (.21)$

         $\qquad\qquad - .0034 \text{ ELAST} - .41 \text{ REG};$
         $\qquad\qquad\ (.0024) \qquad\quad (.23)$

         $\log L = -195.0,\ \text{pseudo-}R^2 = .089,\ \text{linear } R^2 = .274.$

The sample size is much smaller in the second regression because the variable ELAST (the elasticity of demand) is missing in almost 20 percent of the observations. It gets a not-very-significant negative coefficient, indicating that steeper MC functions are associated with less elastic demand curves.

The two regressions show that manufacturers (MFG) are less likely than other firms to have increasing marginal costs, as are firms with substantial costs

Table 4.14   **B7. How Important Is Constant Marginal Cost in Explaining the Speed of Price Adjustment in Your Company? (n = 190)**

Code	Response	Percentage of Firms
1	Totally unimportant*	73.1%
2	Of minor importance	7.2%
3	Moderately important	9.0%
4	Very important	10.6%

Note: Mean response = 1.57. Mean among those with constant marginal cost: 2.19 (n = 90). Rank = ninth.

*This category includes firms that said marginal cost was not constant.

of adjusting prices (ADJ). The variable REG indicates that (partially) regulated firms are more likely to have *falling* MC curves, as is to be expected.

The other significant variable is POINTS. For some reason, firms that have pricing points are also more likely to report rising MC.

Many more variables correlate with a firm's evaluation of the importance of constant MC as an explanation of sticky prices, given that they have constant MC. But here statistical inference starts to get thin because the sample is so small. (Only ninety-two firms report constant MC curves.) The following equation fits (overfits?) the data extremely well:

$$\text{(10)} \qquad \text{OP(B7)} = -3.36 \text{ MFG} + 5.78 \text{ UNION}$$
$$(n = 77) \quad (0.55) \qquad (1.39)$$

$$- .22 \text{ CONTRACTS} - .87 \text{ INTERVAL}$$
$$(.13) \qquad\qquad (.23)$$

$$+ .70 \text{ IMPLICIT} - 1.06 \text{ JUDGE} - 1.21 \text{ POINTS} + 1.25 \text{ LOYAL}$$
$$(.40) \qquad\qquad (0.44) \qquad\qquad (.37) \qquad\qquad (0.37)$$

$$+ 1.61 \text{ INVENTORY} + .77 \text{ ADJ} + .033 \text{ GOVT}$$
$$(0.29) \qquad\qquad (.22) \qquad (.012)$$

$$\log L = -65.9, \text{ pseudo-}R^2 = .407, \text{ linear } R^2 = .737.$$

All of these variables have appeared previously, except for JUDGE—a dummy variable for whether the firm's customers judge quality by price (see the next theory).

Given the tenuous statistical foothold of these estimates, it is probably inadvisable to make much of them. Taken at face value, they say that firms are *more* likely to see constant marginal cost as an important source of sticky prices if they have adjustment costs for changing prices (ADJ), enter into implicit contracts with their customers (IMPLICIT), and have the kind of customer loyalty assumed in the previous theory (LOYAL). These all make intuitive sense, although ADJ gets the opposite sign in equations (8) and (9). But firms also rate the constant-MC theory higher if they are in more unionized industries (UNION), sell more to government (GOVT), and hold inventories of finished goods (INVENTORY); there is no clear explanation for these correlations.

On the negative side, firms attribute *less* importance to the constant-MC theory if they are in manufacturing (which reinforces equations [8] and [9]), if they sell more under written contracts (CONTRACTS), and if they have periodic price reviews (INTERVAL). These findings seem intuitive. But it is far from clear why constant MC should be less important when customers judge quality by price (JUDGE) or have pricing points (POINTS).

4.7   What Price Setters Think about Judging Quality by Price

Few topics in economic theory were hotter in the 1980s than imperfect information, especially *asymmetrically* imperfect information. Literally hundreds of papers were written exploring the implications of adverse selection and moral hazard in such markets. It is only a slight exaggeration to say that the rule book of economic theory was substantially rewritten. Joseph Stiglitz (1987), for example, referred to the repeal of the law of supply and demand.

Adverse selection, in particular, has been offered by Stiglitz and several co-authors as an explanation of why wages, prices, and interest rates do not fall promptly to clear markets. The application to price rigidity is straightforward: firms may hesitate to cut prices in slack markets out of fear that their customers will infer (incorrectly) that product quality has been reduced. Allen (1988) developed an explicit formal model of a related idea in which unobservable quality differences make prices sticky as long as demand shocks are sufficiently serially correlated. I think it fair to say that the notion that judging quality by price might inhibit price reductions has come into common currency.

Unfortunately, no one knows whether this theory has any empirical validity. Do firms really believe that their customers judge quality by price? Is that why prices do not fall in slumps? In a sense, the adverse selection theory is the quintessential example of why I chose the survey method to study price stickiness. The theory is not just *untested,* it is virtually *untestable* by conventional methods. After all, the basic premise is that certain critical dimensions of quality are *unobservable*—even by the people who buy the product. How, then, can any objective data tell the econometrician whether or not the theory is true?

If their own words are to be believed, actual price setters do not believe that judging quality by price inhibits price reductions. This theory was assessed by asking the following question:

B3(a). Another idea is that firms hesitate to reduce their prices because they fear that customers will interpret a price cut as a signal that the quality of the product has been reduced.
(a) Is this idea true in your company?

If (a) was answered in the affirmative, we followed with:

B3. How important is it in discouraging or delaying price decreases in your company?

As table 4.15 shows, this theory rates flat last among the twelve theories tested, with a mean score of just 1.33 on the one-to-four scale. This is an amazingly negative evaluation. The main factor behind this dismal showing is that the vast majority of firms—78.5 percent to be precise—simply do not believe that their customers would "interpret a price cut as a signal that the *quality* of the product has been reduced." Among those that do, the theory attains a respectable average score of 2.56. But there are simply too few such firms to have much of an impact in the aggregate.

These negative results hold more or less across the board. The theory ranks last in manufacturing, utilities, and construction; second to last (with a mean score of only 1.20!) in trade; and third from last in the service sector. The

Table 4.15   **B3. How Important Is Judging Quality by Price in Discouraging or Delaying Price Decreases in Your Company? (n = 200 responses)**

Code	Response	Percentage of Firms
1	Totally unimportant*	81.5%
2	Of minor importance	8.0%
3	Moderately important	6.3%
4	Very important	4.3%

Note: Mean response = 1.33. Mean if quality is judged by price: 2.56 (n = 42). Rank = twelfth.
*This category includes firms that answer "no" to question B3(a).

theory's few boosters seem to be concentrated in the service sector. Of the twenty companies giving the theory a score of 3 or better, eleven sell services.

4.7.1 Correlates of Judging Quality by Price

As these things go, our ability to model econometrically which firms find judging quality by price an important source of price rigidity is reasonable. The best ordered-probit model was (with asymptotic standard errors in parentheses):

(11)   OP(JUDGE) = $-.51$ TRADE -1.14 CON $- .0055$ BUSINESS
(n = 190)   (.36)   (0.61)   (.0041)

$+ .32$ INFL $+ .85$ POINTS $-.21$ RATION $+ .39$ REG;
(.15)   (.27)   (.14)   (.26)

$\text{Log}L = -74.9$; pseudo-R^2 = .200, linear R^2 = .513

The one new variable in this regression is BUSINESS—the fraction of output sold to other businesses. Its negative coefficient indicates that judging quality by price is less prevalent in business-to-business transactions, as is to be expected. The other right-hand variables have appeared before.

- Surprisingly, especially given the negative coefficient on BUSINESS, companies in wholesale and retail trade are *less* likely to believe that their customers judge quality by price.
- There is apparently less judging of quality by price in construction (CON), which may or may not be surprising.
- Firms that believe that their customers have psychological pricing points (POINTS) also tend to believe that their customers judge quality by price. Perhaps psychological manipulability is a generic trait.
- Firms which ration their customers more frequently (RATION) are less likely to report that their customers judge quality by price, perhaps because their products tend to be standardized.
- Judging quality by price is more common among firms that are subject to some sort of regulatory restrictions on pricing.

- INFL is a puzzling variable. The positive coefficient means that "smart" firms are more likely to report that their customers judge quality by price. Have they been reading Joe Stiglitz?

4.8 Summary

Direct survey evidence supports the common macroeconometric finding that changes in P lag behind changes in M. Indeed, almost 80 percent of GDP is repriced quarterly or less frequently. And the typical lag of a price change behind a shock to either demand or cost is about three months. That much price stickiness appears to be enough to give monetary policy a handle on the real economy.

Or is it? The answer depends on the *sources* of all this stickiness. Five theories of sticky prices were popular in the academy during the 1980s, but only one of them is also popular with actual decision makers: coordination failure.

Apparently, many firms hesitate to change their prices for fear that competitors will not follow suit. In fact, this is the most popular theory among the twelve tested in the survey. However, our respondents tell us that the resulting price rigidity is asymmetric in the direction *opposite* from that usually assumed. Firms are more likely to delay price *increases* out of fear that competitors might not match them than they are to delay price *decreases*. Thus, if coordination failure were the *only* source of sticky prices (which it is not), the real effects of monetary expansions would be greater than those of monetary contractions. As Ball and Romer (1991) note, the most obvious policy implication of the model is that more coordinated wage and price setting—somehow achieved—could improve welfare. But if this proves difficult or impossible, the door is opened to activist monetary policy to cure recessions.

The worst of the five theories, according to our respondents, is the notion that firms hesitate to cut prices in slumps because they fear that customers will misconstrue price cuts as signals of reductions in quality. Hardly any of the two hundred firms interviewed believe their customers behave this way; those that do are mostly in services. Although this idea has attracted an enormous following in academia, it seems to have virtually no following in the real world.[27]

The simple theory that flat marginal cost curves underlie price rigidity fares only slightly better. About half of the GDP is apparently produced under conditions of constant MC. But even this group does not see constant MC as a terribly important source of sticky prices. This means that, for many such firms, the markup between price and marginal cost is cyclically variable, not constant. One fascinating finding from the survey is that about 40 percent of GDP is produced under *falling* marginal costs, though it is certainly possible that

---

27. The basic idea of adverse selection may well be important in other contexts. But Blinder and Choi (1990) found similarly negative evidence regarding wage setting.

many respondents confused average with marginal cost in answering this question.

Most modern theories of cyclically sensitive markups make markups *countercyclical,* not *procyclical.* One such theory was tested in the survey and found wanting: the idea that the price elasticity of demand falls in slumps and rises in booms. Our respondents favored the premise by a margin of 58.5 percent to 41.5 percent, but did not view it as a fundamental source of price stickiness.[28]

Last, but not least, the survey taught us a great deal about the nature and validity of the theory that price rigidity stems from adjustment costs.

First, there are strong indications that adjustment costs for changing prices are more often fixed (menu costs) than convex. But since about 20 percent of the economy may have convex adjustment costs, empirical findings that some firms make *very small* price changes should not be construed as rejection of the menu-cost theory.

Second, while the menu-cost idea is symmetric in theory, it appears to be strongly asymmetric in practice. Firms tell us that adjustment costs more often deter price increases than price decreases. This makes it most unlikely that adjustment costs have much to do with printing new price lists, etc.

Third, adjustment costs are an important source of price rigidity within the approximately 40 to 45 percent of the economy that reports nontrivial adjustment costs.

Fourth, the common objection that costs of changing *quantities* must dwarf any costs of changing *prices* has much less validity than is commonly supposed. In fact, many of our decision makers seem to be saying that the former are smaller than the latter.

I cannot resist closing with a conclusion about methodology rather than substance. I think this survey demonstrates that we can learn things of interest by asking actual decision makers to tell us about their behavior. If the survey approach is right, people will cooperate. If the questions are well-posed, people will give thoughtful and coherent answers. Some of the information we can learn through attitudinal surveys can apparently be obtained in no other way.

I would be the last to argue that other more conventional modes of economic inquiry should be abandoned. But the law of diminishing returns suggests that learning by asking, the most underutilized of all economic research tools, may now offer high returns. The total cost of this research project was the equivalent of about two standard National Science Foundation grants to senior researchers. Who doubts that the survey described here added more to our knowledge than two such typical grants?

---

28. I should not overstate the case. Among the 58.5 percent that accept the premise, the theory received modestly good grades. See table 4.13.

References

Allen, Franklin. 1988. A theory of price rigidities when quality is unobservable. *Review of Economic Studies* 55: 139–51.

Azariadis, Costas. 1975. Implicit contracts and underemployment equilibria. *Journal of Political Economy* 83 (December): 1183–1202.

Baily, Martin N. 1974. Wages and employment under uncertain demand. *Review of Economic Studies* 41 (January): 37–50.

Ball, Laurence, and David Romer. 1991. Sticky prices as coordination failure. *American Economic Review* 81 (June): 539–52.

Barro, Robert. 1977. Long-term contracting, sticky prices, and monetary policy. *Journal of Monetary Economics* 3 (July): 305–16.

Bils, Mark. 1989. Cyclical pricing of durable goods. NBER Working Paper no. 3050. Cambridge, Mass.: National Bureau of Economic Research, July.

Blanchard, Olivier, J. 1983. Price asynchronization and price level inertia. In *Inflation, debt and indexation,* eds. R. Dornbusch and M. Simonsen, 3–24. Cambridge: MIT Press.

Blinder, Alan S. 1982. Inventories and sticky prices: More on the microfoundations of macroeconomics. *American Economic Review* 72 (June): 334–48.

Blinder, Alan S., and Don Choi. 1990. A shred of evidence on theories of wage stickiness. *Quarterly Journal of Economics* 105 (November): 1003–15.

Brown, James N., and Orley Ashenfelter. 1986. Testing the efficiency of employment contracts. *Journal of Political Economy,* 94 supp.: S40–87.

Carlton, Dennis W. 1986. The rigidity of prices. *American Economic Review* 76 (September): 637–58.

———. 1990. The theory and the facts of how markets clear: Is industrial organization valuable for understanding macroeconomics? *Handbook of industrial organization,* eds. R. Schmalensee and R. Willig. Amsterdam: North-Holland.

Cooper, Russell, and Andrew John. 1988. Coordinating coordination failures in Keynesian models. *Quarterly Journal of Economics* 103 (August): 441–463.

Gordon, D. F. 1974. A neoclassical theory of Keynesian unemployment. *Economic Inquiry* 12: 431–59.

Gordon, Robert J. 1981. Output fluctuations and gradual price adjustment. *Journal of Economic Literature* 19 (June): 493–530.

———. 1990. What is new-Keynesian economics? *Journal of Economic Literature* 28 (September): 1115–71.

Greene, W. H. 1990. *Econometric analysis.* New York: Macmillan.

Hall, Robert E. 1980. Employment fluctuations and wage rigidity. *Brookings Papers on Economic Activity* 1: 91–123.

———. 1986. Market structure and macroeconomic fluctuations. *Brookings Papers on Economic Activity* 2:285–322.

Kashyap, Anil K. 1992. Sticky prices: New evidence from retail catalogs. University of Chicago, October. Mimeo.

Keynes, John Maynard. 1936. *The general theory of employment, interest, and money* New York: Harcourt, Brace & World.

Mankiw, N. Gregory. 1985. Small menu costs and large business cycles: A macroeconomic model of monopoly. *Quarterly Journal of Economics* 100(May): 529–38.

Okun, Arthur. 1981. *Prices and quantities: A macroeconomic analysis.* Washington, D.C.: Brookings Institution.

Pigou, Arthur C. 1927. *Industrial fluctuations.* London: Macmillan.

Ramey, Valerie A. 1991. Nonconvex costs and the behavior of inventories. *Journal of Political Economy* 99 (April): 306–34.

Rotemberg, Julio J. 1982. Sticky prices in the United States. *Journal of Political Economy* 90, no. 6 (December): 1187–1211.

Shapiro, Matthew D. 1988. The cyclical behavior of price-cost margins: Demand elasticity and marginal cost. Yale University, January. Mimeo.

Stiglitz, Joseph E. 1987. The causes and consequences of the dependence of quality on price. *Journal of Economic Literature* 25 (March): 1–48.

Comment   Olivier Jean Blanchard

On Methodology

In his conclusion, Alan Blinder challenges us: "Who doubts that the survey described here added more to our knowledge than two such typical [National Science Foundation] grants?" As Blinder was embarking on his study, I was sure I would not be among the doubters. I believed that we would get fairly sharp answers as to what firms viewed as important or unimportant, and that this would help focus further theorizing. I must admit to being disappointed by the results.

Look at table 4.4, and take the ratio of column 6, the acceptance rate, to column 7, the proportion of firms for which the premise of the theory is at all applicable. For nine out of twelve theories, the ratio is above 46 percent. For seven out of twelve, the ratio is between 46 percent and 60 percent. The image this evokes and that recurs throughout my reading of the results is, that confronted with the twelve statements, the firms often had the reaction: "Now that you say it, yes, maybe that *is* kind of what we do."

There is, I suspect, a lesson here about the limits of the approach that Blinder has taken in the survey. Firms do think about pricing in their own way. Presented with short summaries of alternative academic theories, they find that most capture something, but that none is quite right. Role reversal may be useful here. Suppose that a businessman decided to find out how economists thought about inflation. Having drawn a list of theories—inflation is due to money growth; inflation is due to changes in relative prices; inflation is due to budget deficits, inflation is due to union militancy, inflation come from depreciation, and so on—he came to Blinder and asked him to rank the theories from 1 to 4. Blinder would boil at the idea of being so constrained in his answers, but would see most statements as having a grain of truth, and would give a lot of 2s and 3s. Being an academic, he would then qualify his answers at length. But businessmen are not academics. They may not have a clear, explicit view of how they set prices, and may not want to spend the time needed to qualify their answers. Thus, they give the 2s and the 3s, do not bother qualifying very much, but it does not quite capture what they do.

Olivier Jean Blanchard is professor of economics at the Massachusetts Institute of Technology and a research associate of the National Bureau of Economic Research.

It is interesting to contrast the approach taken by Blinder to that recently taken by Truman Bewley and Bill Brainard in asking firms about wage setting (Bewley and Brainard 1993). Bewley and Brainard also start from the idea that we can learn a lot from listening to firms. But in sharp contrast to Blinder, Bewley and Brainard act like psychoanalysts, remaining mostly silent as personnel officers explain what they do and why they do it. The picture which comes out is both rich and confusing. Whether and how the arguments used by firms relate to our theories of wage setting is often unclear. But what is clear is that the interviewees would not have felt at ease evaluating the relevance of our various theories of fairness, efficiency wages, and so on, had they been put to them as short statements.

On Price Stickiness

Macroeconomists have long believed in two stylized facts about price-setting by firms. The first is that, given factor costs, prices do not respond to demand shifts very much. The second is that most prices are not set continuously, leading to lags in the response of prices to their underlying determinants. In the 1980s, these two stylized facts have come to be known as "real rigidities" for the first, and "nominal rigidities" for the second. I am not sure the terminology is felicitous. But it is convenient, and I shall use it.

Both facts have been seen as contributing to the slow adjustment of the price level to movements in aggregate demand. But they have also been seen as requiring quite separate explanations. To explain the first, the weak effect of demand shifts on prices given factor prices, most of us have looked for explanations based on imperfect competition. The intellectual challenge here, and not a small one at that, has been perceived to be the development of a theory of imperfect competition which delivered such behavior. In contrast, explaining the second has appeared to most of us to be rather trivial: continuous price setting is obviously very costly. Rather, the challenge has been perceived to show how small lags at the microlevel may, through the interactions between the firms' decisions, lead to large price-level inertia and large macroeconomic costs.

Obviously the dichotomy I have drawn between "real" and "nominal" rigidities is too sharp. Rather trivially, one can only have discrete price setting if there are price setters; there can be price setters only if they have at least transient monopoly power, thus if there is imperfect competition. Also, if firms decide not to change prices in response to demand shifts, then everything else being equal, there is one less reason to change prices, and thus prices will be changed less often. Or, to take yet another interaction, if fluctuations in demand are mean-reverting, then less frequent changes in prices will also mean a smaller average response of prices to demand. But while they interact, they are about two different phenomena.

This distinction is not made explicitly in the survey. Some of the theories are clearly about why prices may not respond to demand given factor prices, and some are about why there may be lags in the response of nominal prices to their determinants. Roughly, theories B1, B4, B8, and B9 are primarily about nominal rigidities, the others primarily about real rigidities. Is it because the distinction is one which economists may see but firms would have had a hard time grasping? I do not think so. Real rigidities correspond to questions such as When you sit down to change prices, how do you take into account changes in demand and changes in factor prices? Do you react differently to changes in demand if they are industrywide or specific to your firm? Nominal rigidities correspond instead to questions such as How often do you change prices? Does this happen on regular dates, or is it triggered by events, such as large changes in factor prices? Do you change most prices at once? Do you try to get the price right now, or later when it is still fixed and inflation has taken place?

I think the survey pays a large cost as a result of not making this distinction. At the presentation stage, organizing theories along those two lines would have helped at least this reader to map the results to macro implications. But the cost is higher. Not making the distinction leads Blinder to ask what I think are incorrectly phrased questions, and thus get what are quite possibly misleading answers. A number of theories which are designed to explain why prices may respond little to demand shifts are phrased in terms of explaining a slow response rather than a lack of response. I shall take one example. Question B7 reads:

> It has been suggested that many firms base prices on costs. Hence firms with constant variable costs per unit have no reason to change prices when production changes.
>   How important is this idea in explaining *the speed of price adjustment* in your company? (emphasis added)

Take a firm which uses a fixed markup rule and has constant variable costs. It may interpret the question as "How important is this idea in explaining why you do not change prices in response to demand?" and answer "Very important." But it may instead interpret the question literally and conclude that flat marginal cost has nothing to do with the speed of adjustment, and thus answer "Totally unimportant."

This point is more than nitpicking. Very surprisingly—at least given my priors—of those firms which declared to have roughly constant variable cost per unit, 73 percent turn out to answer "Totally unimportant" to the question. What do they have in mind? That markups are not constant, or that markups are constant but this has nothing to do with slow adjustment? This takes me to my third set of points.

On the Picture of Price-Setting Which Emerges

Together, the three top-ranked theories point to imperfectly competitive markets, in which (*a*) firms worry about the reaction of other firms to price changes ("coordination failures," ranked first); (*b*) firms rely on simple cost-plus pricing rules, perhaps as coordination devices ("cost-based pricing with lags," ranked second); and, (c) partly in contradiction to the rationale for using simple price rules as coordination devices, goods have many attributes other than price that are adjusted in response to demand ("delivery lags," ranked third). This is a very interesting picture. But in each case one would like to know more.

Blinder emphasizes that he is looking for a particular kind of "coordination failure," one which can emerge even in markets with large numbers of firms. As he himself acknowledges, however, what firms have in mind when they answer "Very important" to that question is in fact unclear. He indicates that a number of firms appear to be thinking of a leader-follower relations. Thus I see those answers as confirming the notion that most firms worry very much about other firms' reactions, but as telling us little beyond that. The black box of short-run movements in prices in response to demand shifts in imperfectly competitive markets remains closed.

What firms mean by cost-based pricing also remains unclear. Do firms have more or less flat marginal cost? The answer to that question is clear. Only 11 percent of the firms report upward sloping marginal cost; the others report either flat or decreasing marginal cost. Do firms use more or less constant markups? Here there are conflicting answers. Of those reporting constant marginal cost, 73 percent dismiss that as "totally unimportant" in explaining the speed of price adjustment. I discussed earlier how we might interpret the answer. One interpretation is that firms do have highly variable markups. But this interpretation is contradicted by the answers to question B6, which describes cost-plus pricing, and finds substantial support among firms, being ranked second overall.

Nominal rigidities do not score high. Costs of adjustment of prices come in in sixth place. But, as I suggested earlier, this is probably as it should be, even if nominal rigidities are important. The theme of the research on nominal rigidities is that they appear to be relatively unimportant to individual price setters, yet they may cumulate to have large macro effects. This may be a case where asking firms is indeed not the way to go. And for the same reasons, namely since they see these aspects of price-setting as minor, asking them to compare the costs of adjusting quantities to those of adjusting prices may not elicit very useful answers.

Where the survey could have been more useful here would have been in asking such questions about whether firms tended to adjust prices at regular intervals, or in response to specific changes in the environment, whether firms adjusted the price to a level which was right at the time of price setting, or took into account future inflation and set the price higher as a result. We have learned that the answers to the first set of questions are of much importance in determining how individual price rigidities get amplified or eliminated in the aggregate. I have come to the conclusion that the answers to the second have important macro implications. If there is positive inflation, and if firms correctly anticipate that their real price will decline throughout the period during which it is set in nominal terms, they will choose a price which is too high today, but right on average. Average profit margins will be roughly invariant to inflation. If instead firms set prices so that they are right at the time of price-setting, then there will be a systematic inverse relation between profit margins and inflation. Recent work I have carried out on the evolution of profits in France suggests to me that some of the large increase in profit margins in France in the 1980s has come from this effect combined with the decrease in inflation (Blanchard and Muet 1993). If I am right, this is an important implication of nominal price-setting. This is clearly a case where we would learn much from asking firms.

References

Bewley, T., and W. Brainard. 1993. A depressed labor market, as explained by participants. Yale University, February. Mimeo.

Blanchard, O., and P.-A. Muet. 1993. Competitiveness through disinflation: An assessment of the French macro-strategy. *Economic Policy* 16 (April): 12–56.

5 What Determines the Sacrifice Ratio?

Laurence Ball

Disinflations are a major cause of recessions in modern economies—perhaps the dominant cause. In the United States, for example, recessions occurred in the early 1970s, mid-1970s, and early 1980s. Each of these downturns coincided with falling inflation caused by tight monetary policy (Romer and Romer 1989).

Is there an iron law that disinflation produces large output losses? Or can favorable circumstances and wise policies reduce or even eliminate these costs? Economists have suggested a wide range of answers to these questions. One traditional view is that disinflation is less expensive if it occurs slowly, so that wages and prices have time to adjust to tighter policy. An opposing view (Sargent 1983) is that *quick* disinflation can be inexpensive, because expectations adjust sharply. Some economists argue that disinflation is less costly if tight monetary policy is accompanied by incomes policies or other efforts to coordinate wage and price adjustment. Finally, a number of authors suggest features of the economic environment that affect the output-inflation trade-off, such as the initial level of inflation (Ball, Mankiw, and Romer 1988), the openness of the economy (Romer 1991), and the nature of labor contracts (Gordon 1982).

Despite this debate, there has been little systematic empirical work on these issues. The speed of disinflation, the nature of incomes policies, and so on

Laurence Ball is professor of economics at Johns Hopkins University and a research associate of the National Bureau of Economic Research.

The author is grateful for research assistance from Rami Amir and Bradley Ruffle, and for suggestions from Benjamin Friedman, David Gruen, N. Gregory Mankiw, David Romer, John Taylor, Stephen Zeldes, and conference participants. He is also grateful to Carlos Seles and Luis Videgaray for pointing out errors in an earlier version of the paper. Financial support was provided by the National Bureau of Economic Research, the National Science Foundation, and the Sloan Foundation.

differ considerably across countries and disinflation episodes, but we do not know whether these differences produce important differences in output behavior. Many studies examine individual disinflation experiences, but few compare sizable numbers of episodes. Those that do consider multiple episodes focus on establishing that the output losses are generally large (e.g., Gordon 1982; Romer and Romer 1989). This paper measures the variation in the costs of disinflation across a sample of episodes, and asks whether this variation can be explained.[1]

I examine disinflations from 1960 to the present in moderate-inflation countries of the Organization for Economic Cooperation and Development (OECD). The sample contains all episodes in which trend inflation (defined as a moving average of actual inflation) falls substantially (usually more than two percentage points). Using quarterly data, I identify twenty-eight episodes in nine countries; with annual data, I identify sixty-five episodes in nineteen countries. I then develop a simple method for estimating the "sacrifice ratio" for each episode: the ratio of the total output loss to the change in trend inflation. This method is based on a new approach to measuring full-employment output during disinflation. Finally, I examine the relation between the sacrifice ratio and the variables that influence it in various theories.

There are two main results. First, the sacrifice ratio is decreasing in the speed of disinflation (the ratio of the change in trend inflation to the length of the episode). That is, as suggested by Sargent, gradualism makes disinflation more expensive. Second, the ratio is lower in countries with more flexible labor contracts. The most important feature of contracts is their duration.

I also examine the effects of initial inflation, incomes policies, and the openness of the economy. For these variables, the results range from negative to inconclusive.

5.1   Constructing Sacrifice Ratios

This section develops a method for identifying disinflation episodes and calculating the associated sacrifice ratios. This approach might prove useful for future studies of disinflation, as well as for the empirical work below.

5.1.1   Motivation

Many authors have estimated sacrifice ratios, but their techniques are not appropriate for the current study. The most common approach is to derive the ratio from an estimated Phillips curve—from the relation between output and inflation in a long time-series (Okun 1978; Gordon and King 1982). A limitation of this approach is that it constrains the output-inflation trade-off to be the same during disinflations as during increases in trend inflation or temporary fluctuations in demand. This restriction is false if the sacrifice ratio

---

1. A recent paper by Schelde-Andersen (1992) also attempts to explain variation in the costs of disinflation. As discussed in the conclusion, the findings are broadly similar to mine.

is influenced by factors specific to disinflations, such as incomes policies or credibility-induced shifts in expectations. Most important, the Phillips-curve approach constrains the sacrifice ratio to be the same for all disinflations within a time series. This paper estimates separate ratios for each episode to see whether the ratio varies systematically, both within the experience of a country and across countries.

A number of authors compute sacrifice ratios for particular episodes based on ad hoc estimates of the change in inflation and output losses. Mankiw (1991), for example, considers the Volcker disinflation. He notes that inflation, as measured by the gross domestic product (GDP) deflator, fell by 6.7 percent between 1981 and 1985. He assumes that the natural rate of unemployment is 6 percent, which implies that unemployment exceeded the natural rate by a total of 9.5 points from 1982 through 1985. Multiplying by an Okun's Law coefficient of two, Mankiw obtains a total output loss of 19 points. The sacrifice ratio for the Volcker episode is 19/6.7 = 2.8.

My estimates of sacrifice ratios are in the spirit of previous episode-specific estimates, but are more systematic. Previous estimates rely on judgment about the dating of episodes and the natural levels of unemployment or output. Applying such judgment on a case-by-case basis is cumbersome and raises the possibility that different episodes are treated inconsistently. I seek an algorithm for calculating sacrifice ratios that generally comes close to conventional estimates but can be applied mechanically to many episodes.

5.1.2   Selecting Episodes

The first step in my procedure is to identify disinflations—episodes in which trend inflation falls substantially. Trend inflation is defined as a centered, nine-quarter moving average of actual inflation: trend inflation in quarter t is the average of inflation from $t - 4$ through $t + 4$. This definition captures the intuition that trend inflation is a smoothed version of actual inflation. I doubt that other reasonable definitions would produce substantially different results.

To identify disinflations in a given country, I first identify "peaks" and "troughs" in trend inflation. A peak is a quarter in which trend inflation is higher than in the previous four quarters and the following four quarters; a trough is defined by an analogous comparison to four quarters on each side. A disinflation episode is any period that starts at an inflation peak and ends at a trough with an annual rate at least two points lower than the peak. These definitions assure that an episode is not ended by a brief increase in inflation in the midst of a longer-term decrease. Figure 5.1 illustrates the procedure by identifying disinflations in the United States, Germany, the United Kingdom, and Japan.

This procedure is meant to separate significant policy-induced shifts in inflation from smaller fluctuations arising from shocks. It appears quite successful. I have checked the historical record for each of the twenty-eight disinflations in my quarterly data set (mainly by reading the OECD *Economic Outlook* and OECD studies of individual countries). In every case, there is a significant

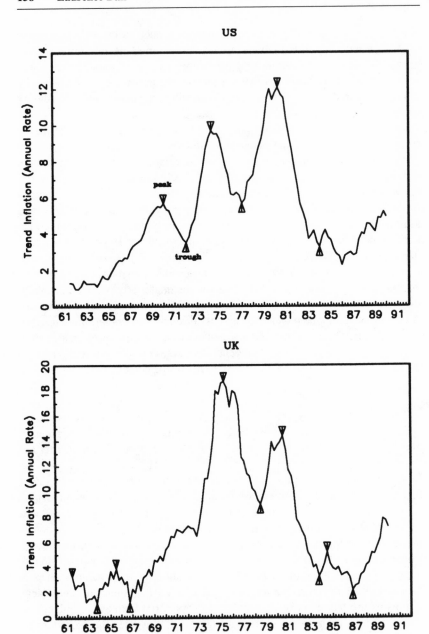

Fig. 5.1   Trend inflation and disinflation episodes

GERMANY

JAPAN

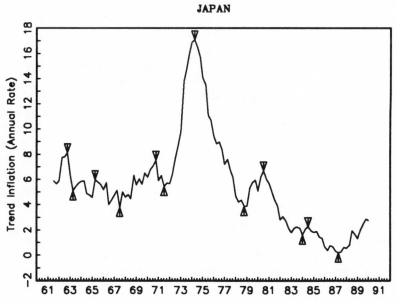

tightening of monetary policy near the start of disinflation. In most cases, the motivation for tight policy is either to reduce inflation or to support the domestic currency. Declines in inflation arising primarily from favorable supply shocks, such as the 1986 decline in oil prices, are too small or too transitory to meet my criteria for disinflation. Intentional demand contractions are essentially the only source of two-point declines in trend inflation.

Indeed, a significant tightening of monetary policy is not only necessary for disinflation but also, it appears, close to sufficient. For the United States and Japan, I have compared my disinflations to the lists of monetary contractions developed by Romer and Romer (1989) and Fernandez (1992). In the United States, policy was tightened in 1968, 1974, 1978, and 1979; if the last two are treated as one episode, there is a close correspondence to the disinflations starting in 1969, 1974, and 1980. Similarly, there is a close correspondence between the six Japanese disinflations and Fernandez's dates.

5.1.3   The Sacrifice Ratio

The denominator of the sacrifice ratio is the change in trend inflation over an episode—the difference between inflation at the peak and at the trough. The numerator is the sum of output losses—the deviations between actual output and its "full employment" or trend level. The most delicate issue is the measurement of trend output, because small differences in fitted trends can make large differences for deviations.

Standard approaches to measuring trend output do not yield appealing results in this application. This point is illustrated by figure 5.2, which shows trend output in the United States and Germany calculated using a log-linear trend split in 1973 and using the Hodrick-Prescott filter. Since these methods minimize deviations from trend, they appear to understate or even eliminate recessions. In the United States, for example, output does not fall below trend during the 1980 recession. In Germany, total deviations from trend during the 1980–86 disinflation are close to zero, whereas traditional accounts of this period include a deep recession without an offsetting boom.[2]

My goal is a definition of trend output that is consistent with conventional views about the costs of various disinflations. After experimentation, I arrive at a definition based on three assumptions. First, output is at its trend or natural level at the start of a disinflation episode—at the inflation peak. This assumption is reasonable because the change in inflation is zero at a peak. The natural level of output is often defined as the level consistent with stable inflation.

Second, I assume that output is again at its trend level four quarters after the end of an episode, that is, four quarters after an inflation trough. The logic behind the first assumption suggests that output returns to trend at the trough,

---

2. Indeed, the HP filter almost always keeps average output over five years or so close to trend. In the United States, average output is close to trend over 1973–78 and 1978–84, which again conflicts with the usual view that these were recessionary periods.

where inflation is again stable. In practice, however, the effects of disinflation are persistent: output appears to return to trend with a lag. Four quarters is a conservative estimate of this lag in a typical disinflation. The return to trend is indicated by above-average growth rates in years after troughs. In the United States, for example, average growth in the four quarters after an inflation trough is 5.7 percent.[3]

My final assumption is that trend output grows log-linearly between the two points when actual and trend output are equal. In graphic terms, trend output is determined by connecting the two points on the log output series. The numerator of the sacrifice ratio is the sum of deviations between this fitted line and log output.

Figure 5.3 plots log output and the fitted trends for the United States, the United Kingdom, Germany, and Japan. The trends are usually close to the lines one would draw by hand if doing ad hoc calculations of the sacrifice ratio.

I interpret the sacrifice ratio as the cost of reducing inflation one point through an aggregate demand contraction. This interpretation relies on two assumptions. First, shifts in demand are the only source of changes in inflation: there are no supply shocks. As discussed above, demand contractions do appear to be the main cause of the disinflations in my sample. Nonetheless, it is likely that supply as well as demand shifts occur during some episodes, and that supply shocks affect the sizes of the output losses and changes in inflation. Thus the sacrifice ratio for a given disinflation is a noisy measure of the effects of the demand contraction. This need not create a problem for my analysis, however. When I regress the sacrifice ratio on explanatory variables, the noise in the ratio can be interpreted as part of the error term.

A second assumption behind my sacrifice ratios is that trend output is unaffected by disinflation: there is no hysteresis. Recent research suggests that demand shifts can reduce output permanently (Romer 1989); that is, contractionary policy reduces trend output as well as causing temporary deviations from trend. In this case, the true undiscounted sacrifice ratio is infinite. With discounting, however, one can calculate a finite ratio with the present value of output losses as the numerator. Moreover, it is plausible that this sacrifice ratio is well proxied by the ratio computed here. My variable measures the deviation from trend output and ignores the change in the trend, but it is likely that these components of the output loss move together: a larger recession leads to a larger permanent loss. In this case, my procedure understates the sacrifice ratio in all disinflations, but accurately identifies the relative costs of different epi-

---

3. Both my first and second assumptions can be derived from the following model. Assume $y = a(\pi - \pi_{-1}) + by_{-1}$, where y is the deviation of output from trend. This equation is a Lucas supply function with lagged inflation proxying for expected inflation. Assume that inflation is stable before the inflation peak and after the trough. Finally, assume that b^4 is approximately zero. These assumptions imply that $y = 0$ at the inflation peak and four quarters after the trough, and that $y < 0$ between these points.

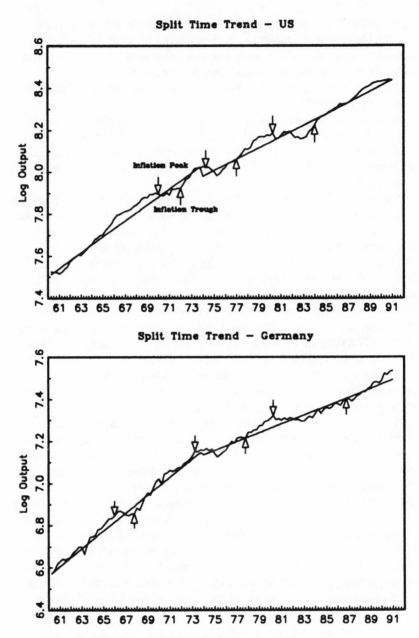

Fig. 5.2   Trend output: standard methods

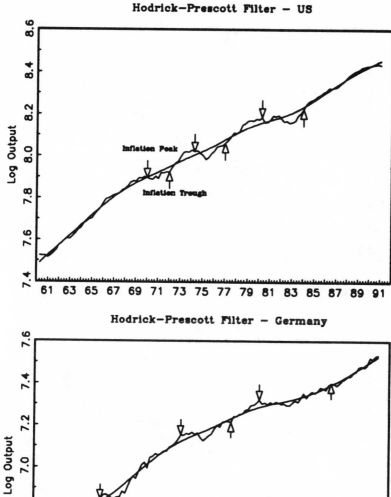

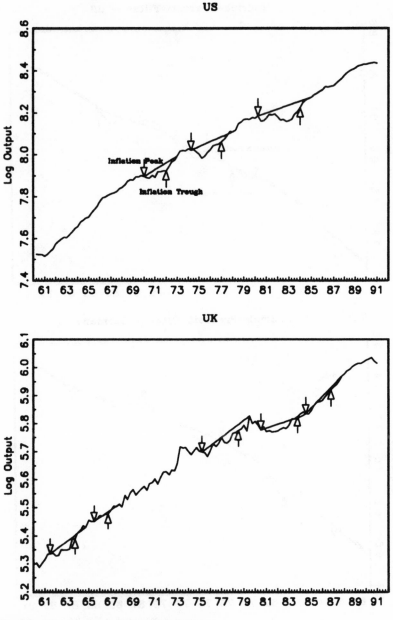

Fig. 5.3   Trend output during disinflations

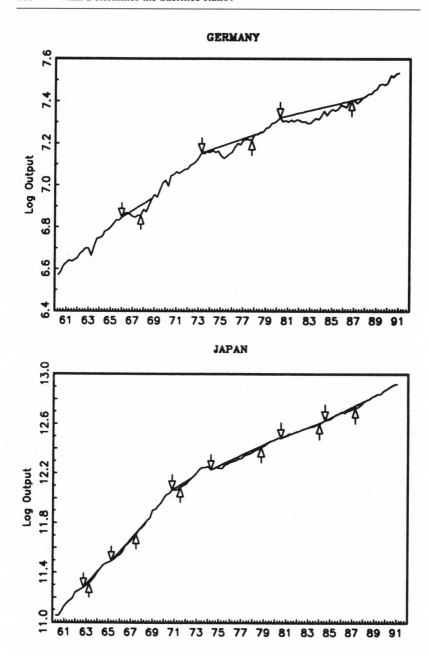

sodes. Thus I can compare episodes without taking a stand on whether disinflation has permanent effects.[4]

5.1.4   Annual Data

For some countries, output data are available only annually. Thus I also use a version of my procedure in which a year is the basic time unit. I define trend inflation for a year as an eight-quarter moving average centered at the year—an average over the four quarters of the year and the two quarters on each side. (Quarterly inflation data are available for all countries.) Year t is an inflation peak (trough) if trend inflation at t is higher (lower) than trend inflation at $t - 1$ or $t + 1$. That is, peaks and troughs are defined with reference to a year on each side rather than four quarters. Trend output is determined by connecting output at the inflation peak to output one year after the trough. Finally, a disinflation occurs when trend inflation falls at least 1.5 percentage points, rather than two points as before. For a given country, this cutoff yields roughly the same number of episodes as I identify with quarterly data. The use of annual data dampens movements in inflation, and the resulting loss of episodes offsets the gain from the lower cutoff.

5.2   A Sample of Sacrifice Ratios

The data on inflation and output are from the International Monetary Fund's *International Financial Statistics.* I examine all OECD countries for which reliable data are available and trend inflation has stayed below 20 percent since 1960. I consider disinflations that begin in 1960 or later and end by 1991. Inflation is measured by the change in the consumer price index (CPI), and output is measured by real gross national product (GNP) or real GDP (whichever is available).

For most countries, my procedure identifies two to five disinflation episodes. The quarterly data yield twenty-eight episodes from nine countries: the United States, the United Kingdom, France, Germany, Italy, Switzerland, Canada, Japan, and Australia. The annual data yield sixty-five episodes in nineteen countries. Twenty-five episodes appear in both the quarterly and annual data sets. Tables 5.1 and 5.2 list all the episodes and their sacrifice ratios.

The average ratio across all episodes is 1.4 for quarterly data and 0.8 for annual data. For the twenty-five episodes in both samples, the averages are 1.5 and 1.1. It appears that the annual data understate output losses because time aggregation smooths the output series. Nonetheless, the two data sets yield similar pictures of the relative costs of different disinflations; for the twenty-five common observations, the correlation between the two ratios is .81.

---

4. In the model of note 3, hysteresis can be introduced by assuming $y^* = y_{-1}^* + cy$, where y^* is trend output and y is the deviation from trend. Under this assumption, a larger deviation implies a larger change in the trend, as suggested in the text.

Table 5.1   **Disinflations: Quarterly Data**

Episode	Length in Quarters	Initial Inflation	Change in Inflation	Sacrifice Ratio
Australia				
74:2–78:1	15	14.60	6.57	0.7234
82:1–84:1	8	10.50	4.98	1.2782
Canada				
74:2–76:4	10	10.60	3.14	0.6273
81:2–85:2	16	11.60	7.83	2.3729
France				
74:2–76:4	10	11.90	2.98	0.9070
81:1–86:4	23	13.00	10.42	0.5997
Germany				
65:4–67:3	7	3.67	2.43	2.5590
73:1–77:3	18	6.92	4.23	2.6358
80:1–86:3	26	5.86	5.95	3.5565
Italy				
63:3–67:4	17	6.79	5.74	2.6539
77:1–78:2	5	16.50	4.30	0.9776
80:1–87:2	29	19.10	14.56	1.5992
Japan				
62:3–63:1	2	8.11	3.00	0.5309
65:1–67:2	9	5.99	2.20	1.6577
70:3–71:2	3	7.53	2.09	1.2689
74:1–78:3	18	17.10	13.21	0.6068
80:2–83:4	14	6.68	5.07	0.0174
84:2–87:1	11	2.29	2.11	1.4801
Switzerland				
73:4–77:4	16	9.42	8.28	1.8509
81:3–83:4	9	6.15	3.86	1.2871
United Kingdom				
61:2–63:3	9	4.24	2.10	1.9105
65:2–66:3	5	4.91	2.69	−0.0063
75:1–78:2	13	19.70	9.71	0.8679
80:2–83:3	13	15.40	11.12	0.2935
84:2–86:3	9	6.19	3.03	0.8680
United States				
69:4–71:4	8	5.67	2.14	2.9364
74:1–76:4	11	9.70	4.00	2.3914
80:1–83:4	15	12.10	8.83	1.8320

For the quarterly data, the sacrifice ratios for individual episodes range from 0.0 to 3.6. The ratio is positive in twenty-seven of twenty-eight cases, suggesting that disinflation is almost always costly. There are sizable differences in average ratios across countries, as shown in table 5.3. The highest average ratios occur in Germany (2.9) and the United States (2.4), and the lowest in France (0.8) and the United Kingdom (0.8). A regression of the ratio on country dummies yields an $\bar{R}^2$ of .47.

Table 5.2   **Disinflations: Annual Data**

Episode	Length in Years	Initial Inflation	Change in Inflation	Sacrifice Ratio
Australia				
61–62	1	1.27	1.52	−0.0399
74–78	4	13.10	6.38	0.4665
82–84	2	9.48	5.46	0.7571
86–88	2	7.80	1.88	0.0824
Austria				
65–66	1	2.18	2.21	−0.5019
74–78	4	8.05	5.16	1.0824
80–83	3	5.93	1.90	1.5339
84–86	2	4.55	3.56	−0.2219
Belgium				
65–67	2	3.60	1.69	0.7376
74–78	4	10.80	7.23	0.4945
82–87	5	7.57	6.54	1.7156
Canada				
69–70	1	3.74	1.54	0.9863
74–76	2	9.08	2.57	0.3822
81–85	4	10.00	6.56	2.2261
Denmark				
68–69	1	6.13	2.94	−0.6939
74–76	2	11.40	3.95	0.5746
77–78	1	9.52	1.74	0.5776
80–85	5	10.60	7.89	1.7621
Finland				
64–65	1	7.27	3.92	−0.3582
67–69	2	7.03	5.22	0.9459
74–78	4	14.70	8.33	1.6569
80–86	6	9.92	6.95	0.6477
France				
62–66	4	5.31	3.63	−0.6765
74–76	2	11.00	3.19	1.0807
81–86	5	11.30	9.05	0.2517
Germany				
65–67	2	3.28	1.78	1.5614
73–78	5	6.31	3.91	3.9174
80–86	6	4.96	5.11	2.0739
Ireland				
64–66	2	5.41	3.37	0.9134
74–78	4	15.90	8.52	0.8147
80–87	7	15.60	13.52	0.4292
Italy				
63–67	4	5.95	4.76	2.2857
76–78	2	14.90	4.30	0.5107
80–87	7	17.60	13.40	1.6448
Japan				
62–64	2	7.55	3.78	−0.6262
74–78	4	15.20	12.51	0.4615
80–82	2	5.44	3.72	−0.1567
83–86	3	1.84	1.99	−0.6117

Table 5.2   (continued)

Episode	Length in Years	Initial Inflation	Change in Inflation	Sacrifice Ratio
Luxemburg				
75–78	3	8.79	6.03	0.5302
Netherlands				
65–67	2	5.44	2.55	1.2767
75–78	3	8.33	4.89	−0.8558
81–83	2	5.92	3.11	1.3973
84–86	2	2.85	3.35	−0.5739
New Zealand				
71–72	1	8.39	2.42	0.5396
75–78	3	13.20	3.73	1.2897
80–83	3	13.50	8.19	0.1752
86–88	2	12.30	7.62	0.1018
Spain				
62–63	1	7.37	2.13	−0.5630
64–69	5	9.95	7.28	−0.2142
77–87	10	18.40	13.86	3.4847
Sweden				
65–68	3	5.59	3.74	1.1134
77–78	1	9.53	2.85	0.3564
80–82	2	11.80	4.35	0.8707
83–86	3	7.61	4.21	−0.5350
Switzerland				
66–68	2	3.58	1.55	1.6060
74–76	2	7.90	6.87	1.3447
81–83	2	4.75	2.12	1.2618
84–86	2	3.22	2.12	−0.7917
United Kingdom				
61–63	2	3.32	2.27	1.7717
75–78	3	16.70	9.71	−0.0682
80–83	3	13.10	9.78	0.5379
84–86	2	4.51	1.84	0.4823
United States				
69–71	2	4.76	1.53	3.3666
74–76	2	8.91	3.63	1.6057
79–83	4	10.40	7.63	1.9362

There is greater variation in the ratio with annual data, and a number of negative ratios. These results probably reflect greater measurement error arising from cruder data. The $\bar{R}^2$ from a regression on country dummies is only .18. Similarly, the $\bar{R}^2$ is lower for annual than for quarterly data in most of the regressions below.

To check the plausibility of my sacrifice ratios, I have compared the ratios for the Volcker disinflation (the last U.S. episode) to previous estimates. Estimates of the Volcker ratio include 4.2 (Blinder 1987), 2.9 (Sachs 1985), 2.8

Table 5.3   **Average Sacrifice Ratios by Country**

Country	Quarterly Data	Annual Data
Australia	1.00	0.32
Austria		0.47
Belgium		0.98
Canada	1.50	1.20
Denmark		0.56
Finland		0.72
France	0.75	0.22
Germany	2.92	2.52
Ireland		0.72
Italy	1.74	1.48
Japan	0.93	−0.23
Luxembourg		0.53
Netherlands		0.31
New Zealand		0.53
Spain		0.90
Sweden		0.45
Switzerland	1.57	0.86
United Kingdom	0.79	0.68
United States	2.39	2.30

(Mankiw 1991), and 1.4 (Schelde-Andersen 1992).[5] My estimates—1.8 with quarterly data and 1.9 with annual data—are within the previous range but lower than average. Two features of my approach explain the relatively low ratios. First, I use the change in consumer price index (CPI) inflation as the denominator of the ratio; most previous authors use the GDP deflator, which yields a smaller inflation gain under Volcker. Second, I assume that output is back at trend in 1984:4 (four quarters after the inflation trough of 1983:4), whereas others assume output losses through 1985.

5.3 The Speed of Disinflation

The next three sections ask whether variation in the sacrifice ratio can be explained. This section shows that the ratio is lower if disinflation is quick.

5.3.1 Background

The optimal speed of disinflation—the choice between "gradualism" and "cold turkey"—is a central issue for macroeconomic policy. One view is that gradualism is less costly because wages and prices possess inertia, and thus need time to adjust to a monetary tightening. This view has been formalized

---

5. Blinder's ratio is 2.1 points of unemployment per point of inflation. An Okun coefficient of two implies an output sacrifice ratio of 4.2.

by Taylor (1983), who presents a model of staggered wage adjustment in which quick disinflation reduces output but slow disinflation does not.[6]

A contrary view is that disinflation is less costly if it is quick. Sargent (1983) argues that a sharp regime-shift produces credibility, and hence a shift in expectations that makes disinflation costless. Gradualism, by contrast, "invites speculation about future reversals," so that expectations do not adjust. Another argument for quick disinflation appears to follow from "menu cost" models of price adjustment. In these models, large shocks trigger greater price adjustment than small shocks; thus a large, one-time shift in monetary policy may be close to neutral, whereas a series of smaller tightenings reduces output substantially. (This idea has not been formalized, however.)

There is currently little evidence on these issues. The two sides make their cases by appealing to historical examples, but the interpretation of individual episodes is controversial. (See, for example, the debate over Sargent's account of the Poincaré disinflation.) This study compares the sacrifice ratio and the speed of disinflation across my sizable sample of episodes.

My basic measure of the speed of disinflation is the change in trend inflation per quarter—the total change from peak to trough divided by the length of the episode. It is not clear, however, that this variable is the right summary statistic; in particular, the numerator and denominator of speed could influence the sacrifice ratio in different ways. In models of staggered price adjustment, the ratio depends only on the length of disinflation relative to the frequency of price adjustment. A larger change in inflation over a given period increases the numerator and denominator of the ratio by the same proportion (Ball 1992). By contrast, Sargent's view suggests that the change in inflation matters: a larger change is more likely to be perceived as a regime-shift, and thus produce a shift in expectations. In my empirical work, I test for separate effects of the inflation change and the episode length.

5.3.2   Basic Results

Table 5.4 presents my basic results about the sacrifice ratio and the speed of disinflation. Columns 1 and 2 report simple regressions of the ratio on speed for the quarterly and annual data sets. In both cases, speed has a significantly negative coefficient: faster disinflations are less expensive. To interpret the coefficients, consider the difference between the fitted sacrifice ratio when speed equals one and when speed equals one quarter. These speeds correspond to a five-point disinflation carried out over five quarters or over twenty quarters (or a ten-point disinflation over ten or forty quarters). For the quarterly data set, the sacrifice ratio is 1.8 when speed is one quarter but only 0.7 when speed is one. The results for annual data are similar. Thus faster disinflation produces substantially lower output losses.

---

6. This result can be criticized on the grounds of theoretical robustness, as well as on the empirical grounds discussed below. See Ball (1992).

Table 5.4   The Sacrifice Ratio and the Speed of Disinflation (dependent variable: sacrifice ratio)

Data Set	(1) Quarterly	(2) Annual	(3) Quarterly	(4) Annual
Constant	2.196 (0.329)	1.512 (0.307)	1.045 (0.325)	0.131 (0.232)
Speed = $\Delta\pi$/length	−1.543 (0.586)	−1.677 (0.637)		
$\Delta\pi$			−0.198 (0.061)	−0.123 (0.057)
Length			0.120 (0.034)	0.106 (0.026)
$\bar{R}^2$	.180	.085	.300	.209
Sample size	28	65	28	65

Note: Standard errors are in parentheses.

Columns 3 and 4 of the table enter the change in inflation ($\Delta\pi$) and the episode length as separate variables. The $\Delta\pi$ coefficient is significantly negative, and the length coefficient is significantly positive. That is, greater speed reduces the sacrifice ratio regardless of whether it results from a larger inflation change over a given period or from a faster completion of a given change. The $\bar{R}^2$'s for this specification are considerably higher than when $\Delta\pi$ and length enter only through their ratio.

I have also estimated the equations in columns 1–4 with the addition of dummy variables for countries. These regressions isolate the within-country comovement of the sacrifice ratio and speed. The results are similar to table 5.4, although somewhat weaker. The coefficient in the simple regression on speed is −0.9 ($t = 1.9$) for quarterly data and −1.2 ($t = 1.8$) for annual data. In the multiple regression, both coefficients are significant for the quarterly sample ($t > 2$), and the length coefficient is significant for the annual sample.[7]

5.3.3   A Potential Bias

As discussed above, the effects of supply shocks on the sacrifice ratio can be interpreted as measurement error. Measurement error in the dependent variable does not generally cause econometric problems, but it does in this application. The problem is that $\Delta\pi$ is both the denominator of the sacrifice ratio and the numerator of the independent variable speed (or, in columns 3 and 4, a separate regressor). For a given demand contraction, a favorable supply shock that increases $\Delta\pi$ will reduce the estimated sacrifice ratio and increase speed,

---

7. I have also experimented with a "random effects" specification, in which the error term contains a component common to episodes from the same country. Generalized least squares (GLS) estimates of this model are very close to the OLS results reported in the text.

Table 5.5   **The Speed of Disinflation: Subsamples (dependent variable: sacrifice ratio)**

	(1) Quarterly through 1972	(2) Quarterly after 1972	(3) Annual through 1972	(4) Annual after 1972
Data Set				
Constant	2.478	2.160	1.932	1.289
	(0.517)	(0.493)	(0.493)	(0.387)
Speed = $\Delta\pi$/length	−1.516	−1.718	−3.024	−1.044
	(0.787)	(0.953)	(1.064)	(0.789)
$\bar{R}^2$	.279	.106	.271	.017
Sample size	8	20	20	45

Note: Standard errors are in parentheses.

creating a spurious negative relation between the two. I now check whether this problem has an important effect on my results.

I take two approaches. First, table 5.5 regresses the sacrifice ratio on speed for disinflations ending by 1972 and disinflations ending after 1972. Aggregate supply was less stable in the second period, and so the negative bias arising from supply shocks should be larger. With quarterly data, however, the speed coefficients for both subsamples are close to the coefficient for the whole sample. With annual data, the coefficient is more negative in the first period than in the second, the opposite of what we would expect if supply shocks had created bias. These results suggest that my basic findings are not driven by supply shocks. Similar results arise if speed is replaced by $\Delta\pi$ and length, or if the sample is split at 1984 (before the 1986 oil price decline).

As a second approach to the supply-shock problem, I estimate the effect of speed using instrumental variables (IV), with length as an instrument. Length is clearly correlated with speed = $\Delta\pi$/length. And length is plausibly uncorrelated with the errors arising from supply shocks. For a given path of aggregate demand, a beneficial supply shock is likely to increase $\Delta\pi$, but not to reduce length: the shock does not cause disinflation to end sooner. Thus, increases in speed resulting from decreases in length should not be negatively correlated with the errors in the sacrifice ratio. (Indeed, beneficial supply shocks near the end of an episode may *increase* its length by extending the inflation decline beyond the end of tight policy. Note that a number of episodes end in the beneficial-shock year of 1986. In this case, the IV coefficient on speed has a positive rather than negative bias.)[8]

8. My approach assumes that the demand contraction during disinflation is exogenous. If policy responds to supply shocks, there are scenarios in which the negative bias in OLS extends to IV. This is the case, for example, if a favorable supply shock causes policymakers to shorten disinflation because an inflation target is met more quickly. In such a case, the identification problem appears insuperable.

Table 5.6   The Speed of Disinflation: Instrumental Variables
            (instrument = 1/length)

	(1) Quarterly Data	(2) Annual Data
Constant	2.077	3.633
	(0.454)	(1.320)
Speed = $\Delta\pi$/length	−1.301	−6.477
	(0.867)	(2.963)
Sample size	28	65

Note: Standard errors are in parentheses.

Table 5.6 presents instrumental variables estimates, with the inverse of length as the instrument. (1/length is more highly correlated with speed than is length.) For the quarterly sample, the coefficient on speed is close to the ordinary least squares (OLS) coefficient. For the annual sample, the coefficient is larger in absolute value, but the difference is not statistically significant. Once again, there is no evidence of negative bias in my basic results.

5.4   Nominal Wage Rigidity

5.4.1   Background

Comparisons of macroeconomic performance in different countries often emphasize differences in nominal wage rigidity (e.g., Bruno and Sachs 1985). These differences are attributed to wage-setting institutions such as the frequency of adjustment, the degree of indexation, and the synchronization of adjustment across sectors. Many authors argue, for example, that three-year staggered contracts make U.S. wages rigid, whereas one-year synchronized contracts make Japanese wages flexible. These differences are used to explain cross-country variation in the costs of disinflation, such as the high costs in the United States and the lower costs in Japan (e.g., Gordon 1982).

In contrast to this tradition, recent "New Keynesian" research has deemphasized wage-setting institutions. New Keynesians argue that monetary nonneutrality arises largely from rigidities in output prices rather than wages (e.g., Mankiw 1990). To the extent that price rigidity determines the cost of disinflation, wage-setting institutions are unimportant.

Once again, the relevant empirical evidence consists mainly of informal comparisons of a few episodes. I now investigate whether wage rigidity helps explain the variation in the sacrifice ratio in my sample.[9]

---

9. Bruno-Sachs and others report extensive cross-country comparisons of wage rigidity and the effects of supply shocks. To my knowledge, however, this study and Schelde-Andersen (1992) are the only papers that compare rigidity and sacrifice ratios.

Table 5.7   **The Sacrifice Ratio and Wage Rigidity (quarterly results)**

	(1)	(2)	(3)	(4)
Constant	2.067	1.593	1.841	1.542
	(0.400)	(0.446)	(0.302)	(0.406)
Wage responsiveness	−0.179	−0.150		
	(0.104)	(0.087)		
Contract duration			−0.313	−0.306
			(0.194)	(0.162)
$\Delta\pi$		−0.190		−0.205
		(0.059)		(0.058)
Length		0.115		0.115
		(0.033)		(0.032)
$\bar{R}^2$	.069	.352	.056	.366
Sample size	28	28	28	28

Note: Standard errors are in parentheses.

5.4.2   Basic Results

My basic measure of wage rigidity is Bruno and Sachs's index of "nominal wage responsiveness." For a given country, Bruno and Sachs assign a value of zero, one, or two to each of three variables: the duration of wage agreements, the degree of indexation, and the degree of synchronization. Higher values mean greater flexibility (that is, shorter, more indexed, and more synchronized agreements). The wage responsiveness index is the sum of the three values, and thus runs from zero to six. I regress the sacrifice ratio on the index, and also experiment with the three components.

The results for quarterly and annual data are presented in tables 5.7 and 5.8. In both cases, I report simple regressions on the responsiveness index and regressions that include $\Delta\pi$ and disinflation length. I also use the duration of agreements in place of the total index. Duration is the only component of the index that is significant by itself.[10]

The results are quite similar across specifications. The coefficients on responsiveness or duration are negative, implying that greater flexibility reduces the sacrifice ratio. The statistical significance of these results is borderline: *t*-statistics range from 1.8 to 2.1 for annual data and from 1.6 to 1.9 for quarterly data. The point estimates imply large effects of flexibility. In column 1 of the annual results, for example, the fitted value of the sacrifice ratio is 1.4 for a responsiveness of zero but only 0.5 for the maximum responsiveness of six. (Switzerland has a rating of zero, and Australia, Denmark, and New Zealand have ratings of six.) The results for duration show that it is the most important component of the index. In column 3 of the annual results, raising duration

10. For these regressions, the annual data set is reduced from sixty-five to fifty-eight observations, because the Bruno-Sachs index is missing for several countries.

Table 5.8   **The Sacrifice Ratio and Wage Rigidity (annual results)**

	(1)	(2)	(3)	(4)
Constant	1.369	0.657	1.280	0.649
	(0.326)	(0.388)	(0.270)	(0.356)
Wage responsiveness	−0.153	−0.130		
	(0.077)	(0.071)		
Contract duration			−0.360	−0.330
			(0.168)	(0.155)
$\Delta\pi$		−0.096		−0.111
		(0.058)		(0.057)
Length		0.096		0.099
		(0.029)		(0.028)
$\bar{R}^2$	.050	.191	.059	.208
Sample size	58	58	58	58

Note: Standard errors are in parentheses.

from zero to two reduces the fitted ratio from 1.3 to 0.6. (Zero means wage agreements of three years, and two means agreements of a year or less.)

5.4.3   A Variation

As an alternative explanatory variable, I use the index of nominal wage rigidity in Grubb, Jackman, and Layard (1983). This variable is quite different from the Bruno-Sachs index: it is constructed from a time-series regression of wages on prices and unemployment. An advantage of the Grubb index is that it flexibly measures the overall rigidity of wages—it does not rely on arbitrary assumptions about the importance of particular contract provisions. An obvious disadvantage is that the Grubb variable is endogenous. Factors that directly influence the sacrifice ratio, such as the initial level of inflation or the prevalence of incomes policies, are likely to influence the speed of wage adjustment that Grubb measures. To address this problem, I estimate the effects of the Grubb index using instrumental variables, with Bruno and Sachs's variables as instruments. This approach isolates the effects of rigidity arising from wage-setting institutions.

Table 5.9 reports results for both quarterly and annual data. Columns 1 and 2 present OLS regressions of the sacrifice ratio on the Grubb index, $\Delta\pi$, and disinflation length. For both data sets, the Grubb variable has a significantly positive coefficient. Columns 3 and 4 report instrumental variables estimates; the instruments are the three components of the wage-responsiveness variable and another Bruno-Sachs index measuring "corporatism" (the extent of unionization, the centralization of bargaining, and so on). The instrumental variables estimates are close to the OLS estimates, although the statistical significance becomes borderline. The results are reasonably stable when various subsets of the instruments are used. Overall, the results confirm the finding that wage rigidity is an important determinant of the sacrifice ratio.

Table 5.9   **The Sacrifice Ratio and Wage Rigidity: Grubb Measure**

	(1) Quarterly Data	(2) Annual Data	(3) Quarterly Data	(4) Annual Data
Procedure	Ordinary Least Squares	Ordinary Least Squares	Instrumental Variables	Instrumental Variables
Constant	0.731	−0.155	0.709	−0.173
	(0.324)	(0.268)	(0.358)	(0.304)
Wage rigidity	0.377	0.578	0.404	0.614
	(0.156)	(0.168)	(0.239)	(0.321)
$\Delta\pi$	−0.201	−0.112	−0.201	−0.112
	(0.056)	(0.054)	(0.056)	(0.054)
Length	0.125	0.101	0.125	0.101
	(0.031)	(0.027)	(0.031)	(0.027)
Sample size	28	58	28	58

Note: Standard errors are in parentheses.

5.5   Other Results

This section reports additional results that are either negative or inconclusive. Future research should explore these issues further.

5.5.1   Initial Inflation

Ball, Mankiw, and Romer (1988) show that trend inflation influences the output-inflation trade-off in New Keynesian models. Higher inflation reduces the extent of nominal rigidity, and thus steepens the short-run Phillips curve. Ball, Mankiw, and Romer show that cross-country evidence strongly supports this prediction. A special case of the prediction is that the sacrifice ratio during disinflation is decreasing in the initial level of trend inflation. I now test this idea with my sample of disinflations. For both quarterly and annual data, table 5.10 reports regressions of the ratio on initial inflation, π_0. I present simple regressions and regressions that include length, $\Delta\pi$, and contract duration (the best-fitting set of variables from the previous section).

The results for the two data sets are rather different. With quarterly data, the simple regression shows a negative effect of π_0, as predicted by theory. The t-statistic is 1.9. The coefficient in the multiple regression is similar in size, but statistically insignificant ($t = 1.0$). This weaker result reflects collinearity between π_0 and $\Delta\pi$: inflation tends to fall more in episodes when it is initially high. (Note that the coefficient on $\Delta\pi$ also becomes insignificant.) Overall, it is difficult to identify separate effects of π_0 and $\Delta\pi$, but the data are at least suggestive that π_0 has a negative effect.

The annual data, by contrast, provide no support for this hypothesis. In both specifications, the coefficient is not only insignificant, but has the wrong sign (positive).

The differences between the quarterly and annual results arise from differ-

Table 5.10   **The Sacrifice Ratio and Initial Inflation (dependent variable: sacrifice ratio)**

	(1) Quarterly Data	(2) Quarterly Data	(3) Annual Data	(4) Annual Data
Constant	2.093	1.884	0.661	0.480
	(0.386)	(0.533)	(0.307)	(0.413)
π_0	−0.067	−0.055	0.014	0.040
	(0.036)	(0.055)	(0.034)	(0.050)
$\Delta\pi$		−0.126		−0.164
		(0.099)		(0.087)
Length		0.097		0.106
		(0.037)		(0.030)
Duration		−0.331		−0.321
		(0.164)		(0.155)
$\bar{R}^2$	.086	.365	.015	.203
Sample size	28	28	58	58

Note: Standard errors are in parentheses.

ences in the samples of countries. When the annual sample is restricted to the countries for which quarterly data exist, the results are similar to the quarterly results. It is not clear why the choice of countries is so important. It is also not clear why the effect of π_0 is weaker than the effect of trend inflation on the Phillips curve found by Ball, Mankiw, and Romer.

5.5.2   Incomes Policies

If inflation possesses inertia, there may be a role for governments to intervene directly in wage- and price-setting during disinflation. By mandating a slowdown in the growth of prices, governments can reduce inertia and thus reduce the sacrifice ratio. This logic has led to wage-price controls or other incomes policies during many disinflations.

To investigate the effects of incomes policies, I must first measure them. For each of the twenty-eight episodes in the quarterly data set, I consulted the historical record to see whether incomes policies were employed. My main sources were the OECD's *Economic Outlook* and surveys of incomes policies (Ulman and Flanagan 1971; Flanagan, Soskice, and Ulman 1983). I create two dummy variables. The first, INCM, equals one if mandatory incomes policies were employed at anytime during the episode. A mandatory policy is defined as one in which legal restrictions are placed on the majority of wages or the majority of output prices. According to my survey, such policies were imposed in six of the twenty-eight episodes (United States 1969–71, Canada 1974–76, France 1974–76, France 1981–86, United Kingdom 1965–66, and United Kingdom 1975–78). The second variable, INCV, equals one if voluntary incomes policies were introduced. These policies are broadly defined to include voluntary guideposts, jawboning, and negotiated settlements with business and labor. Voluntary policies occurred in another twelve of the episodes.

Table 5.11 regresses the sacrifice ratio on INCM and INCV, both with and without additional controls. When both dummies are included, the results are disappointing: INCV has a positive coefficient and INCM has a negative coefficient, and both are insignificant. When INCV is excluded, however, the INCM coefficient is almost significant in the regression with additional controls ($t = 1.8$). The coefficient implies that a mandatory policy reduces the sacrifice ratio by 0.6.

One interpretation of these results is that voluntary policies are ineffective but mandatory policies do reduce the sacrifice ratio. This finding is not very robust, however. The results could be checked by extending the measures of incomes policies to the larger annual sample.

5.5.3   Openness

As stressed by Romer (1991), basic macroeconomics suggests a relation between the output-inflation trade-off and the openness of the economy—the share of imports in total spending. In a more open economy, the exchange-rate appreciation arising from a monetary contraction has a larger direct effect on the price level. Consequently, inflation falls more for a given policy shift: the sacrifice ratio is smaller.

This idea receives no support from my data. Table 5.12 reports regressions of the sacrifice ratio on the imports/GNP ratio (taken from Romer). The effects of imports/GNP are very insignificant for both quarterly and annual data. These results cast doubt on Romer's argument that openness influences average inflation by changing the output-inflation trade-off.

Table 5.11   **The Sacrifice Ratio and Incomes Policies (quarterly data) (dependent variable: sacrifice ratio)**

	(1)	(2)	(3)	(4)
Constant	1.335	1.561	1.539	1.748
	(0.289)	(0.195)	(0.424)	(0.405)
INCM	−0.346	−0.573	−0.351	−0.593
	(0.472)	(0.422)	(0.366)	(0.328)
INCV	0.415		0.449	
	(0.391)		(0.323)	
$\Delta\pi$			−0.223	−0.206
			(0.056)	(0.056)
Length			0.112	0.112
			(0.030)	(0.031)
Duration			−0.285	−0.330
			(0.156)	(0.156)
$\bar{R}^2$	.035	.030	.443	.420
Sample size	28	28	28	28

Note: Standard errors are in parentheses.

Table 5.12   **The Sacrifice Ratio and Openness**

	(1) Quarterly Data	(2) Annual Data	(3) Quarterly Data	(4) Annual Data
Gonstant	1.363	0.828	1.615	0.469
	(0.534)	(0.302)	(0.551)	(0.402)
Imports/gross national product	0.364	−0.096	−0.390	−0.273
	(2.415)	(0.966)	(1.954)	(0.860)
$\Delta\pi$			−0.205	−0.122
			(0.059)	(0.056)
Length			0.116	0.102
			(0.033)	(0.026)
Duration			−0.306	−0.166
			(0.166)	(0.141)
$\bar{R}^2$	−.038	−.017	.339	.218
Sample size	28	61	28	61

Note: Standard errors are in parentheses.

5.6 Conclusion

This paper constructs sacrifice ratios for a sample of disinflations and asks whether variation in the ratio can be explained. I find that the ratio is lower when disinflation is quick, and when wage-setting is more flexible. Openness has no effect on the ratio, and the effects of initial inflation and incomes policies are unclear.

My analysis uses a new measure of the sacrifice ratio based on several assumptions about the behavior of trend output. Future research should check the robustness of the results to variations in my assumptions. Some evidence of robustness is provided by Schelde-Andersen (1992), whose study was carried out independently of mine. Schelde-Andersen estimates sacrifice ratios using a substantially different approach. For example, he measures the ratio using a fixed period for every country (1979–88), and he examines unemployment as well as output losses. His ranking of sacrifice ratios across countries differs considerably from my table 5.3. Nonetheless, Schelde-Andersen and I reach similar conclusions about the determinants of the ratio. In particular, he confirms my findings about both the speed of disinflation and nominal wage rigidity.

Do my results about speed imply that cold-turkey disinflation is preferable to gradualism? This conclusion is warranted only if the cost of disinflation is measured by the total output loss. The welfare loss in a given quarter might be a convex function of the output loss, as macro theorists usually assume. In this case, gradualism has the advantage of spreading the losses over a longer period. Since we do not know the shape of the social loss function, it is difficult to determine the optimal speed of disinflation. At a minimum, however, my results refute the view that gradualism makes disinflation costless.

Another possible implication of my results is that government should encourage greater wage flexibility, for example, by limiting the length of labor contracts. Such a policy is suggested by Bosworth (1981) and others, and can be justified in principle by the negative externalities from long contracts (Ball 1987). My results suggest that the welfare gains from shorter contracts are large: the recessions arising from disinflation are dampened considerably.

References

Ball, Laurence. 1987. Externalities from contract length, *American Economic Review* 77 (September): 615–29.
———. 1994. Credible disinflation with staggered price setting. *American Economic Review.* Forthcoming.
Ball, Laurence, N. Gregory Mankiw, and David Romer. 1988. The new Keynesian economics and the output-inflation trade-off. *Brookings Papers on Economic Activity* 1: 1–65.
Blinder, Alan S. 1987. Hard heads, soft hearts: Tough-minded economics for a just society. Reading, Mass.: Addison-Wesley.
Bruno, Michael, and Jeffrey Sachs. 1985. *Economics of worldwide stagflation.* Cambridge, Mass.: Harvard University Press.
Bosworth, Barry. 1981. Policy choices for controlling inflation. In *Controlling inflation: Studies in wage/price policy, alternatives for the 1980s.* Vol. 1. Center for Democratic Policy. Washington, D.C.: U.S. Government Printing Office.
Fernandez, David G. 1992. Bank lending and the monetary policy transmission mechanism: Evidence from Japan. Princeton University. Manuscript.
Flanagan, Robert J., David W. Soskice, and Lloyd Ulman. 1983. *Unionism, economic stabilization, and incomes policies: European experience.* Washington, D.C.: Brookings Institution.
Gordon, Robert J. 1982. Why stopping inflation may be costly: Evidence from fourteen historical episodes. In *Inflation: Causes and effects,* ed. Robert E. Hall. Chicago: University of Chicago Press.
Gordon, Robert J., and Stephen R. King. 1982. The output cost of disinflation in traditional and vector autoregressive models. *Brookings Papers on Economic Activity* 1: 205–42.
Grubb, Dennis, Richard Jackman, and Richard Layard. 1983. Wage rigidity and unemployment in OECD Countries. *European Economic Review* 21 (March-April): 11–39.
Mankiw, N. Gregory. 1990. A quick refresher course in macroeconomics. *Journal of Economic Literature* 28 (December): 1645–60.
———. 1991. *Macroeconomics.* New York: Worth Publishers.
Okun, Arthur M. 1978. Efficient disinflationary policies. *American Economic Review* 68 (May): 348–52.
Organization for Economic Cooperation and Development (OECD). *Economic Outlook,* various issues.
Romer, Christina D., and David Romer. 1989. Does monetary policy matter? A new test in the spirit of Friedman and Schwartz. *NBER Macroeconomics Annual,* 121–70.
Romer, David. 1989. Comment. *Brookings Papers on Economic Activity* 2: 117–25.
———. 1991. Openness and inflation: Theory and evidence. NBER Working Paper no. 3936, December.

Sachs, Jeffrey D. 1985. The dollar and the policy mix: 1985. *Brookings Papers on Economic Activity* 1: 117–97.

Sargent, Thomas. 1983. Stopping moderate inflations: The methods of Poincare and Thatcher. In *Inflation, debt, and indexation*, eds. Dornbusch and Simonsen. Cambridge, Mass.: MIT Press.

Schelde-Andersen, Palle. 1992. OECD country experiences with disinflation. In *Inflation, disinflation, and monetary policy*, ed. Blundell-Wignell. Reserve Bank of Australia: Ambassador Press.

Taylor, John B. 1983. Union wage settlements during a disinflation. *American Economic Review* 73 (December): 981–93.

Ulman, Lloyd, and Robert J. Flanagan. 1971. *Wage restraint: A study of incomes policies in Western Europe*. Berkeley: University of California Press.

Comment   Benjamin M. Friedman

Laurence Ball's paper is a useful contribution to a literature with old antecedents as well as much contemporary policy import. The central questions at issue are plain: what is the cost of disinflation, and what—if anything—can a country do to reduce that cost? Ball frames these questions within the context of recent contributions by such well known researchers as Arthur Okun, Thomas Sargent, Barry Bosworth, and Robert J. Gordon, but it is also appropriate to recall the earlier incarnation of this discussion in the debate between Friedrich Hayek and Milton Friedman over "gradualism" in disinflation policies, and still prior developments as well. In the United States within the past decade or so, discussion of this issue has mostly focused on the "Volcker disinflation" of the early 1980s, the "Greenspan disinflation" that accompanied the 1990–91 recession, and the proposed (but not enacted) congressional resolution directing the Federal Reserve System to pursue a monetary policy leading to zero inflation.[1] In each case, a central question has been the costs—costs in terms of foregone output, jobs, incomes, profits, capital formation, and so on—that disinflation involves.

At least in the United States, economic thinking about these costs has followed an interesting evolution over the post-World War II era. During roughly the first half of this period, the desire to maintain a higher utilization of the economy's resources (that is, lower unemployment) without incurring ever-increasing price inflation presented macroeconomics with its primary policy objective and, in so doing, motivated the leading topic on the field's research agenda.[2] The conceptual vehicle hypothesized to make greater utilization with-

Benjamin M. Friedman is the William Joseph Maier Professor of Political Economy at Harvard University and director of the Program in Monetary Economics at the National Bureau of Economic Research.

1. See H.R. 409, 101st Cong., 1st sess.

2. The one other macroeconomic objective that commanded perhaps equal attention in the research literature of the time was raising the economy's long-run growth rate, but that idea had much less visible impact on the discussion of actual macroeconomic policy.

out ever-increasing inflation achievable was the Phillips curve: a stable and exploitable trade-off between unemployment and inflation. Given such a trade-off, an appropriate policy could permanently achieve lower unemployment than would be consistent with price stability. Prices would rise, but at a stable rate as long as unemployment was itself steady. Specifically, continually below-normal unemployment need not imply continually increasing inflation.

By the time most economists had given up on the idea of a stable and exploitable unemployment-inflation trade-off, the ongoing U.S. inflation rate had become high by historical peacetime standards. Now the question heading the research and policy agenda in macroeconomics became how to reduce that inflation while holding to a minimum the associated costs. A theory promising costless disinflation, therefore, became to its time what the theory of the stable trade-off had been in its own earlier context.

Macroeconomics again proved up to the challenge. Throughout this period, including the heyday of the stable trade-off and its aftermath, the accepted understanding had been that macroeconomic policy influenced inflation primarily, if not only, by affecting nonfinancial economic activity. Keynesian theory typically summarized the underlying dependence of inflation on the economy's utilization of its real resources via some form of explicit Phillips curve for either prices or wages, importantly including later elaborations that allowed for the role of inflation expectations. The monetarist alternative, couched primarily in terms of money growth and growth of nominal income, was necessarily more vague about the connection to real economic activity, but Friedman and Schwartz's (1963) work and the flood of subsequent studies that it inspired typically showed a substantial effect of monetary policy on real activity before the associated effect on inflation appeared.

By the late 1970s, when U.S. inflation was approaching the double-digit range, this line of thinking connecting disinflation to underutilization of resources had even achieved something of a consensus on the quantitative magnitude of the short-run trade-offs involved. When Okun (1978) surveyed a variety of estimates of the likely real costs of disinflation in the United States, the answer he found was that each one-percentage-point reduction in inflation achieved by monetary policy would require between two and six "point-years" of unemployment, with a median estimate of three point-years. Such an unfavorable trade-off—at the median, fifteen point-years of unemployment to cut the inflation rate by five percentage points—constituted a clear discouragement to an actively disinflationary policy.

By contrast, the radically different view of the way in which monetary policy affects the economy, developed during the 1970s by Lucas (1972, 1973) and Sargent and Wallace (1975), maintained that central-bank actions that are anticipated in advance affect the setting of prices and wages directly through their effect on expectations, with little or no consequence for real economic activity. Hence disinflation is costless as long as the public receives "credible" warning of the central bank's actions, as summarized in the growth of some appropriate measure of the money stock. By announcing its money-growth target in advance, and then ensuring that actual money growth followed the target closely, the central bank could thus achieve any desired reduction in inflation without consequence, adverse or otherwise, to the real economy. It is difficult to judge the exact extent of adherence to this alternative perspective by the outset of the 1980s, or the extent to which it influenced actual monetary policy decisions, but neither appears to have been negligible.

Alas, this exercise in creative optimism proved no more consistent with actual behavior than the claim of a stable trade-off that had preceded it. The Volcker disinflation destroyed the belief of most economists (and probably a still greater proportion of noneconomists) in the prospect of costless disinflation. In the wake of the early 1980s experience, featuring major disinflation accompanied by the largest business recession since the 1930s, it is far more plausible to believe that monetary policy does indeed affect price inflation primarily, if not only, by affecting nonfinancial economic activity—and, further, that the magnitude of these effects is about as was previously supposed. It is to Ball's credit that the notion of costless disinflation never enters his paper. There are few references to "credibility" either.

Although Ball's methodology based on foregone real output delivers more favorable estimates, what is striking about the Volcker disinflation is just how closely in line the resulting unemployment was with prior experience and estimates. Based on a "full employment" benchmark of 6 percent unemployment, the cost of each one percentage point of disinflation for the overall gross domestic product (GDP) deflator in the 1980s experience was about two and one-half point-years of unemployment—slightly better than Okun's median estimate of three, but well within the range of the then-conventional models that he surveyed. On the alternative assumption that the "full employment" unemployment rate was 6 percent at the beginning of the 1980s but declined to 5 percent by mid-decade, the cost per point of disinflation was slightly worse than Okun's median estimate.

By contrast, Ball's estimates based on real output movements show a sacrifice ratio of 1.9 percent for the 1979–83 U.S. experience (1.8 percent in the quarterly data), versus 3.4 percent in 1969–71 and 1.6 percent in 1974–76 (2.9 percent and 2.4 percent, respectively, in the quarterly data). But his use of the loss in real output (relative to trend) in the numerator and the slowing of the consumer price index in the denominator of his ratio presumably leads to an understatement of the costliness of the Volcker disinflation compared with analogous calculations based on unemployment and the GDP deflator. The use of output loss rather than rise in unemployment, as a measure of the cost of disinflation, raises particularly interesting substantive issues. The two measures would result in equivalent comparisons over time if such aspects of macroeconomic activity as productivity growth, labor-force participation, population growth, and the like were constant. But U.S. productivity growth improved in the early years of the 1983–90 expansion, compared with the average experience of the 1970s, and so the cost of disinflation in terms of output was less than the cost in terms of unemployment, even though labor-force growth slowed.

Given that these two measures of "sacrifice" are not equivalent in practice, the most interesting substantive question raised by the choice between them is who is doing the sacrificing. As usual in such matters, if the winners from disinflation could readily compensate the losers, this question would not arise and the output shortfall would be the obvious measure to use. Making such transfers is typically not straightforward (or even possible) in modern industrial societies, however, and so the matter of who gains at the expense of whom is very much to the point.[3]

In contrast to the Volcker disinflation, the Greenspan disinflation featured only a modest unemployment rate (never as great as 8 percent) but extraordinarily slow output growth.[4] In addition to the 2.2 percent drop in output during the 1990–91 recession, which lasted three calendar quarters, output grew by only 2.6 percent in the year and a half before the recession began. Output then expanded by only 2.9 percent in the initial year and a half after the recession ended, versus an average 9.8 percent gain in the comparable stage of the eight previous postrecession recoveries since World War II. Similarly, although slow labor-force growth held unemployment down, *employment* expanded by just 0.1 percent in the first year and a half of recovery in 1991–92, versus an average 5.4 percent gain in the eight prior recoveries. In light of Medoff's (1992a, 1992b) finding that job availability is the macroeconomic variable most highly correlated with standard consumer confidence measures as well as with voting patterns in national elections, the Greenspan disinflation presumably contributed to incumbent president George Bush's loss in the 1992 election.

Several other specifics of Ball's paper bear comment, in addition to the choice of output versus either employment or unemployment to measure cost. First, Ball explicitly focuses only on episodes in which countries have reduced inflation from "moderate" starting points. No inflation observation in his data set is as great as 20 percent. This choice presents a sharp contrast to the approach of Sargent (1982), who, in the spirit of Cagan's (1956) classic study of the demand for money, deliberately focused on hyperinflations. The basic methodological question at issue here is what can be learned about behavior under "normal" conditions from studying extreme situations. The same question is also relevant to the theoretical underpinnings of the debate over costs of disinflation, in that Lucas's (1973) original evidence for a theory of aggregate supply behavior based on producers' inability to distinguish absolute from relative price movements rested mostly on outlier observations for Argentina and Paraguay.

3. See the discussion of this subject in Friedman (1992).
4. Romer and Romer (1992) provide evidence documenting a deliberate tightening of U.S. monetary policy for purposes of disinflation beginning in 1988, and so comparisons between this episode and the Volcker disinflation are apt.

Second, the price-output dynamics that Ball posits require some explanation, to say the least. Ball's procedure assumes that output is at its natural rate at the time that inflation peaks and, subsequently, that output returns to its natural rate a year *after* inflation has bottomed. But if there is no shortfall of output at the peak, why does inflation begin to come down? And, even more puzzling, if there is still an output shortfall at the trough, why does inflation go back up? In both 1972 and 1977, for example, U.S. inflation was rising quite rapidly (see figure 5.1). Yet by Ball's estimate output was still below trend in both instances. In principle, the net impact of these peculiarities of the measurement of the output lost in disinflations could be either to enlarge or to shrink the resulting estimate of the sacrifice ratio for any specific episode. Given the small average size of Ball's estimates, however, the latter seems more likely.

Third, Ball's Hayekian finding that faster disinflations require less sacrifice raises an important problem of potential reverse causation. The basic question at issue in this regard is why central banks do what they do. As in most conventional analysis of the effect of economic policies, Ball takes monetary policy (or whatever negative aggregate demand shocks deliver disinflations) as exogenous with respect to the behavior he is investigating. But what if central banks pursue their presumed goal of disinflation more rigorously when they have reason to believe that the short-run trade-offs associated with doing so are more favorable? Ball partially addresses this question by including country dummies in his regressions, and also by testing for effects of supply shocks, but the issue remains unresolved.

Moreover, even if Ball's conclusion in this regard were persuasively robust, any attempt to find in this result evidence for sacrifice-lessening effects of greater credibility that might be associated with faster disinflation immediately runs afoul of what the specific country comparisons imply in this context. For example, Ball's calculation of a greater sacrifice ratio for Germany (2.1 percent) than for Italy (1.6 percent) in the 1980s is hardly consistent with a large role for credibility effects. Dornbusch's (1990) comparisons based on disinflation and unemployment during this period make the point even plainer: 9.6 point-years of unemployment per point of disinflation in Germany, 7.5 in the Netherlands, 4.0 in France, and 2.2 in Italy. Ball's discussion notwithstanding, comparisons like these are far more suggestive of some form of nonlinearity such that disinflation is less costly when it begins from higher initial inflation levels. (A straightforward extension of the same idea would also incorporate Sargent's finding on the end of hyperinflations.)

Finally, what about the recently fashionable talk in the United States of pressing disinflation to the point of achieving zero inflation? Ball's basic finding brings a useful note of reality to this discussion: "Intentional demand contractions are essentially the only source of two-point declines in trend inflation."

In contrast to this sobering conclusion based on the historical record, the "zero inflation" resolution recently introduced in the U.S. Congress contained not one reference to any loss of jobs, any sacrifice of output, or any shortfall of investment that a successful disinflationary policy would no doubt entail. Instead, the resolution simply stated that "zero inflation will promote the highest possible sustainable level of employment" and "the maximum sustainable rate of economic growth," and, further, that "zero inflation will encourage the highest possible rate of savings and investment." And in contrast to any mention of the higher interest rates that would have to deliver what Ball calls an "intentional demand contraction"—he concludes that "a significant tightening of monetary policy is not only necessary for disinflation but also, it appears, sufficient"—the proposed resolution merely asserted that "zero inflation will reduce interest rates to, and maintain them at, their lowest possible levels."

The problem is not that any of these claims was necessarily wrong as a description of conditions that might prevail once zero inflation were achieved but rather that they signaled no recognition whatever of the economic events that, as Ball's careful analysis shows, past experience indicates would be likely to accompany the path to zero inflation from any given beginning point. To be sure, pursuing the goal of price stability is an appropriate, indeed highly important, priority for public policy. But to do so in a disingenuous manner that obscures rather than confronts the broader implications that such a policy entails is likely, in the end, to prove destructive of just those institutions—including, most prominently, central-bank independence—that can best foster that goal.

References

Cagan, Phillip. 1956. The monetary dynamics of hyperinflation. In *Studies in the quality theory of money,* ed. Friedman. Chicago: University of Chicago Press.

Dornbusch, Rudiger. 1990. Two-track EMU, now! In *Britain and EMU,* eds. Pohl et al. London: London School of Economics, Centre for Economic Performance.

Friedman, Benjamin M. 1992. How does it matter? In *The business cycle: Theories and evidence,* eds. Belongia and Garfinkle. Norwell, Mass.: Kluwer Academic Publishers.

Friedman, Milton, and Anna Jacobson Schwartz. 1963. *A monetary history of the United States, 1867–1960.* Princeton, N.J.: Princeton University Press.

Lucas, Robert E., Jr. 1972. Expectations and the neutrality of money. *Journal of Economic Theory* 4 (April): 103–24.

———. 1973. Some international evidence on output-inflation trade-offs. *American Economic Review* 63 (June): 326–44.

Medoff, James. 1992a. The new unemployment. U.S. Congress, Joint Economic Committee. Mimeo.

———. 1992b. Job growth and the reelection of presidents. Harvard University. Mimeo.

Okun, Arthur M. 1978. Efficient disinflationary policies. *American Economic Review* 68 (May): 348–52.

Romer, Christina D., and David H. Romer. 1992. Monetary policy matters. University of California, Berkeley. Mimeo.

Sargent, Thomas J. 1982. The ends of four big inflations. In *Inflation: Causes and effects*, ed. Hall. Chicago: University of Chicago Press.

Sargent, Thomas J., and Neil Wallace. 1975. "Rational" expectations, the optimal monetary instrument, and the optimal money supply rule. *Journal of Political Economy* 83 (April): 241–54.

Comment   Stephen G. Cecchetti

Laurence Ball's paper examining the impact of monetary policy on output and prices relies on several assumptions that I believe need further consideration. The purpose of this Comment is to highlight these assumptions and then show how small changes can have a large impact on certain aspects of the results. While Ball focuses his attention on the cross-sectional correlation of his estimates of the *sacrifice ratio* with various measures of the economic and political environment, I will direct my attention to the prior problem of calculating the impact of monetary policy on output and prices.

I begin with three points that I believe should guide the analysis. First, Ball presumes that information about monetary influences on the economy exists only in regard to the episodes in which inflation is reduced and output falls. This ignores the periods in which inflation increases and output rises. Why aren't we referring to *these* estimates as the "benefit ratio" from increasing inflation? While there may be an inherent asymmetry in the impact of monetary policy on output and prices, it seems unnatural to presume at the outset that there is no information on policy shifts that move toward monetary loosening. As a practical matter, the question of asymmetry is an empirical one. But it would seem that barring any evidence to the contrary, the episodes in which inflation increases should provide as much information as those in which inflation declines.

The second observation regarding Ball's approach is that it depends on the assumed dynamics of output and inflation in the absence of monetary shocks. In computing the output loss from a particular disinflation, Ball makes an assumption about trend output—namely, that it is at its trend level at the beginning of the episode and returns to the trend level four quarters after the episode. He further assumes that inflation reductions that occur during the episode are permanent. Given these two strong assumptions, that trend output is piecewise linear (in logs) and that the inflation process has no autoregressive component, some sensitivity analysis would seem useful. As we know, assumptions about stationarity and detrending often make a substantial difference in calculations of this type.

Stephen G. Cecchetti is professor of economics at The Ohio State University and a research associate of the National Bureau of Economic Research.

The author thanks Anil Kashyap and Robin Lumsdaine for discussions and comments.

My final observation about the Ball calculations concerns his implicit assumptions about the nature of monetary (and real) shocks. Ball assumes that a monetary shock induces the recessions he observes, and that the path of output and inflation declines during each of the episodes he examines are caused solely by the shift to tight money. But in order to measure the impact of monetary policy, we need to identify the policy shocks. This is not an easy task. How is it that we know that aggregate supply shocks are not occurring during these periods? Ball suggests that such shocks create measurement errors in his estimates of the impact of policy on output and inflation, but I believe that the difficulty is more serious.

To see why, let me give a simple example of the type of information we really need to estimate the quantity of interest. Recall that in making his measurements, Ball examines only cases in which inflation and output move in the same direction. To see how this causes problems, take a case in which an adverse supply shock hits the economy. In the absence of any change in monetary policy, there would be a temporary fall in output and a temporary rise in inflation. But in fact, the monetary authority has the option of accommodating the shock. If monetary policy becomes looser, then inflation will rise and output will *fail* to fall. We actually need to identify these shocks to estimate Ball's sacrifice ratio, otherwise we have no idea whether observed output movements are the consequence of monetary policy shifts or of other shocks to the economy.

I now proceed to use these observations to create an estimate of the sacrifice ratio that is based on a structural identification of aggregate demand and aggregate supply shocks. Once I have estimated the responses of output and inflation to these shocks in a dynamic context, I can estimate the impact of a shock using the impulse response functions, and proceed to study its sensitivity to assumptions about the dynamics of output and inflation.

The structural approach addresses my first and third concerns with Ball's methods. First, it uses information about all output and inflation movements, not just inflation declines associated with recessions. Presumably, we obtain information about the impact of aggregate demand policy on output and prices from upturns as well as downturns. In addition, by identifying the shocks explicitly, we make clear the time path of the effects. Most important, we can allow for effects that last far beyond the cyclical trough and take seriously the implication of recent research on the persistence of output fluctuations which suggests that the effect of demand shocks may be quite long-lived. I will then proceed to my second concern and investigate the importance of assumptions about detrending (or differencing) for the results. Ultimately, the question is whether the data actually give us any useful information about the response of output to policy in this context.

Following Blanchard and Quah (1989), I identify and estimate the aggregate demand shock, and hence the sacrifice ratio, by assuming that aggregate demand shocks have no long-run real effects. I study the following model:

(1)
$$(1 - L)y_t = A_{11}(L)u_t + A_{12}(L)v_t$$
$$(1 - L)\pi_t = A_{21}(L)u_t + A_{22}(L)v_t,$$

where y is the log of output, π is inflation, u is an aggregate supply shock, v is an aggregate demand shock, and the $A_{ij}(L)$s are polynomials in the lag operator L. For the moment, I am assuming that inflation and output are both stationary in first differences. The innovations in (1) are assumed to be i.i.d. and uncorrelated contemporaneously. The Blanchard-Quah restriction that the aggregate demand shocks have no long-run effect on output implies that the long-run effect of v on y is zero, and so $A_{12}(1) = 0$.

Using (1) I can compute the impact of an innovation to v_t on both inflation and the level of output. For inflation, the impact of a unit innovation to v, over a horizon τ, is just the sum of the coefficients in $A_{22}(L)$:

(2)
$$\frac{\Delta\pi}{\Delta v} = \sum_{i=0}^{\tau} a_{22}^i,$$

where a_{22}^i is the coefficient on L^i in $A_{22}(L)$. The impact of v on the *level* of output can be computed from the coefficients in $A_{12}(L)$ as

(3)
$$\frac{\Delta y}{\Delta v} \sum_{i=0}^{\tau} \sum_{j=0}^{i} a_{12}^i.$$

The relative impact of monetary policy on output and inflation is just the ratio of these:

(4)
$$S_v(\tau) = \frac{\Delta y}{\Delta\pi} = \frac{\displaystyle\sum_{i=0}^{\tau}\sum_{j=0}^{i} a_{12}^i}{\displaystyle\sum_{i=0}^{\tau} a_{22}^i}$$

The estimated effect of monetary policy in (4) depends on the assumptions about the degree of differencing necessary to induce stationarity in output and inflation, as well as the horizon τ. To see why, consider the value of $S_v(\tau)$ in the limit as τ tends toward infinity. For the case in (1), where both π and y are assumed to be I(1), the impact of a shock on the level of both inflation and output will be permanent and will tend to some constant. It immediately follows that the cumulative impact of the shock in (3) will become infinite, while the impact on inflation will be finite, and so $\lim_{\tau\to\infty} S_v(\tau)$ will go to infinity.

Alternatively, if we assume that inflation is I(1), while output is stationary about a deterministic trend, since the Blanchard-Quah identification constrains the impact of an innovation to v to be zero in the long run, the result is that (after redefining S_v appropriately) $\lim_{\tau\to\infty} S_v(\tau) = 0$.

This implies that it only makes sense to examine cases in which the horizon is relatively short—I will look at five years. In addition, since the experiment in which Ball is interested is one in which inflation is permanently reduced, it makes no sense to study the case in which inflation is stationary in levels. If one were to assume that π_t were mean-reverting, then by assumption no shock is capable of reducing inflation, and the denominator of S_v would always tend toward zero.

Following in this spirit, I have estimated the value of S_v using the Blanchard-Quah identification, setting τ equal to five years, and approximating the restriction that $A_{12}(1) = 0$ by assuming that the v shocks die out completely after twenty years. Table 5C.1 reports the results for Ball's quarterly data set, which includes GDP or GNP for Australia, Canada, France, Germany, Italy, Japan, Switzerland, the United Kingdom, and the United States. The values in the table should be interpreted as the cumulative output loss experienced during a one-percentage-point decline in inflation. I study two cases, one in which inflation and output are both difference stationary, and another in which I assume that π_t is I(1) while y_t is I(0).

The estimates in table 5C.1 can be compared to those in Ball's table 5.1. Of

Table 5C.1   **Estimates of the Impact of Nominal Shocks on Output and Inflation (cumulative five-year loss in gross domestic product per percentage-point decline in inflation)**

	Cumulative Loss in Percent	
	y_t is I(0)	y_t is I(1)
Australia	0.08	−2.21
59:3–92:3	(1.99)	(4.92)
Canada	1.60	5.69
57:1–92:3	(2.25)	(4.74)
France	−0.76	−3.43
70:1–92:2	(1.31)	(5.50)
Germany	−1.42	8.90
60:1–92:2	(4.17)	(8.85)
Italy	0.68	2.33
60:1–92:1	(1.03)	(1.27)
Japan	−2.62	12.89
57:1–91:1	(4.09)	(7.94)
Switzerland	0.22	−2.23
70:1–92:3	(1.23)	(3.21)
United Kingdom	−0.27	1.45
57:1–92:2	(1.21)	(1.56)
United States	−0.52	8.36
59:1–92:4	(2.30)	(4.32)

Note: Standard errors are in parentheses. The standard errors are computed from the outer product of the numerical derivative of $S_v(\tau)$ with respect to the parameters, including the covariance matrix of v and u, with the covariance matrix estimated by GMM on the exactly identified system. For all of the calculations the vector moving average representation of the VAR is truncated at eighty quarters, so I assume that aggregate demand shocks die out after twenty years. Data are quarterly, from the International Monetary Fund's *International Financial Statistics.* All data are GDP, except for Germany and Japan, for which they are GNP.

the twenty-eight episodes Ball identifies, all fall well into two standard errors of the estimates calculated using my method, and a comparison of the magnitudes suggests that Ball's calculations are much closer to the ones which assume output is stationary. But the main point of the results is that the estimates are both very imprecise and dramatically different depending on the assumption about stationarity. For the United States, for example, the point estimate of the sacrifice ratio is 8.36 if output is I(1), but -0.52 if output is assumed to be I(0). (Keep in mind that as the horizon τ increases, the estimates of $S_y[\tau]$ increase without bound when y_t is I[1]). Furthermore, none of the estimates differ from zero at standard levels of statistical significance. This leads me to conclude that we know very little about the actual size of the impact of policy shocks on output, and so attempts to explain fluctuations in these numbers are unlikely to yield any convincing evidence.

I have one final comment that relates to the nature of the question being posed and how the answer is calculated. This is a more basic conceptual issue. As is clear from equation (4), the calculation of the sacrifice ratio uses the sum of the undiscounted changes in output over some horizon. It seems strange to me to add these things up in this way. Instead, I would suggest that we do something analogous to a cost-benefit analysis of inflation.

From the time path of the output and inflation changes implied by the structural vector autoregression (VAR), and an assumed discount rate, I can compute the present value of the output loss associated with a one-percentage-point decline in inflation. I can then ask what the benefit of this disinflation must be for it to be worth incurring the cost. Since the inflation decline is permanent, we can calculate the necessary inflation benefit, as a percentage of GDP per year forever, that would be needed for us to be willing to pay the output costs. This estimated benefit can then be compared to estimates of the costs of steady inflation.

For the simple case implied by equation (1), we can write this as follows. Assuming that the discount factor (measured at the same frequency as the data) is given by β, then the discounted value of the output loss—the cost—is just

$$(5) \qquad PDV(y) = \sum_{i=0}^{\infty} \beta^i \sum_{j=0}^{i} a^i_{12}.$$

This must be balanced against the inflation reduction. Calling ß the "benefit" of reducing inflation by one percentage point (measured as a percentage of one-year's GDP), we can write the benefit as

$$(6) \qquad PDV(\pi) = ß\left(\sum_{i=0}^{\infty} \beta^i \sum_{j=0}^{i} a^i_{22}\right).$$

Equating $PDV(y)$ to $PDV(\pi)$, I can solve for ß. If one percentage point of steady inflation reduces output by more than ß percent, then it is worth paying the cost to eliminate it. (This calculation has the advantage of getting rid of the need to truncate the sums in order to keep the quantities of interest finite.)

This is a simple calculation, and for the U.S. case, using an annual discount rate of 2 percent, I estimate that the output costs of disinflation equal the benefits of lower inflation when each percentage point of steady inflation has a cost, ß, of 9.05 percent (standard error = 4.86) of a year's GDP! In other words, if one percentage point of inflation costs 9.05 percent or more of GDP per year forever, then it is worth paying the price to reduce it. The reason for this high point estimate is that with this specification the output costs and the inflation benefits both last forever. But again, the lack of precision of the estimate renders it virtually useless.

To conclude, my argument is that in order to even estimate the impact of monetary shocks on output—Ball's sacrifice ratio—we require a structural model in which such shocks are identified. An important element of such a model is a set of assumptions about the time-series properties of output, inflation, and the shocks. After examining one specific model, my conclusion is that the available data are unlikely to yield a convincing set of estimates.

Reference

Blanchard, Olivier J., and Danny Quah. 1989. The dynamic effects of aggregate demand and supply disturbances. *American Economic Review* 79 (September): 655–73.

6   Measuring Core Inflation

Michael F. Bryan and Stephen G. Cecchetti

Discussions of the goals of monetary policy generally focus on the benefits of price and output stabilization. After formulating a loss function that weights these two objectives, the next step is to examine different policy programs and operating procedures in order to achieve the desired outcomes.

But these discussions take for granted our ability to measure the objects of interest, namely, aggregate price inflation and the level of output. Unfortunately, the measurement of aggregate inflation as a monetary phenomenon is difficult, as nonmonetary events, such as sector-specific shocks and measurement errors, can temporarily produce noise in the price data that substantially affects the aggregate price indices at higher frequencies. During periods of poor weather, for example, food prices may rise to reflect decreased supply, thereby producing transitory increases in the aggregate index. Because these price changes do not constitute underlying monetary inflation, the monetary authorities should avoid basing their decisions on them.

Solutions to the problem of high-frequency noise in the price data include calculating low-frequency trends over which this noise is reduced. But from a policymaker's perspective, this greatly reduces the timeliness, and therefore

Michael F. Bryan is economic advisor at the Federal Reserve Bank of Cleveland. Stephen G. Cecchetti is professor of economics at The Ohio State University and a research associate of the National Bureau of Economic Research.

The authors thank Laurence Ball, Ben Bernanke, Giuseppe Bertola, Alan Blinder, John Campbell, William Gavin, Robin Lumsdaine, N. Gregory Mankiw, James Powell, John Roberts, Alan Stockman, Alan Viard, Stephen Zeldes, the conference participants, and anonymous referees and seminar participants at Boston College, New York University, Princeton University, the University of Pennsylvania, and Wilfrid Laurier University, for comments and suggestions. In addition, they thank Edward Bryden and Christopher Pike for research assistance, Robin Ratliff for editorial assistance, and Michael Galka for the artwork. The views stated herein are those of the authors and not necessarily those of the Federal Reserve Bank of Cleveland or of the Board of Governors of the Federal Reserve System.

the relevance, of the incoming data. Another common technique for measuring the underlying or *core* component of inflation excludes certain prices in the computation of the index based on the assumption that these are the ones with high-variance noise components. This is the "ex. food and energy" strategy, where the existing index is reweighted by placing zero weights on some components, and the remaining weights are rescaled.

As an alternative to the consumer price index (CPI) excluding food and energy, Bryan and Pike (1991) suggest computing median inflation across a number of individual prices. This approach is motivated by their observation that individual price series (components of the CPI) tend to exhibit substantial skewness, a fact also noted by Ball and Mankiw (1992), among others.[1]

In this paper, we show that a version of Ball and Mankiw's (1992) model of price-setting implies that core inflation can be measured by a limited-influence estimator, such as the median of the cross-sectional distribution of individual product price inflation first suggested by Bryan and Pike (1991). In the simplest form of the model, price setters face a one-time cross-sectional shock and can pay a menu cost to adjust their price to it immediately. Those firms that choose not to change prices in response to the shock can do so at the beginning of the next "period." Only those price setters whose shocks were large will choose to change, and as a result, when the distribution of shocks is skewed, the mean price level will move temporarily—for example, positive skewness results in a transitory increase in inflation. This structure captures the intuition that the types of shocks that cause problems with price measurement are infrequent and that these shocks tend to be concentrated, at least initially, in certain sectors of the economy.

Removing these transitory elements from the aggregate index can be done easily. The problem is that when the distribution of sector-specific shocks is skewed, the tails of the distribution of resulting price changes will no longer average out properly. This implies that we should not use the mean of price changes to calculate the persistent component of aggregate inflation. Instead, a more accurate measure of the central tendency of the inflation distribution can be calculated by removing the tails of the cross-sectional distribution. This leads us to calculate trimmed means, which are limited-influence estimators that average only the central part of a distribution after truncating the outlying points. The median, which is the focus of much of our work below, is one estimator in this class.

The remainder of this paper is divided into four parts. Section 6.1 provides a brief discussion of the conceptual issues surrounding the measurement of core inflation. We describe a simple model and examine some evidence suggesting that shocks of the type discussed in Ball and Mankiw are likely to affect measured inflation at short horizons of one year or less. Section 6.2 reports estimates of the (weighted) median and a trimmed mean, both calcu-

1. Vining and Elwertowski (1976) discuss this fact at some length.

lated from thirty-six components of the CPI over a sample beginning in February 1967 and ending in December 1992. Section 6.3 presents evidence as to whether our measures conform to a key implication of Ball and Mankiw's view. Differences between core inflation and movements in the CPI should reflect aggregate supply shocks and, to the extent that they are accommodated, should be related to future growth in output. By contrast, core inflation itself should not forecast money growth. We find that these predictions are borne out for the median CPI.

In section 6.4, we examine some additional properties of our estimates, including their ability to forecast inflation at horizons of three to five years. While inflation is very difficult to predict, we find that the core measure based on the weighted-median forecasts future inflation better than either the CPI excluding food and energy or the all items CPI. We conclude this section with the presentation of actual predictions of future inflation. Using our preferred specification, we find that inflation is expected to average approximately 2⅔ percent per year for the five years ending in December 1997.

The final section of the paper offers our conclusions. Briefly, we are encouraged by the performance of the weighted median. Because it is both easy to calculate and simple to explain, we believe that it can be a useful and timely guide for inflation policy.

6.1   Defining Core Inflation

While the term *core inflation* enjoys widespread common use, it appears to have no clear definition.[2] In general, when people use the term they seem to have in mind the long-run, or persistent, component of the measured price index, which is tied in some way to money growth. But a clear definition of core inflation necessarily requires a model of how prices and money are determined in the economy. Any such formal structure is difficult to formulate and easy to criticize, so we will proceed with a simple example that we believe captures much of what underlies existing discussions.[3]

Our goal here is to use existing data on prices to extract a measure of money-induced inflation: that is, the component of price changes that is expected to persist over medium-run horizons of several years. To see how this might be done, assume that we can think of the economy as being composed of two

2. Early attempts to define core inflation can be found in Eckstein (1981) and Blinder (1982).

3. The main conceptual problem in defining core inflation can be described as follows. Any macroeconomic model will imply some quasi-reduced form in which inflation depends on a weighted average of past money growth and past permanent and transitory "shocks." If money were truly exogenous, one could measure core inflation by estimating this reduced form and then looking only at the portion of inflation that is due to past money growth and the permanent component of the shocks. But in reality, money growth responds to the shocks themselves, so measuring the long-run trend in prices requires estimating the monetary reaction function. In fact, this suggests that measuring core inflation necessitates that we identify monetary shocks as well as the shocks to which money is responding.

kinds of price setters. The first have flexible prices in the sense that they set their prices every period in response to realized changes in the economy. The second group of price setters set their prices infrequently, and face potentially high costs of readjustment.[4] These price setters are the familiar contracting agents of the New Keynesian theory, who set their prices both to correct for past unexpected events and in anticipation of future trends in the economy. From the point of view of measuring inflation, we might think of the first group, the realization-based price setters, as creating noise in inflation measured using existing price indices, as their price paths can exhibit large transitory fluctuations. Because they can change their prices quickly and often, these firms have little reason to care about the long-run trends in aggregate inflation or money growth.

By comparison, the expectations-based price setters have substantially smoother price paths, since they cannot correct mistakes quickly and at low cost. Our view is that the expectations-based price setters actually have information about the quantity we want to measure. If we knew who these people were, we could just go out and measure their prices. But since we do not, we must adopt a strategy in which we try to infer core inflation from the data we have.

A simple model of our view of price-setting behavior draws on Ball and Mankiw's study of the skewness of the distribution of price changes and its relationship to aggregate supply shocks. They examine price-setting as a single-period problem that can be described as follows. Each firm in the economy adjusts its price at the beginning of each period, taking into account anticipated future developments. Following this initial adjustment, each firm is then subjected to a mean zero shock and can pay a menu cost to change its price a second time. Only some firms will experience shocks that are large enough to make the second adjustment worthwhile. As a result, the observed change in the aggregate price level will depend on the shape of the distribution of idiosyncratic shocks. In particular, if the shock distribution is skewed, the aggregate price level will move up or down temporarily.

We concentrate here on a single-period problem in order to highlight the fact that we are interested in the impact of infrequent shocks. In effect, we are presuming that at the beginning of the single period under study, all price setters have completed their responses to the last disturbance of this type. This is really an assumption about the calendar time length of the model's "period." Some evidence of this is provided below.

To make the model a bit more specific, assume that the economy is composed of a large number of firms, that trend output growth is normalized to zero, and that velocity is constant.[5] Furthermore, take money growth ($\dot{m}$) to be

---

4. Different firms will fall into these two groups for a number of reasons. We would expect, for example, that the flexible-price group will be composed of firms with some combination of low costs of price adjustment and high variance of shocks.

5. In this simple framework, we are not able to address the problems created by transitory velocity shocks.

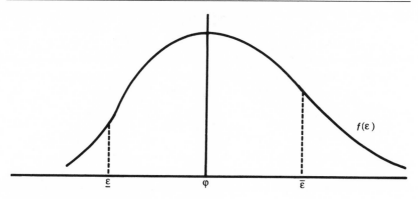

Fig. 6.1   Distribution of relative price shocks

exogenously determined and given by a known constant (although this is not necessary). Under these conditions, each firm will initially choose to change its price by $\dot{m}$, and aggregate inflation will equal monetary inflation. It follows that we can define core inflation as

$$(1) \qquad\qquad \pi^c = \dot{m}.$$

If we were to further assume that money growth follows a random walk, then π^c would be the best forecast of future inflation.[6]

Following this initial price-setting exercise, each firm experiences a shock, ε_i, to either its production costs or its product demand. The distribution of these shocks, $f(\varepsilon_i)$, has some arbitrary shape, such as the one drawn in figure 6.1. If each firm were to reset its prices following the realization of the ε_i's instead of before, they would have changed them by

$$(2) \qquad\qquad \pi_i = \dot{m} + \varepsilon_i.$$

But this is no longer possible without paying a menu cost. As a consequence, only firms with large $|\varepsilon_i|$ will choose to change again. With further structure on the problem, it would be possible to calculate the critical values of ε_i that lead to this action.[7] For purposes of exposition, we assume that all firms face the same menu costs, and thus will all have the same threshold values for ε. These are labeled $\underline{\varepsilon}$ and $\bar{\varepsilon}$ in figure 6.1. It is only those firms with $\bar{\varepsilon} < \varepsilon_i < \underline{\varepsilon}$ that will change their prices. (These thresholds will differ with the cost of price adjustment, and so, in general, they will differ across firms.)

We can now examine the resulting distribution of observed price changes. First, all of the firms that chose not to act based on the realized shocks will

6. The level of core inflation will also be the level of inflation at which actual output, y, equals the natural rate, y^*. Any deviations of inflation from π^c will result in changes in real money balances and move y away from y^*. A simple interpretation of this definition is that we are attempting to measure the point at which the current level of aggregate demand intersects the long-run (vertical) aggregate supply curve.

7. See Ball and Mankiw (1992), section III, for an example.

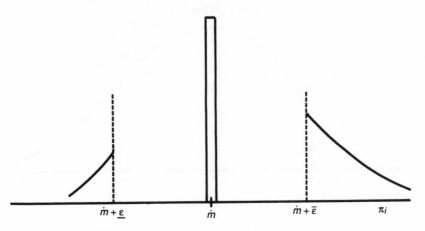

$$\dot{m}+\underline{\varepsilon} \qquad \dot{m} \qquad \dot{m}+\bar{\varepsilon} \qquad \pi_i$$

Fig. 6.2   Distribution of nominal price changes

have changed their prices by $\dot{m}$. This results in a spike in the cross-sectional price-change distribution. On the other hand, the firms that did pay the menu cost and adjusted to the shock will have nominal price changes that are in the tails above and below this spike. The result is pictured in figure 6.2.

In computing aggregate observed inflation, π, we would naturally average over all of the prices in the economy. When the distribution of ε_i is symmetrical, this yields $\pi = \pi^c = \dot{m}$. But when the distribution of shocks is skewed, observed inflation is not going to equal π^c. In fact, π will be greater than or less than π^c depending on whether $f(\varepsilon_i)$ is positive or negatively skewed.[8]

Because our goal is to measure π^c from the available price data, this simple analysis leads us to an estimate that can be computed directly from the data. Instead of averaging over the entire cross-sectional distribution of price changes, consider trimming the distribution by averaging only the central part of the density. From figure 6.2 it is clear that if we average the central portion of the distribution—in the example this is the spike at $\dot{m}$—then we obtain an accurate estimate of π_c. As a result, we are led to compute limited-influence estimates of inflation, such as the median. These estimators are calculated by trimming the outlying portions of the cross-sectional distribution of the component parts of aggregate price indices.

The results of this simple example suggest that we examine the median, but the model is extremely specific. The implications of the analysis certainly remain valid if we assume that the shocks under consideration are infrequent and

8. The impact of the shape of $f(\varepsilon_i)$ lasts for at least two periods. To see this, note that at the beginning of the period following a shock, when all of the Ball-Mankiw price setters have the opportunity to adjust again, the relationship between measured and core inflation will depend on the distribution of shocks in the past period. When $f(\varepsilon_i)$ is positively skewed, current-period inflation will be above core inflation, while in the period following the shock, measured inflation will be below core inflation.

that the economy has fully adjusted to the last one by the time the next one arrives. But if shocks of this type arrive every period, then we need to consider a multiple-period dynamic model, one that is substantially more difficult.[9] A completely satisfactory presentation would incorporate staggered price-setting explicitly, and the results are likely to imply more complex time-dependent and parametric measures of core inflation.[10] Nevertheless, we feel that the intuition we gain from this exercise is useful, and that it guides us to explore a new estimator for inflation that is easy to calculate.

There is a way to use the available price information to estimate the frequency—that is, every month, once per year, etc.—at which these difficulties are likely to arise. To see how this can be done, rewrite equation (2) with time subscripts, and replace money growth with average aggregate inflation:

(3) $$\pi_{it} = \pi_t + \varepsilon_{it}.$$

Now consider measuring average per period inflation in each sector over a horizon of K periods. Using (3), we can write this as

(4) $$\pi_{it}^K = \sum_{j=1}^K \pi_{i,t+j} = \pi_t^K + \frac{1}{K}\sum_{j=1}^K \varepsilon_{i,t+j},$$

where π_t^K is average aggregate inflation per-period over the K-period horizon. Next, examine the distribution of π_{it}^K, computed cross-sectionally over the sectors. If the skewness disappears as K increases, this suggests that there is a horizon at which the problems caused by the asymmetric shocks disappear.

Using data on thirty-six components of the all urban consumers CPI (seasonally adjusted by the Bureau of Labor Statistics) from February 1967 through December 1992, and measuring inflation as the change in the natural log of the price level, we have computed the cross-sectional skewness in the price change distribution using overlapping data for K going from one to forty-eight months.[11] Throughout, we define inflation as the change in the log of the price index level. The results are reported in table 6.1. We have conducted a Monte Carlo experiment in order to determine if a particular level of skewness is surprising. Using the null that each sector's relative price change is drawn from a normal distribution with mean zero, and variance equal to the uncondi-

9. We have examined a simple multiple-period version of the Ball and Mankiw model, and find that as long as the shocks are temporally independent, the price-change distribution remains bunched at $\dot{m}$, but the bias in the mean depends on the change in the skewness, rather than its level—for example, the bias is positive when the skewness increases. While this may seem disappointing at first, there is empirical evidence that skewness changes substantially over time (see, for example, Ball and Mankiw's table II).

10. While such measures will have the advantage of being grounded in a more realistic structural model, they are likely to have the disadvantage of requiring imposition of a time-invariant stochastic structure on the data. Such methods are always vulnerable to the standard critiques.

11. The data set was chosen so that there would be a reasonably large number of component series, and at the same time we retain complete coverage of the components in the index. Skewness is calculated using the 1985 fixed expenditure weights.

Table 6.1   Frequency Distribution of Skewness (computed using overlapping observations of K months)

K	Average of Skewness	Percent Rejected at			
		1%	5%	10%	20%
1	0.346	0.09	0.15	0.19	0.39
3	0.348	0.05	0.09	0.16	0.34
6	0.230	0.03	0.09	0.14	0.30
9	0.253	0.02	0.08	0.13	0.24
12	0.239	0.02	0.06	0.10	0.28
24	0.171	0.00	0.03	0.07	0.26
36	0.029	0.00	0.01	0.03	0.14
48	−0.070	0.00	0.00	0.02	0.14

Note: Frequency distribution is computed from the percentiles of the skewness distribution based on ten thousand draws of 36 $N(0, \sigma_i^2)$ variates, weighted by the 1985 consumer price index weights. The variance, σ_i^2, is set equal to the unconditional time-series variance of inflation in each of the components in the data computed for each value of K.

tional variance of that sector's K-period price changes over the entire sample, we compute the empirical distribution of the skewness for ten thousand draws. The results are then used to evaluate the observed skewness in the data. The calculations in table 6.1 show clearly that at frequencies of twelve months or shorter, some periods have substantial skewness in the price change distribution.[12] From this we conclude that the problems in inflation measures that we wish to eliminate exist at frequencies of one year and perhaps longer.[13]

It is important to note that the definition of core inflation as the rate of money growth presumes that there is no monetary accommodation. In order to derive these very simple results, we have assumed that $\dot{m}$ does not depend in any way on the ε's. As such, we are proposing a measure of core inflation that forecasts the level of future inflation in the absence of monetary response to supply shocks.

We conclude this discussion with two additional remarks about the median and related estimators. First, the computation of a limited-influence estimator from the cross-sectional distribution of price changes each period has a number of potential advantages over standard methods. In particular, measures such as the median are robust to the presence of many types of noise. For example, to the extent that some price-change observations contain a combination of sampling measurement errors and actual price-setting mistakes, both of which are likely to be short-lived, this noise creates misleading movements in the

12. These results are sensitive to the specific assumptions about the heteroskedasticity of the shock distributions. For example, if we were to assume that all the relative price shocks were drawn from the same normal distribution, then we would continue to observe a substantial number of large values for the skewness until K equals seventy-two months.

13. We note, but cannot explain, the fact that as K becomes large, the observed distribution is becoming more concentrated than the empirical distribution would suggest.

aggregate index only when it is far from the central tendency of the distribution. Estimating a trimmed mean or a median will downweight the importance of this effect and result in a more robust measure of inflation. In addition, calculation of the median is a natural way to protect against problems such as the energy price increases of the 1970s—we do not need to know which sector will be subjected to the next large shock.

Finally, calculation of the median can give us additional information about price-setting behavior in the sectors covered by the indices we study. In particular, we can count how often a particular good is in the middle of the cross-sectional distribution. If the median good were selected randomly each month, this sample frequency would equal the unconditional probability of the good being the median good. Sample probabilities above or below the unconditional probability suggest that a sector is dominated by either expectations-based, inertial behavior or by realization-based, auction behavior.

6.2   Estimates of Core Inflation

Using the data on the CPI described above, we now examine various measures of inflation. We compute two trimmed means using the fixed 1985 CPI weights as measures of the number of prices in each category. In other words, in computing the histogram for inflation in each month, we assume that the weight represents the percentage of the distribution of all prices that experienced that amount of inflation. We report results for the weighted median and for a 15 percent trimmed mean. The median is measured as the central point, as implied by the CPI expenditure weights, in the cross-sectional histogram of inflation each month. The 15 percent trimmed mean is computed by averaging the central 85 percent of the price-change distribution each month. Obviously, we could report results for an index computed by trimming any arbitrary percentage of the tails of the distribution. We have chosen 15 percent because it has the smallest monthly variance of all trimmed estimators of this type.[14]

Table 6.2 reports the summary statistics for the all items CPI, the CPI excluding food and energy, the weighted median, and the 15 percent trimmed mean. As one would expect, the variance of the core measures is substantially lower than that of the CPI measures. In fact, the standard deviation of the median and the 15 percent trimmed mean are both on the order of 25 percent less than that of the total CPI, and 10 percent less than that of the CPI excluding food and energy. Furthermore, all of the series show substantial persistence, although the standard Dickey-Fuller test fails to reject stationarity in all of the series (the 10 percent critical value is -3.12).[15]

14. The 15 percent trimmed mean also has the highest first-order autocorrelation of all the trimmed estimators.

15. The results of testing for a unit root in inflation are extremely sensitive to the sample period chosen. Using data from 1960 to 1989, for example, Ball and Cecchetti (1990) model inflation as nonstationary.

Table 6.2   **Comparison of Various Measures of Inflation, 1967:2 to 1992:12 (computed from monthly data measured at annual rates)**

	All Items Consumer Price Index	Consumer Price Index Excluding Food and Energy	Weighted Median	15% Trimmed Mean
Mean	5.67	5.71	5.64	5.56
Standard deviation	3.79	3.25	2.95	2.86
1st-order autocorrelation	0.64	0.60	0.68	0.76
Dickey-Fuller (24)[a]	−2.85	−2.59	−2.44	−2.46
	Correlation Matrix			
All items Consumer price index	1.00	0.73	0.75	0.84
Consumer price index excluding food and energy	0.73	1.00	0.80	0.87
Weighted median	0.75	0.80	1.00	0.93
15% trimmed mean	0.84	0.87	0.93	1.00

[a]Dickey-Fuller tests are based on examining the coefficient on the lagged price level in the regression given by $\Delta p_t = a + bp_{t-1} + \sum_{i=1}^{k} c_i \Delta p_{t-i} + v_t$, where p is the log of the price level, Δp is the first difference in the log of the price (inflation), v is a random error, and the remaining terms are parameters. The null hypothesis is that the log of the price level (p_t) has a unit root, namely, that $b = 0$. (See Dickey and Fuller 1981.) The reported results, for $k = 24$, are unaffected by setting $k = 12$.

Figure 6.3 presents a plot of the twelve-month lagged moving average of each of the series—an observation plotted at date t is the sum of monthly inflation from $t - 11$ months through t. The graph reveals a number of interesting patterns in the core measures, in addition to demonstrating how they are less variable. First, both the median and the 15 percent trimmed mean show lower peaks. Furthermore, the core measures display substantially lower inflation than either the all items CPI or the CPI excluding food and energy during the high-inflation period of 1979 to 1981. Finally, the results clearly demonstrate that the low inflation of 1986 was largely the consequence of transitory shocks to relative prices.

As we mentioned at the end of section 6.1, the sample frequency a good is at the median provides us with interesting information about the nature of price-setting in various sectors. Table 6.3 reports the unconditional probability of each good being the median together with the sample probability that the good is the median. The unconditional probability of a good being the median cannot be computed in a simple analytic way. Instead, we calculate the quantity of interest using a Monte Carlo experiment in which we draw 1.5 million random sample orderings and tabulate the frequency each good is at the median.

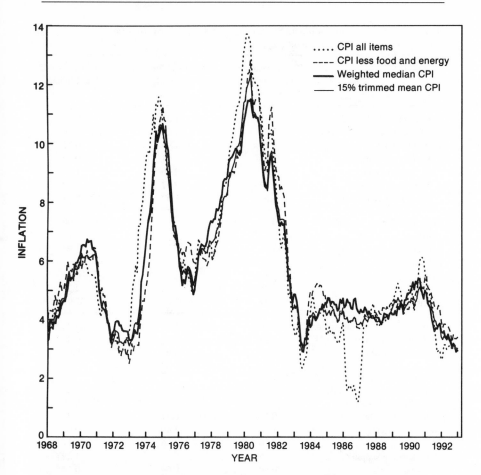

Fig. 6.3   Comparison of inflation measures (twelve-month moving averages, 1968 to 1992)

The results show several intriguing properties.[16] The most striking is that the shelter component of the index, with an unconditional probability of 37.01 percent (the CPI weight is 27.89), is the median good 47.04 percent of the time. Food away from home (unconditional probability = 5.42, sample frequency = 9.65) and medical care services plus commodities (unconditional probability = 5.89, sample frequency = 9.65) are also in the center of the distribution more often than random chance suggests they should be. All of these

16. The results are the same for both the 1967 to 1979 sample period and the 1980 to 1992 sample period.

Table 6.3   **Unconditional Probability and Sample Frequency for Median Good (%)**

Description	1985 Consumer Price Index Weight	Unconditional Probability Good Is at Median	Frequency Good Is at Median
Cereals and bakery products	1.43	1.22	0.96
Meats, poultry, fish, and eggs	3.03	2.63	0.96
Dairy products	1.23	1.05	0.32
Fruits and vegetables	1.85	1.61	0.32
Other food at home	2.38	2.06	1.93
Total food at home	**9.92**	**8.57**	**4.49**
Food away from home	**6.08**	**5.42**	**9.65**
Fuel oil and other household fuels	0.42	0.36	0.00
Gas and electricity (energy services)	3.64	3.20	1.93
Motor fuel	3.30	2.88	0.32
Total energy	**7.36**	**6.44**	**2.25**
Shelter	**27.89**	**37.01**	**47.91**
Medical care commodities	1.26	1.09	3.22
Medical care services	5.43	4.80	6.43
Total medical care	**6.69**	**5.89**	**9.65**
Men's and boys' apparel	1.45	1.27	0.96
Women's and girls' apparel	2.52	2.21	2.25
Infant and toddler apparel	0.22	0.19	0.00
Other apparel commodities	0.55	0.47	0.32
Alcoholic beverages	1.62	1.40	0.64
House furnishings	3.70	3.26	1.61
Housekeeping supplies	1.15	0.99	1.29
Footwear	0.80	0.69	0.64
New vehicles	5.03	4.44	4.18
Used cars	1.13	0.98	1.29
Other private transportation commodities	0.68	0.59	0.00
Entertainment commodities	2.03	1.76	0.64
Tobacco and smoking products	1.66	1.43	0.96
Toilet goods and personal care appliances	0.63	0.55	0.32
Schoolbooks and supplies	0.24	0.21	0.00
Total other commodities	**23.41**	**20.44**	**15.10**
Apparel services	0.56	0.48	0.32
Housekeeping services	1.47	1.26	1.29
Auto maintenance and repair	1.52	1.33	1.29
Other private transportation services	3.85	3.41	1.93
Public transportation	1.49	1.27	0.00

Table 6.3   (continued)

Description	1985 Consumer Price Index Weight	Unconditional Probability Good Is at Median	Frequency Good Is at Median
Entertainment services	2.33	2.02	1.61
Personal care services	0.55	0.49	0.64
Personal and education services	3.58	3.13	2.89
Other utilities and public services	3.27	2.85	0.96
Total other services	**18.62**	**16.24**	**10.93**

Note: Calculations use thirty-six components of the consumer price index (CPI), monthly from February 1967 to December 1992. Unconditional Probability Good Is at Median is calculated from a Monte Carlo experiment with 1.5 million draws using the 1985 CPI weights. Frequency Good Is at Median simply counts the number of months a particular good is the median good, and divides by the total number of months. Sums of unconditional probabilities are estimates assuming independence.

are markets in which long-term contracts or customer relationships are important.[17]

The results in table 6.3 also shed some light on the practice of excluding food and energy arbitrarily. We find that both food at home and energy are in the center of the distribution much less frequently than their weights would suggest. If we assume independence and simply sum the probabilities and the sample frequencies, then food at home plus energy has an unconditional probability of 15.01, but the goods in these groups are at the median a total of only 6.74 percent of the time. From this we conclude that if we were to construct an index that removed food and energy components, it would retain "food away from home" and be an "excluding food at home and energy" index.

Our next task is to demonstrate the usefulness of these proposed measures of core inflation and to show that they are superior estimates of money-induced inflation. In the following sections, we examine a series of characteristics of the core measures. First, we study the relationship between money and inflation directly. Then we consider the ability of the alternative price measures to

17. We have also computed the percentage of the months in which each commodity lies in the central half of the cross-sectional distribution, and they are consistent with those reported in the table. If goods were ordered randomly, then a component with weight w_i should appear in the middle of the distribution approximately $50 + 2w_i$ percent of the time. Food away from home, with a weight of 6.08, is in the middle 50 percent of the distribution in 82.5 percent of the months of the sample, far more than the 62 percent that would result from random chance. By contrast, the inflation in energy prices and the prices of food at home appear in the center of the distribution far less than half of the time—motor fuel, for example, has a weight of 3.30 and is present in only 14.2 percent of the months.

forecast CPI inflation over long horizons under the assumption that, since supply disturbances affect measured CPI inflation only in the short run, current core inflation should provide useful information about future aggregate price increases.

6.3 Core Inflation and Money Growth

A primary motivation for our study of core inflation is to find a measure that is highly correlated with money growth. To test our success in this endeavor, we first consider the ability of money growth to forecast each of the alternative inflation measures in simple regressions.

A straightforward way of evaluating the relationship between money growth and various measures of inflation employs the following simple regression:

$$(5) \qquad \frac{1}{K}(\ln p^r_{t+K}) - \ln p^r_t = \alpha + \sum_{i=1}^{m} \beta_i \, [\ln M_t - \ln M_{t-i}] + \varepsilon_t,$$

where M is a measure of money.

We look at the ability of the monetary base, M1, and M2 to forecast the average level of inflation over the next one to five years. The results for $m = 24$ months, which are representative, are presented in table 6.4, where we report the R^2's of the regressions (5). The table shows that the past year's money growth is most highly correlated with changes in the weighted median, with the 15 percent trimmed mean a close second.

Next, we conduct a series of Granger-style tests to establish where changes in money growth actually forecast changes in inflation, once we take account of the ability of past inflation to forecast itself. Curiously, previous research has found that tests of this type show that the forecasting relationship (and the direction of causality) between the CPI and money operates in the opposite direction—from inflation to money growth. A recent study by Hoover (1991), for example, provides substantial evidence for this counterintuitive result. We might interpret Hoover's conclusions as suggesting that movements in standard aggregate price indices are dominated by supply disturbances that influence both prices and money. Purging the price statistics of these distortions should reveal the money-to-inflation relationship that is otherwise obscured.

In order to test whether a candidate variable y forecasts x in the Granger sense, we examine the coefficients on x in the regression

$$(6) \qquad y_t = \alpha + \sum_{i=1}^{m} b_i y_{t-i} + \sum_{i=1}^{m} c_i x_{t-i} + u_t.$$

We report results for testing whether all of the c_i's are zero simultaneously. This can be interpreted as a test for whether x forecasts y, once lagged y is taken into account.

Table 6.4   **Forecasting Long-Horizon Inflation with Money Growth (1967:02 to 1992:12)**

Horizon (K)	All Items Consumer Price Index	Consumer Price Index Excluding Food and Energy	Weighted Median	15% Trimmed Mean
		M = Monetary Base		
12	0.16	0.19	0.19	0.18
24	0.16	0.22	0.22	0.21
36	0.13	0.19	0.17	0.17
48	0.07	0.14	0.10	0.10
60	0.03	0.11	0.06	0.06
		M = M1		
12	0.03	0.03	0.04	0.03
24	0.01	0.01	0.01	0.01
36	0.02	0.01	0.03	0.02
48	0.10	0.07	0.11	0.10
60	0.17	0.12	0.18	0.16
		M = M2		
12	0.19	0.12	0.22	0.18
24	0.24	0.23	0.32	0.28
36	0.24	0.27	0.33	0.30
48	0.18	0.25	0.26	0.24
60	0.10	0.16	0.15	0.14

Note: The table reports the R^2 from a regression of twenty-four lags of money growth on inflation over the next K months. See equation (5).

Results for $m = 12$ are presented in table 6.5.[18] These clearly suggest that both M1 and M2 growth forecast core inflation as measured by the weighted median and the 15 percent trimmed mean. But, as we expect, the deviations of actual inflation from the 15 percent trimmed mean and the weighted median both forecast M1, while the weighted median forecasts M2 growth. Unfortunately, the results for the monetary base are less compelling.

While these tests have a number of well-known problems that prevent us from interpreting them as evidence of true causality, we find the results tend to confirm our measures and interpretation. Specifically, the reason that others have found that inflation forecasts money growth appears to be a sign of the monetary accommodation of the aggregate supply shocks that we measure as the deviations of the all items CPI from the core measure. Furthermore, the

18. The results are unaffected by increasing m to 24.

Table 6.5   Tests of Granger-Style Forecasting Ability: Money and Inflation
                   (1967:03 to 1992:06)

	Monetary Base		M1		M2	
Inflation Measure	M to π	π to M	M to π	π to M	M to π	π to M
All items consumer price index	0.13	0.57	0.72	0.03	0.34	0.00
Consumer price index excluding food and energy	0.05	0.53	0.01	0.03	0.03	0.04
Weighted median	0.11	0.34	0.01	0.18	0.00	0.30
15% trimmed mean	0.35	0.36	0.01	0.05	0.00	0.11
Consumer price index-2	0.15	0.62	0.18	0.24	0.36	0.06
Consumer price index-3	0.19	0.91	0.39	0.00	0.25	0.05
Consumer price index-4	0.28	0.96	0.37	0.04	0.52	0.15

Note: Values are p-values for Granger F-tests.

fact that core inflation is forecast by money growth, but does not itself forecast money growth, suggests a measure of inflation that is in some sense tied to monetary policy.

6.4   Forecasting CPI Inflation

It is typically difficult to forecast medium- and long-term inflation in either a univariate or multivariate setting. Nevertheless, we set out to examine the ability of these different price measures to forecast actual inflation over horizons of one to five years. In this section we proceed in two related directions. First, we study univariate forecasts of CPI inflation over horizons of one to five years. The univariate forecasts reported in section 6.4.1 show that recent core inflation does a slightly better job than inflation in either the all items CPI or the CPI excluding food and energy. Section 6.4.2 examines the marginal forecasting power of core inflation when it is added to a multivariate equation including money, output, and interest rates with essentially the same result.

6.4.1   Univariate Methods

The results in section 6.1, table 6.1 suggest that short-run problems in measurement of aggregate inflation are likely to disappear over horizons of one year or more. This suggests that the all items CPI provides an accurate measure of inflation over longer horizons and thus is useful as a benchmark for forecasting inflation. Using equation (4), we identify the object of interest as

$$(7) \qquad \Pi_t^K = \frac{1}{K}[\ln(\text{CPI}_{t+K}) - \ln(\text{CPI}_t)],$$

where K might indicate one, two, or three years.

If we were simply interested in constructing the best estimate of Π_t^K possible, then we could continue in a number of directions, such as constructing a multivariate vector autoregression. But since our main interest is in the informativeness of the measures of core inflation, we proceed slightly differently.[19] Restricting ourselves to price data alone, we examine our alternative measures of inflation and see which of them forecasts Π_t^K best. To do this, consider the following simple regression of the average CPI inflation at horizon K on inflation in a candidate index over the previous year:

$$(8) \qquad \Pi_t^K = \alpha + \beta(\ln p_t^r - \ln p_{t-12}^r) + \varepsilon_t^K,$$

where p^r is the one of the four indices: all items CPI, CPI excluding food and energy, the weighted median, and the 15 percent trimmed mean. We provide two sets of comparisons. In the first, we estimate (8) from monthly data through December 1979 and then use the fitted regression to forecast from January 1980 through the end of the sample (which will vary depending on the choice of the horizon K).[20] The second exercise examines the forecast error when the forecast is simply cumulative inflation over the prior twelve months. We report results for this naive rule over the entire available sample.

Table 6.6 reports the root mean square errors for each of these forecasting exercises, along with summary statistics for Π_t^K.[21] The results suggest two conclusions. First, we confirm the general impression that it is difficult to forecast inflation. For horizons of two years or longer over the sample beginning in 1980, the root mean square errors of the forecasts are more than half the mean of the series being forecast.

Second, the core measures provide the best forecasts at long horizons. Among the alternatives, the weighted median yields the best forecast of long-horizon CPI inflation. One view of core inflation, then, is that it is a forecast of future inflation over the next three to five years.[22]

6.4.2 Multivariate Methods

An alternative to the univariate forecasting equation (8) is to examine the marginal forecasting power of prices in an equation that includes a set of variables Z:

$$(9) \qquad \Pi_t^K = \alpha + \sum_{i=0}^{11}\beta_i(\ln p_t^r - \ln p_{t-1}^r) + \gamma Z_t + \varepsilon_t^K.$$

---

19. Yet another alternative would be to define core inflation as the optimal forecast of Π_t^K. This has the disadvantage that it is difficult to calculate in real time. In addition, such a definition would force revision of the entire history of estimates with the arrival of each new month's data.

20. The estimates of β in (8) are very close to one for most of the cases, implying that the current twelve-month moving average of the index is the best forecast of long-horizon inflation.

21. We have restricted the constant in equation (8) to zero, as this reduces the root mean square forecast errors. This is consistent with the general notion that inflation is highly persistent.

22. All of our results are robust to either adding lags of the right-hand-side variable to the forecasting regression (8), or including many lags of single-period inflation rather than twelve-month averages.

Table 6.6   **Comparison of Forecasts of Long-Horizon Consumer Price Index Inflation (1967:02 to 1992:12)**

	Root Mean Square Error Horizon K in Months				
Candidate Index	12	24	36	48	60
	Forecasts Beginning 1980:01				
All items consumer price index	2.25	2.72	3.07	3.40	3.82
Consumer price index excluding food and energy	2.58	3.02	3.41	3.79	4.25
Weighted median	2.08	2.48	2.80	3.10	3.49
15% trimmed mean	2.21	2.62	2.99	3.32	3.74
	Summary Statistics for Π_t^K during Forecasting Period				
Mean	4.51	4.32	4.18	4.10	4.01
Standard deviation	2.14	1.52	1.06	0.89	0.71
	Full Sample				
All items consumer price index	2.17	2.71	2.95	3.05	3.08
Consumer price index excluding food and energy	2.64	2.94	3.02	3.00	3.00
Weighted median	2.30	2.58	2.67	2.67	2.66
15% trimmed mean	2.32	2.64	2.76	2.76	2.75
	Summary Statistics for Π_t^K during Forecasting Period				
Mean	5.83	5.90	5.96	6.02	6.10
Standard Deviation	2.86	2.63	2.40	2.21	2.05

Note: The top panel of the table reports the root mean square error of forecasts of inflation beginning in 1980:01 constructed from an equation estimated over the period from 1967:02 through 1979:12. The bottom panel reports the root mean square error of forecasts of inflation over the entire available sample, based on the previous twelve months.

We examine the case in which the Z's are twelve monthly lags of money growth, the growth in industrial production, the nominal interest rate on a constant K-month maturity U.S. government bond, and inflation in the CPI itself. To test the proposition of interest, we compare the P-values from F-tests that all the β's are zero simultaneously when the equation is estimated over the entire available sample period.

The results are reported in table 6.7. As the table clearly shows, the weighted median is consistently informative about future changes in the CPI, *over and above* the information contained in the past changes in the CPI itself. The result is robust to both the horizon and the choice of how money is measured. Interestingly, the CPI excluding food and energy appears to contain little additional information useful in predicting future inflation.

As a final exercise, we use the estimated multivariate forecasting equation (9) to compute actual forecasts of inflation from 1993 to 1997. Table 6.8 reports the fitted values for regressions over various horizons, with different measures of money and core inflation, using actual data through December 1992. We also present estimates of the standard errors of these forecasts.

The estimated forecasts vary substantially depending on the definition of money and the measures of inflation included in the simple linear regression. But the weight of the evidence thus far suggests that we should focus on results for M2 and the weighted median. Using this preferred combination, we find that inflation is forecast to average 3.76 percent for 1993, 3.02 percent for the three years ending December 1995, and 2.68 percent over the five years ending December 1997. The standard errors of all of these estimates are a bit over 1 percent, so a 95 percent confidence interval for the five-year horizon would be (0.3,5.1). Thus, in the absence of accommodation of any future shocks, current monetary policy will result in inflation that is roughly comparable to that of the past decade (1983 to 1992), when price increases averaged approximately 4 percent per year.

Table 6.7   **Multivariate Forecasts of Inflation: The Marginal Contribution of Past Inflation (1967:02 to 1992:12)**

	K		
	12	36	60
	Monetary Base		
Consumer price index excluding			
food and energy	0.61	0.03	0.48
Weighted median	0.07	0.00	0.09
15% trimmed mean	0.37	0.33	0.58
	M1		
Consumer price index excluding			
food and energy	0.01	0.16	0.56
Weighted median	0.63	0.00	0.00
15% trimmed mean	0.14	0.71	0.05
	M2		
Consumer price index excluding			
food and energy	0.50	0.93	1.00
Weighted median	0.02	0.00	0.00
15% trimmed mean	0.22	0.40	0.50

Note: The table reports the p-values for the F-tests associated with adding twelve lags of the candidate index to a regression of average inflation K months into the future on twelve monthly lags of the nominal interest and the growth rates of either the monetary base, M1 or M2, industrial production, and the CPI.

Table 6.8   Forecasts of Inflation: 1993 to 1997 (average annual rates, standard
                   errors in parentheses)

	Annual Average from December 1992 to		
	December 1993	December 1995	December 1997
	Monetary Base		
Consumer price index excluding	4.62	6.22	5.95
food and energy	(1.31)	(1.32)	(1.32)
Weighted median	4.30	5.30	5.47
	(1.25)	(1.22)	(1.27)
15% trimmed mean	4.69	6.01	5.85
	(1.29)	(1.28)	(1.33)
	M1		
Consumer price index excluding	4.98	5.66	4.56
food and energy	(1.14)	(1.25)	(1.19)
Weighted median	4.49	4.60	3.79
	(1.20)	(1.31)	(1.22)
15% trimmed mean	4.91	5.38	4.29
	(1.17)	(1.27)	(1.19)
	M2		
Consumer price index excluding	3.80	3.59	3.36
food and energy	(1.25)	(1.25)	(1.18)
Weighted median	3.76	3.02	2.68
	(1.22)	(1.25)	(1.19)
15% trimmed mean	3.80	3.36	3.11
	(1.24)	(1.26)	(1.17)

Note: The table reports the forecasts using a regression of average inflation K months into the future on twelve monthly lags of the nominal interest and the growth rates of either the monetary base, M1, or M2, industrial production, the CPI, and the candidate measure of inflation. Included are the fitted value for the forecast using data through December 1992 and standard errors that incorporate parameter uncertainty with the covariance matrix of the coefficient estimates computed using the Newey and West (1987) procedure with $K + 1$ lags.

6.5 Conclusion

This paper examines the use of limited-influence estimators as measures of core inflation. Specifically, we study the CPI excluding food and energy, and several estimates based on trimming the outlying observations of the cross-sectional distribution of inflation in each month, including the weighted median. Our use of these estimators is motivated by the observation that non-monetary economic shocks can, at least temporarily, produce noise in reported inflation statistics. As an example, we show how, when the distribution of sector-specific supply shocks is asymmetric, costly price adjustment can result in transitory movements of average inflation away from its long-run trend.

We are encouraged by the finding that the limited-influence estimators are superior to the CPI in several respects. They have a higher correlation with past money growth and provide improved forecasts of future inflation. Furthermore, unlike the all items CPI, the limited-influence estimates appear to be unrelated to future money growth.

Within the class of inflation measures we consider, the weighted median CPI fares best in virtually all of the statistical criteria we examine. Such a finding is not particularly surprising, given the nature of the problem we have outlined. A disproportionate share of the noise in the price data comes from the extreme tails of the distribution of price changes, and so systematically eliminating the tails of the distribution should give us a more robust measure of the persistent component of inflation.

What is missing from our analysis is a fully satisfactory model of the money growth–inflation relationship. This prevents us from addressing a number of interesting propositions, such as the degree to which monetary policy reacts to temporary aggregate supply and aggregate demand shocks. Also absent from consideration is the related issue of long-run bias in inflation measurement that results from permanent changes in the expenditure weights. From the perspective of a policymaker interested in short-run indicators of monetary inflation, we suspect that such biases are of secondary importance. Nevertheless, we believe that the long-run properties of limited-influence estimators of inflation remain an important area for future research.

References

Ball, Laurence, and Stephen G. Cecchetti. 1990. Inflation and uncertainty at short and long horizons. *Brookings Papers on Economic Activity* 21 (1): 215–45.

Ball, Laurence, and N. Gregory Mankiw. 1992. Relative-price changes as aggregate supply shocks. NBER Working Paper no. 4168. Cambridge, Mass.: National Bureau of Economic Research, September.

Blinder, Alan S. 1982. The anatomy of double-digit inflation. In *Inflation: Causes and effects,* ed. Robert E. Hall, 261–82. Chicago: University of Chicago Press.

Bryan, Michael F., and Christopher J. Pike. 1991. Median price changes: An alternative approach to measuring current monetary inflation. *Economic Commentary,* Federal Reserve Bank of Cleveland, 1 December.

Dickey, David A., and Wayne A. Fuller. 1981. Likelihood ratio statistics for autoregressive time series with a unit root. *Econometrica* 49 (July): 1057–72.

Eckstein, Otto. 1981. *Core inflation.* Englewood Cliffs, N.J.: Prentice-Hall.

Hoover, Kevin. 1991. The causal direction between money and prices. *Journal of Monetary Economics* 27 (June): 381–423.

Newey, Whitney K., and Kenneth D. West. 1987. A simple, positive definite, heteroskedasticity and autocorrelation consistent covariance matrix. *Econometrica* 55 (May): 703–8.

Vining, Daniel R., and Thomas C. Elwertowski. 1976. The relationship between relative prices and the general price level. *American Economic Review* 66 (September): 699–708.

Comment   Stephen P. Zeldes

Bryan and Cecchetti provide an alternative method of summarizing the vast amount of information in the many components of consumer prices. Rather than looking at reported aggregate consumer price index (CPI) inflation, which is approximately a weighted average of the inflation rates of all of the individual components, they calculate the median inflation and the 15% trimmed mean inflation. Bryan and Cecchetti (BC) refer to these measures as estimates of "core inflation." These measures turn out to have intriguing properties: they have a lower variance and higher persistence than the CPI inflation, they can be used to improve on forecasts of future inflation, and they are related to past money growth yet do not forecast future money growth.

BC document these intriguing properties, but they are not very clear as to what these measures are supposed to represent; that is, they never really define core inflation. My main comment at the conference has been partially addressed here but remains partly relevant. Reading the paper is like watching the television game show "Jeopardy." The category is inflation. BC have provided us with the answer: the trimmed mean. Now, for two hundred dollars, what is the question to which this is the answer? Unfortunately, the buzzer rang before either they or I could completely figure it out.

In the previous literature, there seemed to be two different notions of core inflation. First, Otto Eckstein defines core inflation as "the trend increase in the cost of the factors of production. It originates in the long-term expectations of inflation in the minds of households and businesses, in the contractual arrangements which sustain the wage-price momentum, and in the tax system." He essentially considers a Phillips curve augmented by inflation expectations and supply shocks. The core inflation rate corresponds to the inflation expectations term: what inflation would be if there were no supply shocks, and unemployment were at the natural rate. He was trying to get at the persistence of inflation in order to say something about future inflation.

The other popular usage of the term *core inflation* is in the popular press: the rate of change of CPI excluding food and energy. The intuition is that the persistence of the food and energy component is less than the rest, so this measure can provide a better indicator of future inflation than looking at total inflation.

BC consider an alternative measure. They compute inflation rates for each of thirty-six components of the CPI, and calculate two types of trimmed means, in each case eliminating the outliers on each side of the distribution. These measures are the 15 percent trimmed mean and the median (or 50 percent trimmed mean).

The first question one probably should ask is of what use is a summary

Stephen P. Zeldes is associate professor of finance at the Wharton School of the University of Pennsylvania and a research associate of the National Bureau of Economic Research.

statistic such as core inflation? It is unlikely that any one statistic is going to be a sufficient statistic, that is, that it will completely summarize all of the relevant information in relative price movements. But if one statistic can capture, even imperfectly, the information in a large volume of data, it can clearly be of use to economists, policymakers, and the general public.

One of the goals of the paper is to generate an inflation measure that is useful for formulating monetary policy. Exactly what information would monetary policymakers like to have, and how does this relate to core inflation? Presumably, they would like the answer to the following very broad question: For each possible path of monetary policy, what is the expected path of real output and inflation? For example, holding the growth of the monetary base constant, what is the expected rate of inflation and real output growth in each of the next ten years? Or consider another example. The inflation rate has been constant at an annualized rate of 4 percent for a number of quarters. In the current quarter inflation turns out to be 6 percent. Does this merit a change in monetary policy? Presumably, the answer depends on the persistence of the inflation innovation in the absence of any change in monetary policy, that is, on some conditional forecast of the path of future inflation.

All of the proposed measures of core inflation relate in some way to expectations about future inflation, although none is strictly formulated as a rational forecast conditional on an information set. One way of formulating a measure of core inflation might be: what is the expected path of future inflation given a future path of monetary policy and the past behavior of all individual price indices? This is not exactly what BC do, and doing so would require taking a stand on the underlying economic model.

BC argue that their measures should yield a better estimate of the underlying inflation in the economy, that is, that their measures provide more information about future inflation than simply looking at the current inflation rate. The theoretical argument requires a few steps, involving the link between outliers and persistence. These steps are as follows: (*a*) skewness in the distribution of the shocks to relative prices causes a change in aggregate inflation, and (*b*) these changes, and only these changes, are transitory.

Consider each step in turn. The first link clearly needn't be true. In a competitive model with no sticky prices and where relative prices adjust fully to changes in demand and supply, the aggregate price level is tied down by the demand and supply of money, and money is neutral. In this model it makes no sense to look at the individual components: if, given money growth, food prices have a large increase because of a drought, then the price of other commodities will grow sufficiently less slowly to keep the overall inflation rate at the same rate it would have been in the absence of a drought. In this model, relative price changes are independent of aggregate price changes, so it would be misleading to eliminate or downweight the relative price changes that are outliers.

BC rely instead on the Ball-Romer model with sticky prices, in which skewed changes in relative prices can change aggregate inflation. BC show that in a simple version of this type of model, the trimmed mean provides an estimate of what inflation would be in the absence of these supply shocks. An important extension of this paper would be to derive the properties of the trimmed mean in a fully specified dynamic model of this type. It is unclear whether the results presented here would continue to hold in such a model.

Even if the trimmed mean eliminates supply shocks, there is still the second link: are the aggregate shocks to inflation resulting from skewed relative price shocks transitory while other sources are not? BC argue that in a version of the Ball and Romer model with the simplest dynamics included, the supply shocks would be transitory. However, in a different model, one could imagine permanent shocks to inflation causing skewness in the underlying distribution of relative price changes. In this case it would be misleading to eliminate these shocks from our measure of inflation. It is also clearly possible to have transitory money supply and money demand shocks, as well as other types of transitory aggregate demand shocks.

The overall message here is that the appropriate measure of core inflation must be model based. Additional work needs to be done deriving the properties of the trimmed mean in more general models of inflation.

Next, turn to the empirical properties of the trimmed means. First, the univariate properties. Relative to the standard CPI inflation, BC show that their measures have lower variance and higher persistence (first order serial correlation). They are also slightly lower during the 1979 to 1981 period, and do not fall during the transitory 1986–87 slowdown in CPI inflation. Next, BC find that for M1 and M2 growth, money growth Granger-causes trimmed mean inflation, but trimmed mean inflation does not Granger-cause money growth. Although I'm not quite sure why this occurs, the results suggest that the trimmed means might be able to avoid some of endogeneity problems of previous work. Finally, BC regress long horizon (one to five year) inflation against different inflation measures over the previous twelve months. They find that using the median or trimmed mean provides a moderately better forecast of future inflation than does standard CPI inflation or the CPI excluding food and energy. Also, in some cases the median or trimmed mean helps predict future inflation even after including past money growth and other past variables. These results are very intriguing.

Although I am still not sure what is meant by the term core inflation, I think BC have taken an important first step in documenting that the median and trimmed mean are measures that can provide some important summary information about future inflation. It is impressive that we learn about the time-series properties of aggregate inflation using only the cross-sectional distribution in relative price changes. We can therefore add this to the list of possible sources of information about inflation expectations that were mentioned during the conference: forecasts of professional forecasters, commodity prices, bond prices (comparing nominal bonds to hopefully-soon-to-be-issued indexed bonds), and univariate aggregate time-series models. The results of this paper should interest policymakers and will likely promote future theoretical and empirical research on this topic.

7 Monetary Policy and Bank Lending

Anil K. Kashyap and Jeremy C. Stein

In this paper, we survey recent theoretical and empirical work that relates to the "lending" channel of monetary policy transmission. To begin, we need to define clearly what is meant by the lending channel. It is perhaps easiest to do so by contrasting the lending view of monetary policy transmission with the simpler, and better-known, "money" view.

In what we take to be the polar, pure money version of the monetary transmission mechanism, there are effectively only two assets—money and bonds. In this world, the banking sector's only special role has to do with the liability side of its balance sheet—the fact that it can create money by issuing demand deposits. On the asset side of their balance sheets, banks do nothing unique—like the household sector, they too just invest in bonds.

In this two-asset world, monetary nonneutrality arises if movements in reserves affect real interest rates. The transmission works as follows: a decrease in reserves reduces the banking sector's ability to issue demand deposits. As a matter of accounting, this implies that the banking sector must also hold (on net) fewer bonds. Thus the household sector must hold less money, and more bonds. If prices do not adjust fully and instantaneously, households will have less money in *real* terms, and equilibrium will require an increase in real

Anil K. Kashyap is associate professor of business economics at the University of Chicago's Graduate School of Business and a faculty research fellow of the National Bureau of Economic Research. Jeremy C. Stein is professor of finance at the Massachusetts Institute of Technology's Sloan School of Management and a research associate of the National Bureau of Economic Research.

The authors thank Ben Bernanke, Martin Eichenbaum, Mark Gertler, Bruce Greenwald, and Eugene Fama for helpful conversations, Owen Lamont for research assistance, Michael Gibson for kindly providing data, and Maureen O'Donnell for help in preparing the manuscript. We are also grateful to the Federal Reserve Bank of Chicago, the University of Chicago IBM Faculty Research Fund, the National Science Foundation, and MIT's International Financial Services Research Center for research and financial support.

interest rates. This in turn can have real effects on investment, and ultimately, on aggregate economic activity.

Note that as we have defined the pure money view of the transmission mechanism—solely by reference to the fact that it is characterized by the simple two-asset feature—there is a wide range of alternative formulations that capture its essence. These include the textbook IS-LM model, as well as the dynamic equilibrium/cash-in advance models of Rotemberg (1984), Grossman and Weiss (1983), Lucas (1990), and Christiano and Eichenbaum (1992). Although these two classes of models differ along a number of dimensions (for example, in the way they generate incomplete price adjustment), they share the two-asset feature.

By contrast, we say there is a distinct lending channel of monetary policy transmission when the two-asset simplification is inappropriate in a specific sense. In the lending view, there are three assets—money, publicly issued bonds, and intermediated "loans"—that differ from each other in meaningful ways and must be accounted for separately when analyzing the impact of monetary policy shocks. The banking sector now can be special in two relevant ways: in addition to creating money, it makes loans, which (unlike buying bonds) the household sector cannot do.

In this three-asset world, monetary policy can work not only through its impact on the bond-market rate of interest, but also through its *independent* impact on the supply of intermediated loans. To think about the distinction between the money and lending channels, take an extreme example where households view the two assets that they do hold—money and bonds—as very close substitutes. In this case, a decrease in reserves that leads to a decline in the money supply will have a minimal impact on the interest rate on publicly held bonds. Thus the money channel is very weak. However, the decrease in reserves can still have important real consequences, if it leads banks to cut back on loan supply: the cost of loans *relative* to bonds will rise, and those firms that rely on bank lending (say, because they do not have access to public bond markets) will be led to cut back on investment. Put differently, monetary policy can have significant real effects that are not summarized by its consequences for open-market interest rates.

A couple of points about the lending view should be emphasized right away, to prevent further confusion. First, as we have defined it, the lending view centers on the premise that bank loans and publicly issued bonds are not perfect substitutes. It *does not* hinge critically on whether or not there is quantity rationing in the loan market. As a matter of practical reality, shifts in bank loan supply may well be accompanied by variations in the degree of rationing, but this is not necessary for there to be a meaningful lending channel.

Second, much like with the pure money view, the essence of the lending view can probably be captured in a wide range of models. This may not be immediately apparent, because the lending channel has received much less modeling attention than the money channel. Indeed, the only recent modeling attempts that we know of are essentially extensions of the IS-LM framework, most notably Bernanke and Blinder (1988). However, as we will argue below, the important aspects of the lending view transcend the specific IS-LM style formulation adopted by Bernanke and Blinder; for example, they could in principle be captured in dynamic equilibrium/cash-in-advance models also.

Having defined (loosely) what we mean by the distinction between the money and the lending channels, much of the remainder of this paper focuses on the following two sets of questions:

1. As a matter of theory, what "microfoundations" are required for a distinct lending channel to exist? Does it appear that the necessary preconditions for a lending channel are satisfied in today's financial environment? Are they apt to be satisfied in the future?

2. Is there any direct evidence that supports the existence of a distinct lending channel? If so, how important in magnitude is the lending channel?

Before proceeding, however, there is a logically prior question that must be addressed, namely: Why is the distinction between the money and lending channels an interesting or important one? Although we must defer a complete answer until later in the paper, we can offer several brief observations:

1. If the lending view is correct, monetary policy can have important effects on investment and aggregate activity without moving open-market rates by much. At the least, this suggests that one might wish to look to alternative indicators to help gauge the stance of policy.

2. Standard investment and inventory models—which typically use open-market rates as a measure of the cost of financing—may give a misleading picture of the extent to which different sectors are directly affected by monetary policy. For example, most empirical work fails to find a significant connection between inventories and interest rates. As we argue below, it is probably wrong to conclude from this work that tight monetary policy cannot have a strong direct impact on inventory behavior.

3. The quantitative importance of the lending channel is likely to be sensitive to a number of institutional characteristics of the financial markets (for example, the rise of "nonbank banks," the development of the public "junk bond" market, etc.). Thus understanding the lending channel is a prerequisite to understanding how innovation in financial institutions might influence the potency of monetary policy.

4. Similarly, the aggregate impact of the lending channel may depend on the financial condition of the banking sector. As we argue below, when bank capital is depleted (and particularly when bank loan making is tied to risk-based capital requirements), the lending channel is likely to be weaker. This has obvious implications for the ability of monetary policy to offset particular sorts of adverse shocks.

5. Finally, the lending view implies that monetary policy can have distributional consequences that would not arise were policy transmitted solely through a money channel. For example, the lending view suggests that the

costs of tight policy might fall disproportionately on smaller firms that are unable to access public capital markets. Such distributional considerations may be important to bear in mind when formulating policy.

Although this list is far from exhaustive, it hopefully gives some idea of the potential usefulness of understanding and quantifying the lending view. With this motivation in mind, the remainder of the paper is organized as follows. Section 7.1 gives a very brief history of the thought surrounding the lending view. Section 7.2 examines its microfoundations. Section 7.3 reviews the evidence that bears most directly on the lending view.

7.1 Early Work on the Lending View

The lending view of monetary policy transmission has, in one form or another, been around for a long time. Much of the early work tended to blur together two logically distinct issues: (*a*) whether monetary policy works in part by changing the relative costs of bank loans and open-market paper; and (*b*) whether such shifts in bank loan supply are accompanied by variations in the degree of nonprice credit rationing.

Roosa's (1951) "availability doctrine" is a classic example of this line of thinking. He takes issue with the simple money channel view that "changes in market rates of interest provided a satisfactory explanation for cyclical economic disturbance. . . . The postwar experience suggests that yield changes of scarcely ⅛ of 1 percent for the longest-term bonds have considerable market effects." Rather, Roosa argues, "it is the lender, neglected by the monetary theorists, who does most to put new substance in the older doctrine. . . . Rate changes brought about by the open market operations of the central bank influence the disposition or the ability of lenders to make funds available to borrowers. . . . It is principally through effects upon the position and decision of lenders . . . that central bank action . . . achieves its significance." Although Roosa's observations came in the midst of the debate over whether monetary policy effectiveness after the impending Federal Reserve-Treasury Accord would necessitate large swings in open-market interest rates, the importance of bank credit continued to be a hotly debated topic long after the accord was signed.

Over the next dozen years the argument was refined, and a number of investigators, notably, Tobin and Brainard (1963), Brunner and Meltzer (1963), and Brainard (1964), proposed models that included as a central feature the imperfect substitutability of various assets including bank loans. Thus, Modigliani (1963) was able to more precisely summarize the role of banks in a world of imperfect information: "Suppose the task of making credit available to units in need of financing requires specialized knowledge and organization and is therefore carried out exclusively by specialized institutions which we may label financial intermediaries. . . . Intermediaries in turn lend to final debtors of the economy at some rate . . . [which] adjusts at best only slowly to market conditions. . . . The single rate of the perfect market model is replaced by a plurality of rates."[1]

Despite the fact that the Modigliani rendition of the lending view is very close to the one we are now advocating, the lending view began to fall out of favor during the 1960s. In part, this lack of acceptance seems attributable to the fact that many early accounts relied heavily (and unnecessarily, in our view) on a credit-rationing mechanism, while at the same time failing to provide a satisfying theoretical role for such rationing to exist. For example, Samuelson rebutted Roosa by arguing that the credit rationing implicit in the availability doctrine was at odds with profit maximization by lenders (see testimony of Samuelson in U.S. Congress 1952). More importantly, as Gertler (1988) points out, the Modigliani and Miller results on the irrelevance of capital structure seemed to undermine the basic premise that lending arrangements could be important. Furthermore, on the empirical front, Friedman and Schwartz (1963) were supplying strong evidence in favor of the money view.

As we will discuss in the remainder of the paper, each of these objections has subsequently been addressed. For instance, work by Jaffee and Russell (1976), Stiglitz and Weiss (1981), and many others has demonstrated that credit rationing can occur in models where all agents are maximizing.[2] More generally, as we argue in the next section, research in the theory of credit-market imperfections and financial intermediation has helped put the lending view on much firmer microfoundations. Still, the failure of the lending view to be widely embraced cannot be completely ascribed to theoretical discomfort—it has also suffered until recently from a lack of clear-cut, direct empirical support. Thus, perhaps even more so than the theoretical developments, the recent empirical work reviewed in section 7.3 has helped to renew interest in the lending view.

7.2   Building Blocks of the Lending View

Perhaps the best-known recent formulation of the lending view is a model due to Bernanke and Blinder (1988). Their model makes it clear that there are three necessary conditions that must hold if there is to be a distinct lending channel of monetary policy transmission:

1. Intermediated loans and open-market bonds must not be perfect substitutes for some firms on the liability side of their balance sheet. In other words, the Modigliani-Miller capital-structure invariance proposition must break down in a particular way, so that these firms are unable to offset a decline in the supply of loans simply by borrowing more directly from the household sector in public markets.

1. See also Tobin and Brainard (1963) and Brainard (1964) for early general equilibrium models of financial intermediation with imperfect substitutability across assets.

2. Indeed, Blinder and Stiglitz (1983) and Fuerst (1992b) outline models of monetary policy transmission that capture the credit-rationing aspects of Roosa's (1951) availability doctrine.

2. By changing the quantity of reserves available to the banking system, the Federal Reserve must be able to affect the supply of intermediated loans. That is, the intermediary sector as a whole must not be able to completely insulate its lending activities from shocks to reserves, either by switching from deposits to less reserve-intensive forms of finance (for example, certificates of deposit [CDs], commercial paper, equity, etc.) or by paring its net holdings of bonds.

3. There must be some form of imperfect price adjustment that prevents any monetary policy shock from being neutral. If prices adjust frictionlessly, a change in nominal reserves will be met with an equiproportionate change in prices, and both bank and corporate balance sheets will remain unaltered in real terms. In this case, there can be no real effects of monetary policy through either the lending channel or the conventional money channel.

If either of the first two necessary conditions fails to hold, loans and bonds effectively become perfect substitutes, and we are reduced back to the pure money view of policy transmission. If condition 1 fails, Modigliani-Miller corporations will completely arbitrage away any cost differentials between loans and bonds. If condition 2 fails, intermediaries will do the arbitrage. In either case, the net result will be that loans and bonds will always be priced identically in equilibrium.

Although the Bernanke-Blinder formulation is very helpful in illustrating the necessary conditions that are required for the existence of a distinct lending channel, it does not directly address whether each of these three conditions can be given solid microfoundations. Nor does it ask whether any such micro-foundations appear plausible given the current financial environment. For example: what sort of technological and/or informational assumptions must one make about the structure of intermediation to generate condition 2? Do these assumptions seem reasonable in light of what we actually observe?

In the rest of this section, we take up these questions relating to microfoundations. To preview the discussion a bit: We begin by arguing that condition 1 is probably easiest to justify, both in the context of a widely accepted, well-articulated theoretical paradigm, and in terms of what is observed in practice. On the other hand, condition 2 is quite a bit trickier—there are a number of possible factors that could conceivably limit the Fed's ability to affect the supply of intermediated loans. Our bottom line here is that it is nonetheless highly unlikely that condition 2 will fail to hold completely, although one can imagine circumstances in which Fed policy might have only a small impact on aggregate loan supply.

Finally, the question of the microfoundations for condition 3 is much broader in scope than just the lending channel—this question is central to *any* account of monetary policy, and has accordingly received an enormous amount of attention. Thus we do not attempt a detailed treatment here. Instead, we focus on a much narrower issue: the *interaction* between the microfoundations for condition 3 and those for conditions 1 and 2. In particular, we focus on a class of models—those of the dynamic equilibrium/cash-in-advance variety—

where the frictions driving imperfect price adjustment can be one and the same as those driving intermediary lending policy. We ask whether these sorts of models are likely to be successful in providing a realistic account of both price adjustment and intermediary lending patterns.

7.2.1 Why Do Some Firms "Depend" on Intermediated Loans?

In the last decade or so, a large body of theoretical literature has developed on the subject of financial intermediation. One broad theme of this work (seen, for example, in Diamond 1984; Boyd and Prescott 1986; and Fama 1990) is that intermediaries can represent efficient vehicles for conserving on the costs of monitoring certain types of borrowers. The basic idea is this: Due to asymmetric information and/or moral hazard, lending without any monitoring can involve large deadweight costs. Given these costs, it would be efficient to devote some resources to monitoring activities. However, if there are a large number of lenders—that is, if the credit is extended in public markets—free-rider problems will confound attempts to monitor. Thus it can make sense to create an intermediary to serve as a single "delegated monitor," thereby circumventing these free-rider problems and conserving on aggregate monitoring costs.

While ultimately correct, this argument is, by itself, incomplete. Although having a single intermediary do all the monitoring would seem to represent an obvious cost savings, there is a potential difficulty, namely, the introduction of a second layer of agency. This point is addressed by Diamond (1984), who asks the critical question: "Who monitors the delegated monitor?" In other words, what is to prevent the intermediary from taking investors' money and squandering it by making bad loans (that is, by lending without going to the effort of actually doing any monitoring)? Diamond shows that this second-tier agency problem can be mitigated if the intermediary holds a large, diversified portfolio of loans, and finances itself largely with publicly issued debt.

Diamond's conclusions about the optimal capital structure for an intermediary raise an issue that is central for monetary policy. Although Diamond argues that intermediaries ought to be largely debt-financed, there is nothing in his model—or in many of the other models of financial intermediation—that suggests that intermediaries must be financed with demand deposits. Indeed, the institutions in many of these models can equally well be thought of as "nonbank banks," that is, finance companies such as G.E. Capital that makes loans but do not finance themselves at all with deposits.

Thus while it seems relatively straightforward to argue from first principles that some firms—particularly those for whom monitoring costs are likely to be high—will be to some degree *intermediary dependent,* it is less obvious that they will necessarily be *bank dependent,* in the sense of relying on institutions that themselves are financed with demand deposits. In terms of the necessary conditions we have defined above, this distinction implies some initial doubts about whether one should expect condition 2 to hold across a wide range of circumstances. If intermediation can just as easily be done through institutions that fund themselves with nonreservable forms of finance (for example, commercial paper, long-term debt, etc.), then it is unclear how the Federal Reserve could ever affect the aggregate supply of intermediated loans. This question will be taken up in detail in section 7.2.2 below; for the moment we will put aside the important distinction between deposit-taking banks and intermediaries more generally.

In addition to the theoretical work, there have recently been a number of empirical papers that support the notion that intermediated loans are "special" for some borrowers. First, Fama (1985) and James (1987) show that bank borrowers effectively bear the cost of reserve requirements, which suggests that they are getting a service which cannot be replicated by nonbank providers of finance, such as the public markets. Second, James (1987) and Lummer and McConnell (1989) find that bank loans agreements are taken as "good news" by the stock market, consistent with the notion that banks provide an information-gathering function. Finally, Hoshi, Kashyap, and Scharfstein (1991) show that Japanese firms with close banking relationships are less likely to be liquidity constrained. This finding fits with the argument that monitoring by intermediaries reduces the information and/or incentive problems that typically create a wedge between the costs of internal and external finance.

It is one thing to believe that certain firms will be dependent on the services of the intermediary sector. It is quite another to believe that firms may come to rely on a *particular* intermediary with whom they have an established relationship—in other words, that there are lock-in effects that make it costly to switch lenders. However, as we argue below, if lender-specific lock-in does indeed exist, it can have important consequences for the transmission of monetary policy—all else equal, such lock-in will tend to make the lending channel more potent.

A few recent papers, both theoretical and empirical, provide some support for the hypothesis that banking relationships involve a degree of lock-in. On the theoretical side, Sharpe (1990) and Rajan (1992) argue that the very fact that a bank does monitoring creates the potential for lock-in. In the course of a relationship, a bank will acquire an informational monopoly with respect to its client, a monopoly which puts other potential lenders at a comparative disadvantage.

On the empirical side, Sushka, Slovin, and Polonchek (1993) conduct an interesting event study of Continental Bank's customers during the period when Continental was in danger of failing and was ultimately bailed out by the government. During this time, their customers' stock prices moved in concert with Continental's own fortunes, falling with bad news about Continental, and rising sharply with the announcement of the bailout. This suggests that these customers were somewhat locked in to Continental, and could not costlessly switch to another lender. Further evidence for the importance of banking relationships comes from Petersen and Rajan (1992). They find that the availability of credit to a small business is, all else equal, an increasing function of the length of its relationship with its bank.

Of course, even if one accepts that condition 1 is both theoretically and empirically plausible, there remains the question of its aggregate importance, not only today, but looking into the future. Certainly there are a substantial number of U.S. firms that cannot be considered intermediary dependent in any sense. Moreover, the evidence from the United States as well as other countries suggest that there is a strong secular trend away from intermediated finance, and toward securities markets.

In spite of such trends, the data show that intermediaries—and banks in particular—continue to play a dominant role in financing U.S. corporations, particularly medium-sized and smaller ones. (We review some evidence to this effect below.) Thus it seems reasonable to believe that shocks to the supply of intermediated loans might have important aggregate implications, even in today's environment.

7.2.2   Can the Fed Affect the Supply of Intermediated Loans?

The second necessary condition for the existence of a distinct lending channel is that the Fed be able to affect—by manipulating the amount of reserves available to the banking sector—the aggregate supply of loans made by intermediaries. We examine four factors that could conceivably weaken or even break the link between reserves and loan supply: (*a*) the existence of nonbank intermediaries; (*b*) banks' ability to react to changes in reserves by adjusting their holdings of securities rather than loans; (*c*) banks' ability to raise funds with nonreservable forms of financing; and (*d*) the existence of risk-based capital requirements.

The Significance of Nonbank Intermediaries

As noted above, many theories of financial intermediation leave open the possibility that lending to "information-intensive" borrowers could be accomplished by nondeposit-taking institutions. If such institutions play an important role, the link between Fed policy and aggregate loan supply might be weakened, or even severed. First, and most obviously, if nonbank intermediaries are responsible for most of the lending volume in the economy, the Fed will be unable to have much of an impact on the overall supply of intermediated loans, even if it can influence *bank* loan supply.

Second, and more subtly, one might argue that even if nonbank intermediaries do not have a large market share, they may effectively be the "marginal" lenders in the economy—that is, they may be able to pick up much of the slack if bank loan supply is cut back. However, we view this marginal lender argument as not completely compelling, particularly with regard to its short-run implications. It implicitly assumes that there are negligible costs incurred when borrowers switch from one lender to another. As seen in the previous section, there are both theoretical and empirical reasons to believe that such

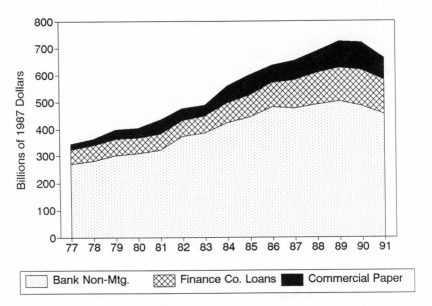

Fig. 7.1 Composition of Credit (nonfinancial corporations)

an assumption is inappropriate—that there is indeed a significant degree of lock-in between specific banks and their customers.

Thus if one is interested in understanding relatively short-run behavior, there may be something useful to be learned from comparing the relative sizes of the bank and nonbank intermediary sectors.

Figure 7.1 addresses this question, showing how the composition of intermediated loans to nonfinancial corporations breaks down into bank Commercial and Industrial loans (C and I loans) and finance-company loans over the period 1977–91. In addition, the figure also sheds some light on the issue raised above—the substitution of open-market borrowings for intermediated loans—by including data on the growth of the commercial paper market over this period.

The figure illustrates that while both finance-company loans and commercial paper have grown very rapidly in percentage terms over the last fifteen years, traditional commercial banks are still by far the most important of these three sources of finance, representing over 68 percent of the combined total in 1991. (The share was on the order of 78 percent in 1977). Thus it would be premature to say that growth in either the commercial paper market or in the nonbank intermediary sector has rendered the commercial banking sector of significantly less aggregate importance than it was, say, a couple of decades ago.

Table 7.1 presents more detail on how corporate financing patterns have evolved over the last twenty or so years. Using data from the *Quarterly Finan-*

Table 7.1   **Bank and Nonbank Sources of Debt for Manufacturing Corporations, 1973, 1991**

	1973:4				1991:4			
	Total	Large	Medium	Small	Total	Large	Medium	Small
Bank debt/Total debt								
Short-term	78.8%	64.9%	93.1%	84.0%	44.9%	22.8%	77.0%	82.9%
Long-term	24.6%	17.1%	36.1%	43.3%	31.2%	21.1%	51.7%	59.3%
Total	34.4%	23.4%	49.8%	55.3%	33.0%	21.3%	54.9%	65.5%
Commercial paper as % of								
Short-term debt	12.7%	26.1%	2.1%	1.7%	N.A.	62.8%	6.9%	N.A.
Nonbank short-term								
debt	59.7%	74.3%	31.0%	10.4%	N.A.	81.3%	30.1%	N.A.
Total debt	2.3%	3.4%	0.5%	0.5%	N.A.	7.5%	0.9%	N.A.
Total nonbank debt	3.5%	4.5%	1.0%	1.1%	N.A.	9.6%	1.9%	N.A.

Source: Quarterly Financial Report.

Note: In 1991:4, Small was under $25 million (20.6 percent of total manufacturing assets), Medium was $25 million–$1 billion (7.9 percent), and Large was above $1 billion in assets (71.4 percent). In 1973:4, Small was under $5 million (10.4 percent of total), Medium was $5–250 million (22.7 percent), and Large was above $250 million (66.9 percent). N.A. = not available.

cial Report, we break down manufacturing firms into three size categories— small, medium, and large—and look at how the balance sheets of firms in each category have changed between 1973 and 1991.

Again, the most striking finding is that if we take the overall manufacturing-wide ratio of bank debt to total debt, there is virtually no change over time. Bank debt represents 34.4 percent of total debt in 1973, and 33.0 percent in 1991. This aggregate number reinforces the conclusion drawn above—that one should not exaggerate the extent to which changes in financing practices have diminished the role of banks.

Of course, banks have lost substantial ground in some areas. First, if one focuses only on short-term lending, banks have seen their overall share fall from 78.8 percent to 44.9 percent. (This is offset by the fact that banks have actually gained share in overall long-term lending.) Moreover, this loss of short-term market share is almost exclusively concentrated among large corporations—the one place where the commercial paper market has made very substantial inroads.[3] Short-term bank loans as a fraction of all short-term debt of large manufacturing corporations fell from 64.9 percent in 1973 to 22.8 percent in 1991.

---

3. These figures may somewhat overstate the true economic extent of disintermediation, as approximately 8 percent of commercial paper issues are backed by irrevocable standby letters of credit from banks (see Gorton and Pennacchi 1990). In such cases, banks still bear the full credit risk, and presumably engage in monitoring. More generally, a number of other financial innovations—for example, the loan sales market—have blurred the line between intermediated and public-market sources of finance.

While the gains of the commercial paper market among large borrowers are certainly impressive, their aggregate impact should not be overstated. Commercial paper has not yet penetrated the medium- and small-firm categories to any perceptible degree, and banks' share of short-term debt for these firms is still overwhelming, at 77.0 percent and 82.9 percent, respectively.

The Future of Nonbank Intermediaries

Looking to the future, the rise of nonbank intermediaries documented in figure 7.1 raises a number of difficult questions. At one extreme, some observers—particularly advocates of "narrow banking"—have concluded that there is no longer any reason (other than perhaps historical accident or bad regulation), to glue together in a single institution the deposit-taking and loan-making functions, as opposed to their being carried out separately, say, by money market mutual funds and finance companies, respectively. What exactly, ask these observers, are the synergies between deposit taking and loan making? If no clear-cut synergies can be identified, one might expect the nonbank sector to grow rapidly in the future, thereby diluting the potency of any lending channel of policy transmission. (See Gorton and Pennacchi 1990 for a forceful rendition of this argument.)

The work of Diamond and Dybvig (1983) provides something of a counterpoint to the Gorton-Pennacchi argument. The Diamond-Dybvig model suggests that there may indeed be a link between the deposit-taking and loan-making functions of banks. In their model, banks perform a "liquidity transformation" role. All individual investors would like to invest in highly liquid assets, because they may suddenly wish to consume all of their wealth. But the economy's productive investment opportunities require tying up resources in long-lived projects. In this setting, it is optimal for a bank to issue demand deposits—thereby satisfying individuals' liquidity needs—and to invest the proceeds in the long-lived assets.[4]

Thus a synergy between deposit taking and loan making arises out of a fundamental mismatch between individuals' desire to hold liquid assets and the economy's need to invest in illiquid projects. However, the Diamond-Dybvig model probably overstates the importance of the liquidity transformation synergy, since it simply *assumes* that all investment opportunities are long-term and all savers want to keep all their wealth in liquid assets. In reality, there may not be nearly as much of a mismatch between savers' portfolio preferences and the underlying investment technology—there will be both some investment opportunities that are relatively short-term, and some investors who are not unwilling to tie up their assets for a longer period of time. Gorton and Pennacchi present some evidence that bears on this point. One fact they emphasize is

---

4. Diamond and Dybvig show that, in this setting, bank deposits perform a role that cannot be duplicated by other tradable claims, such as equity shares issued against the long-lived projects.

that the sum of outstanding Treasury bills and nonfinancial commercial paper is now roughly twice as large as the level of checkable bank deposits. This is a recent development—bank deposits were larger until around 1980—and it suggests that it might soon be possible to have a world in which deposit taking is done largely by institutions (like money market mutual funds) that invest primarily in high-quality, short-term liquid assets. Inevitably, however, these sorts of thought exercises run into difficult general equilibrium considerations. As Gorton and Pennacchi themselves point out, simply showing that the volume of T-bills and commercial paper greatly exceeds bank deposits is not conclusive proof that there is no role in equilibrium for traditional "liquidity transforming" banks in the Diamond-Dybvig spirit. After all, T-bills and commercial paper outside the deposit-taking system may already be satisfying some of the economy's demand for liquidity, so it would be wrong to posit that one could take them and use them as backing for deposits without losing anything.

Our own view is that while the Gorton-Pennacchi argument has a great deal of merit, it is hard to predict with any confidence that we will soon see anything like a disappearance of traditional dual-function commercial banks. Perhaps the greatest uncertainties have to do not with the economic considerations sketched above, but with regulation. Even if one completely accepts the hypothesis that there are no real economic synergies holding deposit taking and loan making together, government regulations can provide a powerful glue. For example, deposit-insurance subsidies may be effectively larger for those banks that invest in risky loans rather than T-bills, thereby encouraging a combination of the two activities.

In this regard, one important regulatory innovation is the introduction of risk-based capital requirements. As we discuss below, these may have the effect of accelerating any natural separation of deposit taking and loan making.

Banks' Holdings of Securities as a Buffer against Reserve Shocks

Even ignoring the issues raised by the existence of nonbank intermediaries, it is still possible that bank lending might be decoupled from open-market operations. Suppose that as a result of a monetary tightening, a bank finds that its deposits have been reduced by one dollar. How will the bank respond? Basically, it can adjust along one of three dimensions: (*a*) it can cut back on the number of loans it makes; (*b*) it can sell some of its securities holdings (for example, T-bills); or (*c*) it can attempt to raise more nondeposit financing (for example, CDs, medium-term notes, long-term debt, or equity). In order for condition 2 to be satisfied, it must be that the bank wishes (for a given configuration of rates on the different instruments) to do some of the adjustment by reducing loans. Or said differently, it must be that the bank is not wholly indifferent to variations in the quantity of T-bills and/or CDs, and thus does not use such variations to completely "shield" its loan portfolio from monetary shocks. (Note that selling T-bills and issuing CDs are closely related strategies—either can be thought of as reducing the bank's net holding of "bonds," broadly defined.)

Why might a bank not be indifferent to variations in T-bills or CDs? We will start with T-bills. The argument here is straightforward, and has been made by many authors. (See, for example, Bernanke and Gertler 1987.) At any point in time, a bank faces the possibility of random depositor withdrawals. If the bank holds all its assets (other than required reserves) in illiquid loans, it will have a difficult time accommodating these withdrawals while still meeting reserve requirements. In particular, it will be forced to liquidate loans on short notice, which could be very costly. By holding easily marketable securities such as T-bills, the bank avoids these illiquidity costs.

Of course, there is a trade-off involved in holding T-bills, since they offer a lower return than intermediated loans. This suggests that for any given level of deposits, and any given configuration of interest rates on loans and bills, there will be a unique optimal quantity of bill holdings. In other words, banks will not be indifferent to the amount of T-bills they hold.[5]

Table 7.2 presents some data on banks' holdings of securities, taken from the *Call Reports*. The data show that there are persistent cross-sectional differences in banks' portfolio composition. In particular, large banks—those in the top 1 percent as measured by total assets—hold significantly less in the way of securities than do medium-sized banks, who in turn hold less than small banks. These well-defined cross-sectional patterns would be very unlikely if portfolio composition was a matter of indifference to banks. In contrast, they are exactly what one might expect if banks traded off the liquidity of securities against their lower returns: smaller banks, with fewer depositors, are more vulnerable to large (percentage) withdrawals, and hence must protect themselves by holding more securities.[6]

Banks' Ability to Make Use of Nonreservable Forms of Finance

We now turn to the question of why a bank does not offset a loss in deposits solely by issuing more CDs—that is, why it is not indifferent to variations in the quantity of CDs it has outstanding. Romer and Romer (1990) argue that banks *are* likely to be indifferent, which would mean that condition 2 fails to hold.

However, the Romer-Romer argument embodies a highly simplified view of the CD market. Implicitly, it assumes that the supply of CDs available to any bank is perfectly elastic at the current market rate—that is, a bank can issue

5. See Greenwald and Stiglitz (1992) for an extension of these arguments and a general analysis of the consequences of risk aversion by banks.

6. Another reason one might expect small banks to hold more securities is if information problems made it more difficult for them to raise nondeposit external finance on short notice. See the arguments below.

Table 7.2   **Median Securities-to-Assets Ratios, for Banks in Different Size Classes, 1976–1990**

	Large Banks (largest 1 percent)	Medium Banks (75–99 percentile)	Small Banks (below 75 percent)
1976	18.1%	26.5%	27.2%
1978	17.4%	23.7%	24.0%
1980	17.2%	25.3%	26.4%
1982	15.7%	24.8%	27.8%
1984	12.4%	23.5%	27.6%
1986	15.2%	22.3%	26.5%
1988	15.0%	21.8%	28.5%
1990	15.1%	22.3%	28.9%

Source: Call Reports.

as many CDs as it wants without paying any premium. There are a number of reasons why this is unlikely to be true in practice.

Given that large-denomination CDs (or other instruments that a bank might use to finance itself in the public capital markets, such as medium-term notes, long-term debt, or equity) are not federally insured, investors must concern themselves with the quality of the issuing bank. If there is some degree of asymmetric information between the bank and investors, the standard sorts of adverse selection problems (see, for example, Myers and Majluf 1984) will arise. These considerations will tend to make the marginal cost of external financing an increasing function of the amount raised.[7]

All the available evidence supports the notion that default risk is important in the pricing of wholesale CDs. Large banks' CDs are evaluated by five rating agencies, and the rates paid by different quality issuers can vary considerably. Moreover, there is considerable intertemporal variation in the spread between average marketwide CD rates and the rate on riskless T-bills. To take just one example, the troubles of Continental Illinois in 1984 led to widespread worries about bank health, and an increase in this spread from 40 basis points in April to nearly 150 basis points in July.[8]

The implications of increasing marginal costs of CD financing can be illustrated with a very simple partial-equilibrium model. (The model also captures the earlier argument that banks need to hold some securities for liquidity pur-

---

7. See Lucas and McDonald (1992) for a recent model of the banking sector in which adverse selection problems interfere with banks' ability to raise nondeposit external finance.

8. See Cook and Rowe (1986). Fama (1985) documents that CD rates move very closely with commercial paper rates. Indeed, both appear to rise relative to T-bill rates during times of tight monetary policy (Stigum 1990). In the case of CDs, one possible interpretation is that banks attempt to issue more CDs as a substitute for deposits during periods of tight money, and that this increased supply pushes up the rates they must pay.

poses.) Consider a representative bank that holds as assets reserves (R), loans (L), and bonds (B), and finances itself with deposits (D) and CDs (C). The bank seeks to maximize

(1) $\text{Max } r_L L + r_B B - r_C C,$

where r_L, r_B, and r_C represent the interest rates on loans, bonds, and CDs, respectively. (This formulation assumes that demand deposits are non-interest bearing.) The bank is a price taker with respect to the first two rates, but perceives r_C to be an increasing function of C. The bank faces the following constraints:

(2) $R \geq kD$ (reserve requirement)

(3) $R + B \geq jD$ (liquidity constraint)

(4) $R + L + B = C + D$ (assets = liabilities)

Inequality (2) implicitly assumes that CDs are not subject to any reserve requirement, but it is easy to generalize the argument to the case where they are just subject to a lower requirement than deposits. Inequality (3) is meant to capture in as simple a fashion as possible the sorts of liquidity arguments for holding bonds made in the previous section. To justify it, one might imagine that a fraction j of the bank's deposits may be redeemed at any point in time, and that it is prohibitively costly to liquidate loans immediately. Thus the bank must hold enough bonds so that the sum of bonds and reserves is sufficient to meet redemptions.[9] Clearly, one can develop a somewhat more sophisticated version of this story if one is interested in making the portfolio demand for bonds less degenerate.

So long as $r_B < r_L$, all three constraints will be met with equality, and the bank's first order condition is given by

(5) $r_L - r_C = C r_C'.$

If, as assumed by Romer and Romer, there are no increasing marginal costs of CD financing, then the loan rate must be exactly equal to the CD rate in equilibrium—in other words, loans and CDs (or, alternatively, loans and bonds) are perfect substitutes from the perspective of the banking sector, and condition 2 fails.

Things are very different when banks perceive increasing costs of CD issuance. Now, if the spread between loan and CD rates remains unchanged, then the *quantity* of CDs is pinned down. Thus the "first-round" response of the banking sector to a one-dollar decrease in reserves is to decrease deposits by $1/k$, bonds by $(j/k - 1)$, and loans by $(1-j)/k$, while leaving CDs fixed. Of course, in general equilibrium, these effects may be attenuated, as the spread

---

9. Bernanke and Gertler (1987) derive something very similar to our liquidity constraint in the context of a much more fully specified model of the banking sector.

between loan rates and CD rates may widen, thereby encouraging more CD issuance. But in any case, loans and CDs are no longer perfect substitutes, and the spread between them will be affected by shocks to reserves.[10]

The Impact of Risk-Based Capital Requirements

We argued above that a bank's asset mix of loans and securities was likely to represent an interior optimum of a portfolio choice problem. The important implication that follows from this is that the bank will not want to do all of the adjustment to a contractionary shock by selling securities—in order to preserve optimality, it will also wish to decrease its holdings of loans. However, there is an important caveat to this argument. Risk-based capital requirements (of the sort that have been phased in over the last several years under the Basle Accords) can tie a bank's ability to extend loans to its level of equity capital. If a bank's lending is constrained by such regulation, then it may do all of its marginal adjustments by buying and selling securities.

This can be easily illustrated in the context of the model sketched above. Risk-based capital requirements essentially impose an additional constraint of the form

$$(6) \qquad\qquad pL \leq E,$$

where p is the capital requirement on loans, and E is the bank's equity. This simple version of the constraint implicitly (and realistically) assumes that T-bills are not subject to *any* capital requirement.

If it is costly for a bank to adjust the amount of equity financing it has (say because of the information problems that accompany new equity issues—see Myers and Majluf 1984), then (6) may bind. It is easy to see that in this case, the liquidity constraint in (3) will be slack—that is, the bank will hold more bonds than it needs for liquidity purposes. This is simply because it does not have enough capital to support more of the higher-yielding loans. Under these circumstances, monetary policy will have no effect on the bank's desire to invest in loans. Loans are tied down by (6), and all marginal changes in the bank's portfolio are accomplished by buying and selling T-bills. (See Bernanke and Lown 1991 for empirical evidence that bank capital can be a constraining factor in lending behavior.)

Of course, it is highly unlikely that all or even most banks will face binding capital constraints at any point in time. What is the effect of such unconstrained banks? At one extreme, it might be argued that as long as there are any capital-unconstrained banks, they will effectively be the "marginal" lenders in the economy, and hence the banking sector as a whole will behave as if it were capital-unconstrained. However, such an argument runs into the sorts of

10. The magnitude of the ultimate general equilibrium effect will depend on the magnitude of r_c'. If r_c' is very small, loan rates will rise only slightly relative to CD rates, and a large volume of new CD issuance will take place. Conversely, if r_c' is large, loan rates will rise by relatively more, and fewer new CDs will be issued.

problems raised earlier—it implicitly disregards the potential for switching costs when borrowers attempt to move from one bank to another. Our view is that even if just a fraction of the banks in the economy are capital-constrained, this will affect the potency of monetary policy. Essentially, we are saying that if Bank A is capital constrained, then Fed easing will not have the same expansionary effects it otherwise might, because Bank A will not lend any more than it already is, and because Bank A's customers cannot frictionlessly switch to another unconstrained bank that is easing its lending policy.

This sort of logic may help to explain why monetary policy was thought by many to be relatively ineffectual during the 1990–91 recession. To the extent that many (though certainly not all) banks found their capital positions impaired by large losses on their existing loan portfolios, and hence found (6) to be binding, the lending channel of monetary transmission would be weakened. More subtly, if regional shocks were in part responsible for the loan losses, then monetary policy might have a more powerful effect in some parts of the country—those less hard hit by the adverse shocks—than in others.

Similar reasoning also suggests that accounting and regulatory decisions can have important effects on the potency of monetary policy. If regulators are more aggressive in forcing banks to acknowledge loan losses, this will tend to reduce bank capital, and again dilute the effectiveness of the lending channel. Conversely, if capital requirements are relaxed, monetary policy might be made somewhat more potent.

Looking to the future, risk-based capital requirements may also play a significant role in the evolution of the banking system. We noted earlier that an important open question for monetary policy is the extent to which deposit taking and loan making will tend to grow apart in the years to come. Risk-based capital requirements would seem to have the potential to accelerate any natural separation of the two activities. In the past, there was a regulation-induced reason to keep the two together—by taking deposits and making risky loans, a bank could raise the value of the subsidy it received from the Federal Deposit Insurance Corporation (FDIC). Risk-based capital requirements reduce this incentive, as would risk-based insurance premiums.

7.2.3 Imperfect Price Adjustment and the Lending View

As noted earlier, the requirement of imperfect price adjustment is not unique to the lending view—it is a prerequisite for *any* theory in which monetary policy has real effects. Accordingly, we do not attempt to survey the enormous literature on the microfoundations of imperfect price adjustment. Rather, we focus on a much narrower issue: the extent to which the frictions responsible for imperfect price adjustment might *interact* with those responsible for conditions 1 and 2.

The Bernanke-Blinder formulation of the lending view, like traditional IS-LM models, implicitly assumes that prices are sticky, without providing any explicit microeconomic justification for this assumption. Moreover, the sticky-price assumption is completely separated from the assumptions driving firms' and intermediaries' preferences across loans and bonds—one can imagine varying the horizon over which prices adjust without modifying the rest of the model in any substantive way.

As we have already emphasized, however, the essence of the lending view can probably be captured in a wide range of models. For example, if one is uncomfortable with simply assuming that prices are temporarily fixed, one might appeal to the type of "limited participation" dynamic general equilibrium models introduced by Grossman and Weiss (1983) and Rotemberg (1984) to generate imperfect price adjustment, while still preserving the other necessary building blocks for the lending view.[11]

Although we are not aware of any limited participation models that explicitly set out to capture the distinction between the money and lending channels, there are a couple that seem to be quite close to addressing it. Two recent papers by Fuerst (1992a, 1992b) are especially relevant. In both papers the monetary mechanism works roughly as follows: There are "households," "firms," and "intermediaries." Both households and firms are subject to cash-in-advance constraints in all of their transactions.

A monetary shock takes the form of the central bank injecting cash directly into the intermediary sector. The important distinction between households and firms is that firms are "closer" to the intermediary sector, in the sense that they can transact with intermediaries without any time lag. Households, in contrast, must wait a period to revise their investment decisions. This implies that the immediate consequence of a monetary injection is that the firms wind up holding all the extra cash for one period. In other words, the firms are the only participants in this limited participation model, and monetary injections are funneled to them via the banking sector.

Monetary policy is nonneutral in this setting (thanks to the limited participation feature), and it has compositional effects. The interest rate in the firm lending market will be lower after a positive monetary shock than the (shadow) interest rate in the household market, since the firms absorb all of the shock in the short term. In one version of the model (Fuerst 1992a), the interest rate clears the firm lending market; in the other there is some degree of credit rationing.

Although Fuerst does not suggest that these models bear specifically on the lending channel, it seems to us that with a bit of reinterpretation, they might be thought of in this way. Suppose we relabel Fuerst's "firms" as "bank-dependent firms," and his "households" as "non-bank-dependent firms." The model would now have very much the feeling of the lending view. In particular, the effects of monetary policy would be transmitted via bank lending policy, and these effects would fall more heavily on the shoulders of bank-dependent firms.

11. We are unaware of any empirical evidence that supports the limited-participation assumption. Thus, both the IS-LM and limited-participation models can be criticized for the mechanisms used to produce price rigidity.

It is interesting to see where our necessary conditions (1, 2, and 3) would show up in such a model. It turns out that all three are actually embedded in a single timing assumption—namely, that only bank-dependent firms and intermediaries can transact with each other without any lag. First, note that since bank-dependent and non-bank-dependent firms are effectively "walled off" from each other in the short run, they cannot arbitrage away differences in borrowing costs. This is condition 1. Second, intermediaries are also walled off from non-bank-dependent firms in the short run. Thus they can only unload a central-bank injection on bank-dependent firms, and they too cannot arbitrage away differences in borrowing costs across the bank-dependent and non-bank-dependent markets. So condition 2 is satisfied. Finally, as we have already seen, the limited participation feature also generates the imperfect price adjustment required in condition 3.

In one sense, such a formulation of the lending view is quite elegant, since it traces everything back to a single friction—the (exogenous) cost that prevents non-bank-dependent firms from participating continuously in the bank lending market. However, this compact elegance may come at a cost in terms of empirical realism. For example, banks' portfolio "preferences" in this sort of model are purely a short-run phenomenon—in the short run, banks have no choice other than to funnel all of an injection to a subset of firms, but this changes completely once a "period" elapses. This implies that if monetary policy is ever going to impact the volume of bank lending, we should see these effects unfold very quickly. As will be shown in section 7.3 below, this implication runs counter to what is seen in the data.

In contrast, in the Bernanke-Blinder formulation of the lending channel, banks (and firms) are assumed to have well-defined *long-run* portfolio preferences between loans and bonds. This formulation therefore does not carry with it the strong implication that any of the changes in bank-lending volume that accompany a monetary policy shock should be manifested immediately. Thus on this score at least, it does a better job of fitting the facts.

We do not at all mean to suggest that the limited participation/dynamic equilibrium class of models will ultimately be unable to capture the salient aspects of the lending view. Rather, we are simply pointing out that there may be some problems in interpreting *current versions* of these models as providing an accurate and complete description of the lending view, even if they capture some of its basic essence. Richer formulations, which still use limited participation as a device to generate imperfect price adjustment, but that provide a more detailed account of intermediary portfolio choice, may well prove to be very successful in modeling the lending view.

7.3 Empirical Work on the Lending Channel

There are a variety of ways to organize a discussion of the evidence that pertains to the lending channel. We will begin by reviewing some suggestive, simple correlations that are open to many interpretations and then progressively introduce more focused tests that can be used to distinguish between competing explanations. Most of the literature either exclusively considers time-series correlations or cross-sectional correlations. While we too divide our discussion along these lines, we believe it is important to keep both bodies of evidence in mind in assessing the overall plausibility of the lending channel. After reviewing the evidence, we wrap up with some simple calculations aimed at quantifying the importance of the lending channel.

7.3.1   Tests Using Aggregate Time-Series Data

Perhaps the simplest implication of the lending channel is that bank loans should be closely correlated with measures of economic activity. Figure 7.2 graphs the change in nonfarm inventories (as reported in the National Income and Product Accounts) along with the change in commercial and industrial bank loans. The two series are highly correlated—the correlation is 0.4. Similar pictures can be drawn to show a strong correlation between bank loans and unemployment, gross national product (GNP), and other key macroeconomic indicators.

In terms of establishing support for the lending channel, however, such correlations are inconclusive, because although they are consistent with the implications of conditions 1 and 2, they also admit other interpretations. For example, it may be that the correlations are driven by changes in the demand for bank loans rather than the supply of bank loans (as required by condition 1).

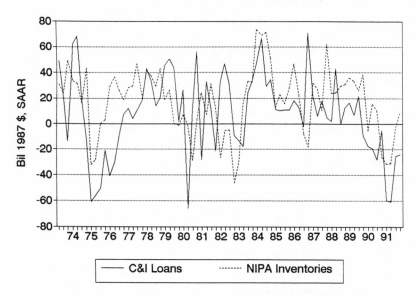

Fig. 7.2   C and I loans and National Income and Product Accounts (NIPA) nonfarm inventories (changes, in billions of 1987 dollars, SAAR)

That is, bank loans and inventories might move together because banks always stand willing to lend, and firms finance desired changes in level of inventories with bank loans. And even if the evidence does in part reflect the impact of variations in loan supply, it does not establish that these variations can be attributed to changes in monetary policy, as required by condition 2.

We thus start by reviewing the data that bear more directly on condition 1— the question of whether shifts in loan supply matter. In fact, there is considerable evidence that disruptions in the banking sector and the attendant shifts in bank loan supply are sometimes responsible for significant fluctuations in economic activity. One of the most influential of these studies is Bernanke's (1983) examination of the Great Depression in the United States. Bernanke examines the extent to which the money view of monetary policy transmission can account for the decline in U.S. output between 1930 and 1933. He finds that while a standard monetary model would predict a large drop in output, a significant amount of the decline cannot be explained by appealing purely to monetary influences. Moreover, not only can much of the unexplained decline be rationalized by recognizing the disruptive effects of bank panics, but these panics (and associated financial crises) also seem capable of explaining the persistence of the Depression. The Bernanke interpretation has become part of the conventional explanation for the depth and persistence of the Depression in the United States and is one of the strongest pieces of evidence supporting the view that shifts in loan supply can be quite important.

Bernanke, in subsequent work with James (1991), has extended this work to analyze the role of Depression-era banking panics in countries besides the United States. Studying a sample of twenty-four countries, Bernanke and James (1991) find that there are large output declines during periods of banking panics that cannot be explained by standard factors, such as trade effects, interest rates, fiscal policy, etc. Similar results have been uncovered in studies of different historical episodes in a number of countries.

The literature on credit controls also suggests that disruptions of the lending process can be quite important (see Owens and Schreft 1992). Perhaps the clearest example is the 1980 Credit Controls initiated by President Carter. Although the six-point credit-restraint program was only in place from March 14 through July 3, it had a remarkable effect on borrowing and purchasing patterns (see Schreft 1990 for details). While the controls sought to discourage all types of credit extensions, in Schreft's words, "the consumer credit controls were largely symbolic and without teeth." However, the impact on bank lending was very powerful. She reports that bank loans, which had been growing at an annualized rate of between 15 and 20 percent prior to the controls, dropped to an annual growth rate of only 2.5 percent for the month of March. In April, total bank loans outstanding fell 5 percent (at an annual rate). The decline in activity was equally sharp. Real gross domestic product (GDP) contracted at a 9.9 percent annual rate in the second quarter of the year. Once the controls were lifted, loan growth and GDP growth resumed at a healthy pace.

Finally, evidence from structural vector autoregressions (VARs) also supports the notion that shocks to loan supply have significant real effects. A noteworthy example is Bernanke (1986). Bernanke proceeds by imposing enough covariance restrictions on the disturbance terms in his equations to allow him to identify a structural shock to the intermediation process. A representative example of his restrictions is that shocks to aggregate loans are contemporaneously uncorrelated with shocks to military spending and money. Thus his identifying assumptions permit a direct investigation of whether condition 1 holds. As he notes, a change in monetary policy is one of several candidates for factors that might disturb the lending process. The resulting instrumental-variable estimates suggest that lending shocks do seem to have a sizable effect on aggregate demand. In a similar vein, Kuttner (1992) also finds that lending shocks are important for spending.

Of course, for the lending view to be relevant we must go one step further and demonstrate that condition 2 also holds, that is, that monetary policy has the power to shift loan supply. This observation suggests examining the comovements in the stance of monetary policy, loans, and activity, which in turn requires one to quantify the stance of monetary policy. Fortunately, the conclusions do not seem very sensitive to the use of any particular indicator of policy. For instance, Bernanke and Blinder (1992) find that increases in the federal funds rate (their measure of the stance of Federal Reserve policy) lead banks to slowly downsize by shedding loans, and that as loans decline the economy slows. These findings are reproduced in figure 7.3.[12]

Others researchers have also found that loans adjust gradually (but noticeably) following a shift in policy. For instance, Romer and Romer (1990) report a similar finding when they date shifts in policy by studying the language in Federal Open Market Committee directives. Thus, there does seem to be solid evidence that loan volume responds (albeit with a lag) to changes in the stance of monetary policy.

The slow adjustment of loans to policy may initially seem to undercut the plausibility of important effects coming through shifts in loan supply. For example, King (1986) runs a horse race between loans and monetary aggregates and finds that the latter do a better job of predicting activity; or said differently, money tends to lead output while loans tend to move roughly contemporaneously with output. Romer and Romer (1990) find similar results, and interpret them as cutting against the lending view. And recently, Ramey (1992) has reconfirmed these findings using a horse race based on a set of error-correction models.[13]

---

12. These results seem to be a bit sensitive to the choice of loan series. Bernanke and Blinder look at a loan series that captures all types of bank lending. If one instead focuses on lending to businesses (for example, Commercial and Industrial loans), loan volume initially increases following an interest-rate hike, but then turns around and begins to decline. As we discuss later, Morgan's (1992) work suggests that this is due largely to the presence of loan commitments.

13. Most of these contests show that M2 is the best monetary aggregate for predicting future output movements. However, from a theoretical perspective, M2 contains many nontransaction components and therefore is not the most obvious candidate to use to defend the money view.

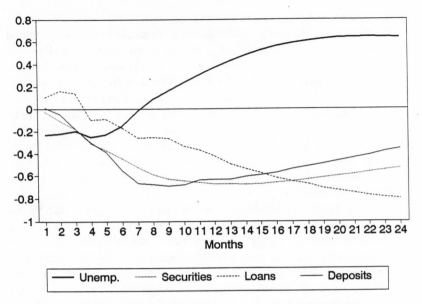

Fig. 7.3   Responses to increase in funds rate (estimated 59:12–90:12)

However, for a couple of reasons we do not think these timing differences are particularly damaging for the lending view. First, it is natural to believe that the most immediate consequence of a slowdown would be an undesired buildup of firms' inventories. This would lead to a short-run increase in the demand for loans to finance the excess inventories. Thus even if loan supply is contracting, we may not observe a rapid decline in loan volume.[14]

A second consideration, emphasized by Bernanke and Blinder, is that the contractual nature of loan agreements limits the speed with which loan volume can shrink. Recent work by Morgan (1992) confirms that much of the sluggishness in loan volume is indeed due to loan commitments. Specifically, Morgan contrasts movements in C and I loans made *under commitment* with movements in C and I loans made *without any commitment*. In figure 7.3, we saw that rising interest rates are often followed initially by slightly lower unemployment (higher activity); and Morgan finds that the loans made under commitment largely track these movements in activity. In contrast, he finds that customer loans that do not have commitments begin to fall relatively quickly, responding about as fast and as sharply as monetary aggregates. Thus, the response of loan supply to movements in monetary policy does seem quite plausible.

However, even taking the effect of loan commitments into account, it ap-

14. Diamond (1991) also offers a theoretical model that suggests that the demand for intermediated credit should increase during a downturn.

pears that loan supply responds to monetary policy with some lag. This is important to note if one is interested in applying the Lucas-Fuerst style models discussed in section 7.2.3 to capture the lending view. As noted earlier, current versions of these models generally predict very rapid responses of loans to monetary policy: the nonparticipation constraints implicit in these models are temporary. Thus, one challenge in applying this class of models in this context will be to come up with a plausible modification that can rationalize the timing patterns between shifts in policy and changes in lending and output.

Unfortunately, the observation that changes in monetary policy are followed by changes in both loan quantities and economic activity still does not prove that condition 2 holds. For example, one way to read these results is that tight monetary policy operates through standard interest channels to depress economic activity and to reduce the *demand* for credit. Consequently, there can be an induced correlation between activity and bank lending even if there is no lending channel.[15] This identification problem means that although correlations between policy indicators, bank loans, and activity are consistent with the view that monetary policy works through loan supply, such evidence cannot provide unambiguous support of the lending view.

One approach to dealing with this identification problem is proposed by Kashyap, Stein, and Wilcox (1993) (KSW). They consider the relative fluctuations in bank loans and a leading substitute for bank loans: commercial paper. The central KSW insight is that movements in substitutes for bank financing should contain information about the demand for bank financing. For example, if bank loans are falling while commercial paper issuance is rising, then KSW infer that bank loan supply has contracted.

Having made this identifying assumption, KSW propose testing both conditions 1 and 2. To verify that the central bank can affect loan supply (condition 2), KSW examine movements in the "mix" between bank loans and loan substitutes following changes in the stance of monetary policy.[16] Using both the Federal Funds rate and the Romers' policy proxy, KSW find that when the Fed tightens, commercial paper issuance surges while loans (slowly) decline—that is, the move in the mix indicates loan supply has shifted inward.[17] To study whether the implied shifts in loan supply are important (conditions 1 and 3), they add their mix variable to a set of structural equations for inventory and fixed investment. Their tests boil down to checking whether the proxy for loan-

15. However, this alternative explanation has to be stretched to explain Morgan's findings: one must argue that the demand for loans from noncommitted borrowers falls much faster than the demand of the borrowers with commitments.

16. KSW define their mix variable to be the ratio of bank loans to the sum of bank loans plus commercial paper.

17. Miron, Romer, and Weil (chap. 8 in this volume) find that movements in the CP-loan mix are less clear cut in response to earlier historical episodes of tight policy, for example, those in the early part of the century. However, given the very different institutional makeup of the markets in these periods, it is unclear whether the results are directly comparable with those of KSW. See also Bernanke's Comment on chap. 8.

supply shifts has any additional explanatory power for investment once other fundamental factors such as the cost of capital are taken into account.[18]

KSW find that the mix does seem to have independent predictive power for investment, particularly inventory investment. Since swings in inventory investment are central to business cycles and because conventional interest-rate effects have proved difficult to find for inventories, these results are note-worthy. In other words, the KSW findings provide some support for the view that monetary policy and financial factors may be important for inventory movements even though standard security market interest rates do not have much predictive power for inventories.

Hoshi, Scharfstein, and Singleton (1991) conduct an analogous set of tests using aggregate Japanese data. Specifically, they compare the behavior of bank loans which were subject to informal control by the Bank of Japan with loans from insurance companies which were the main alternative to bank financing. They find that when the Bank of Japan tightens, the fraction of industrial loans coming from banks drops noticeably, confirming condition 2. They also find that in a four-variable VAR (which includes interest rates) the mix is a signifi-cant determinant of both fixed investment and finished goods inventories. Thus, the Japanese and U.S. data give the same basic message.[19]

An alternative way of using information regarding substitutes for bank loans to resolve the identification problem is to study movements in *relative prices* rather than *relative quantities*. Specifically, changes in loan supply could be identified by checking whether the price of loans increases relative to the price of an alternative such as commercial paper. However, some care must be taken here since the nonprice terms of bank credit (for example, collateral, cove-nants, etc.) may vary systematically over time. In this case, one might expect data such as the prime rate to be relatively uninformative about the true cost of bank loans, and hence less useful in resolving the identification problem.[20]

Perhaps surprisingly, KSW also find evidence supporting both conditions 1 and 2 using the gap between the prime rate and the commercial paper rate to gauge loan supply: when the Fed tightens, the prime rate rises relative to the commercial paper rate. Furthermore, movements in this spread help forecast investment, even controlling for the cost of capital. In contrast, however, Kuttner (1992), using simple VAR-type causality tests, shows that the spread between the prime rate and the commercial-paper rate is a poor predictor of output (much worse than the KSW quantity-based mix variable, which contin-

18. A similar approach could be used to extend the work by Morgan. For instance, with an additional assumption that the demand for credit is the same for firms with and without bank commitments, the difference between the loans extended to the two sets of firms could be used to isolate shifts in loan supply. The gap between the two types of loans could then be used as a proxy for loan supply instead of the KSW mix variable.

19. Arguably, the Japanese evidence is less surprising since the Bank of Japan appears to exert some direct control over loan volume in addition to any indirect control that might come from changing reserves.

20. See Kashyap, Stein, and Wilcox (1993) for further discussion on this point.

ues to perform strongly in the VAR-type tests.)[21] Thus, the tests with price-based indicators lead to qualitatively similar conclusions as the tests using quantity-based indicators, although the findings with the rate spreads seem to be less robust.

Overall, we find the existing results based on aggregate data fairly supportive of the lending view. We see a coherent body of evidence, starting with very simple correlations and moving through a fairly precise set of tests, that suggests that monetary transmission operates at least partially through induced shifts in loan supply. However, we also recognize some important limitations that accompany this type of time-series analysis. For instance, one difficulty is that there are relatively few episodes where monetary policy shifts. In almost all of these cases, the shifts occur near recessions, so that many of the correlations we have discussed also could be uncovered by contrasting behavior during booms and busts. Since this sort of ambiguity is likely to be very difficult to resolve using only aggregate data, we think it is essential to examine other types of evidence.

7.3.2   Tests Using Cross-Sectional Data

There are good reasons to believe that studying cross-sectional data might be particularly helpful in this respect. For one, there is added variation that can be exploited in cross-sectional data. More specifically, there are a rich set of cross-firm implications of the lending view that are masked at the aggregate level. One key example is that not all firms are likely to be bank dependent, so some of the hypothesized effects implied by the lending view should occur for some firms but not for others. The combination of more data and more precise implications of the theory suggests a powerful set of tests using microdata that can be used to complement the aggregate findings.

While tests using cross-sectional data do offer considerable promise, they also come at a higher cost because these data require more effort to work with than do aggregate time-series data. At this point there has been relatively less work using microdata to specifically examine the lending view. A couple of notable exceptions are the recent papers by Gertler and Gilchrist (1992) and Oliner and Rudebusch (1992) that use information from the *Quarterly Financial Report,* a survey of over seven thousand manufacturing firms, to contrast the behavior of small and large firms. Under the assumption that small firms

---

21. Work by Friedman and Kuttner (1992, 1993) and Stock and Watson (1989) suggests that a different interest-rate spread, the difference between commercial paper and Treasury-bill rates, is a very reliable predictor of activity. These results might be interpreted as providing some indirect evidence on the lending view. For instance, if monetary policy does move loan supply and thus changes firms' financing patterns, then it seems likely that part of the movement in the bills/paper spread is due to shifts in monetary policy (see Bernanke 1990 and Friedman and Kuttner 1993 for details). However, in terms of the lending view, it is not clear why the bills/paper spread would perform so much better than the paper/prime spread in different forecasting contests. This suggests that one area for future work will be to combine the information in different price and quantity indicators to provide a more complex assessment of the lending view.

are much more likely to be bank dependent than larger firms, the comparisons bear on the lending view.

Gertler and Gilchrist (1992) begin by showing that bank loans to small firms decline significantly when the Fed raises interest rates, while large firms' aggregate external financing actually rises. One explanation for the Gertler and Gilchrist findings might be that some large firms issue commercial paper to finance trade credit that they want to offer to their smaller customers, who have been cut off from bank financing. In this case, commercial paper and bank loans are aggregate substitutes (as assumed by KSW) even though only certain firms can directly issue commercial paper.[22]

Moreover, Gertler and Gilchrist find that the inventory investment of small firms is much more sensitive to monetary policy shocks than that of large firms. This finding is compatible with the KSW aggregate evidence on inventories, and we will return to it shortly when we attempt to calibrate the magnitude of the lending channel. Oliner and Rudebusch (1992) conduct a similar investigation using imputed investment data for small and large manufacturing firms. They too find that small firms' investment is more sensitive to movements in a proxy for the stance of the monetary policy.

While this line of work produces conclusions that fit with the cross-sectional implications of the lending view, the relatively coarse level of disaggregation leaves open some other possibilities. For example, it might simply be that for technological reasons, small firms are more recession sensitive than large firms.[23] This sort of objection can be partially addressed by using firm-level data.

Several recent papers can be interpreted as firm-level tests of the lending view. In each case, the authors first identify a set of liquidity-constrained firms and then investigate whether these liquidity constraints become more binding in the wake of a shift in monetary policy. To the extent that the liquidity-constrained firms are to some degree bank dependent, this evidence bears on the lending view.

Hoshi, Scharfstein, and Singleton (1991) (HSS) focus on a set of Japanese firms that would be susceptible to being cut off from banks during times of tight credit—firms that are not part of bank-centered industrial groups. HSS investigate whether these "independent" firms' fixed investment becomes more sensitive to cash flow when monetary policy tightens. Until recently in Japan, assessing the stance of monetary policy was relatively straightforward because the Bank of Japan (BOJ) explicitly made suggestions to banks about how much

22. KSW do not commit to any particular microeconomic story to rationalize their assumption of the substitutability of commercial paper and bank loans. However, as long as the substitution of trade credit for bank loans is imperfect, the KSW story makes sense. In other words, the KSW story in no way hinges on the existence of marginal firms that shift between borrowing through banks or borrowing through the commercial paper market.

23. See, however, Gertler and Hubbard (1989), who take issue with the view that small firms are more recession sensitive than large firms.

lending to undertake. When the BOJ wanted to tighten it would urge banks to curtail their lending. And indeed, HSS find that when monetary policy is tight, liquidity is more important for independent firms' investment than in normal times.

Gertler and Hubbard (1989) conduct a similar study with U.S. data. They build on the Fazzari, Hubbard, and Petersen (1988) (FHP) result that the fixed investment of firms that do not pay dividends is much more sensitive to cash flow and liquidity than is the fixed investment of firms that have high dividend payout ratios. Accepting the FHP interpretation that this is evidence of liquidity constraints, it is possible to ask whether such constraints become more severe during periods of tight money.

Studying the FHP sample from 1970 to 1984, Gertler and Hubbard find that the investment of the low-payout firms does indeed become more sensitive to cash flow during the 1974–75 and 1981–82 recessions. Given that tight monetary policy was a factor in both recessions (see Romer and Romer 1990), these findings lend further support to the lending view. However, as Gertler and Hubbard note, the following alternative interpretation is also possible. If information about some borrowers is incomplete, they may be able to borrow more easily by posting collateral. During a recession, it may be that collateral values fall. In this case, even if bank loan supply does not shift inward, the decrease in collateral values would lead banks to lend less in equilibrium. Discriminating between this "collateral shock" explanation for the Gertler and Hubbard finding and the lending view is not easy. Both explanations stress the importance of a cutoff in bank lending as a contributing factor to the decline in investment, and differ only with respect to the source of this cutoff.

Kashyap, Lamont, and Stein (1992) (KLS) conduct a similar set of tests using firm-level inventory data. They focus on the differences between publicly traded companies that do and do not have bond ratings. The nonrated companies are typically much smaller than the rated companies and are likely bank dependent. Because of the myriad of evidence suggesting that Federal Reserve policy was restrictive prior to 1982, KLS begin their study with an examination of the 1982 recession. They find that during this episode, the inventory movements of the nonrated companies were much more dependent on their own cash holdings than were the inventory movements of the rated companies. (In fact, there is no significant liquidity effect for the rated companies.)

In contrast, KLS find that during subsequent periods there is little relation between cash holdings and inventory movements for the nonrated companies. For instance, during 1985 and 1986, when KLS argue that monetary policy was particularly loose, the correlation between inventory investment and cash holdings is negative and completely insignificant. These findings further support the KSW suggestion that financial factors beyond those captured by open-market interest rates play an important role in inventory movements during recessions.

As with the Gertler and Hubbard results, however, the KLS finding might also be interpreted as supporting the importance of collateral shocks rather than the lending view. KLS present some additional tests that try to distinguish between the two explanations. KLS reason that if the collateral deterioration story is correct, then the cutoff in bank lending ought to be more pronounced for firms that have high debt levels (that is, firms that have limited amounts of uncommitted collateral available). However, KLS find no systematic relation between debt levels (relative to total assets) and the sensitivity of inventory investment to cash holdings.

Overall, we read the firm-level evidence as echoing the story that emerges from both the aggregate data and the partially disaggregated *Quarterly Financial Report* data. Several different studies yield the same basic conclusion: during periods when monetary policy is tight, it appears that bank-dependent firms' spending becomes more closely tied to the availability of internal finance.

7.3.3   Quantifying the Impact of the Lending Channel

While we are quite confident in asserting that the lending channel exists, we are much less certain about its overall quantitative significance. The ideal way to assess the strength of the lending channel would be to estimate a fully specified structural model that captures both the lending and money channels and then to simulate the impact of tightening of monetary policy. Unfortunately, at this point no such model exists. As a second best alternative, we discuss three imperfect but quite different approaches to calibrating the importance of the lending channel.

One set of estimates can be inferred from the work of Kashyap, Stein, and Wilcox. Recall that they use a set of standard structural models for inventory and fixed investment—that already control for open-market interest rates and output—and test whether their financing mix variable provides any additional explanatory power. The rough idea is that the mix captures that part of overall financing costs attributable to the lending channel. KSW find that the coefficients on the mix are sufficiently big that a shock similar to the one that followed the Fed's October 1979 shift in policy results in an extra 1 percent decline in GNP. As noted earlier, most of this extra adjustment takes place in inventories. It is also worth noting that by construction this estimate ignores any possible effects that might operate through other channels, such as consumers' expenditures on durables.

An alternative strategy would be to begin with the Gertler-Gilchrist comparison of the inventory behavior of small and large manufacturing firms. Using a VAR framework, they find that there is a sharp difference in the way the two types of firms respond to a Romer date impulse: eight quarters after a Romer date, large-firm inventories are usually up by 5 percent, while small-firm inventories are typically down by about 11 percent. The cumulative impact of the small firms is significant: they bring the aggregate inventory accumulation down from 5 percent to roughly 2 percent.

Making the (perhaps strong) assumption that the large-small differential is entirely attributable to the lending channel, this result suggests that the lending channel causes manufacturing inventories to be 3 percent lower than they would be otherwise. This implies a fairly modest effect in terms of GNP. For example, considering again the October 1979 shift in Fed policy, according to the *Quarterly Financial Report* the stock of manufacturing inventories was roughly 250 billion as of the fourth quarter of 1979. A 3 percent decline in this stock therefore represents about 0.30 percent drop in GNP. According to Blinder and Maccini (1991, 76) manufacturing firms held an average of about 60 percent of total manufacturing and trade inventories (between 1959 and 1986). So, if one assumes further that the inventory behavior of the nonmanufacturing firms is similar to that of the manufacturing firms, then the total economywide inventory effect would be about 0.5 percent of GNP (.5 = .30/.60). Thus, the size of the effect as calibrated from the Gertler-Gilchrist data is roughly consistent with the effect reported by KSW using aggregate data.

Finally, to take a different tack, one might ask how much of the potency of monetary policy can be confidently ascribed to the money view of transmission. In other words, one might try to calibrate the magnitude of the lending view by working backwards: make an estimate of the importance of monetary policy, decide how much of this can be traced to open-market interest-rate effects, and then impute any remaining effects to the lending channel. Of course this approach puts the "burden of proof" squarely on the money view, and therefore highlights the choices that one implicitly must make in calibrating the size of these effects.

This example is particularly provocative because interest-rate effects are notoriously hard to find for many categories of investment spending. For instance, Blinder and Maccini (1991, 82), in surveying the literature on inventories conclude that empirical research "generally fails to uncover any influence of real interest rates on inventory investment, especially for finished goods in manufacturing." Given the large role of inventories in cyclical fluctuations, this should force a diehard believer in the money view to ask whether it is plausible to maintain that monetary policy has no direct effect on inventories.

Similarly, direct attempts to estimate the relationship between real interest rates and aggregate output (usually under the guise of estimating the slope of the IS curve) often find that there is little relationship between the two. For instance, Hirtle and Kelleher (1990) survey the literature on the interest sensitivity of the economy (and how it might have changed because of financial market deregulation) and note that there is little consensus on whether real interest rates matter much. For instance, their own results suggest that there is no significant relationship between (short-term) real interest rates and output. This sort of finding suggests that one could take an extreme stand and claim that all of monetary policy's potency comes via a lending channel! While we think this claim is too strong, we think it is equally disingenuous to tilt a calculation so that the money channel by default gets the bulk of any unexplained variation.

On the whole, the literature on the lending channel thus far does not very precisely pin down the quantitative importance of the effects. Some of this problem arises because there is still no widely accepted theoretical model that both satisfactorily captures all the important potential channels and can be estimated. Not surprisingly the result is that one can come up with a wide range of estimates. The KSW and Gertler-Gilchrist numbers suggest a meaningful though moderate impact, while the "name the residual strategy"—claiming all of the non-interest-rate effects for the lending channel—suggests a potentially huge impact. More careful attempts to narrow the range are likely to be one of the leading topics of work in this area.

7.4 Conclusions

This paper was designed to accomplish three goals. First, we wanted to clarify what is meant by the lending view of monetary policy transmission. Ultimately, the lending view boils down to the two-part assertion that (*a*) open-market operations affect the supply of bank loans; and (*b*) that these loan supply shifts in turn affect both the magnitude of aggregate output and its composition. The essential ingredient that underlies this mechanism is the imperfect substitutability of bank loans and publicly issued bonds, both as corporate liabilities *and* as bank assets.

In contrast, quantity rationing in the loan market is not necessary for there to be a meaningful lending channel, although in practice such rationing is likely to be present to some degree. Thus, as we have defined things, the lending view of monetary policy transmission is a subset of the larger literature that connects financial market imperfections and the real economy. Of course, even if our narrow version of the lending channel does not apply, there may be other ways in which financial market imperfections shape the consequences of monetary policy (for example, Bernanke and Gertler 1989).

Similarly, the lending view need not imply that the more traditional money channel of policy transmission is inoperative; clearly the two channels can coexist and can complement each other. Nonetheless, the distinction between the two is an important one: as we have stressed, the existence of a lending channel can influence both the potency and the distributional consequences of monetary policy, as well as the information content of a variety of indicators that policymakers look to.

A second goal of the paper was to outline the microfoundations that are needed to rationalize the existence of the lending channel. The bottom line here is that while the large existing literature on financial contracting and intermediation already provides much of what is needed, there remain some thorny problems that have thus far received little formal modeling attention. One particular area that would appear to require further work is that which corresponds to condition 2—the link between Fed-induced shocks to reserves and the aggregate supply of intermediated loans.

Our final goal was to collect the empirical evidence that bears on the lending view. In our view, the evidence for the *existence* of a lending channel is already quite strong—there are a number of papers that document facts that would be very difficult to explain under the pure money view of monetary policy transmission. Importantly, this evidence comes from a number of sources, uses both aggregate and cross-sectional data, and for the most part produces results that complement each other.

While there is surely more work to be done in terms of building a definitive case for the existence of the lending channel, a perhaps more important (and difficult) task for future research is to provide a relatively precise assessment of its quantitative importance. At this point, we remain quite uncertain about the exact magnitude of the lending channel impacts across a variety of sectors. Learning more about these magnitudes will be of vital importance if this line of research is ever to provide anything more than qualitative help to policymakers.

References

Bernanke, Ben S. 1993. Nonmonetary effects of the financial crisis in the propogation of the Great Depression. *American Economic Review* 73:257–76.

———. 1986. *Alternative explanations of the money-income correlation.* Carnegie-Rochester Conference Series on Public Policy, vol. 25: 49–100. Amsterdam: North-Holland.

———. 1990. On the predictive power of interest rates and interest rate spreads. *New England Economic Review,* November-December, 51–68.

Bernanke, Ben S., and Alan S. Blinder. 1988. Credit, money, and aggregate demand. *American Economic Review, Papers and Proceedings* 78:435–39.

———. 1992. The federal funds rate and the channels of monetary transmission. *American Economic Review* 82:901–21.

Bernanke, Ben S., and Mark Gertler. 1987. Banking and macroeconomic equilibrium. In *New approaches to monetary economics,* eds. William A. Barnett and Kenneth J. Singleton, 89–111. Cambridge: Cambridge University Press.

———. 1989. Agency costs, net worth and business fluctuations. *American Economic Review* 79 (March): 14–31.

Bernanke, Ben S., and Harold James. 1991. The gold standard, deflation and financial crises in the Great Depression: An international comparison. In *Financial markets and financial crises,* ed. R. Glenn Hubbard, 33–68. Chicago: University of Chicago Press.

Bernanke, Ben S., and Cara S. Lown. 1991. The Credit Crunch. *Brookings Papers on Economic Activity* 2:205–39. Washington, D.C.: Brookings Institution.

Blinder, Alan S., and Louis J. Maccini. 1991. Taking stock: A critical assessment of recent research on inventories. *Journal of Economic Perspectives* 5(1): 73–96.

Blinder, Alan S., and Joseph E. Stiglitz. 1983. Money, credit constraints and economic activity. *American Economic Review, Papers and Proceedings* 73:297–302.

Boyd, John, and Edward Prescott. 1986. Financial intermediary-coalitions. *Journal of Economic Theory* 38, no. 2 (April): 221–32.

Brainard, William, C. 1964. Financial intermediaries and a theory of monetary control. *Yale Economic Essays* 4:431–82.

Brunner, Karl, and Allan H. Meltzer. 1963. The place of financial intermediaries in the transmission of monetary policy. *American Economic Review* 53:372–82.

Christiano, Lawrence, and Martin Eichenbaum. 1992. Liquidity effects and the monetary transmission mechanism. *American Economic Review, Papers and Proceedings* 92:346–53.

Cook, Timothy Q., and Timothy D. Rowe. 1986. *Instruments of the money market.* 6th ed. Richmond, Va: Federal Reserve Bank of Richmond.

Diamond, Douglas. 1984. Financial intermediation and delegated monitoring. *Review of Economic Studies* 51 (July): 393–414.

———. 1991. Monitoring and reputation: The choice between bank loans and directly placed debt. *Journal of Political Economy* 99(4): 689–721.

Diamond, Douglas, and Philip Dybvig. 1983. Bank runs, deposit insurance and liqudity. *Journal of Political Economy* 91(3): 401–19.

Fama, Eugene F. 1985. What's different about banks. *Journal of Monetary Economics* 15:29–39.

———. 1990. Contracting costs and financing decisions. Part 2. *Journal of Business* 63(1): S71–91.

Fazzari, Stephen, R. Glenn Hubbard, and Bruce Petersen. 1988. Financing constraints and corporate investment. *Brookings Papers on Economic Activity* 1:141–95. Washington, D.C.: Brookings Institution.

Friedman, Benjamin, and Kenneth Kuttner. 1992. Money, income, prices and interest rates. *American Economic Review* 82 (June): 472–92.

———. 1993. Why does the paper-bill spread predict real economic activity? In *Business cycles, indicators, and forecasting,* eds. James H. Stock and Mark W. Watson. Chicago: University of Chicago Press.

Friedman, Milton, and Anna Schwartz. 1963. *A monetary history of the United States, 1867–1960.* Princeton, N.J.: Princeton University Press.

Fuerst, Timothy S. 1992a. Liquidity, loanable funds and real activity. *Journal of Monetary Economics* 29:3–24.

———. 1992b. "The availability doctrine. Northwestern University, Kellogg School of Management. Mimeo.

Gertler, Mark. 1988. Financial structure and aggregate economic activity. Part 2. *Journal of Money, Credit and Banking* 20 (August): 559–88.

Gertler, Mark, and Simon Gilchrist. 1992. Monetary policy, business cycles and the behavior of small manufacturing firms. NBER Working Paper no. 3892. Cambridge, Mass.: National Bureau of Economic Research, rev. November.

Gertler, Mark, and R. Glenn Hubbard. 1989. Financial factors in business fluctuations. In *Financial market volatility: Causes, consequences, and policy recommendations.* Kansas City, Mo.: Federal Reserve Bank of Kansas City.

Gorton, Gary, and George Pennacchi. 1990. Financial innovation and the provision of liquidity services. University of Pennsylvania, Wharton School. Mimeo.

Greenwald, Bruce, and Joseph E. Stiglitz. 1992. Towards a reformulation of monetary theory: Competitive banking. NBER Working Paper no. 4117. Cambridge, Mass.: National Bureau of Economic Research.

Grossman, Sanford, and Laurence Weiss. 1983. A transactions-based model of the monetary transmission mechanism. *American Economic Review* 73 (December): 871–80.

Hirtle, Beverly, and Jeanette Kelleher. 1990. Financial market evolution and the interest sensitivity of output. *Federal Reserve Bank of New York Quarterly Review,* summer, 56–70.

Hoshi, Takeo, Anil Kashyap, and David Scharfstein. 1991. Corporate structure, liquidity and investment: Evidence from Japanese industrial groups. *Quarterly Journal of Economics* 106:33–60.

Hoshi, Takeo, David Scharfstein, and Kenneth Singleton. 1991. Japanese corporate investment and bank of Japan guidance of commercial bank lending. MIT Sloan School of Management. Mimeo.

Jaffee, Dwight, and Thomas Russell. 1976. Imperfect information and credit rationing. *Quarterly Journal of Economics* 90:651–66.

James, Christopher. 1987. Some evidence on the uniqueness of bank loans. *Journal of Financial Economics* 19:217–36.

Kashyap, Anil K., Owen Lamont, and Jeremy C. Stein. 1992. Credit conditions and the cyclical behavior of inventories. MIT Sloan School of Management. Mimeo. Forthcoming in *Quarterly Journal of Economics.*

Kashyap, Anil K., Jeremy C. Stein, and David W. Wilcox. 1993. Monetary policy and credit conditions: Evidence from the composition of external finance. *American Economic Review* 83(1): 78–98.

King, Stephen R. 1986. Monetary transmission: Through bank loans or bank liabilities? *Journal of Money, Credit and Banking* 18:290–303.

Kuttner, Kenneth. 1992. Monetary policy and external finance: The implications of short-term debt flows. Federal Reserve Bank of Chicago. Mimeo.

Lucas, Deborah J., and Robert L. McDonald. 1992. Bank financing and investment decisions with asymmetric information about loan quality. *RAND Journal of Economics* 23(1): 86–105.

Lucas, Robert E., Jr. 1990. Liquidity and interest rates. *Journal of Economic Theory,* 50, no. 2 (April):237–64.

Lummer, Scott L., and John J. McConnell. 1989. Further evidence on the bank lending process and capital market response to bank loan agreements. *Journal of Financial Economics* 25(1): 99–122.

Modigliani, Franco. 1963. The monetary mechanism and its interaction with real phenomena. *Review of Economics and Statistics* 45(1): 79–107.

Morgan, Donald P. 1992. Monetary policy and loan commitments. Work in progress. Kansas City, Mo.: Federal Reserve Bank of Kansas City.

Myers, Stewart, and Nicholas Majluf. 1984. Corporate financing and investment decisions when firms have information that investors do not have. *Journal of Financial Economics* 13:187–221.

Oliner, Stephen, and Glenn Rudebusch. 1992. The transmission of monetary policy: Evidence from the mix of external debt and the importance of internal finance. Federal Reserve Board. Mimeo.

Owens, Raymond E., and Stacey Schreft. 1992. Identifying credit crunches. Federal Reserve Bank of Richmond. Mimeo.

Petersen, Mitchell, and Raghuram G. Rajan. 1992. The benefits of firm-creditor relationships: A study of small business financing. University of Chicago, Graduate School of Business. Mimeo.

Rajan, Raghuram. 1992. Insiders and outsiders: The choice between relationship and arm's length debt. *Journal of Finance* 47:1367–1400.

Ramey, Valerie. 1992. How important is the credit channel of monetary transmission? University of California, San Diego. Mimeo.

Romer, Christina D., and David H. Romer. 1990. New evidence on the monetary transmission mechanism. *Brookings Papers on Economic Activity* 1:149–213. Washington, D.C.: Brookings Institution.

Roosa, Robert V. 1951. Interest rates and the central bank. In *Money, trade and economic growth: Essays in honor of John H. Williams.* New York: Macmillan.

Rotemberg, Julio. 1984. A monetary equilibrium model with transactions costs. *Journal of Political Economy* 92 (February): 40–58.

Schreft, Stacey. 1990. Credit controls: 1980. *Federal Reserve Bank of Richmond Economic Review* 76(6): 25–55.

Sharpe, Steve. 1990. Asymmetric information, bank lending and implicit contracts: A stylized model of consumer relationships. *Journal of Finance* 45:1069–87.

Sushka, Marie E., Myron B. Slovin, and John A. Polonchek. 1992. The value of bank durability: Borrowers as bank stakeholders. *Journal of Finance* 48, no. 1 (March): 247–66.

Stiglitz, Joseph, and Andrew Weiss. 1981. Credit rationing in markets with imperfect information. *American Economic Review* 71(2): 393–410.

Stigum, Marcia. 1990. *The money market.* Homewood, Ill.: Dow Jones Irwin.

Stock, James H., and Mark W. Watson. 1989. New indices of coincident and leading economic indicators. *NBER Macroeconomics Annual* 4:351–94.

Tobin, James, and William Brainard. 1963. Financial intermediaries and the effectiveness of monetary control. *American Economic Review* 53:383–400.

U.S. Congress. 1952. Joint Committee on the Economic Report. *Monetary policy and the management of public debt: Their role in achieving price stability and high-level employment.* 82d Cong., 2d sess.

Comment   Martin Eichenbaum

This paper provides a useful survey of recent theoretical and empirical work on what has become known as the "lending view" of the monetary transmission mechanism. My Comment focuses on two related questions pertaining to the empirical side of the paper. First, what is the nature of the identification problem involved in trying to evaluate the importance of the "lending channel" that is emphasized in the lending view? Second, how convincing is the empirical evidence that the lending channel plays a quantitatively important role in the monetary transmission mechanism?

My basic conclusions are as follows. The identification problems involved in isolating a lending channel are quite severe. Moreover, substantive inference seems to be quite sensitive to the set of identifying assumptions used. When all is said and done, there is very little evidence to directly support the notion that the lending channel plays an important role in propagating the effects of changes in monetary policy. What evidence there is, is equally consistent with alternative interpretations that stress the economic determinants of the observed heterogeneity among economic agents, like small and large firms. Dis-

Martin Eichenbaum is professor of economics at Northwestern University, a senior consultant at the Federal Reserve Bank of Chicago, and a research associate of the National Bureau of Economic Research.

The author thanks Lawrence Christiano, Michael Horvath, and Jonas Fisher for useful conversations in preparing this Comment.

tinguishing between these alternatives will require a detailed analysis of microeconomic data. As things stand though, the empirical claims made for the lending view have not been substantiated.

According to Kashyap and Stein, all that is needed for the lending channel to be operative is that (*a*) some agents view bank credit as special, and (*b*) open-market operations shift the supply of bank credit. The vast majority of theoretical papers in this area make these concepts operational by supposing that there are important asymmetric information problems in credit markets that lead to credit rationing of a subset of agents in the economy.

To find evidence of the lending channel, you have to confront two identification problems. First, you need to make identifying assumptions to isolate a measure of exogenous movements in monetary policy. Usually, this involves taking a stand on the monetary policy rule in effect over the sample period being considered. Second, you need to make a set of identifying assumptions to argue that the supply, rather than the demand for credit, has moved in response to a monetary policy shock. Typically this amounts to finding a differential response of two sets of agents in the economy to a change in monetary policy and arguing that the differential response reflects the presence of the lending channel. The usual identifying assumption here is that, absent credit market imperfections, the agents would have reacted in the same way. The fact that they reacted differently is taken to be evidence of an operative lending channel.

Keeping in mind these identification issues, what kind of evidence do Kashyap and Stein present? First, they point to a variety of unconditional correlations between economic activity and different loans. This is not helpful, as Kashyap and Stein themselves admit, since neither of the two identification problems is dealt with. Second, the authors present evidence that real shocks to the financial intermediation sector matter. While very interesting, this is irrelevant to the issue at hand. Everyone agrees that output would decline if we blew up all the banks or imposed a large tax on what they produced. The question is not whether the activities of banks and financial intermediaries affect the economy. Of course they do. The question is how these activities respond to open-market operations. Third, Kashyap and Stein cite Bernanke and Blinder's (1992) findings that following a shock to monetary policy, measured as an orthogonalized innovation to the Federal funds rate, total bank lending and aggregate output fall. I agree with Kashyap and Stein that this is a very interesting finding. But nothing whatsoever about the empirical importance of the lending channel can be inferred from it. Absent further identifying assumptions, we do not know if the fall in loans reflects a fall in the demand for loans or a fall in the supply of loans.

Fourth, the authors discuss their own work with Wilcox, which analyzes relative fluctuations in bank loans and a leading substitute for bank loans, commercial paper. The basic idea is that if bank loans fall after a monetary policy shock while the stock of commercial paper rises, then we can conclude that the supply of bank loans has contracted. Kashyap, Stein, and Wilcox find that, for their measures of shocks to monetary policy, the mix of bank loans (B) to the sum of bank loans plus commercial paper (C) falls, that is, $\dfrac{B}{B+C}$ declines after a contractionary monetary policy shock. This is interpreted as strong evidence for the importance of the lending channel.

A critical problem with this evidence is that Gertler and Gilchrist (1993) and Oliner and Rudebusch (1993) show that the fall in $\dfrac{B}{B+C}$ does not reflect the substitution of any one agent from bank loans into commercial paper. Instead the fall in bank loans and the rise in commercial paper occurs among two separate groups of borrowers. To begin with, all forms of large-firm debt (bank loans, commercial paper, and "other") go *up*, not down, after a contractionary monetary policy shock. This may reflect the need to finance the rise in inventories that occurs at the beginning of a recession. The only debt that actually goes down is small-firm bank loans. Since the fall in bank loans and the rise in commercial paper pertain to different economic agents, the mix variable emphasized by Kashyap, Stein, and Wilcox cannot be viewed as a legitimate proxy for the supply of bank loans. It follows that the decline in the mix, $\dfrac{B}{B+C}$, cannot be interpreted as evidence for the importance of the lending view.

Still it is true that large and small firms appear to react differently to changes in monetary policy. Just how differently though depends on how we measure shocks to monetary policy. Suppose we identify shocks to monetary policy with one of the measures used by Oliner and Rudebusch, namely, quarterly first differences of the Federal Funds rate. This corresponds to the (incredible) identifying assumption that all changes in the Federal Funds rate are policy induced and that the information set which the Federal Reserve uses when making those changes is uncorrelated with standard economic data. Proceeding as Oliner and Rudebusch did, I computed the sum of the coefficients on the lagged policy variables and the t-statistics of that sum. In one regression I used the total (short-term) indebtedness of large manufacturing firms. In the other I used the total indebtedness of small manufacturing firms. In each case, total indebtedness consisted of the sum of bank loans, commercial paper, and "other" debt. The data were the same as in Gertler and Gilchrist (1993).

The sums of the coefficients and associated t-statistic for the large-firm regression are .019 and 1.48, respectively. The corresponding numbers for the small-firm regression are −.017 and 3.00. These results are consistent with Oliner and Rudebusch. In particular, the negative and highly significant sum of coefficients for the small firms is consistent with the view that after a monetary contraction, small firms face a constriction of bank credit that is not made up from other sources. Large firms increase their total indebtedness.

I then considered a different and (to me) less incredible way of identifying

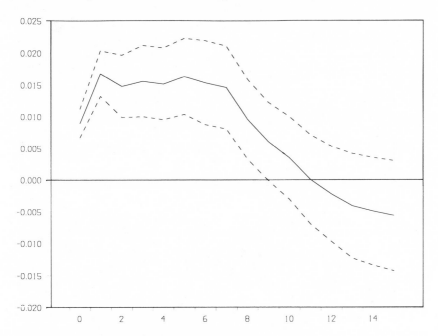

Fig. 7C.1   The response of large-firm loans

monetary policy shocks. Proceeding as in Bernanke and Blinder (1992), I assumed that the monetary authority sets the Federal funds rate as a function of current and past values of real GNP, the GNP deflator as well as past values of the Federal funds rate and total indebtedness of large and small manufacturing firms. A policy shock is identified with the least squares residual that arises when the Federal funds rate is regressed against these variables.[1] All data were quarterly and cover the period 1975:1 to 1991:2.

Figures 7C.1 and 7C.2 display the dynamic response function of total dollar loans to large and small manufacturing firms following a positive orthogonalized innovation to the Federal funds rate. The dotted lines denote a one standard error band around the dynamic response function, that is, a 70 percent confidence interval. Notice that total short-term indebtedness of small firms actually *rises* for roughly one and a half years after the shock to policy.[2] In light of this result it seems very difficult to maintain the view that credit constraints on small firms become much more binding after a monetary contrac-

1. Specifically, I regressed the Federal funds rate on current and six lagged values of real GNP and the GNP deflator as well as six lagged values of the Federal funds rate and total indebtedness of large and small manufacturing firms.
2. The same pattern emerges if we look at the total short-term indebtedness of corporate and noncorporate firms. Both rise in a statistically significant manner after a monetary contraction, although indebtedness of corporate firms rises by more.

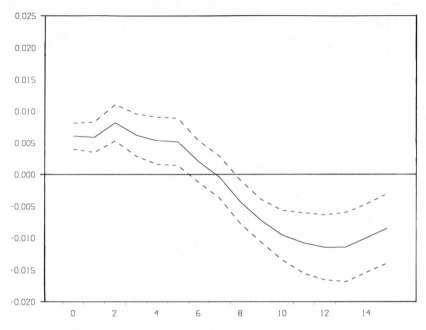

Fig. 7C.2   The response of small-firm loans

tion. After all, small firms do manage to increase their total indebtedness after a monetary contraction.

Even if the qualitative responses of small and large firms to monetary policy shocks are not very different, it is true that their quantitative responses are different. This can be interpreted as evidence in favor of the lending view if we make the identifying assumption that, absent credit constraints, small firms would increase their total debt as much as large firms. This amounts to saying that the *only* factor distinguishing small and large firms is the degree to which they face credit constraints, that is, it is a matter of historical accident that some firms are large and some are small. Under this interpretation, what happens after a monetary contraction is that the inventories of all firms rise after a contractionary shock to monetary policy.[3] Firms need to finance these inventories and all firms, large and small, are able to do so. But small firms obtain less financing, perhaps because they are forced to go to higher-cost sources of credit. The presumption is that this somehow contributes to the propagation of monetary shocks. Unfortunately, no explicit model of this effect has been developed nor has any evidence been offered regarding the quantitative importance of this effect.

A different interpretation builds on the notion that small firms are small for a reason. For example, the size distribution of firms across different industries

3. The lending view has nothing to say about why this might be the case.

may be quite different. Small firms could be concentrated in cyclically sensitive industries or in industries were inventories do not build up as quickly at the onset of a recession. Then the differential response of small and large firms to changes in monetary policy has nothing to do with the frictions emphasized in the lending view. It simply reflects the underlying reasons for the size distribution of firms. As far as I know, the empirical plausibility of this interpretation has not yet been investigated. Until it has though, the current findings regarding the behavior of small and large firms cannot be used as evidence in favor of the lending view.

Finally, I ought to say something about Kashyap and Stein's analysis of the connection between the lending view and limited-participation models of the sort considered by Robert Lucas, Tim Fuerst, and Lawrence Christiano and myself. Frankly I found the discussion somewhat forced. Perhaps this is because I think that any fully articulated version of the lending view will inevitably involve credit market imperfections. And there is no logical connection between limited participation and credit constraints. Fisher's (1993) model is very interesting precisely because it allows for credit market imperfections in a limited participation setup. Among other things, this allows him to carefully distinguish and quantify the roles which the different frictions play in a general equilibrium model.

In conclusion, I found the Kashyap and Stein paper useful along a number of dimensions. Certainly it clarified a number of issues for me. Still, I remain far from convinced that there is much evidence to support the notion that the credit or lending channel is a quantitatively important part of the monetary transmission mechanism. It may be. But the evidence to substantiate that position has not yet been developed.

References

Bernanke, Ben, and Alan Blinder. 1992. The federal funds rate and the channels of monetary transmission. *American Economic Review* 82:901–21.
Fisher, Jonas. 1993. Credit market imperfections and the monetary transmission mechanism. Northwestern University. Manuscript.
Gertler, Mark, and Simon Gilchrist. 1993. Monetary policy, business cycles and the behavior of small manufacturing firms. New York University. Manuscript.
Oliner, Stephen D., and Glenn D. Rudebusch. 1993. The transmission of monetary policy to small and large firms. Board of Governors of the Federal Reserve System. Manuscript.

8   Historical Perspectives on the Monetary Transmission Mechanism

Jeffrey A. Miron, Christina D. Romer, and David N. Weil

In recent years, macroeconomists have devoted renewed attention to understanding the monetary transmission mechanism. According to the standard "money" view, an open-market sale of bonds by the central bank forces up interest rates because bond holders must be compensated with higher interest income for holding a less liquid combination of assets. Although textbook presentations of this view often assume that banks are involved in the transmission of the open-market sale, the presence of banks, and particularly bank loans, is in no way necessary.

The alternative "lending" view of the monetary transmission mechanism assumes that bank loans are a special form of external finance. Banks do not regard loans and bonds as perfect substitutes on the asset side of their balance sheets, and firms do not regard bank loans as equivalent to other sources of funds on the liability side of their balance sheets. Since banks faced with a loss of reserves prefer to reduce the interest-bearing component of their portfolio partly via loans and partly via securities, and since firms do not view securities as perfect substitutes for bank loans, the interest rate on loans must increase relative to that on securities. This increase in the "spread" reflects an additional contractionary effect of restrictive monetary policy that is absent in the pure money view of the transmission mechanism.

This paper provides historical perspective on the monetary transmission

Jeffrey A. Miron is professor of economics at Boston University and a research associate of the National Bureau of Economic Research. Christina D. Romer is professor of economics at the University of California, Berkeley, and a research associate of the National Bureau of Economic Research. David N. Weil is associate professor of economics at Brown University and a faculty research fellow of the National Bureau of Economic Research.

The authors thank Ben Bernanke, Charles Calomiris, Philip Jefferson, Gregory Mankiw, David Romer, Anna Schwartz, and David Wilcox for helpful comments on earlier drafts of this paper. They are indebted to Matthew Jones for excellent research assistance.

mechanism. Several recent papers attempt to determine whether the special nature of bank lending impinges on the monetary transmission mechanism (Bernanke 1983; Calomiris and Hubbard 1989; Bordo, Rappaport, and Schwartz 1992; Kashyap, Stein, and Wilcox 1993; Romer and Romer 1990; Hall and Thomson 1993), and a number of these examine the transmission mechanism in particular historical episodes (Calomiris and Hubbard 1989; Bordo, Rappaport, and Schwartz 1992; Bernanke 1983). None of these papers, however, explores changes in the nature of the transmission mechanism over time. In this paper we directly examine the changes in financial market institutions over the last one hundred years, and we show how these changes can be used to assess the importance of the lending channel of monetary transmission.

Section 8.1 presents the basic analytical framework. We use the Bernanke and Blinder (1988) model of the monetary transmission mechanism to show under what conditions the response of the economy to a monetary contraction should be especially sensitive to the presence of a lending channel. Each of the conditions we identify can be examined in the data over long historical periods. We can therefore determine whether the lending channel appears to be important in periods when theory combined with evidence on the financial structure suggests it should be important.

Section 8.2 examines empirically those features of bank and firm balance sheets that our theoretical discussion suggests are most relevant to the quantitative importance of the lending channel. In particular we document how such factors as the structure of reserve requirements and the composition of external firm finance have changed over time. Our analysis shows that the lending channel should have played a much greater role in the pre-1929 era than during the early part of the post–World War II period.

In section 8.3 we present new evidence on the lending channel by determining whether measures of the importance of bank lending behave differently across periods characterized by differences in those factors that our theoretical discussion suggests determine the strength of the lending channel. The measures we consider are the spread between the interest rate on bank loans and the interest rate on commercial paper, the ratio of bank loans to other sources of credit (the "mix"), and the relation between bank loans and output after monetary contractions and in more ordinary times. We find little evidence that these measures of the importance of the lending channel change across time periods in the ways implied by changes in financial structure and institutions.

Section 8.4 concludes the paper. The evidence we present can be interpreted in at least two ways. On the one hand, it may indicate that traditional indicators of the importance of the lending channel are not useful. On the other hand, it may indicate that the lending channel has not been particularly important in any sample period. Our analysis does not rule decisively on which of these two explanations is correct. However, since the most obvious indicators of the lending channel fail to provide consistent evidence of its importance, we believe proponents of this view are likely to have a difficult time providing a compelling case for its empirical relevance.

8.1 Framework for Analysis

We begin by laying out a model of the monetary transmission mechanism that considers the relative importance of different financing channels. The model is a modified version of the one presented in Bernanke and Blinder (1988). We use the model to highlight the role of various institutional features in determining the importance of the lending channel.

8.1.1 The Model

We begin by considering the more familiar model in which loans play no role. The only assets are money, m, and bonds, b. Our notation is that small letters signify quantities, capital letters signify functions, subscripts signify derivatives, and superscripts signify subsets of quantities (for example, b is bonds while b^b is bonds held by banks). Since the price level and the inflation rate are held fixed throughout, we normalize them to 1 and 0, respectively. All variables are therefore in real terms.

The demand for money depends on output, y, and the bond interest rate, i,

$$(1) \qquad m = D(i,y).$$

As in the standard *IS* curve, output depends negatively on the interest rate,

$$(2) \qquad y = Y(i).$$

Differentiating (1) and (2) yields

$$(3) \qquad \frac{dy}{dm} = \frac{Y_i}{D_i + D_y Y_i}.$$

Equation (3) shows the effect of money on output when only the money channel is operational.

Theories of the lending channel begin by recognizing the existence of another asset, loans, l. The banking sector's balance sheet is then

$$(4) \qquad m = b^b + l + r,$$

where r is reserves and b^b is net holdings of bonds by banks. Note that we treat time deposits and certificates of deposit (CDs) as bank-issued bonds, which are subtracted from bank holdings of bonds in calculating b^b. All money is held in the form of deposits, which are liabilities of banks. Nonbank holdings of nominally denominated assets, w, are given by

$$(5) \qquad w = b^p + m - l,$$

where b^p is net bond holdings of the nonbank public. Note that we include both firms and households in the nonbank sector. This formulation assumes that in the short run the stock of nominally denominated assets held by the nonbank sector is fixed.

Introducing a third asset requires introducing a second interest rate. Rather than including the interest rate on loans directly, we introduce the difference between the loan interest rate and the bond interest rate, δ, which affects investment demand. Thus (2) becomes

$$(6) \qquad\qquad y = Y(i,\delta),$$

where $Y_i < 0$ and $Y_\delta < 0$. The demand for loans by the nonbank public is

$$(7) \qquad\qquad l = L(\delta,i,y),$$

where $L_\delta < 0$. We discuss the signs of L_i and L_y below.

Banks hold deposits as liabilities, and loans and reserves as assets. Combining the models of Romer and Romer (1990) and Bernanke and Blinder (1988), we allow banks to hold bonds as either assets or liabilities, with time deposits and CDs defined as bank-issued bonds. We define b^b as banks' net holdings of bonds. As discussed by Romer and Romer, bond issues by banks may or may not require significant reserve holdings. We assume that if reserve requirements are imposed on bond issue, then banks will not both hold and issue bonds, except for small quantities of bonds held for liquidity purposes. Thus the reserve requirement holds on the net issue of bonds.

We take the fraction of bank deposits held as reserves against demand deposits to be constant at some level τ_1 that can be thought of as required or desired reserves. Reserves against bond issues are taken to be constant at rate τ_2. Banks choose the fraction of nonreserve assets held in the form of loans as a function of the loan-bond interest differential,

$$(8) \qquad\qquad \frac{l}{l + b^b} = \lambda = \Lambda(\delta),$$

where $\Lambda_\delta > 0$.[1] If λ is less than one, banks hold bonds on net. If λ is greater than one, banks issue bonds on net.

In the case where banks are net holders of bonds, the supply of loans is

$$(9) \qquad\qquad l = \Lambda(\delta)(1 - \tau_1)m.$$

In the case where banks are net issuers of bonds, the supply of loans is

$$(10) \qquad\qquad l = \left(\frac{\Lambda(\delta)(1 - \tau_1)}{1 + (\Lambda(\delta) - 1)\tau_2}\right)m.$$

Note that if the reserve requirement on bond issues is zero, then equations (9) and (10) are the same. Thus in the rest of this section, we assume that reserves

---

1. Bernanke and Blinder (1988) assume that the desired fraction of the bank's nonreserve portfolio held in the form of loans is a function of the rates of interest on loans and bonds separately. We believe nothing rests on our simplification.

are held on net bond issues and then discuss the cases where no such reserves are held by setting τ_2 to zero.

Equating the supply and demand for loans yields

$$(11) \qquad L(\delta,i,y) = \left(\frac{\Lambda(\delta)(1 - \tau_1)}{1 + (\Lambda(\delta) - 1)\tau_2}\right)m.$$

Equations (1), (6), and (11) determine the levels of y, i, and δ given the level of m. Totally differentiating the three equations, the effect of a change in the money supply on output is

$$(12) \quad \frac{dy}{dm} = \frac{\left(\frac{\Lambda_\delta}{\lambda}\left(\frac{1 - \tau_2}{1 + (\lambda - 1)\tau_2}\right) - \frac{L_\delta}{l}\right)\left(\frac{Y_i}{Y_\delta}\right) + \left(\frac{L_i}{l}\right) - \left(\frac{D_i}{m}\right)}{\left(\frac{\Lambda_\delta}{\lambda}\left(\frac{1 - \tau_2}{1 + (\lambda - 1)\tau_2}\right) - \frac{L_\delta}{l}\right)\left(\frac{D_i + D_y Y_i}{Y_\delta}\right) + \left(\frac{L_i D_y - L_y D_i}{l}\right)}.$$

This equation shows the effects of an open-market sale that reduces m and raises either b^b or b^p, holding w constant, when both a lending channel and a money channel are operational.

8.1.2   Simplifying Assumptions

We now add further assumptions to simplify expression (12). We begin with the interest elasticities of the nonbank public's demands for different assets. Starting from the nonbank sector's holdings of nominally denominated assets, we have the usual adding up constraint

$$(13) \qquad 0 = B_i^p + D_i - L_i,$$

where $B^p(\cdot)$ is the nonbank public's demand for bonds. Dividing by the total amount of deposits and rearranging gives

$$(14) \qquad \frac{D_i}{m} = \frac{L_i}{l}\frac{l}{m} - \frac{B_i^p}{b^p}\frac{b^p}{m}.$$

This equation relates the percentage change in deposits in response to an interest-rate increase to the percentage changes in loan and bond holdings in response to an interest-rate increase and to the relative sizes of the three nominal assets held by the nonbank sector. When interest rates rise, the nonbank public wants to hold less money. It can accomplish this by holding more bonds ($B_i^p > 0$) or fewer loans ($L_i < 0$) or both.

To go further, we assume that the percentage changes in the holdings of the two assets in response to interest-rate changes are equal. Thus,

$$(15) \qquad \frac{L_i}{l} = -\frac{B_i^p}{b^p}.$$

The relationship between the interest elasticities of money and loan demand is therefore

(16)
$$\frac{L_i}{l} = \left(\frac{D_i}{m}\right)\left(\frac{m}{l + b^p}\right).$$

Substituting this expression into equation (12) eliminates one term in the numerator.

We now turn to the income elasticities of money, loan, and bond demand. The adding up constraint means that

(17)
$$0 = B_y^p + D_y - L_y.$$

The standard assumption is that D_y is positive, and we add the assumption that in response to an increase in income, bond and loan demand adjust by the same percentage, so

(18)
$$\frac{L_y}{l} = -\frac{B_y^p}{b^p}.$$

We thus derive an expression for the relationship between the income elasticities of money and loan demand analogous to (16) above,

(19)
$$\frac{D_y}{m} = \left(\frac{L_y}{l}\right)\left(\frac{l + b^p}{m}\right).$$

Combining (16) and (19) gives

(20)
$$D_i L_y = L_i D_y,$$

which eliminates one term in the denominator of the expression for dy/dm derived above.[2]

Incorporating these assumptions about elasticities, the derivative of output with respect to money becomes

(21)
$$\frac{dy}{dm} = \frac{\left(\frac{\Lambda_\delta}{\lambda}\left(\frac{1 - \tau_2}{1 + (\lambda - 1)\tau_2}\right) - \frac{L_\delta}{l}\right)\left(\frac{Y_i}{Y_\delta}\right) - \left(\frac{b^p + l - m}{b^p + l}\right)\left(\frac{D_i}{m}\right)}{\left(\frac{\Lambda_\delta}{\lambda}\left(\frac{1 - \tau_2}{1 + (\lambda - 1)\tau_2}\right) - \frac{L_\delta}{l}\right)\left(\frac{D_i + D_y Y_i}{Y_\delta}\right)}.$$

This expression shows the effects of money on output when a lending channel is operational, assuming our simplifying assumptions are approximately correct. Several comments about this expression are in order.

The conditions for a lending channel to be operational are that $\Lambda_\delta < \infty$,

2. The conditions under which the last term in the denominator drops out are more general than the assumptions made here. For example, rather than assuming that private bond holdings and loans both adjust by the same percentage (in response to changes in either i or y), we could assume that the ratio of their percentage adjustments is the same in either case.

$L_\delta > -\infty$, and $Y_\delta < 0$. If any of these conditions fails to hold, then (21) collapses to (3). The first of these conditions states that banks do not regard loans and bonds as perfect substitutes in their portfolios; the second states that firms do not regard loans and bonds as perfect substitutes in their portfolios; and the third states that firms' investment decisions depend on both the loan and bond interest rates.

The condition for money to have a greater effect on output when the lending channel is operational (that is, the condition for the expression in [21] to exceed the expression in [3]) is that

(22) $$b^p + l - m > 0.$$

Since this term can be positive or negative, the lending channel can exacerbate or moderate the money channel's effect on output. From the bank's balance sheet,

(23) $$l - m = -b^b - r.$$

So, the condition for the lending channel to exacerbate the effect of money on output is that

(24) $$b^b + r < b^p.$$

We assume in what follows that this condition is satisfied.

8.1.3   The Determinants of dy/dm

Having laid out the basic model, we now consider how observable features of the institutional and financial structure of the economy are likely to affect the impact of money on output, assuming a lending channel is operational. Our discussion focuses on two broad areas: the structure of bank balance sheets and the structure of firm finance.

The first factor likely to determine the magnitude of money's effect on output is the structure of bank assets. Assuming that condition (24) is satisfied, dy/dm is largest when Λ_δ/λ is small, that is, when banks do not adjust the fraction of their assets made up of loans in response to a change in the loan-bond differential. Under the assumption that Λ_δ does not vary significantly with λ, this would imply that dy/dm is increasing in the fraction of their portfolios that banks hold in loans.

More generally, the effect of changes in λ on Λ_δ/λ depends on the underlying model of bank portfolio preferences. One case where one can determine the magnitude of Λ_δ/λ is when there is a significant reserve requirement on the issue of bonds by banks, and λ (the fraction of the bank's portfolio made up of loans) is near one. In this case banks are likely to be at a corner, where the marginal cost of one less loan (the interest rate on holding bonds, which is the opportunity cost of making loans) could be much less than the marginal cost of one more loan (that is, the bond interest rate adjusted for the cost of holding reserves against bond issue). In such a case, the elasticity of the portfolio share with respect to the loan-bond differential is likely to be near zero, and thus, other factors held constant, dy/dm should be large.

The second factor affecting the size of dy/dm is the structure of firm finance. Expression (21) indicates that the fraction of firms' capital coming from loans relative to bonds likely affects the magnitude of the lending channel by changing the semielasticity of loan demand with respect to the loan-bond differential, L_8/l. As loans increase as a fraction of firm finance, we expect L_8/l to fall, thus increasing dy/dm.

A third factor in the size of dy/dm is the relative size of the sensitivities of investment to the bond interest rate and to the loan-bond differential. Holding Y_i constant, an increase in the ratio of Y_8 to Y_i raises the value of dy/dm. This ratio will be affected both by the different fractions of investment being financed at the loan and bond rates and by the potential for substitution between the two. If, for example, "small" firms invest using loans while "large" firms invest using bonds, if there is no substitution between the two sources of financing, and if the two size firms have the same interest elasticity of investment, then Y_8/Y_i will just equal the fraction of firms that are small. Differences in the interest elasticities of investment between large and small firms will affect the ratio of Y_8 to Y_i. If small firms are more interest sensitive than large firms, dy/dm will be bigger. Finally, if firms are able to substitute between loans and bonds in their financing, this will reduce Y_8 and thus reduce dy/dm.

8.2   Changes in Financial Structure

According to the model presented in section 8.1, changes in the financial structure of the economy have important implications for the importance of the lending channel in the transmission of monetary shocks. Therefore, to see whether the importance of the lending channel is likely to have changed over time in the United States, we examine evidence on how various aspects of financial structure have changed between 1900 and 1988. In particular, we look at structural changes in the balance sheets of banks and firms.

The major finding of this analysis of institutions is that the lending channel of the monetary transmission mechanism should have been stronger before 1929 than in the first two decades after 1945. We find that important changes in financial structure occurred between the pre-Depression and post–World War II eras and that, at least up through 1970, essentially all of these changes imply a weakening of the lending channel. After 1970 the evidence is more complicated, with some changes further weakening the lending channel and others potentially strengthening it.

8.2.1   Banks

Assets

Annual data on bank balance sheets from 1896 to the present are available from the Federal Reserve. These data reflect a major effort by the Federal Re-

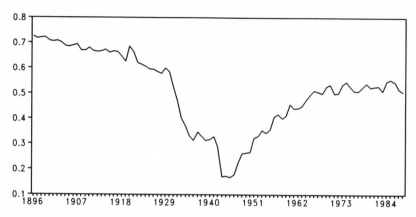

Fig. 8.1   Ratio of bank loans to total interest-bearing bank assets, 1896–1988
Note: Real estate loans are excluded from bank loans.

serve to adjust the historical statistics for the prewar era (from the Comptroller of the Currency) to be as consistent as possible with postwar statistics. This adjustment mainly involves inflating the data for nonnational banks to compensate for underreporting by state banks in the period before 1938. In this section we use the version of the Federal Reserve data corresponding to all commercial banks.[3]

Figure 8.1 shows the ratio of total bank loans less real estate loans to total interest-bearing bank assets for 1896 to 1988. This ratio declined slowly over the first three decades of the twentieth century, from 72 percent in 1896 to 60 percent in 1929. It then fell dramatically during the Great Depression and World War II, reaching 17 percent in 1945. Between 1945 and 1970 it rose steadily, reaching 27 percent in 1950, 46 percent in 1960, and 53 percent in 1970. Since 1970 non–real estate loans as a fraction of total bank assets have hovered around 52 percent.

Mirroring this fall over time in the loan ratio is a rise over time in the fraction of bank assets accounted for by government securities. Government securities accounted for between 5 and 7 percent of interest-bearing bank assets during most of the pre–World War I era. After the war this number was higher; in 1929, for example, government securities accounted for 10 percent of total assets. During World War II banks increased their holdings of U.S. government securities by a factor of four. This came on top of a threefold increase between 1929 and 1936. As a result, government securities accounted for 73 percent of total interest-bearing assets in 1945. Banks' holdings of government securities then fell steadily in the first two decades of the postwar era as loans rose. However, as the behavior of the loan ratio suggests, the fraction of bank assets

3. The data for 1896–1970 are from U.S. Bureau of the Census (1975, ser. X588–X609). Data after 1970 are from the *Annual Statistical Digest* of the Federal Reserve for various years. For all years we use total loans excluding interbank loans. Data prior to 1970 are for June 30 or the nearest available date; data thereafter are for the last Wednesday in June.

accounted for by government securities never returned to its pre–World War I level; in 1988 government securities were still 14 percent of total bank assets.

This pattern suggests that loans were, on average, a substantially larger fraction of total interest-bearing bank assets in the pre-Depression era than in the post–World War II period. Even at the postwar peak, the fraction of bank assets accounted for by non–real estate loans was more than ten percentage points smaller than the average fraction in the pre-1929 period. In terms of the model given in section 8.1, holding other factors constant, this change implies that the lending channel was substantially more important before 1929 than after 1945.[4]

The implications of the low loan holdings during the period 1929–1944 are harder to determine because the period is short and dominated by the Great Depression. The plummeting of the fraction of bank assets accounted for by loans between 1929 and 1936 almost surely reflects the tremendous fall in output, rather than some instantaneous change in the importance of the lending channel. Thus, a reasonable view is that the lending channel was as important during the declining phase of the Depression as it was in the three decades before 1929. On the other hand, after the recovery was firmly under way, it seems possible that the continued low loan ratios, including the additional declines associated with World War II, imply that the lending channel was considerably weaker in the late 1930s and early 1940s than previously. Once banks had switched so thoroughly out of loans and into other assets, a decline in reserves should have had less effect on bank lending.

Liabilities

The structure and level of reserve requirements has changed dramatically over time. Figure 8.2a shows the ratio of the reserve requirement on time deposits to the reserve requirement on demand deposits over the last century. Figure 8.2b shows the level of the reserve requirement on time deposits. Construction of these figures is somewhat complicated due to changes in the definition of time deposits and to the variation in state regulations before the founding of the Federal Reserve in 1914. For the period before 1917, we analyze reserve requirements for national banks, as set by the National Banking Act of 1864 and various amendments. These figures are also complicated by the fact that the definition of deposits was changed substantially by the Monetary Control Act of 1980.[5]

---

4. In the preceding discussion we examined total loans less real estate loans. This measure was motivated by the presumption that most real estate loans are to households and that the lending channel works mainly through loans to firms. However, if one includes real estate loans the results are qualitatively similar. The only difference is that the loan ratio including real estate loans nearly reaches pre-1929 levels in the 1980s.

5. The data on reserve requirements under the National Banking Act are from Bordo, Rappaport, and Schwartz (1992, 211). The data for 1917–80 are from U.S. Board of Governors of the Federal Reserve System (1983, 236–37). For the period 1917–62, we use the reserve requirements on

Under the National Banking Act no distinction was drawn between time deposits and demand deposits; there was a uniform reserve requirement on all deposits. Thus, the ratio of the reserve requirement on time deposits to that on demand deposits for national banks was one from 1874 until the founding of the Federal Reserve. Effective in 1917, the Federal Reserve Act distinguished between time and demand deposits, setting the ratio of the reserve requirements on the two at an initial level of roughly one to three. Though there was some variation in this ratio during the interwar and early postwar eras, it remained at roughly one to three until the mid-1960s. The relative size of the requirement on time deposits was lowered significantly in 1967, and the ratio hovered around ⅙ through the 1970s. After 1980 the ratio rose to ¼, but this change is somewhat hard to interpret because of the change in the definition of deposits.

The change in the ratio of reserve requirements on time and demand deposits in the postwar era is even more dramatic if one considers special time deposits rather than ordinary savings accounts. An important development of the 1960s was the advent of certificates of deposit.[6] While CDs had roughly the same reserve requirements as savings deposits in the late 1960s, in the 1970s their reserve requirement fell from 3 percent to 1 percent. In 1980, under the Monetary Control Act, the reserve requirement on CDs over a certain level was set to zero. As a result of this change, banks in the late 1970s and 1980s had a way of raising funds that was free of reserve limitations.

The level of the reserve requirement on time deposits follows almost the same pattern as the ratio of the reserve requirement on time deposits to that on demand deposits. Under the National Banking Act the reserve requirement on time deposits was not only the same as that on demand deposits, it was also very high (25 percent). With the advent of the Federal Reserve, the reserve requirement on time deposits fell dramatically (to 3 percent). This level rose somewhat during the Great Depression and the early postwar era (to between 5 and 7.5 percent), before returning to 3 percent in 1967. Once again, if special time deposits are considered rather than savings accounts, changes occur again in 1975 and 1980 when the reserve requirement on CDs was lowered and then eliminated.

As mentioned above, the discussion of reserve requirements for the pre–World War I era is complicated by the presence of state banks that were subject to individual state reserve requirements. In the period before World War I there

---

demand deposits for reserve city banks and time deposits for all classes of banks. For the period 1966–72 we use the requirements on demand deposits for reserve city banks with deposits over $5 million and on savings deposits. For 1972–80, we use the requirements on net demand deposits for banks with deposits over $400 million and on savings deposits. After 1980, we use the requirements on net transactions accounts over $28.9 million and on nonpersonal time deposits of maturity less than one and one-half years.

6. Kaufman (1992, 62) states that CDs "were developed in 1961 to provide commercial banks with a means of competing . . . for the temporary excess money balances of larger corporations."

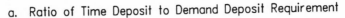

a. Ratio of Time Deposit to Demand Deposit Requirement

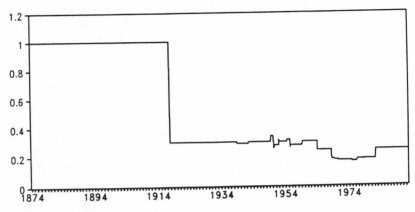

b. Reserve Requirement on Time Deposits

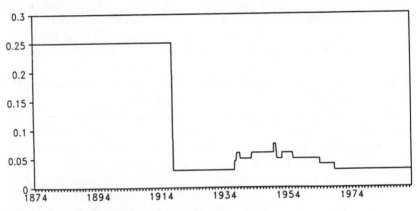

Fig. 8.2   Reserve requirements, 1874–1991

was substantial variation in state regulations. Before detailing the differences between state and national bank regulations, it is important to note that national banks account for a large fraction of total bank assets in the early period. National banks accounted for 42 percent of total bank assets in 1896 and 43 percent in 1910.[7] Thus, nearly half of bank deposits in the prewar era certainly had equal reserve requirements on demand and time deposits.

A systematic study of state reserve requirement legislation by Rodkey (1934) indicates that most state banks had similar reserve requirements on demand and time deposits during the period before the founding of the Federal Reserve. However, Rodkey lists eleven states that passed legislation distin-

7. The data on national and nonnational bank assets are from U.S. Bureau of the Census (1975, ser. X635, X657).

guishing between the different types of deposits in the setting of reserve requirements. These states were (in the order of the date of legislation) Maine, New Hampshire, Nebraska, Iowa, North Carolina, Oregon, Pennsylvania, Connecticut, Vermont, Utah, and Colorado. In most of these states, however, the ratio of the reserve requirement on time deposits to that on demand deposits was much closer to one than in the post–Federal Reserve period, and the level of reserve requirements on time deposits was substantial. For example, in the Pennsylvania statute passed in 1907, the reserve requirement on time deposits was 7.5 percent and that on demand deposits was 15 percent. In the Utah statute passed in 1911, the reserve requirement on time deposits was 10 percent and that on demand deposits was 15 percent.

Those states that had similar reserve requirements on time deposits and demand deposits typically set fairly high reserve requirements. A study by Welldon (1909) of state regulations in 1909 found that reserve requirements on time and demand deposits in state banks were usually between 15 and 25 percent. However, Welldon found that in 1909, fourteen states had zero reserve requirements on both time and demand deposits. Since reserve requirements were becoming more common over time, the number of states with no reserve requirements was surely much larger in the 1870s and 1880s.

Given that the majority of state banks set equal and high reserve requirements on time and demand deposits in the pre–Federal Reserve era, it is reasonable to conclude that the ratio of the reserve requirement on time deposits to that on demand deposits fell substantially between the pre-1914 era and the interwar and postwar periods. Furthermore, within the post–World War II period, the ratio fell even more. The level of reserve requirements on time deposits almost surely showed the same pattern.

To look directly at the importance of time deposits to bank balance sheets, figure 8.3a presents the ratio of time deposits to total interest-bearing assets of commercial banks.[8] The relative size of time deposits, though small, rose through the pre–Federal Reserve period and continued to rise through the onset of the Depression. The relative magnitude of time deposits fell during World War II, but then rose swiftly during the postwar period, with time deposits (including CDs) becoming the dominant liability of commercial banks in the 1970s and 1980s.

The change in the structure of reserve requirements over time and the corresponding rise in the importance of time deposits suggest that the lending channel should have been weakened between the pre-1914 and post–World War II periods. In the pre–Federal Reserve era, banks had little opportunity to raise funds to counteract a fall in reserves because all deposits were covered by the same reserve requirements. Thus, loans had to contract in response to a fall in reserves. In contrast, in the 1980s banks could issue CDs which have no reserve

---

8. Data on time deposits, which include CDs and savings accounts, for 1896–1970 are from U.S. Bureau of the Census, 1975, ser. 606; data for 1971–90 are from the Federal Reserve's *Annual Statistical Digest*. All data are for the end of June or the last Wednesday in June.

a. Ratio of Time Deposits to Total Interest—Bearing Assets

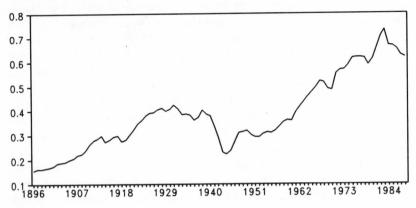

b. Ratio of Bank Loans to Net Interest—Bearing Assets (Lambda)

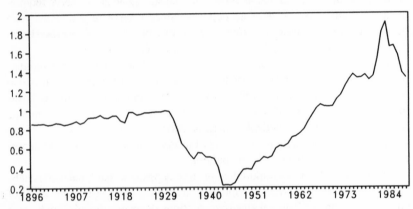

Fig. 8.3   Composition of bank portfolios, 1896–1988

requirement. As a result, loans no longer need to fall in response to a decline in reserves.

Figure 8.3b plots our summary measure of banks' portfolios, λ, which is the ratio of loans to net interest bearing assets (loans plus net bond holdings). During the period before the Great Depression, λ remained near one, reflecting the fact that banks' net holdings of bonds were near zero. During the first part of this period, when there were substantial reserve requirements on time deposits, we suspect that banks were at a corner with respect to the fraction of their net assets made up of loans. More generally, the fact that λ was so near to one *and* showed so little variation suggests that banks were reluctant to change the composition of their portfolios in response, for example, to a change in the loan-bond differential. In such a case, according to the model laid out above, the lending channel will be particularly potent. Over the postwar period, λ rose steadily, reflecting both an increase in loans on the asset side and an increase in time deposits as liabilities. The effect of these changes in λ on the importance of the lending channel in the postwar era is ambiguous. On the one hand, the high values of λ in the latter half of the period might suggest that Λ_g/λ was small and the lending channel was important. On the other hand, the large range of values over which λ varied might suggest that banks were not reluctant to adjust their portfolios, and thus that the lending channel was not important.

8.2.2 Firms

According to the model given in section 8.1, changes in the composition of firm finance and the relative size of large and small firms over time would cause the importance of the lending channel of monetary transmission to change as well. If firms use fewer loans relative to other liabilities to finance investment, this should decrease the importance of the lending channel. This is true because a lower emphasis on loan finance means that firms are less sensitive to changes in the loan-bond interest differential. Since small firms are likely to be more constrained in their alternatives to bank credit, a fall in the proportion of firms that are small implies that the lending channel is likely to have become less important also.[9]

Aggregate Behavior

Perhaps the simplest measure of the importance of bank loans in the financing of firms is the ratio of total bank loans (less real estate loans) to the capital stock. This measure provides an indication of whether bank loans grew faster, slower, or at just the same rate as the capital which such loans are designed to finance. The data on total non–real estate bank loans are taken from the balance sheet for all commercial banks described above. The capital stock series used shows the net stock of fixed, nonresidential private capital.[10] Since the loan series is in current dollars, we use the current–cost valuation capital stock series as well. Because the capital stock series starts in 1925, we can look only at the ratio starting at the end of the pre-Depression era.

Figure 8.4 shows the ratio of total non–real estate bank loans to the capital stock. As can be seen, in the late 1920s this ratio was between 26 and 29 percent. During the Depression, the ratio plummeted as loans fell dramatically. The ratio remained below 20 percent until 1960. During the early 1970s, it reached levels close to the typical value in the late 1920s. In the late 1970s and early 1980s, the ratio of loans to the capital stock fell again, to values close to 20 percent. This picture certainly suggests that loans were a more important source of firm finance at the end of the pre-Depression era than in the postwar

9. Gertler and Gilchrist (1991) and Oliner and Rudebusch (1992) suggest that monetary contractions affect the economy by reducing the availability of bank loans to small firms.

10. These data are described in U.S. Bureau of Economic Analysis (1974). We use the most recent version of the data available from the National Trade Data Bank.

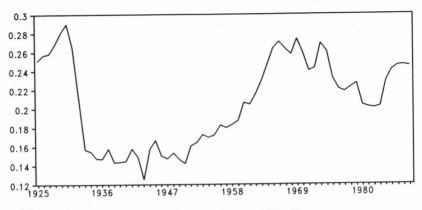

Fig. 8.4   Ratio of bank loans to the capital stock, 1925–88

era. However, what happened during the early years of the twentieth century cannot be discerned.

The fact that bank loans have not grown as rapidly as the capital stock at an aggregate level since 1925 is important because it provides a way of gauging the plausibility of the sectoral balance sheets discussed below. Given the aggregate behavior of loans, it would be impossible for several important sectors to show a marked increase in the importance of bank loans unless other sectors show a substantial decline. At a more fundamental level, the decline in the aggregate importance of bank loans over time suggests that the lending channel of monetary transmission is likely to have become less important over time. If more capital was financed using bank loans in the pre-1929 era than in the postwar era, it is likely that the lending channel was stronger in the past than today.

Corporations

More detailed information about the importance of bank lending in the financing of firms can be found in the sectoral balance sheet of the nonfinancial corporate sector and the nonfarm, unincorporated business sector of the U.S. economy. The annual balance sheet data are constructed by merging the data from Goldsmith, Lipsey, and Mendelson (1963) for selected years between 1900–45 with those from the Flow of Funds Accounts of the Federal Reserve for 1945–90. The data from Goldsmith, Lipsey, and Mendelson, while similar in concept to those of the Federal Reserve, differ in many practical ways from the modern data. Furthermore, the Flow of Funds data from the Federal Reserve on assets and liabilities have been revised over time, so that data from the early postwar era are not strictly comparable with more recent data. To deal with these problems of comparability, we make several adjustments to the various series. These adjustments are described in the appendix.

The bank loans n.e.c. (not elsewhere classified) entry in the sectoral balance

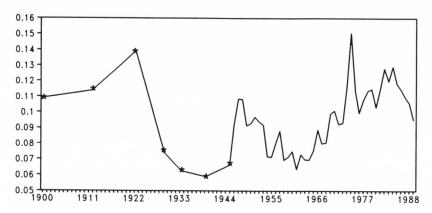

Fig. 8.5   Ratio of loans to total liabilities for corporations, 1900–89
Note: Before 1945 data are available only for starred observations; after 1945 the data are annual.

sheet is the best available measure of total bank loans to corporations. There are surely other bank loans made to corporations, but they are lumped in with the loans of other financial intermediaries in such categories as mortgages and loans on securities. To gauge the changes in the importance of bank loans, we compare bank loans with the sum of total liabilities of corporations, less trade debt and the market value of corporate equities. While gross trade debt is typically included in total liabilities, it is not a large net source of finance for the corporate sector because firms owe most of it to each other. Therefore, we exclude gross trade debt from total liabilities. Figure 8.5 shows the ratio of bank loans n.e.c. to total liabilities less trade debt plus equities for nonfinancial corporations.

This graph shows that the loan ratio of corporations rose over the course of the pre-Depression era, from 11 percent in 1900 to 14 percent in 1922. By 1929, however, it had fallen back to 8 percent because of the explosion in the market value of corporate equities. It then fell further during the Depression, reaching 6 percent in 1933. The corporate loan ratio started the postwar era fairly high, reaching 11 percent in 1947, but then dropped substantially in the 1950s. During the 1950s and 1960s, the ratio hovered around 7 percent. It then rose in the 1970s, but, with the exception of 1974, it did not reach its pre-Depression peak value. Based on this graph, it appears that the loan ratio for corporations was noticeably higher in the pre-Depression era than in the first two decades of the postwar era. After 1970, loans increased in importance, but they are still less important than in the first decades of the 1900s.

The decreased role of bank loans in the postwar era has various sources. One widely cited change in corporate finance between the pre–World War I era and the interwar and postwar periods is the expansion of the commercial paper market (see, for example, Cargill 1991, 140, and Greef 1938). However, even though the commercial paper market expanded significantly, especially after 1960, it is still a very small fraction of total liabilities. Thus, it is not the main source of the decreased importance of loans. The more important change is the expansion of corporate equities. Corporate equities increased much faster between the pre-1929 and postwar eras than did loans or total liabilities (less trade debt). Indeed, the ratio of loans to total liabilities (less trade debt) was roughly the same in the early 1900s and the early postwar era.[11] Thus, the main source of the decline in the importance of bank finance for corporations is the expansion of equity finance.

Unincorporated Businesses

As described in the appendix, the balance sheet for nonfarm, unincorporated businesses cannot be made consistent over time. However, the data from Goldsmith, Lipsey, and Mendelson for 1900 to 1945 show some interesting trends. Figure 8.6 shows the ratio of bank loans to total liabilities (less trade debt) for unincorporated businesses before 1945. As with corporate finance, loans became a much smaller fraction of total liabilities of unincorporated businesses beginning in 1929 and this decline continued through the Great Depression. The decline in the loans to total liabilities ratio was also substantially larger for unincorporated businesses than for corporations. The level to which the loan ratio for unincorporated businesses returned in 1945 is much lower than its pre-Depression level. While one would not want to deduce a postwar trend from 1945 alone, there is certainly no evidence of a rapid postwar expansion of bank loan finance for unincorporated businesses.

As mentioned above, the ratio of total bank loans to the capital stock imposes some constraints on what could plausibly have happened to the importance of loans for the unincorporated business sector over the postwar era. We know that bank loans became less important at an aggregate level in financing the capital stock between the prewar era and the first two decades of the postwar era. After 1970, bank loans increased in importance, but loans were still a less important form of finance than in the pre-Depression era. The loan ratio of corporations shows exactly the same pattern as the aggregate ratio. Therefore, unless some other sector showed a great decrease in the importance of loans, the unincorporated business sector could not have greatly increased its loan ratio over the postwar era.

The fact that in the postwar era bank loans have become a smaller fraction of total liabilities, certainly for corporations and probably for unincorporated businesses, makes it likely that the lending channel of the transmission mechanism has weakened over time. In terms of our model, if there are more substitutes for bank loans in the postwar era than in the pre-1929 era, then the sensitivity of investment to the loan-bond spread should have diminished. This in

---

11. The ratio of loans to total liabilities, including gross trade debt, shows a noticeable fall between the pre-Depression and postwar eras. This is because trade debt has also expanded rapidly.

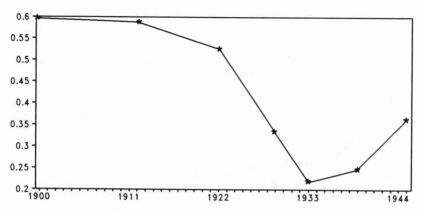

Fig. 8.6   Ratio of loans to total liabilities for unincorporated businesses, 1900–45
Note: Data are available only for starred observations.

turn implies that the relative importance of the lending channel should have declined as well.

The fact that loans have become a more important source of firm finance over the course of the postwar era suggests that the relative importance of the lending channel may not have been constant between 1945 and 1990. Indeed, judging just from the facts about firm finance, it appears quite likely that the lending channel became more important after 1970 than it was in the 1950s and 1960s, though not as important as in the pre-Depression era.

Relative Size of Corporations and Unincorporated Businesses

While the classification of particular liabilities for unincorporated businesses cannot be made consistent over time, the data for total liabilities and equities do appear to be comparable across time periods. Therefore, it is possible to use this information to gauge the relative size of the corporate and unincorporated sectors.[12] Since corporations are typically much larger than unincorporated businesses, this comparison can give some indication of changes in the distribution of large and small firms over time. Figure 8.7 graphs the ratio of total liabilities (less gross trade debt) of unincorporated businesses to the sum of total liabilities (again, less gross trade debt) of corporations and corporate equities.

Judging from this measure, the corporate sector grew more rapidly than the unincorporated sector between 1900 and 1945; the ratio of total liabilities of unincorporated businesses to total liabilities plus equities of corporations fell

---

12. Total assets would be a more obvious way to compare the sizes of the two sectors. Unfortunately, the balance sheets give only total financial assets, which are not a good indicator of relative size.

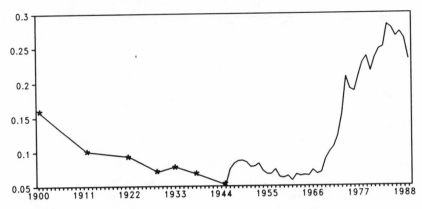

Fig. 8.7   Ratio of total liabilities of unincorporated businesses to total liabilities of corporations, 1900–89

Note: Before 1945 data are available only for starred observations; after 1945 the data are annual.

steadily over this period. In the early postwar era, the ratio hovered at roughly the same level as in 1929. After 1970, this ratio rose substantially, reflecting the greater growth of total liabilities for unincorporated businesses.

If this ratio truly reflects the relative size of the two sectors, and if the lending channel is more important the larger the bank-dependent unincorporated sector, then the fall in the ratio between 1900 and 1945 suggests that the lending channel of monetary transmission was weakening over this period. It then remained at its 1929 level during the early postwar era. The subsequent rise in the relative size of the two sectors suggests that the lending channel has become more important again in the last two decades.

8.2.3   Summary

Taken together, the various changes in the structure of financial institutions suggest that the lending channel should have decreased in importance between the pre-1929 and the post-1945 eras. Both the structure of bank balance sheets and the structure of firm balance sheets suggest that loans were more important before the Great Depression than after. Within the pre-Depression era, the differentiation of reserve requirements on time deposits and demand deposits and the large decline in the level of reserve requirements on time deposits at the time of the founding of the Federal Reserve suggest that the lending channel should have been stronger before 1914 than after.

Within the postwar era, the fact that bank loans have become a larger fraction of total bank assets and total firm liabilities after 1970 than in the first two decades of the postwar era suggests that the lending channel may have been increasing in importance. The relative importance of unincorporated (and presumably bank-dependent) businesses also rose in the second half of the post–World War II era, again suggesting an increased importance of the lending channel. However, the ratio of the reserve requirement on time deposits to that on demand deposits and the level of reserve requirements on time deposits fell in the late postwar era, and time deposits and CDs rose to become the dominant liability of commercial banks over the postwar period. These factors would tend to lessen the importance of the lending channel. Thus, while it is clear that the lending channel should have weakened between the pre-Depression era and early postwar eras, the relative strength of the lending channel in the early and late postwar eras is ambiguous.

8.3 Historical Evidence on the Lending Channel

In this section we examine the behavior since the late nineteenth century of various indicators of the strength of the lending channel. In particular, we look at the spread between the loan and bond rates, the mix of credit market instruments between loans and commercial paper, and the correlation between output and lending. The analysis of section 8.1 and previous analytical work suggest that these measures should behave differently after monetary contractions than in more ordinary times if the lending channel is important. Since the institutional analysis of section 8.2 suggests that the strength of the lending channel should have declined over time, our hypothesis is that the response of these variables to monetary shocks should have declined as well. If they have not, this could either be evidence that these measures of the strength of the lending channel are not very good, or evidence that the lending channel has not been important in any era.

Since the response of these variables to monetary contractions is the measure of the strength of the lending channel, identifying monetary contractions is an important step in the analysis. The monetary contractions that we consider consist of three pre–Federal Reserve financial panics (1890:8, 1893:5, and 1907:10); four interwar contractions consisting of Friedman and Schwartz's (1963) three crucial experiments plus the bank holiday (1920:1, 1931:10, 1933:2, and 1937:1); and seven post–World War II episodes identified by Romer and Romer (1989, 1994) as anti-inflation interventions by the Federal Reserve (1947:10, 1955:9, 1968:12, 1974:4, 1978:8, 1979:10, and 1988:12). The extent to which each of these episodes constitutes an exogenous monetary contraction has been debated at length elsewhere (Friedman 1989; Schwartz 1989; Hoover and Perez 1994; Dotsey and Reid 1992); we do not repeat that discussion here.

8.3.1 The Spread

According to the model presented above, one key indicator of the strength of the lending channel is δ, the spread between loan rates and bond rates. In response to a monetary contraction, the spread should increase as banks contract loans, and thus force firms to use bonds as an imperfect, alternate source of finance. Using the framework in section 8.1, and incorporating the simpli-

a. 1890–1909

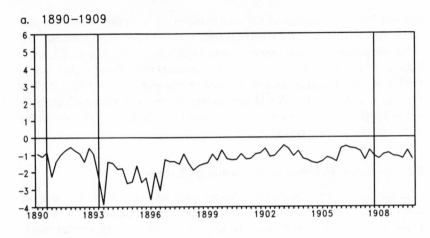

b. 1910–1929

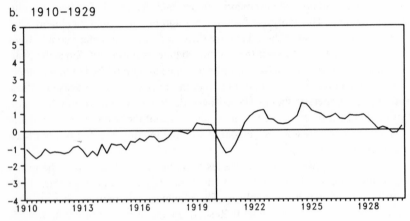

c. 1930–1938

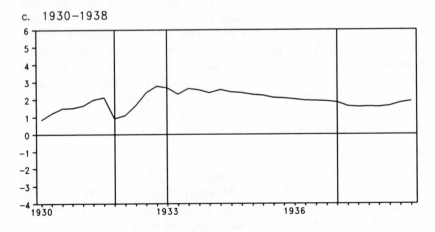

d. 1947–1970

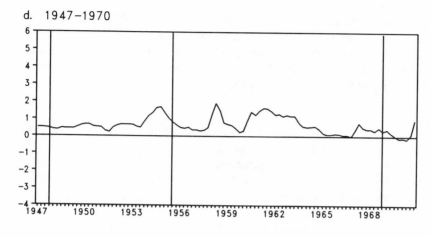

e. 1971–1991

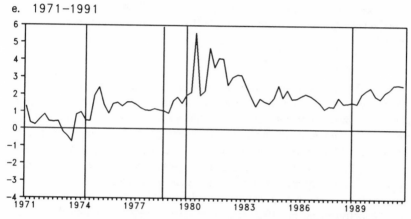

Fig. 8.8   Loan-bond interest-rate spread and monetary contractions, 1890–1991
Note: Vertical lines denote the dates of negative monetary shocks.

fying assumptions used there, the response of the spread to a change in the money stock is

(25)
$$\frac{d\delta}{dm} = \frac{-\left(\dfrac{b^p + l - m}{b^p + l}\right)\left(\dfrac{1}{m}\right)}{\left(\dfrac{\Lambda_\delta}{\lambda}\left(\dfrac{1 - \tau_2}{1 + (\lambda - 1)\tau_2}\right) - \dfrac{L_\delta}{l}\right)}.$$

The factors that imply a large response of the spread to money are a subset of those that lead to a large value of dy/dm in equation (21) above. The less willing banks and firms are to substitute between loans and bonds in response to changes in the spread, the larger the effect of money will be on the spread.

Similarly, in the case where banks are net issuers of bonds, the larger the reserve requirement on CDs and time deposits, the larger the effect of money on the spread. On the other hand, the sensitivities of investment to the bond interest rate and to the spread, which affect the size of dy/dm, do not affect the sensitivity of the spread to money shocks.

Data

Figure 8.8 presents a measure of the spread for the period 1890–1991. The loan rate series is the time-loan rate on six-month time loans for the period 1890–1918, the rate charged on customer loans by banks in principal cities for the period 1919–27, the rate charged on commercial loans by banks in principal cities for the period 1928–39, and the prime interest rate for the period 1947–91.[13] The bond rate series is for six-month prime commercial paper. All data are quarterly averages of monthly data. The figure indicates that the spread rose on average over the forty years prior to the Great Depression and that it was generally higher in the second half of the postwar period than in the first half.

Results

Rather than focus on long-term trends in the spread, we instead look at the behavior of the spread in monetary contractions. Figure 8.8 also shows the dates of negative monetary shocks so that we can evaluate the path of the spread following each of the fourteen monetary contractions we consider. Given the model presented in section 8.1, one should expect the spread to increase following monetary contractions. Given the evidence presented in section 8.2, and assuming that the magnitude of monetary contractions has been roughly similar over time, one should expect relatively large increases in the spread following pre-1929 monetary contractions and relatively modest increases in the spread following early postwar contractions.[14]

The data presented in the figure do not bear out these expectations. Note first that, looking across the entire sample, the spread does not consistently increase following monetary contractions. In nine of fourteen cases, the spread remains approximately unchanged or decreases slightly during the two years following the onset of a contraction. In three of the five cases where the spread does increase, the magnitude of this increase is only about one hundred basis points. The two episodes that display significant increases in the magnitude of the spread are dominated by the second quarter of 1980, when the Fed imposed credit controls that limited the rate of growth of bank lending (Schreft 1990;

13. The time loan rate data are from Mankiw, Miron, and Weil (1987, 1990). The customer and commercial loan rate data are from U.S. Board of Governors (1976a, 463–64, tables 124–25). The prime rate data are from Data Resources, Inc. (DRI).

14. The fact that consistent measures of aggregate output and unemployment show that recessions were of roughly the same size before 1929 and after 1945 is one indicator that monetary contractions were probably not radically different in the two eras.

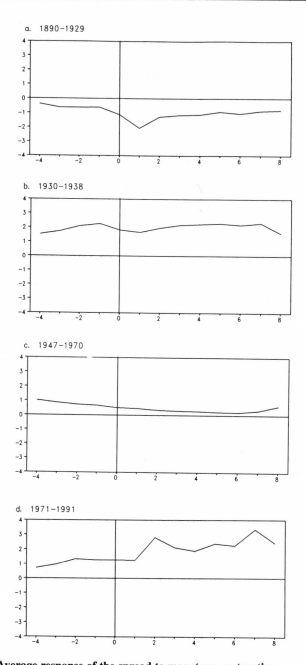

Fig. 8.9   Average response of the spread to monetary contractions

Note: The vertical line denotes the date of a negative monetary shock. The average behavior of the spread is calculated for four quarters before to eight quarters after the monetary shock.

Owens and Schreft 1992). Averaging over the entire sample, the spread increases by only twenty-one basis points at the one-year horizon and by thirty-nine basis points at the two-year horizon.[15]

Figure 8.9 shows the average behavior of the spread in each of four subsamples corresponding to different "lending regimes." The first regime is 1890–1929, the second is 1930–38, the third is 1947–70, and the fourth is 1971–91. According to the evidence presented in section 8.2, one ought to expect the most dramatic response of the spread during the pre-1929 period and the least dramatic during the 1947–70 period, assuming the magnitude of monetary contractions is roughly similar across the regimes.

The differences in the response of the spread across regimes only partially bear out this expectation. At the one-year horizon, the spread increases on average by one basis point during the 1890–1929 regime, falls by twenty-five basis points during the 1947–70 regime, and rises by sixty-two basis points during the 1971–91 regime. Thus, while post–World War II changes in the response of the spread to monetary contractions are consistent with the evidence presented in section 8.2, the difference in the behavior of the spread in the pre-Depression and post–World War II periods is not.

Changes in the Commercial Paper Market

Given that the spread does not consistently rise after monetary contractions in the pre–World War I and interwar eras, it is reasonable to ask whether there have been changes in the commercial paper market that could make this variable a less reliable indicator of the strength of the credit channel before World War II than after. Our judgment is that there have not.

This is not to say that the commercial paper market has not changed over time. Most obviously, it has grown tremendously. Much of this growth has been in commercial paper issued by finance companies and directly placed, which is not considered in this paper.[16] Nevertheless, the nominal value of dealer-placed commercial paper increased by a factor of roughly 230 between December 1919 and December 1991. For comparison, the nominal value of bank loans increased by a factor of roughly 95 over the same period. This rapid growth, however, does not imply that the early commercial paper market was backward. According to Greef (1938), by 1890 the commercial paper market was national in scope and dominated by large commercial paper houses that were efficient and modern.

---

15. Kashyap, Stein, and Wilcox (1993) report that in both bivariate VARs and trivariate VARs that include GNP, Romer dates or Romer dates plus a 1966 credit-crunch dummy are statistically significant predictors of the interest-rate spread considered here. Their sample period is 1963–89. The results given above suggest that the Kashyap-Stein-Wilcox results are dominated by a few observations corresponding to the 1980 credit controls.

16. To give a sense of magnitudes, in December 1988, total commercial paper outstanding was approximately $455 billion and dealer-placed finance company paper and nonfinancial company paper were $261 billion.

There have also been some changes in the type of firms which issue commercial paper. In the nineteenth century, it was often the less established or less well regarded firms that issued commercial paper; firms with stronger reputations borrowed from banks.[17] This pattern changed gradually, and by the end of World War I it was typically large firms with solid credit ratings that issued commercial paper. This is still the case today. This change in the quality of borrowers in the commercial paper market is the obvious explanation for the change from negative to positive values of the spread over the last century, shown in figure 8.8.

It is hard to see how either of these changes (the growth of the commercial paper market or the switch to higher quality borrowers) could have caused the spread to fall after some monetary contractions in the early period if the lending channel were important. The market for commercial paper was certainly large enough and established enough by 1890 that it could absorb a significant increase in the supply of commercial paper without extreme movements in interest rates. Similarly, even if less high quality firms typically issued commercial paper in the earlier years than in the interwar or post–World War II periods, a decline in bank lending which made it harder for all firms to get loans would be expected to raise the loan rate relative to the commercial paper rate. Thus, neither of the major changes in the commercial paper market is likely to have made the spread fall after monetary contractions if the lending channel was important.

One institutional factor that could account for the peculiar behavior of the spread after financial panics is the fact that banks held a substantial fraction of the stock of commercial paper in the pre-1929 era. Greef (1938, 62) argues that a banking panic which strapped banks for reserves caused their demand for commercial paper to decline. If this effect were large enough, it could cause the commercial paper rate to rise and thus could cause the spread between the loan rate and the commercial paper rate to rise less than it otherwise might, or conceivably, even to fall. However, it is important to note that this explanation does not account for the very large fall in the spread following the monetary contraction of 1920 because in this episode there was little or no distress in the financial system.

There are alternative hypotheses that could also explain the fall in the spread after early monetary contractions. Most obviously, if the spread merely indicates default risk, then one might expect the spread to fall in the late 1800s and early 1900s because commercial paper was the more risky asset. This same reasoning could explain why the spread rises after monetary contractions in the postwar era, since today commercial paper is the less risky asset. This alternative, while consistent with the data, is not consistent with the view that the spread provides an indication of the strength of the lending channel in any period since it implies that movements in the spread are driven significantly by

17. See, for example, Macaulay (1938, A335).

movements in default risk rather than by movements in the supply of loans relative to bonds.

8.3.2   The Mix

One factor that potentially complicates the interpretation of our results on the behavior of the spread is the fact that since there are other dimensions to a loan besides the interest rate—collateral, for example—the observed interest rate may not be an accurate measure of its price. Or course, as long as the reported interest rate is one component of the price of a loan, the spread should still vary in the direction implied by the lending channel if this component of the transmission mechanism is empirically important. Nevertheless, this consideration implies the presence of possibly substantial noise in the relation between monetary contractions and the behavior of the spread.

In response to this problem of using observed spreads, Kashyap, Stein, and Wilcox (1993) suggest examining quantity variables as indicators of the strength of the lending channel. In particular, they note that if both banks and firms regard loans and securities as imperfect substitutes, a monetary contraction should lower the quantity of bank loans relative to total credit extended. This implication is immune to the criticism that a decline in output for any reason will endogenously tend to induce a decline in bank loans, since even in the face of declining output the lending hypothesis implies that monetary contractions induce a substitution by firms away from bank borrowing toward commercial paper issuance.[18] Kashyap, Stein, and Wilcox test this implication by examining the ratio of bank loans to bank loans plus commercial paper outstanding immediately following four of the Romer and Romer (1989) episodes. They show that this variable, referred to as the mix, tends to fall after Romer dates, consistent with the implications of the lending hypothesis. We extend this approach to early post–World War II and interwar data.

Data and Specification

The mix variable is calculated by taking the ratio of bank loans outstanding to the sum of commercial paper and bank loans outstanding. In calculating the mix we examine quarterly averages of monthly data. Monthly data on the nominal value of commercial paper outstanding are available from the Federal Reserve starting in 1919.[19] Over time, however, there have been changes in the definition and breakdown of the commercial paper data. To the extent possible, we use only data on dealer-placed, non-bank-related commercial paper. Dealer-placed financial company commercial paper is included in the total,

---

18. Gertler and Gilchrist (1991) discuss possible problems of interpretation with the Kashyap-Stein-Wilcox approach.

19. The data for 1919–40 are from U.S. Board of Governors (1976a, 465–67, tables 126–27). The data for 1941–69 are from U.S. Board of Governors (1976b, 714–18, tables 12.10–12.11). The data for 1970–78 are from the Federal Reserve's *Annual Statistical Digest* (1980, 73–74, table 22). The data after 1978 are from yearly issues of the *Annual Statistical Digest.*

but most financial company paper is directly placed and therefore excluded. Whenever there are changes in definition or data collection procedures and a period of overlap is given, we use ratio splices to prevent discrete jumps in the series.[20]

For the period 1919 to 1991 we use loans data from the asset statement of Weekly Reporting Member Banks in Leading Cities collected by the Federal Reserve.[21] This series reports total loans of reporting banks every Wednesday of the year. We use the data for the last Wednesday of the quarter as the quarterly observation.[22] Because there are some changes in definition and sample over time, we again use ratio splices when there is an obvious break in the series and an observation of overlap is available.[23]

Results

Figure 8.10 displays the mix for the period since 1919. Although we use slightly different data series in order to enhance comparability over time, our results for the second half of the postwar period are quite similar to those presented by Kashyap, Stein, and Wilcox. After the monetary shocks in 1968, 1974, 1978, 1979, and 1988 the mix declines consistently. One should note that during the period from about 1965 on the mix displays a general downward trend, but the declines following the five most recent Romer and Romer dates appear somewhat faster than implied by the negative trend.

In the early postwar and interwar periods, however, the mix does not generally behave as predicted by the lending hypothesis. During the 1947 and 1955 contractions the mix remains approximately constant, and subsequent to the 1931 and 1920 contractions the mix rises. It does fall slightly although briefly in 1937 and declines more consistently after the bank holiday in 1933.

In light of the information presented in section 8.2, the behavior of the mix is most anomalous in the 1920 episode. According to all the measures considered there, the lending channel should have been stronger in the 1920s than during any later period. Yet, during the one monetary contraction in the 1920s the mix behaves exactly contrary to the implications of the lending hypothesis. The behavior of the mix in 1931 is also difficult to reconcile with the lending view. Although bank loans had declined as a fraction of bank assets by 1931, most of this decline presumably reflected an endogenous response of lending

20. Splices are done in January 1970, August 1959, and December 1952.

21. The data for 1919–41 are from U.S. Board of Governors (1976a, 132–62, table 48). The data for 1942–70 are from U.S. Board of Governors (1976b, 256–82, table 4.1). The data after 1970 are from various issues of the *Annual Statistical Digest* of the Federal Reserve.

22. We have examined both seasonally adjusted and unadjusted data. Since the differences between the results were extremely small, we present only the unadjusted results for comparability with Kashyap, Stein, and Wilcox.

23. The two cases where we are able to do splices are in June 1969, when there was a change in the reporting form, and in January 1972, when all of the data back to 1972 were revised to conform to a new coverage basis started in 1979.

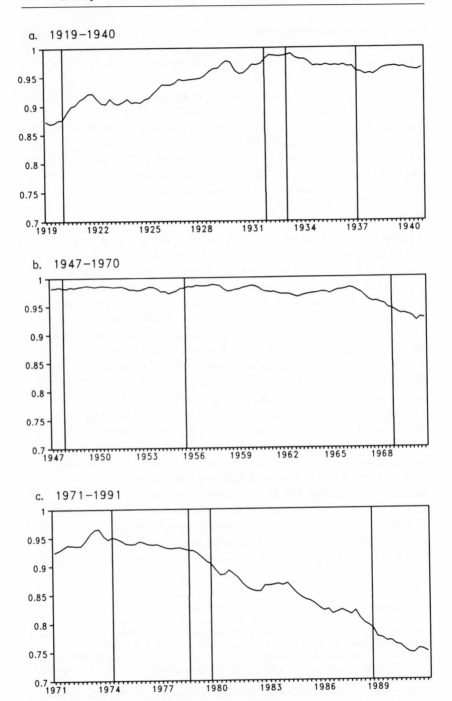

Fig. 8.10   The mix and monetary contractions, 1919–91
Note: The mix is calculated as the ratio of bank loans outstanding to the sum of bank loans and commercial paper outstanding. Vertical lines denote the dates of negative monetary shocks.

to the fall in output, rather than a structural change in the importance of the lending channel. Therefore, the mix should have fallen rather than risen in this episode.

Changes in the Commercial Paper Market

As with the spread, it is important to consider whether there is anything peculiar about the commercial paper market that could explain the dramatic rise of the mix in 1920. First, at a general level, the argument that the expansion and improvement in the quality of commercial paper should not have affected the behavior of the spread also applies to the mix. The commercial paper market was large enough and comprised of high enough quality borrowers by the end of World War I that a monetary contraction which reduced the ability of firms to borrow from banks should have led to a rise in commercial paper issued relative to bank loans.

The effect on the commercial paper market of the establishment of the Federal Reserve is a complicated topic that may be related to the behavior of the mix in 1920. The Federal Reserve Act of 1913 made commercial paper eligible for rediscount by the Federal Reserve banks for their member banks. According to Greef, this "created a broader and more continuous market for notes handled by dealers and thus gave them a greater degree of liquidity than they had possessed at any previous time" (1938, 143). This presumably encouraged the growth of the commercial paper market. At the same time, however, the Federal Reserve sought to encourage the development of the bankers' acceptances market by also allowing member banks to accept bills of exchange for rediscount.[24] Both Greef and Macaulay (1938) argue that this development may have had little effect on the commercial paper market because acceptances were typically used for financing transactions very different from those for which commercial paper was used. Greef thinks that changes in firm operating practices, the boom in the stock market, and the generally unsettled condition of business in the 1920s were the more important sources of a decline in the volume of commercial paper issued in the 1920s.

Even if the policies of the Federal Reserve were a factor in the long-term rise in the mix in the interwar era, it is hard to see how this could explain the dramatic rise in the mix in 1920. As can be seen in figure 8.9, the rise in the mix in 1920 and 1921 exceeds any reasonable estimate of the usual trend behavior of this series.

8.3.3   The Correlation between Output and Lending

A final test of the strength of the lending channel in different eras involves examining the correlation between output and lending both after monetary contractions and in other periods. In any time period there is likely to be a positive correlation between lending and output because lending has a substantial endogenous component: investment and loans tend to go up when the econ-

---

24. Bankers' acceptances are two-name paper; they are a direct liability of the firm issuing them and a contingent liability of the bank guaranteeing funds at maturity.

omy is doing well and fall when the economy is declining. However, if lending also has an independent component which declines in monetary contractions and actually causes a fall in output, the correlation between lending and output should be even higher than usual soon after monetary contractions, because both the usual endogenous response and the independent lending channel will be operating. This reasoning suggests that the differential in the correlation between output and lending after monetary contractions and in other times provides information about the importance of the lending channel. If there is a large difference between the two correlations, this is evidence that there is a lending channel to the monetary transmission mechanism. Comparing this differential across eras can indicate whether the lending channel used to be stronger in the past than it is today.

Data and Specification

For these calculations we use quarterly data on lending and industrial production. The lending data that we use for this calculation come from two sources. For the period 1884 to 1929 we use data collected by the Comptroller of the Currency. These data show the quantity of loans held by national banks on particular call dates during the year.[25] While this series does not show data for the same dates each year or for every month, there is almost always one call date in each quarter of the year. When there is more than one call date in a quarter, we use the later of the two as the observation for the quarter.[26] Furthermore, as discussed above, since national banks account for nearly half of all bank assets in the pre-1929 era, this loan series has reasonably broad coverage. For the period 1919 to 1991 we use the loans data from Weekly Reporting Member Banks discussed in section 8.3.2.

The industrial production series for 1919–91 is from the Federal Reserve Board. Before 1919 we use a smoothed version of the index of industrial production compiled by Miron and Romer (1990). This series is smoothed based on a regression of the Federal Reserve Board index for 1920–29 on the Miron-Romer series.[27]

Since the relationship between lending and output is presumably more complicated than a simple contemporaneous correlation we use the following regression to estimate the correlation. We first detrend and seasonally adjust both lending and industrial production by regressing the percentage changes on quarterly dummy variables and a linear trend and then taking the residuals. We then regress the residuals for industrial production on the contemporaneous

---

25. The data for 1884–1918 are given in U.S. Comptroller of the Currency, 1919, *Annual Report* (pp. 276–303). The data for 1919 are from the 1924 *Annual Report*. The data for 1920–24 are from the 1927 *Annual Report*. The data for 1925–32 are from the 1932 *Annual Report*. Since the early data lump total loans and discounts together with overdrafts, we include overdrafts in the total when they begin to be reported separately in 1898.

26. After 1924 it is often the case that there is no call date in the third quarter of the year but instead two observations for the fourth quarter. For these cases we take the first call date for the fourth quarter (which is typically in early October) as the observation for the third quarter.

27. See Romer (1994) for a full discussion of this adjustment.

Table 8.1 R^2's from Regressions of Industrial Production on Lending

Sample Period	0–12 Quarters after a Monetary Contraction	All Other Times
	Comptroller of the Currency Lending Data	
1885:1–1929:4	0.32	0.08
1885:1–1914:4	0.35	0.13
1920:1–1929:4	0.56	0.10
	Weekly Reporting Banks Lending Data	
1920:1–1929:4	0.59	0.06
1920:1–1940:4	0.65	0.35
1948:1–1991:2	0.29	0.12
1948:1–1970:4	0.36	0.13
1971:1–1991:2	0.29	0.21

value and three lags of the residuals for lending. The R^2's of the regressions are a measure of the explanatory power of lagged and contemporaneous lending for movements in real output. We run this regression both for the sample period that includes only the twelve quarters after monetary contractions and for the sample period that consists of all other times. We estimate this pair of regressions for different eras, including our main periods of comparison, 1885–1929 and 1948–91.

Results

The R^2's of these regressions for different eras are given in table 8.1. First, because the lending data change between the pre-1914 and post-1948 period, it is important to compare the results for the period 1919 to 1929, when both lending series exist. As can be seen from the table, the two lending series give very similar results for the 1920s; the R^2's for both regressions are nearly identical using the two different lending series.

Because data differences do not seem to matter, it is reasonable to compare the data before 1929 with those after 1948. For the period 1885–1929, the spread between the R^2 for the regression for the period twelve quarters after monetary contractions and that for all other times is 0.24. For the period 1948–91, the spread in R^2's is 0.17. These results suggest that there has been little change in the spread in R^2's over time. To the degree that there is any difference, the spread in the R^2's is slightly larger before 1929 than after 1948. The results also show that the absolute spread is fairly small in both eras, on the order of 0.2. To put this spread in perspective, the same type of regression for money (using data on M1) yields spreads of between 0.3 and 0.4 for various sample periods in the postwar era.[28]

---

28. The data on M1 for 1919–58 are from Friedman and Schwartz (1963, 709–21, table A-1, col. 7). The data for 1959–91 are from the Citibase data bank, July 1992 update. A ratio splice is

There is some variation in the relationship between the R^2's when one looks at certain shorter sample periods. First, the spread between the R^2 for the regression estimated for the sample period after monetary contractions and that for all other times is substantially bigger for the 1920s than for the period before 1914: the spread is roughly 0.5 for the 1920s and 0.2 for the three decades before 1914. This finding should be interpreted with caution, however, because there is only one monetary contraction during the 1920s (1920:1). Second, within the postwar era, the results are somewhat different for the two decades before 1970 than for the two decades after. The spread between the R^2's for the two regressions before 1970 is 0.23, almost identical to that in the pre-1929 era. For the period 1971–91, however, the spread is only 0.08. This suggests that, if anything, the lending channel has gotten weaker over the postwar era.

8.4 Conclusions

Our goal in this paper has been to use historical data to shed light on the importance of the lending channel of monetary transmission. We began by laying out a model in which shocks to the money supply affect aggregate demand through both the money and lending channels. We used this model to analyze the effect of structural changes on the importance of the lending channel. We showed that increasing the fraction of bank assets made up of loans and raising the reserve requirement on bank issue of liabilities, such as time loans or CDs, increases the importance of the lending channel. Similarly, raising the fraction of firm finance made up of bank loans or the fraction of investment done by bank-dependent small firms makes the lending channel more important.

Armed with the results of this modeling exercise, we then analyzed the historical changes in the structure of finance. We found that several changes in financial structure over the past one hundred years should have had major effects on the importance of the lending channel. The fraction of bank portfolios held in the form of loans declined dramatically during the Depression and World War II eras and rose during the latter half of the post–World War II era to nearly its pre-Depression level. Both absolute and relative reserve requirements on time deposits and CDs fell dramatically with the founding of the Federal Reserve and fell further in the post–World War II period. Similarly, the ratio of bank loans to the capital stock fell dramatically with the onset of

---

used to connect the two series in January 1959. The usual money-output relationship breaks down after the 1988 monetary contraction: the movements in money are much larger and further behind the movements in output than after other monetary contractions. For this reason, the spread in the R^2's for money is small for sample periods that include the post-1987 period, but large for the pre-1986 era.

the Great Depression and did not return to its pre-1929 level until the second half of the post–World War II era. The relative importance of unincorporated firms, which are presumably more dependent on banks than are corporations, fell over the first seventy years of the twentieth century, although it rose in the 1970s and 1980s to levels higher than those experienced before the Depression. The overall effect of these changes should have been to weaken the lending channel in the early post–World War II period compared to the pre-Depression era. The lending channel may have been stronger in the second half of the post–World War II era than in the first half, but whether it should have been as strong as the pre-Depression era is not clear.

We then turned to the data to see whether we could find evidence of the changes in the importance of the lending channel predicted by our model given the observed changes in financial structure. The results of this exercise were striking. The systematic increase in the interest-rate spread between loans and bonds that the lending channel predicts should follow a monetary contraction does not appear in the data. The mix, which declined following monetary contractions in the later post–World War II period, fails to do so in the one pre-Depression contraction for which we have evidence. Finally, the difference between the R^2's of regressions of output on lending inside and outside of contractionary episodes is no larger in the pre-Depression period than in the post–World War II period.

Our failure to find evidence of the systematic changes in the response of these indicators to monetary contractions predicted by our model of the lending channel is subject to two interpretations. First, the indicators we examine may simply be poor measures of the importance of the lending channel. In this case, much of the evidence in favor of the existence of a strong postwar lending channel would have to be questioned. Alternatively, it may be that changes in the importance of the lending channel have not been reflected in these measures because the lending channel itself is very weak. As a result, most of the movement in these indicators would be due to noise or random events, not to changes in the specialness of bank loans over time. Our analysis does not rule decisively on which of these two explanations is correct. However, both of these interpretations suggest that the empirical relevance of the lending channel has yet to be demonstrated.

Appendix
Balance Sheet Data for Firms and Households

The data come from three basic sources: Goldsmith, Lipsey, and Mendelson (1963), the U.S. Board of Governors of the Federal Reserve System (1973), and the U.S. Board of Governors of the Federal Reserve System (1990). These sources are referred to as GLM, FRB 1973, and FRB 1990, respectively, in the following descriptions. We line up the data from GLM on nonfinancial corporations with the FRB series on corporate, nonfinancial business, and the data from GLM on nonfarm unincorporated businesses with the FRB series on nonfarm, noncorporate business.

The general strategy is to line up particular components of the balance sheet that are of interest, such as total liabilities, bank loans not elsewhere classified, and bonds and notes, from the different sources and then ratio splice them together. The ratio splices are necessary because the series do not line up exactly due to slight changes in concepts and measurement techniques over time. The data for 1966–89 are from FRB 1990 and are taken as they are. The data for 1946–66 are from FRB 1973 and are ratio spliced to the modern data in 1966. The data for 1900–45 are from GLM and are spliced on in 1945.

Nonfinancial Corporations

The balance sheet data for 1900–45 are given in GLM (1963, 146, table III-4b). The data for 1945–66 are from FRB (1973, 85–87). The data for 1966–89 are from FRB (1990, 9–10). The GLM data include commercial paper liabilities in the bonds and notes category, while the FRB reports bonds and open-market paper separately (GLM, p. 10). We combine the two to be the extension of the GLM series. Trade debt is gross for both sources. The data for corporate equities for 1900–45 is from GLM (1963, 318–19, table IV-b-17b). The equities data for 1945–66 are from FRB (1973, 117–19) and for 1966–89 are from FRB (1990, 9–10).

Nonfarm, Unincorporated Businesses

We had hoped to form a continuous balance sheet for nonfarm, unincorporated businesses as well as for corporations. However, in 1945, the one year of overlap between the two series, bank loans n.e.c. are roughly nine times larger in the GLM data than in the FRB data. Much of this difference appears to be due to how total liabilities are allocated among categories. For this reason, we do not examine the individual elements of the unincorporated business sector. We do, however, use the data on total liabilities. The data for 1900–45 are from GLM (1963, 128, table III-2a). Data for 1945–66 are from FRB (1973, 85–87) and for 1966–89 from FRB (1990, 7–8). Adjustment of the FRB series is needed because for 1945–66 the total liabilities series includes net trade debt, while GLM and the later FRB series includes gross trade debt (GLM, p. 9). For these years we subtract net trade debt from total liabilities, and add in gross trade debt.

References

Bernanke, Ben S. 1983. Nonmonetary effects of the financial crisis in the propagation of the Great Depression. *American Economic Review* 73:257–76.

Bernanke, Ben S., and Alan S. Blinder. 1988. Credit, Money, and Aggregate Demand. *American Economic Review* 78:435–39.

Bordo, Michael D., Peter Rappaport, and Anna J. Schwartz. 1992. Money versus credit rationing: Evidence for the National Banking Era, 1880–1914. In *Strategic factors in nineteenth century American economic history: A volume to honor Robert W. Fogel,* eds. Claudia Goldin and Hugh Rockoff. Chicago: University of Chicago Press.

Calomiris, Charles, and R. Glenn Hubbard. 1989. Price flexibility, credit availability, and economic fluctuations: Evidence from the United States, 1894–1909. *Quarterly Journal of Economics* 104:429–52.

Cargill, Thomas F. 1991. *Money, the financial system, and monetary policy.* 4th ed. Englewood Cliffs, N.J.: Prentice-Hall.

Dotsey, Michael, and Milton Reid. 1992. Oil shocks, monetary policy, and economic activity. Federal Reserve Bank of Richmond. Manuscript.

Friedman, Benjamin M. 1989. Comment on Romer and Romer: Does monetary policy matter? *NBER Macroeconomics Annual* 4:177–82.

Friedman, Milton, and Anna J. Schwartz. 1963. *A monetary history of the United States, 1867–1960.* Princeton, N.J.: Princeton University Press.

Gertler, Mark, and Simon Gilchrist. 1991. Monetary policy, business cycles and the behavior of small manufacturing firms. NBER Working Paper no. 3892. Cambridge, Mass.: National Bureau of Economic Research.

Goldsmith, Raymond W., Robert E. Lipsey, and Morris Mendelson. 1963. *Studies in the national balance sheet of the United States.* Vol. 2. Princeton, N.J.: Princeton University Press.

Greef, Albert O. 1938. *The commercial paper house in the United States.* Cambridge, Mass.: Harvard University Press.

Hall, Brian J., and James D. C. Thomson. 1993. Are bank loans really special? Evidence on the lending view. Harvard University. Manuscript.

Hoover, Kevin D., and Stephen J. Perez. 1994. Post hoc ergo propter hoc once more: An evaluation of "Does monetary policy matter?" in the spirit of James Tobin. *Journal of Monetary Economics* 34.

Kashyap, Anil K., Jeremy C. Stein, and David W. Wilcox. 1993. Monetary policy and credit conditions: Evidence from the composition of external finance. *American Economic Review* 83:78–98.

Kaufman, George G. 1992. *The U.S. financial system.* 5th ed. Englewood Cliffs, N.J.: Prentice-Hall.

Macaulay, Frederick R. 1938. *The movements of interest rates, bond yields, and stock prices in the United States since 1856.* New York: NBER.

Mankiw, N. Gregory, Jeffrey A. Miron, and David N. Weil. 1987. The adjustment of expectations to a change in regime: A study of the founding of the Federal Reserve. *American Economic Review* 77:358–74.

———. 1990. The adjustment of expectations to a change in regime: Reply. *American Economic Review* 80:977–79.

Miron, Jeffrey A., and Christina D. Romer. 1990. A new monthly index of industrial production, 1884–1940. *Journal of Economic History* 50:321–37.

Oliner, Stephen D., and Glenn D. Rudebusch. 1992. The transmission of monetary policy to small and large firms. Board of Governors of the Federal Reserve. Manuscript.

Owens, Raymond E., and Stacey L. Schreft. 1992. Identifying credit crunches. Federal Reserve Bank of Richmond. Manuscript.

Rodkey, Robert G. 1934. *Legal reserve in american banking. Michigan Business Studies,* vol. 6, no. 5: 362–483. Ann Arbor: University of Michigan Press.

Romer, Christina D. 1994. Remeasuring business cycles. *Journal of Economic History* 54.

Romer, Christina D., and David H. Romer. 1989. Does monetary policy matter? A new test in the spirit of Friedman and Schwartz. *NBER Macroeconomics Annual* 4:121–70.

————. 1990. New evidence on the monetary transmission mechanism. *Brookings Papers on Economic Activity* 1:149–213.

————. 1994. Monetary policy matters. *Journal of Monetary Economics* 34.

Schreft, Stacey L. 1990. Credit controls: 1980. *Federal Reserve Bank of Richmond Economic Review* 76 (November/December): 25–55.

Schwartz, Anna J. 1989. Comment on Romer and Romer: Does monetary policy matter? *NBER Macroeconomics Annual* 4:170–76.

U.S. Board of Governors of the Federal Reserve System. 1973. *Flow of funds accounts 1945–1972: Annual total flows and year-end assets and liabilities.* Washington, D.C.

————. 1976a. *Banking and monetary statistics, 1914–1941.* Washington, D.C.

————. 1976b. *Banking and monetary statistics, 1941–1970.* Washington, D.C.

————. 1983. *Annual report of the Board of Governors of the Federal Reserve System.* Washington, D.C.

————. 1990. *Flow of funds accounts: Financial assets and liabilities, year end, 1966–1989.*

————. *Annual Statistical Digest.* Various years.

U.S. Bureau of the Census. 1975. *Historical statistics of the United States: Colonial times to 1970.*

U.S. Bureau of Economic Analysis. 1974. *Fixed nonresidential business capital in the United States, 1925–73.*

U.S. Comptroller of the Currency. *Annual Report.* Various years.

Welldon, Samuel A. 1909. *Digest of state banking statutes.* Washington, D.C.: U.S. Government Printing Office.

Comment   Ben S. Bernanke

It will probably not come as a surprise that I find the evidence found by these authors against the "lending" view of monetary policy transmission to be less compelling than they do, and I will devote most of this Comment to explaining why. But Miron, Romer, and Weil (MRW) are nevertheless to be commended for bringing the historical approach to bear on the question of how monetary policy changes are transmitted to the economy. Given the inherent difficulties of discriminating among hypothesized channels of monetary transmission, it is certainly worthwhile to see whether the important changes that have occurred in financial institutions, markets, and regulations over the last century can provide any identifying power. In a similar spirit, international differences

Ben S. Bernanke is professor of economics and public affairs at Princeton University and a research associate of the National Bureau of Economic Research.

in financial markets and institutions existing at a given time might also prove useful for identifying the channels of monetary transmission.

The meat of this article is to be found in sections 8.2 and 8.3, in which MRW attempt to build an empirical case against the existence of a lending channel. In brief, the logic of their case is as follows: First, in section 8.2, MRW use historical information about changes in financial institutions, financial regulation, and portfolio behavior to argue that the lending channel, if it ever existed, is likely to have become weaker over time. Second, in section 8.3, they examine some empirical indicators of the lending channel, looking for changes in the behavior of these indicators across different subperiods. Since they do not find that these indicators differ across subperiods in the way suggested by their analysis of section 8.2, they conclude that the lending channel was probably not important in any period.

I think both steps of this argument are subject to question. Let me take them in order, beginning with the proposition that the lending channel has become less important.

Most of section 8.2's conclusion that the lending channel has weakened over time depends on treating endogenous variables (such as the ratios of loans to securities in the banking sector, or the share of capital financed by bank loans) as if they were exogenous. For the type of argument MRW want to make, however, it is not enough to know that the values taken on by certain endogenous variables have changed over time; it is crucial also to know *why* the endogenous variable changed, and what else was changing in the system at the same time.

For example, the finding that over some period loans fell relative to the capital stock—the result, MRW argue, of the increased development of the equity market—does not necessarily imply that the lending channel became less important, as the authors conclude.[1] It could just as well be argued, for example, that the withdrawal of large firms from the use of bank credit resulted in the typical bank borrower having fewer alternative credit sources and less internal finance available than before. This change would imply a sharper effect of a given contraction of bank lending on spending, since borrowers denied bank credit would have nowhere else to go.

Similarly, the increased share of loans in banks' portfolios in the latter postwar period does not necessarily imply that the lending channel was strengthening after 1970, as the MRW methodology would suggest: rather, it is likely that this increase in loan share was driven by developments such as securitization that increased the liquidity of bank loans, as well as improvements in money markets that reduced banks' precautionary demand for securities. These changes might well have weakened the lending channel on net by increasing

---

1. Inventory stocks would be a more reasonable denominator than the capital stock in this application, since bank loans are typically used to finance working capital rather than long-term fixed capital.

banks' willingness to reduce securities holdings to low levels in times of tight money.

The bottom line is that, to make the case for regime changes, it is important to focus on fundamental institutional or regulatory changes rather than on endogenous choice variables of banks or firms, as MRW have done in a number of cases.

A second general objection to the analysis of section 8.2 is its asymmetry: it looks at only the institutional changes affecting the potency of the lending view but not those affecting the potency of the money view. In fact, a number of changes—most notably, the development of a variety of close money substitutes—would lead one to guess that the "money channel" has weakened over this period as well. Thus it is possible that the *relative* contribution of the lending channel to the overall impact effect of monetary policy changes has risen or stayed the same instead of falling. It seems to me that the failure to control for changes in the money channel vitiates the tests of section 8.3, which implicitly assume that the potency of the money channel has not changed.

A final comment to be made about the historical analysis has to do with truth in advertising: although there are qualifications in the paper, when interpreting or summarizing their results MRW tend to overstate the degree to which the weakening of the lending channel can be found in the data. For example, in their introduction they write, "Our analysis shows that the lending channel should have played a *much greater* role in the pre-1929 era than during the post–World War II period, *especially* the early part of this period" (italics mine). I think any reasonable parsing of that sentence gives the meaning that the strength of the lending channel was definitely lower after 1970 than before 1929, even though the difference might have been less than the difference between the early postwar period and the pre-1929 period. Yet, even if we accept MRW's methodology (which I have suggested we should not), this claim is not well supported by what they find. For example, figures 8.4, 8.5, and 8.7 of their paper suggest that the lending channel was approximately as strong after 1970 as it was pre-1929. The implication is that MRW's tests of section 8.3 must rely heavily, not on obvious differences between the pre-1929 and post-1945 eras, but rather on the outlying observations generated by the experience of the 1950s and early 1960s.

In section 8.3, as I have noted, MRW examine the behavior of some indicators of the lending channel across the "regimes" identified in section 8.2. Not finding the differences in behavior across regimes that they expect, they conclude that the lending view must have never been relevant. I find this logic strange. As an analogy, consider a scientist with two beakers (metaphors for the prewar and postwar periods). Suppose that the scientist has pretty good a priori reasons (based on historical analysis) to believe that a certain compound (the lending view) is in beaker A (the prewar period), but is unsure about whether the compound is in beaker B (the postwar period) as well. Using instruments of uncertain quality (the lending-view indicators), the scientist tests beaker B for the compound. Not receiving a definitive answer, she then uses the same instruments to test beaker A, again not finding anything definitive. What should the scientist conclude? MRW seem to think that the right conclusion is that the compound is in neither beaker, despite the a priori reasons to believe that the compound was in beaker A. It seems to me that the right conclusion is instead that the instruments aren't any good.

In fact, the "instruments" used by MRW to detect a lending channel are quite tenuous. I discuss each of MRW's three indicator variables briefly:

The Loan Rate—Commercial Paper Rate Spread

The authors use this interest-rate spread to proxy for the loan-bond spread in the theoretical model, a spread which the model predicts should rise when monetary tightening reduces the relative supply of bank loans. Unfortunately, this proxy is a poor one: First, the empirical bank-loan rate does not measure the marginal cost of bank funds to a constant-quality borrower, as it would have to do to match the theoretical construct. Rather, factors such as changing borrower mix, changes in collateral and other nonprice terms, and possibly rationing may make the empirical loan rate behave very differently from its theoretical counterpart. In particular, counter to a claim of the paper, it is plausible that the theoretical and empirical spreads do not even have to move in the same direction. For example, there is good evidence that banks drop smaller and riskier borrowers in favor of larger, safer ones during a recession. This "flight to quality" effect alone could explain the sometimes perverse movements of the empirical loan rate.

As the empirical loan rate is a poor proxy for the loan rate in the theory, so is the commercial paper rate a poor proxy for the safe rate in the model. Commercial paper (CP) is not a safe (or even completely liquid) asset; early in the MRW sample there were periods in which the CP rate actually exceeded the loan rate. In the postwar period, the commercial paper rate (and the CP rate–Treasury-bill rate) has been a sensitive indicator of monetary contractions and credit crunches, probably because of imperfect liquidity of the CP market. Thus using the CP rate as a proxy for the safe rate is likely to be highly misleading.

The reader of this comment may suspect that my criticism of the loan rate–CP rate spread as an indicator arises in part because I don't like the results of the test. On the contrary, the empirical problems with using this spread as an indicator have been understood in the literature for a long time. In my 1983 paper, for example, I wrote

> It would be useful to have a direct measure of the CCI [the bank's loan rate less the cost of funds]; unfortunately, no really satisfactory representation of this concept is available. Reported commercial loan rates reflect loans that are actually made, not the shadow cost of bank funds to the representative potential borrower; since banks in a period of retrenchment make only the

safest and highest-quality loans, measured loan rates may well move in-
versely to the CCI. (Bernanke 1983, 264)

I have made similar observations in a number of subsequent papers, as have
other people working on this topic.

The Correlation between Output and Lending

As the basis for another test of the lending view, MRW argue that, if the
lending view is true, loans and output should be more strongly correlated during periods of monetary restriction than otherwise. However, they do not present any formal explanation of why we should take the simple correlation of
two endogenous variables as evidence for a structural hypothesis. Indeed, there
are forces working in the opposite direction of their claim: for example, most
studies of the response of loans to a monetary contraction find that loans actually rise in the short run, a pattern that appears to be the result of larger firms
taking down their lines of bank credit in order to finance unintended inventory
accumulations. This pattern is not inconsistent with a role for the lending channel in the medium run (indeed, small firms without lines of credit feel the brunt
in the short run); yet the "perverse" movement of loans immediately following
a monetary contraction could rationalize even a decline in the correlation of
loans and output during periods of monetary stringency. More broadly, as I
have argued in much greater detail in a Comment on Ramey (1993), it is generally not the case that reduced-form correlations or timing relationships among
output, money, and loans can identify the channels of monetary transmission.

As it happens, however, MRW do find a stronger relationship between industrial production and bank lending during the three years following a monetary contraction than at other times (their table 8.1). Rather than emphasize
this finding, however, MRW look at the *differences of differences of R^2's* (of
the regression of output on lending) across the various regimes, arguing that
the differential link of output and lending (between tight money periods and
other periods) should be stronger where the lending channel is stronger. At this
point, noise in the data must be the dominant factor. Incredibly, and swallowing
all the logical steps leading up to this test, the MRW results don't look that bad
for the lending view: the differential R^2's do seem to fall over time, as predicted
by the premise that the lending channel has weakened over time. Nevertheless,
without statistical or other rationales, MRW conclude that these results are
somehow not favorable to the lending view. I don't understand why not, given
the logic of the test.

The Mix between Bank Loans and Commercial Paper

In an innovative paper, Kashyap, Stein, and Wilcox (1993) showed that the
ratio of loans to commercial paper fell sharply in periods of monetary stringency, a result they interpreted as confirming the lending view's implication
that tight money forces borrowers away from banks toward other credit

sources. MRW reproduce these results for the postwar period but find them to be less evident in other periods. In particular, during the 1920 tight money episode loans actually rose relative to commercial paper.

Of the three indicators that MRW use, I think the "mix" variable is the most legitimate, and the only one of the three that can be called (in MRW's phrase) a "traditional" indicator of the lending view. Thus I find MRW's evidence, particularly the anomalous 1920 episode, to be intriguing and worth exploring further. My guess is, though, that the explanation for 1920 will turn out to lie in differences in institutions between then and now. In particular, in 1920 commercial paper was not backed by bank lines of credit (as it almost always is today), and commercial paper borrowers often posed as much credit risk as bank borrowers. Thus it is possible that the "flight to quality" phenomenon worked in the opposite direction in 1920 than it does today.

In challenging MRW's specific tests, I do not mean to imply by any means that the existence of the lending channel is not a testable proposition. On the contrary, there is now quite a large body of evidence—including observations on the nature of institutional arrangements, historical experiences, and more formal econometric studies—that confirms various aspects of the lending view hypothesis. This evidence is discussed very completely by Kashyap and Stein in chapter 7 of this volume, so I will not restate those points here. But MRW's implication that there exists no positive evidence for a lending channel—even a lending channel that plays a relatively small role in the overall monetary policy transmission process—is clearly not correct.

This brings me to a final general point, which again concerns the asymmetry of the testing procedure followed by MRW. MRW implicitly treat the conventional money view as the null hypothesis; when their tests do not turn up convincing evidence for the lending view, they seem happy to ascribe all of the (unexplained) impact of monetary policy to the money channel. But MRW never offer any positive evidence for the money view!

What if we were to turn the exercise around and make the lending view the null hypothesis, thereby putting the burden of proof on the money view? I think the money view would do badly. First of all, as I discussed in the previous paragraph, there is a respectable set of arguments and evidence making the positive case for the existence of the lending view. (The case for the lending view becomes even stronger when its definition is broadened to include other imperfect capital markets phenomena, such as balance sheet and cash flow effects.) In contrast, the proposition that the money channel is powerful runs into some challenging empirical problems. These difficulties include (*a*) the increasing prevalence of money substitutes, which reduces the leverage of the money channel on interest rates; (*b*) the "term structure problem," that is, the relative inability of the Fed to control long-term as opposed to short-term interest rates (presumably, long-term rates are the ones relevant to most firm investment decisions); and (*c*) the "cost of capital problem," that is, the consistent finding that small to moderate changes in interest rates don't seem to affect investment decisions very much. A serious defense of the conventional money view should address these issues as well as attack the lending view.

I have tried to refute what I believe to be invalid or fragile conclusions drawn by this paper, particularly the rather implausible claim that the lending channel should be given literally no weight at all in the monetary transmission process. Evidence and common sense tell us that both the money and lending channels must be operative to some degree. The real question (both for economists and Federal Reserve policymakers) is quantitative: how big are the two channels and by how much has their relative importance changed over time? We should try to develop and estimate general models of bank, depositor, and borrower behavior that will allow us to get at these questions.

References

Bernanke, Ben S. 1983. Nonmonetary effects of the financial crisis in the propagation of the Great Depression. *American Economic Review* 73:257–76.
Kashyap, Anil K., Jeremy C. Stein, and David Wilcox. 1993. Monetary policy and credit conditions: Evidence from the computation of external finance. *American Economic Review* 83:78–98.
Ramey, Valerie. 1993. *How important is the credit channel in the transmission of monetary policy?* NBER Working Paper no. A285. Cambridge, Mass.: National Bureau of Economic Research, March.

9   Federal Reserve Policy: Cause and Effect

Matthew D. Shapiro

The Federal Reserve periodically makes decisions to reduce the rate of inflation. Romer and Romer (1989, also 1990), in a recent and influential study, identify six dates since World War II when Federal Reserve policy became explicitly disinflationary. They have recently added a seventh date (Romer and Romer 1992).[1] They find evidence of the effectiveness of Fed policy consistent with the predictions of the neo-Keynesian model. The disinflations are followed by periods of substantial output and employment loss.

Romer and Romer, in both their historical and econometric methodology, treat the changes in Fed policy as exogenous events. In their examination of the Federal Open Market Committee (FOMC) minutes, they look explicitly for innovations in Fed policy concerning the steady-state rate of inflation. They deliberately avoid an examination of economic conditions in dating the Fed decisions. In their econometric work, they treat these changes in Fed policy as observed exogenous impulses that determine the course of real economic activity and inflation. Hence, the impact of the policy shifts is estimated by ordinary least squares. The dynamic multipliers implied by these estimates are thus taken as the impact *per se* of the policy.

Matthew D. Shapiro is associate professor of economics and faculty associate of the Survey Research Center at the University of Michigan and faculty research fellow of the National Bureau of Economic Research.

The author is grateful to Robert Barsky, Charles Fleischman, Lung-Fei Lee, Bennett McCallum, N. Gregory Mankiw, David Romer, anonymous reviewers, and the conference participants for helpful comments on preliminary drafts. Carlos Quintanilla provided able research assistance. This research was undertaken while he was an Alfred P. Sloan Fellow.

1. The dates identified in Romer and Romer (1989) are 1947:10, 1955:09, 1968:12, 1974:04, 1978:08, and 1979:10. Romer and Romer (1992) adds 1988:12. The preliminary research for this paper was carried out before the Romers identified this latest date. The estimates in this paper, however, incorporate the new Romer date. Makadok (1988) also uses the narrative of Federal Reserve policies to study their cause and effect.

Romer and Romer's perspective of treating policy variables as exogenous is part of a long tradition. Most studies of the effectiveness of monetary policy use time-series indicators of monetary policy such as growth rates of money stocks or interest rates as predictors of aggregate economic outcomes. By ignoring the feedback of the economy to policy, these studies treat policy changes as random shocks.

But, of course, decisions by the FOMC to change policy take place with explicit consideration of economic conditions. A decision to disinflate is meaningful only if there is a precondition of existing high inflation, either actual or expected. Therefore, there must be feedback from the economy to policy making. Even if the Fed's actions can be regarded as predetermined, they are certainly not strictly exogenous. The FOMC is reacting to the economy and hoping to affect it.

The first part of this paper examines the effects of the Fed's decision to disinflate. That these decisions are followed by substantial declines in real activity is well documented in the Romers' papers. Previous work does not, however, examine the effect on inflation of the disinflationary shifts in policy. Since disinflation is the Fed's explicit objective, I develop quantitative estimates of the disinflationary effect of the policy change in order to study systematically the decision to undertake it.

The second part of the paper uses what is learned about the effects of a decision to disinflate to examine its determinants. It constructs measures of variables driving the Fed's decision to disinflate. It then develops a discrete-choice model that shows how these variables explain the Fed's actions.

9.1 Effects

In discussions of cause and effect, cause usually comes before effect. Yet, at least insofar as the empirical work for this paper is concerned, the effects of disinflation need to be studied first. Presumably, the Fed has an estimate of the impact of its policy before undertaking it. But in order to model that decision, I must first construct similar estimates of the costs and benefits of the decision.

Surprisingly, the literature has not addressed the very basic question, what is the consequence *for inflation* of a decision by the Fed to disinflate? Empirical work by Romer and Romer documents the costs of a decision to disinflate. They show forecasts of production and unemployment responding to these Federal Reserve policy shifts. Taken for granted is that the disinflationary episodes have a favorable impact on inflation. For the empirical modeling of the decision to disinflate, I need, however, a quantitative estimate of the benefits as well as the costs. Therefore, I will examine in some detail the anti-inflation consequences of the disinflations.

9.1.1 Specification of the Inflation Process

The variables I consider are inflation measured by the consumer price index, the civilian unemployment rate, and the Romer dummies.[2] The goal of this section is to develop forecasts of inflation and unemployment conditional on a policy change. These forecasts will then be used as an input into the model of Fed decisions in section 9.2.

Since the aim of this section is to develop forecasts, it relies on simple time-series models of inflation and unemployment conditional on their own lags and lags of the Romer dummies. I present both univariate estimates and bivariate estimates, where lags of the unemployment rate appear in the inflation equation and vice versa.

Figure 9.1 presents the basic data. The unemployment rate has a clear and well-known upward trend for most of the sample. In the econometric work that follows, the unemployment rate is detrended with a linear trend. The trend arises because of labor-market phenomena not closely linked to short-run Fed policy, so abstracting from the trend seems appropriate.

Specification of the inflation process is more problematic. As a matter of theory, it is desirable to allow for persistent impacts of the decision to disinflate on the level of inflation. Only finite lags of the Romer dates are entered into the equations. Hence, in an equation that has the level of inflation as the left-hand-side variable, a policy change will have only temporary, although possibly very persistent, impacts on the inflation rate. In a specification where the difference of inflation is the dependent variable, they will in general have permanent effects, although the long-run effect could be small.

Of course, the empirical persistence of the inflation process must be considered. Previous work has found post–World War II inflation, in contrast with earlier samples (see Barsky 1987), to be very persistent. The persistence of inflation is, however, very sensitive to the sample period. As we get more and more observations after the Volcker disinflation, inflation looks more mean-reverting. But even more important is how the earlier years of the postwar period are treated. The period 1947–52 has dramatic swings in inflation associated with the post–World War II and Korean War business cycles and with price controls and their aftermath. Consequently, estimates in this paper are carried out over the period beginning in 1953. No claim is made that the results are robust to inclusion of the 1947–52 period. Quite the contrary, the results are very sensitive to inclusion of this period. Since there are strong a priori grounds for expecting the early period to be different from the later, including

---

2. The data are quarterly. The monthly Romer dummies are converted to quarterly as dummies for quarters during which a Romer date occurs. The inflation rate is measured as the three-month percent change (log-differences at annual rate) for the quarter. The unemployment rate is the average for the quarter. The sample period is from 1953:1 to 1992:4 (see below for discussion of sample period). The sample period refers to the range of the dependent variables in any equation estimated, so in those involving lags, the appropriate presample data are used.

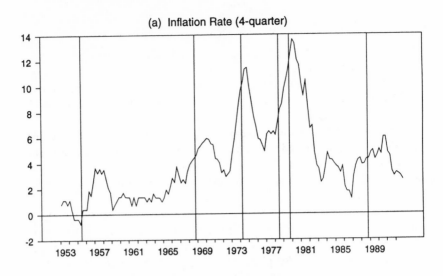

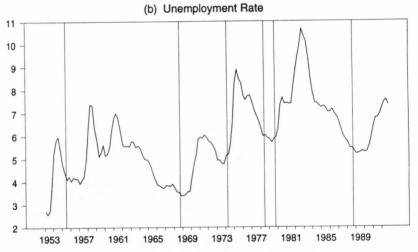

Fig. 9.1   Inflation, unemployment and the decision to disinflate

Note: Inflation is the four-quarter change in the consumer price index for all urban consumers. Unemployment is the civilian unemployment rate. Vertical lines are the Romer dates.

it in the sample would not shed much light on the behavior of the economy during the bulk of the postwar period.

Table 9.1 documents this sensitivity of the inflation process to the sample period. It reports the regression results of the change of inflation on seven of its own lags and the lagged level. The table reports the implied largest autoregressive root of the level of inflation and its *t*-statistic for the null that it is unity. Both these statistics have Dickey-Fuller (1981) distributions. The first three rows report results starting in 1947. These document the instability of the

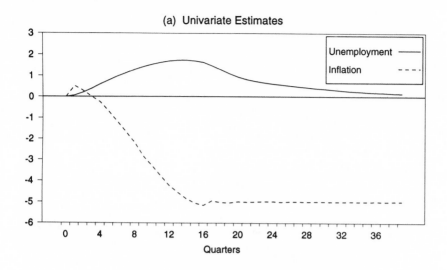

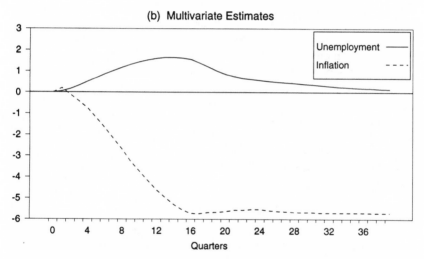

Fig. 9.2   Response of unemployment and inflation to a Romer date: inflation nonstationary

Note: Estimates from (a) table 9.2 and (b) table 9.4.

inflation process in the early period. For both the 1947–92 and 1947–79 periods, inflation is estimated to be rapidly mean-reverting (largest roots of 0.68 or 0.66). But the next rows show that much of the mean-reversion over the postwar period arises from the 1947–52 period. This period had very unpersistent inflation (root of 0.19). On account of this very different behavior, together with the Korean War price controls, I start the sample in 1953.

In the 1953–92 period, inflation is just on the boundary between accepting

Table 9.1   **Persistence of Inflation: Various Samples since 1947**

Sample	Largest Autoregressive Root	t-statistic
1947:1–1992:4	0.68	−4.96
1947:1–1979:4	0.66	−4.10
1947:1–1952:4	0.19	−2.92
1953:1–1992:4	0.84	−2.97
1953:1–1979:4	0.92	−1.26

Note: Table reports Dickey-Fuller (1981) regression of the change of inflation (seven lags) and a constant (no trend). It reports the implied largest autoregressive root of the level of inflation and the Dickey-Fuller t-statistic for the null hypothesis that it is unity.

and rejecting the unit-root hypothesis. The largest autoregressive root is 0.84; the Dickey-Fuller t-statistic of −2.97 is marginal at conventional significance levels. The last row shows that even in the 1953–92 period, there are important changes in the persistence of inflation. In the 1953–79 period, the root is much closer to unity and the t-statistic is in the region of nonrejection. Inflation looked very persistent over this period. Since the Volcker disinflation of the 1980s, it looks more mean-reverting. As I will argue later in this section, the Volcker disinflation is a singular event, so it is hard to predict its lasting consequences for the process of inflation.

In light of the sensitivity of the inflation process to specification and sample period, many of the results of this paper will be presented for specifications using both the level and difference of inflation. It is already clear from table 9.1 that certain results, those concerning inflation, will be sensitive to the specification of its process. But other results, in particular those relating to unemployment, are not.

9.1.2 Results: Effects of Policy Changes

Let π_t be the inflation rate and u_t be the employment rate. The equations to estimate what happens after a Romer date are specified as follows:

$$(1) \quad \Delta\pi_t = \beta_\pi \pi_{t-1} + A_{\pi\pi}(L)\Delta\pi_{t-1} + A_{\pi u}(L)u_{t-1} + D_\pi(L)R_{t-1} + \varepsilon_{1t}$$
$$u_t = \beta_u \pi_{t-1} + A_{u\pi}(L)\Delta\pi_{t-1} + A_{uu}(L)u_{t-1} + D_u(L)R_{t-1} + \varepsilon_{2t},$$

where $\Delta\pi_t$ is the change of the inflation rate, R_t is the dummy variable that is one on a Romer date and zero otherwise, and $A(L)$ and $D(L)$ are polynomials in the lag operator. The $A(L)$ polynomials are eighth-order and unrestricted.[3] The $D(L)$ polynomials, which capture the impact of the Romer dates, include lags one through sixteen and are estimated as fourth-order polynomially dis-

---

3. The $A_{u\pi}(L)$ polynomial also is such that the current value π_t of the inflation rate is included in the equation for unemployment. This is merely a normalization to make the error terms uncorrelated. It is equivalent to using the triangularization popular in the literature on vector autoregressions.

tributed lags with the far endpoint restricted to zero.[4] When estimated as unrestricted, the lag distributions are noisier, but have basically the same dynamics.

The coefficients β are constrained to be zero in the nonstationary specification of inflation and freely estimated when inflation is allowed to be stationary. Including the lagged level of inflation in the equations is equivalent to respecifying the equations in terms of the level of inflation. This normalization facilitates comparison of the estimated coefficients across the specifications of the inflation process.[5]

Univariate Estimates

The results for the univariate estimates are presented in table 9.2 and 9.3 and figures 9.2a and 9.3a. Consider first the estimates for unemployment (the same in both tables).[6] Unemployment has the hump-shaped dynamics that are typical of real aggregates. After a shock to unemployment, it continues in the same direction for several quarters before slowly reverting to trend. The Romer dates increase unemployment gradually. Figure 9.2a shows the convolution of the Romer dates and the own-lags of unemployment. Following a Romer date, unemployment gradually increases to a peak level of 1.73 in the fifteenth quarter after the shocks and then slowly reverts to trend. As subsequent figures show, these dynamics are essentially invariant to the specification of the inflation rate and to whether a univariate or bivariate system is estimated. They replicate the findings presented by Romer and Romer (1989). The tables give the F-statistic for the null hypothesis that the all of the coefficients of the Romer dates are zero.[7] For unemployment, this hypothesis is rejected at the 0.03 level.

The constant of the unemployment rate equation has an interesting interpretation. Since the variable u_t is zero mean, it would be zero but for the inclusion of the dummies for disinflation. The estimated coefficient indicates that the Romer dates increase the average unemployment rate by about one-tenth of one percentage point.

Now consider the estimates of the inflation process. Even conditioning on the Romer dates, inflation is persistent. The coefficient of the lagged level of inflation in table 9.3 is not significantly different from zero. Hence, inclusion of the Romer dummies does not affect the unit-roots tests reported in table 9.1. Inflation is, however, less persistent than a random walk (see the negative coefficients of the lagged $\Delta\pi$). The coefficients of the lagged Romer dates

---

4. Sixteen lags is long enough so that the endpoint restriction is not strongly binding.

5. To make the nonstationary and stationary models have the same degrees of freedom, when inflation is allowed to be stationary by including the lagged level π_{t-1}, I include only seven lags in the polynomials in $\Delta\pi_{t-1}$.

6. Recall that here and throughout, u_t is the deviation of unemployment from a linear trend.

7. Because the lags of the Romer dates are estimated as a fourth-order polynomial with a far endpoint constraint, the hypothesis has only three restrictions.

Table 9.2   **Estimated Response of Inflation and Unemployment (inflation nonstationary, univariate estimates)**

Independent Variables	Lags	$\Delta\pi$		u	
Constant		0.40	(0.22)	−0.07	(0.03)
$\Delta\pi$	1	−0.63	(0.08)		
$\Delta\pi$	2	−0.40	(0.10)		
$\Delta\pi$	3	−0.04	(0.11)		
$\Delta\pi$	4	−0.04	(0.10)		
$\Delta\pi$	5	0.01	(0.10)		
$\Delta\pi$	6	0.03	(0.10)		
$\Delta\pi$	7	0.08	(0.09)		
$\Delta\pi$	8	−0.12	(0.07)		
u	1			1.61	(0.08)
u	2			−0.77	(0.15)
u	3			0.02	(0.16)
u	4			−0.08	(0.16)
u	5			0.19	(0.16)
u	6			0.06	(0.16)
u	7			−0.22	(0.15)
u	8			0.11	(0.08)
R	1	0.51	(0.71)	0.07	(0.10)
R	2	0.11	(0.50)	0.09	(0.07)
R	3	−0.23	(0.41)	0.11	(0.06)
R	4	−0.50	(0.39)	0.12	(0.06)
R	5	−0.72	(0.39)	0.13	(0.06)
R	6	−0.89	(0.39)	0.15	(0.06)
R	7	−1.00	(0.38)	0.15	(0.06)
R	8	−1.07	(0.36)	0.16	(0.06)
R	9	−1.10	(0.35)	0.16	(0.06)
R	10	−1.09	(0.36)	0.16	(0.06)
R	11	−1.04	(0.38)	0.15	(0.06)
R	12	−0.96	(0.41)	0.15	(0.07)
R	13	−0.85	(0.44)	0.12	(0.07)
R	14	−0.72	(0.44)	0.12	(0.07)
R	15	−0.56	(0.41)	0.09	(0.06)
R	16	−0.39	(0.33)	0.07	(0.05)
S.E.E.		1.97		0.30	
$\bar{R}^2$		0.33		0.95	
$F(3,140)$		3.26		3.09	
p-value		0.02		0.03	

Note: Autoregression of change of inflation ($\Delta\pi$) and detrended unemployment (u) on own lags and Romer dates (R). Standard errors are in parentheses. S.E.E. is standard error of regression. $\bar{R}^2$ is adjusted coefficient of determination. $F(3,140)$ and p-value are the F-statistic and rejection probability for the hypothesis that the coefficients of R are jointly zero.

Table 9.3   **Estimated Response of Inflation and Unemployment (Inflation stationary, univariate estimates)**

Independent Variables	Lags	$\Delta\pi$		u	
Constant		0.65	(0.28)	−0.07	(0.03)
π	1	−0.09	(0.08)		
$\Delta\pi$	1	−0.56	(0.11)		
$\Delta\pi$	2	−0.33	(0.12)		
$\Delta\pi$	3	0.02	(0.12)		
$\Delta\pi$	4	0.01	(0.11)		
$\Delta\pi$	5	0.05	(0.11)		
$\Delta\pi$	6	0.12	(0.10)		
$\Delta\pi$	7	0.17	(0.07)		
u	1			1.61	(0.08)
u	2			−0.77	(0.15)
u	3			0.02	(0.16)
u	4			−0.08	(0.16)
u	5			0.19	(0.16)
u	6			0.06	(0.16)
u	7			−0.22	(0.15)
u	8			0.11	(0.08)
R	1	0.68	(0.74)	0.07	(0.10)
R	2	0.27	(0.55)	0.09	(0.07)
R	3	−0.07	(0.48)	0.11	(0.06)
R	4	−0.33	(0.47)	0.12	(0.06)
R	5	−0.53	(0.49)	0.13	(0.06)
R	6	−0.67	(0.50)	0.15	(0.06)
R	7	−0.75	(0.49)	0.15	(0.06)
R	8	−0.79	(0.49)	0.16	(0.06)
R	9	−0.79	(0.48)	0.16	(0.06)
R	10	−0.75	(0.48)	0.16	(0.06)
R	11	−0.69	(0.49)	0.15	(0.06)
R	12	−0.60	(0.50)	0.15	(0.07)
R	13	−0.50	(0.50)	0.13	(0.07)
R	14	−0.39	(0.49)	0.12	(0.07)
R	15	−0.28	(0.44)	0.09	(0.06)
R	16	−0.17	(0.35)	0.07	(0.05)
S.E.E.		1.98		0.30	
$\bar{R}^2$		0.33		0.95	
$F(3,140)$		1.24		3.09	
p-value		0.30		0.03	

Note: Autoregression of change of inflation ($\Delta\pi$) and detrended unemployment (u) on own lags and Romer dates (R). Lagged level of inflation included to render inflation stationary. See also note to table 9.2.

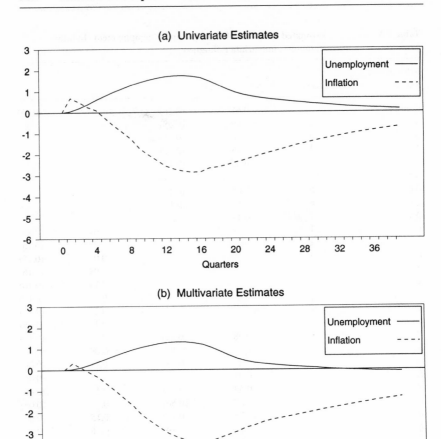

Fig. 9.3   Response of unemployment and inflation to a Romer date: inflation stationary

Note: Estimates from (a) table 9.3 and (b) table 9.5.

have similar patterns in table 9.2 and table 9.3. Following a Romer date, inflation continues to accelerate for two quarters and then decelerates. The joint test that the coefficients of the Romer dates are all zero rejects for the nonstationary, but not for the stationary specification.

The dynamic response of inflation to the Romer dates is again easiest to see in the figures. Figure 9.2a gives the response for the univariate, inflation-nonstationary model; figure 9.3a gives it for the univariate, inflation-stationary model. Both figures report the response of the *level* of inflation to a Romer date. For the nonstationary specification in figure 9.2a, inflation continues to accelerate for several quarters. It then decelerates until it levels off after about four years at a level five percentage points lower than where it began. This change is economically significant. The standard error of the inflation equation is about two percentage points, so the reduction is two and one-half times the innovation's standard error. But as will be shown below, the magnitude of the change is attributable largely to the Volcker disinflation.

The pattern for the stationary-inflation model in figure 9.3a is similar, although the magnitudes are not. The maximum reduction in inflation is only about three percentage points, and, of course, it is temporary. Moreover, recall that the coefficients of the Romer dates are not significantly different from zero in the estimates reported in table 9.3, so the projected disinflation is not statistically significant.

Multivariate Estimates

Table 9.4 and 9.5 and figures 9.2b and 9.3b report the results of estimating the multivariate model where the change in inflation and the level of unemployment are regressed on their own lags and lags of the unemployment rate.[8] Both nonstationary- and stationary-inflation models are again estimated.

Figures 9.2b and 9.3b report the total responses to a Romer date. That is, for inflation, the changes in lagged unemployment are taken into account and vice versa. The estimated response of unemployment and inflation to disinflations is very similar to the corresponding estimates for the univariate models in the (a) panels of the figures. The similarity of the univariate and multivariate estimates of the response of inflation and unemployment to a disinflation disguises interesting differences that are revealed in the estimates of the equations reported in the tables. In the unemployment equation, the coefficients of the Romer dates do not change much between tables 9.2 and 9.4. Including the lagged changes in inflation only slightly attenuates the coefficients of the Romer dates in the unemployment equation in table 9.4. They remain statistically significant, although at the 0.06 rather than the 0.03 level.

On the other hand, when lags of unemployment are included in the equation for the change in inflation in table 9.4, the coefficients of the Romer dates get considerably smaller than those in the univariate model in table 9.2. Moreover, the coefficients of the Romer dates in the inflation equation in table 9.4 are jointly statistically insignificant (p-value of the F-statistic is 0.51). Hence, the impact on inflation of the Romer dates in the multivariate system operates indirectly through the impact of lagged unemployment rather than directly in the inflation equation. Since the estimated equations are reduced form, they need to be interpreted with caution. Yet, the absence of an independent impact of

---

8. Also, the current change in inflation is included in the unemployment rate regression to normalize the residuals to be uncorrelated.

Table 9.4   **Estimated Response of Inflation and Unemployment (inflation nonstationary, multivariate estimates)**

Independent Variables	Lags	$\Delta\pi$		u	
Constant		0.23	(0.21)	−0.06	(0.03)
$\Delta\pi$	0			−0.01	(0.01)
$\Delta\pi$	1	−0.73	(0.08)	0.00	(0.02)
$\Delta\pi$	2	−0.47	(0.10)	0.01	(0.02)
$\Delta\pi$	3	−0.10	(0.11)	−0.02	(0.02)
$\Delta\pi$	4	−0.06	(0.11)	0.00	(0.02)
$\Delta\pi$	5	0.05	(0.11)	0.01	(0.02)
$\Delta\pi$	6	0.16	(0.10)	0.00	(0.02)
$\Delta\pi$	7	0.19	(0.09)	0.01	(0.01)
$\Delta\pi$	8	−0.03	(0.07)	0.00	(0.01)
u	1	−2.73	(0.50)	1.60	(0.09)
u	2	3.42	(0.95)	−0.71	(0.16)
u	3	−0.83	(1.02)	−0.07	(0.17)
u	4	−1.13	(1.02)	−0.09	(0.17)
u	5	1.56	(1.01)	0.34	(0.17)
u	6	−1.22	(1.04)	−0.06	(0.17)
u	7	1.60	(0.95)	−0.19	(0.16)
u	8	−0.88	(0.50)	0.12	(0.08)
R	1	0.20	(0.65)	0.06	(0.11)
R	2	−0.01	(0.46)	0.08	(0.08)
R	3	−0.18	(0.38)	0.09	(0.06)
R	4	−0.31	(0.36)	0.11	(0.06)
R	5	−0.41	(0.37)	0.12	(0.06)
R	6	−0.48	(0.37)	0.13	(0.06)
R	7	−0.52	(0.37)	0.14	(0.06)
R	8	−0.53	(0.35)	0.15	(0.06)
R	9	−0.53	(0.35)	0.15	(0.06)
R	10	−0.50	(0.36)	0.15	(0.06)
R	11	−0.46	(0.38)	0.15	(0.06)
R	12	−0.41	(0.40)	0.14	(0.07)
R	13	−0.35	(0.42)	0.13	(0.07)
R	14	−0.28	(0.42)	0.12	(0.07)
R	15	−0.20	(0.39)	0.10	(0.06)
R	16	−0.13	(0.32)	0.07	(0.05)
S.E.E.		1.78		0.30	
$\bar{R}^2$		0.45		0.95	
$F(3,140)$		0.78		2.59	
p-value		0.51		0.06	

Note: Vector autoregression of change of inflation ($\Delta\pi$) and detrended unemployment (u) on own lags and Romer dates (R). Current $\Delta\pi$ included in equation for u to triangularize the system. See also note to table 9.2.

Table 9.5   **Estimated Response of Inflation and Unemployment (inflation stationary, multivariate estimates)**

Independent Variables	Lags	$\Delta\pi$		u	
Constant		0.35	(0.26)	−0.08	(0.04)
π	1	−0.05	(0.07)	0.01	(0.01)
$\Delta\pi$	0			−0.01	(0.01)
$\Delta\pi$	1	−0.69	(0.11)	−0.00	(0.02)
$\Delta\pi$	2	−0.43	(0.12)	0.00	(0.02)
$\Delta\pi$	3	−0.06	(0.13)	−0.02	(0.02)
$\Delta\pi$	4	−0.03	(0.12)	0.00	(0.02)
$\Delta\pi$	5	0.08	(0.11)	0.01	(0.02)
$\Delta\pi$	6	0.19	(0.10)	−0.00	(0.02)
$\Delta\pi$	7	0.21	(0.07)	0.01	(0.01)
u	1	−2.73	(0.50)	1.60	(0.09)
u	2	3.41	(0.94)	−0.71	(0.16)
u	3	−0.81	(1.02)	−0.07	(0.17)
u	4	−1.15	(1.02)	−0.08	(0.17)
u	5	1.57	(1.01)	0.34	(0.17)
u	6	−1.18	(1.04)	−0.06	(0.17)
u	7	1.57	(0.95)	−0.19	(0.16)
u	8	−0.87	(0.49)	0.12	(0.08)
R	1	0.32	(0.68)	0.04	(0.11)
R	2	0.12	(0.51)	0.06	(0.09)
R	3	−0.03	(0.45)	0.07	(0.08)
R	4	−0.15	(0.45)	0.09	(0.08)
R	5	−0.24	(0.47)	0.10	(0.08)
R	6	−0.30	(0.48)	0.11	(0.08)
R	7	−0.33	(0.47)	0.12	(0.08)
R	8	−0.34	(0.47)	0.12	(0.08)
R	9	−0.33	(0.46)	0.13	(0.08)
R	10	−0.31	(0.46)	0.13	(0.08)
R	11	−0.27	(0.46)	0.13	(0.08)
R	12	−0.23	(0.47)	0.12	(0.08)
R	13	−0.18	(0.47)	0.11	(0.08)
R	14	−0.13	(0.46)	0.10	(0.08)
R	15	−0.09	(0.41)	0.08	(0.07)
R	16	−0.05	(0.33)	0.06	(0.05)
S.E.E.		1.78		0.29	
$\bar{R}^2$		0.45		0.95	
$F(3,140)$		0.27		0.97	
p-value		0.85		0.40	

Note: Vector autoregression of change of inflation ($\Delta\pi$) and detrended unemployment (u) on own lags and Romer dates (R). Lagged level of inflation included to render inflation stationary. Current $\Delta\pi$ included in equation for u to triangularize the system. See also note to table 9.2.

the Romer dates on inflation does suggest that disinflations operate through the Phillips curve rather than by independent shifts in the inflationary regime.

Including the lagged unemployment rates in the equation for inflation in the stationary specification has a similar effect (compare tables 9.3 and 9.5). The coefficients of the Romer dates in the inflation equation in table 9.5 are substantially smaller than those in table 9.3. But they are insignificant in both the univariate and multivariate equations, so the difference in the magnitudes of the coefficient estimates should not be overinterpreted.

Disinflations Episode by Episode

In the inflation-nonstationary specification, the estimates reported in this section imply that the disinflations have, on average, a substantial, permanent effect on the inflation rate. These come at a cost of high unemployment for a period of years. But as Feldstein (1979) points out, a permanent gain from lower inflation could well outweigh the temporary output loss.

The estimates based on the regressions for the whole period have important limitations. Specifically, they impose that the magnitude of the disinflation is the same across episodes.[9] It could well be that certain episodes represented much more substantial contractions than others. In this subsection, I present evidence that reveals what success the Fed had in reducing the rate of inflation following each Romer date.

To examine the impact of the disinflations episodically, I use the following simple, nonparametric procedure. I estimate a univariate autoregression of the change of inflation over the entire sample. The equation includes a constant and eight lags of $\Delta\pi_t$, but no Romer dummies. Figure 9.4 shows graphs of the cumulative forecast error for the *level* of inflation from the quarter before each Romer date.[10] The solid lines are the forecast errors, the dashed lines are the one-standard-deviation error bands. For example, in figure 9.4c, inflation is almost 8 percent lower in 1976:1, eight quarters after the Romer date, than it was forecast to be in 1974:1, the quarter before the decision to disinflate.

Figure 9.4 shows that, except for the October 1979 Volcker disinflation, none of the decisions to disinflate had a permanent impact on the level of inflation. (Figure 9.4d credits the August 1978 disinflation with a long-run impact, but the forecast errors do not turn negative until after the October 1979 date.) Forecast errors after the September 1955 (figure 9.4a) episode were large and positive. After the December 1968 (figure 9.4b) episode, the errors were small—first positive and then negative. In the disinflation following the first OPEC price increase (figure 9.4c), there were persistent and large negative forecast errors. Over the two-year horizon, there were substantial reductions in the realized rate of inflation relative to expectation, but these begin to dissipate in 1976. By early 1978 (note that this date is before the second OPEC oil price

---

9. I am grateful to Saul Hymans and Phil Howrey for stressing this issue to me.
10. Romer and Romer (1989, figure 3) provide an analogous figure for the unemployment rate.

increase), inflation is close to its predisinflation expected value. Hence, if this episode is to be counted as a success, there must be some offsetting failure subsequent to it. Moreover, the failure of the OPEC I disinflation to have lasting benefits cannot be blamed on OPEC II. Any success had dissipated before the second oil shock.

Figure 9.4d tells the story of the August 1978 disinflation. It totally failed to affect the forecast errors. They remain positive in the first six quarters. The subsequent reductions in inflation occurred after the 1979 episode.

The October 1979 episode is the outstanding success. It heralded a sustained, large reduction in the rate of inflation. Five years after it, the rate of inflation was 8.5 percentage points lower than would have been forecast in the quarter before the decision to disinflate. From figure 9.4, it is clear that this data point is virtually alone in driving the estimates of the long-run effect of the Romer dummies on inflation presented in the previous subsections.

Finally, figure 9.4f reports the effect of the most recent episode. After bouncing around for several years, the forecast error does settle down below zero, but it is well within the one-standard-deviation band.

Discussion

The large estimated response of the inflation rate to the decision to disinflate is driven by the success of the Volcker disinflation. Following the 1955, 1968, 1978, and 1988 decisions, forecast errors for inflation were positive or mixed. The 1974 episode was a temporary success, but inflation reasserted itself even before the second round of OPEC price increases. Perhaps it should not be surprising that the Volcker episode looks uniquely successful. Figure 9.1a shows how inflation continued to rise after each disinflation, even if there was a temporary retreat. Moreover, had the previous episodes been successful, the conditions that fostered the Volcker change in policy would not have been present.

These results do not necessarily imply, however, that the future rate of inflation is not a primary variable of concern in motivating the Fed to disinflate. The Fed could act in the hope of having a success along the lines that Volcker did, even if in most cases these hopes are not realized. This issue of how the Fed reacts to inflation is addressed in the next section.

9.2   Cause

This section attempts to model the decision of the Fed to disinflate. In it I first calculate measures of the costs and benefits of the decision to disinflate. The estimates of the previous section are inputs into these calculations. I then estimate a discrete-choice model of the decision to disinflate based on these measures of costs and benefits.

The structure of the model is as follows. Let R_t^* be the Fed's intolerance of inflation. This is an unobserved, continuous variable. When it exceeds a thresh-

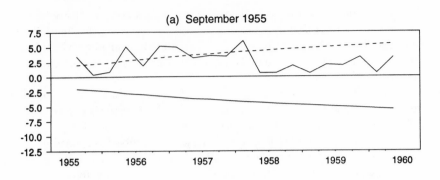

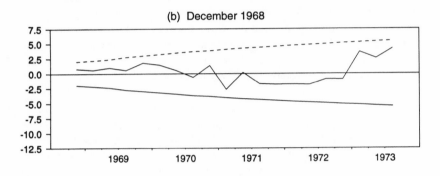

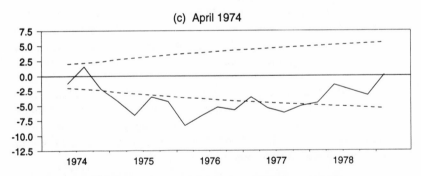

Fig. 9.4   Forecast error for inflation following decisions to disinflate
Note: Cumulative forecast errors of the level of inflation estimated on an AR(8) model for $\Delta\pi_t$.
Dashed line is one-standard-deviation error band.

old (normalized to be zero), the Fed decides it is worthwhile to subject the
economy to a disinflation. The structure of the econometric specification paral-
lels that of the discrete-choice literature. The latent intolerance to inflation is
modeled as a linear function of observables, X_t:

$$(2) \qquad\qquad R_t^* = X_t\beta + v_t.$$

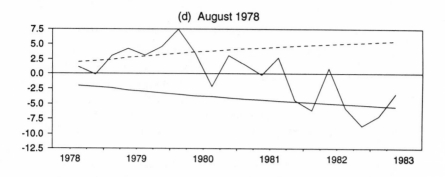

(d) August 1978

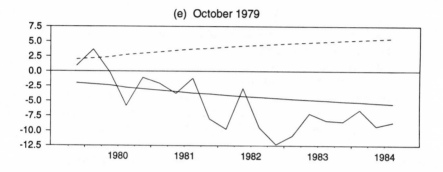

(e) October 1979

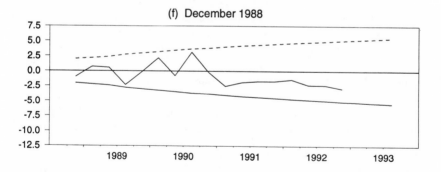

(f) December 1988

When the intolerance exceeds the threshold, the Fed decides to change policy. That is,

$$(3) \qquad\qquad R_t = 1 \text{ when } R_t^* > 0.$$

In this section, I first consider the variables that determine the decision to disinflate (X_t). Then I use those variables to estimate the discrete-choice model.

9.2.1 Variables Determining the Decision to Disinflate

This section of the paper develops variables that are meant to explain the Fed's decision to disinflate. The obvious candidates are measures relating to unemployment (the cost of disinflation) and inflation (the potential benefit). In periods of high inflation, the Fed should more likely be contemplating a disinflation. In periods of high expected unemployment, the cost of disinflating is higher, so the Fed is less likely to make the economy suffer from a disinflation.

One approach would be to make the determining variables X_t simply lags of the unemployment and inflation. But such a model would be misspecified on several grounds. First, presumably what the Fed is contemplating is the impact of its decision on future economic outcomes. Hence, the variables should be forward looking, although they should not use future information.

Second, inflation and unemployment are inertial. The quarter after a decision to disinflate, they will be about the same as they were when the decision was made. If the X_t were based on the current values of unemployment and inflation, equations (2) and (3) would continue to predict changes in policy even after they had taken place. To avoid this misspecification, the variables X_t must ratchet as a consequence of a previous decision to disinflate. Again, this can be accomplished by making them forward looking. Forecasts of unemployment and inflation can react instantaneously even if the actual variables are sluggish.

Several other considerations about the specifications of X_t are driven by the fact that there are only a few episodes of policy change. The list of variables must be short. With an unparsimonious specification and only six disinflations in the sample, it would be very easy to overfit the model. Moreover, again because of the small number of episodes, there is little scope to let the data guide the choice of variables without running the risk that all fit is spurious.

With these considerations in mind, I use the following two measures as determinants of Federal Reserve decisions to disinflate. They are the *expected present discounted value of the level of inflation* and the *expected present discounted value of unemployment.*

These variables capture what one hopes are the central concerns of the Fed when it contemplates a change in aggregate policy. They are forward looking but based on current information and they summarize parsimoniously the current outlook conditional on whether a disinflation has recently occurred. Moreover, they are highly correlated with other variables that might be considered as candidates for driving the Fed's decision. I will discuss below the robustness of the posited measures to various changes in the specification.

These variables are calculated using the estimates developed in section 9.1. The relevant variables are forecast into the indefinite future for each point in the sample. The summary measures are calculated based on these forecasts. I then calculate their expected present discounted value using a 2 percent per quarter discount rate. The robustness of the measures to the discount rate is also considered below.

Note that the present value of the inflation rate might be a key determinant of the decision to disinflate despite the limited effect of the disinflations on inflation in most episodes. The Fed might react to the inflation rate even if it turns out it does not, in practice, succeed in changing it.

Estimates of the Present Discounted Value of Forecasted Inflation and Unemployment

Figure 9.5 gives the estimated determinants of the decision to disinflate. The estimates are based on the multivariate system presented in table 9.4.[11] They are normalized by multiplying by one minus the discount rate so that the units are roughly at annual rate. In this section of the paper, only estimates based on the nonstationary inflation model will be presented. In the next subsection, I show that the present discounted value of forecast inflation is not that sensitive to the stationarity versus nonstationarity of inflation.

Figure 9.5a graphs the present discounted value of the forecasted inflation rate. Its low frequency movements track the actual inflation rate. The variable does ratchet down after Romer dates, but there are also fairly large changes not associated with Romer dates. Recall that the permanent effect of a Romer date is only two and one-half times the standard deviations of the inflation innovation, so large swings independent of the Romer dates are to be expected.

The present discounted value of expected unemployment is given in figure 9.5b. It falls steadily until a Romer date is encountered and then ratchets up once the disinflation occurs. Unlike inflation, the Romer dates appear to be the predominate factor in unemployment's business-cycle movements.

Robustness

As noted above, there is little scope for experimentation with the variables to be included in the model for estimating the probability of disinflation. Yet there is also little theoretical guidance as to the precise form of these variables. Therefore, one should be concerned whether the measures of the variables driving the Fed's decisions are robust to plausible perturbations of their specification. In this subsection, I consider how various alternative measures correlate with the ones used in the probit estimates.

A plausible alternative measure of the inflation rate would be the long-run or asymptotic forecast of its level.[12] This measure is very highly correlated

11. The equation for unemployment does not include the current change in inflation when it is used in this section.
12. Earlier drafts of this paper used this measure.

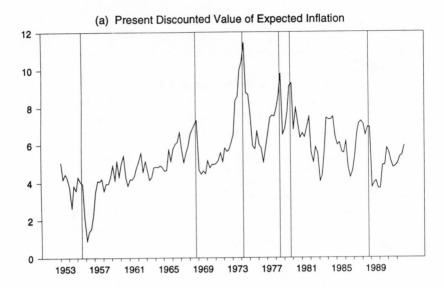

(a) Present Discounted Value of Expected Inflation

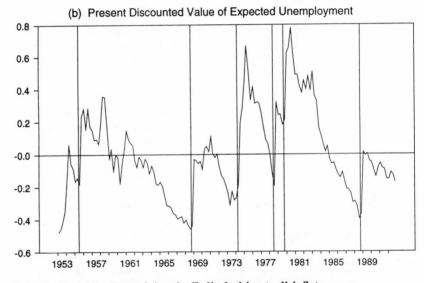

(b) Present Discounted Value of Expected Unemployment

Fig. 9.5   Variables determining the Fed's decision to disinflate

Note: Present discounted value (discount rate of 2 percent per quarter) of forecasted inflation and unemployment. Estimates based on multivariate forecasts with inflation nonstationary (see text). Vertical lines are Romer dates.

Table 9.6   **Decision to Disinflate: Probit Estimates**

	Model 1	Model 2	Model 3
Constant	−4.04	−1.92	−4.24
	(0.82)	(0.23)	(0.89)
PDV inflation	0.35		0.36
	(0.11)		(0.12)
PDV unemployment		−1.62	−1.61
		(0.92)	(0.99)
Log likelihood	−19.98	−23.69	−18.29

Note: Probit estimates using values of the expected present discounted value (PDV) of inflation and unemployment as explanatory variables for Fed decisions to disinflate. See text for details. Standard errors in parentheses.

with the one used in the present paper. Indeed, the correlation is 0.987, so the measures are roughly interchangeable.

In section 9.1, very different results were obtained for the stationary versus nonstationary specifications of the inflation rate. Two factors militate against there being much of a difference between these specifications for calculating present discounted values. First, the pattern of the change for the first four years is about the same. Second, discounting makes the differences in the distant years not matter much. Consequently, the correlation between the present discounted value of expected inflation for inflation-stationary and nonstationary is 0.986 for the discount rate of 0.02 per quarter.[13]

Finally, over plausible ranges of discount rates, the expected present discounted values remain highly coherent. This paper uses a 0.02 quarterly discount rate in calculating the expected present discounted value of inflation and unemployment. Compare these to those calculated with an extremely high discount rate, say 0.10 per quarter: the correlation of the inflation measure discounted with 0.02 versus 0.10 is 0.965; for unemployment, it is 0.964.

9.2.2 Estimated Probability of Disinflation

The models in equations (2) and (3) are estimated using a probit specification of the disturbance. The explanatory variables are the lagged values of the expected present discounted value of inflation and unemployment.[14] (See table 9.6.) Model 1 uses just the inflation variable, model 2 uses just the unemployment variable, model 3 uses both. Expected inflation has the predicted impact on the decision to disinflate. Higher inflation raises the probability. The coefficient is strongly statistically significant. Likewise, expected unemployment

13. This calculation should be taken with a grain of salt, however, because of the statistical insignificance of the Romer dates in the stationary specification of inflation. For this reason, I focus on the inflation nonstationary model.

14. Makadok (1988) estimates a multinominal model (for expansionary, neutral, and contractionary policy) based on lagged macroeconomic variables.

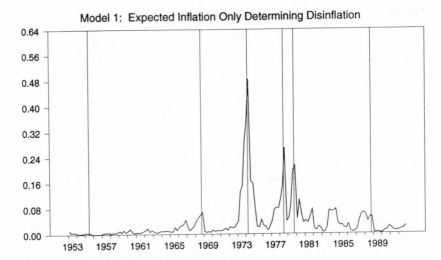

Fig. 9.6   Estimated probability of disinflation
Note: Estimates based on equation reported in table 9.6, model 1. Vertical lines are Romer dates.

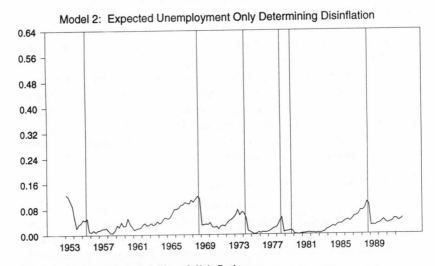

Fig. 9.7   Estimated probability of disinflation
Note: Estimates based on equation reported in table 9.6, model 2. Vertical lines are Romer dates.

also has the predicted impact. Lower unemployment raises the probability of disinflation, but the estimate is only marginally statistically significant. Including both variables does not much alter the magnitude of the estimated coefficients, indicating that they have an independent impact on the probability of a disinflation.

The estimated probit coefficients are difficult to interpret. Figures 9.6

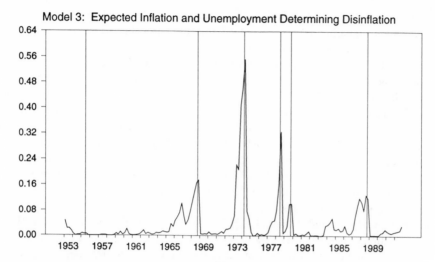

Fig. 9.8   Estimated probability of disinflation

Note: Estimates based on equation reported in table 9.6, model 3. Vertical lines are Romer dates.

through 9.8 give the implied probability of disinflation period by period for the three models. Except for the first disinflation, which this specification totally fails to predict, the probabilities have local peaks around the Romer dates. For the models including inflation, for just one date—the 1974 disinflation—does the probability of a disinflation exceed one-half. Hence the model does not do a good job of pinpointing *the particular quarter* when the disinflation will take place. But the probability is high over adjacent quarters, so the model does attribute a high probability to a disinflation taking place in the year that they occur.[15]

Given the low *t*-statistic of the unemployment variable in the estimates, it does not do a good job of tracking the decisions. Yet figure 9.7 illustrates the role it has in explaining disinflation. The probability slowly increases as unemployment falls prior to a Romer date. Since unemployment is so persistent, the variable does little to pinpoint that particular quarter of the disinflation. Hence the low *t*-statistic. Yet, the integral of the probability over the quarters leading up to the disinflation would indicate the strong probability of a disinflation *sometime* during the period of low unemployment.

Consider the episodes in turn. As has already been noted, the 1955 episode is not explained by the model. Neither was unemployment expected to be particularly low nor inflation particularly high.

15. Recall that the disinflations are rare. In a sample of 180 quarters, only seven occur. Hence, the unconditional probability of one occurring in any given quarter is less than 4 percent. The fitted probabilities should thus be judged against this baseline, not a baseline developed for cross-section studies where the number of zeros and ones in the explanatory variable are of the same order of magnitude.

The probability of disinflation grew steadily in the late 1960s until the 1969 episode. Comparing figures 9.6 and 9.7, this fitted probability is mainly associated with the unemployment variable.

The 1974 decision is the one most sharply predicted by the model. It combined the maximum expected inflation with fairly low expected unemployment (see figure 9.7).

The next two best-predicted decisions are in the late 1970s. Inflation is the driving factor. Indeed, once unemployment is taken into account, the Volcker disinflation in 1979 has a lower fitted probability than when only inflation is included in the model (compare figures 9.6 and 9.8). Why is the most successful disinflation not the most likely? It is precisely because expected unemployment was fairly high in late 1979, partially as a consequence of the failed disinflation of the previous year.

Finally, Romer and Romer (1992) have dated a seventh post–World War II disinflation in late 1988. The model concurs. It begins to predict a disinflation in 1987 based on the drift downward in the unemployment rate beginning in the mid-1980s. As with the 1969 episode, low unemployment rather than high inflation is the primary explanatory factor.[16]

Figure 9.9 presents estimates of a model that is *intentionally misspecified.* It uses estimates of the expected present discounted value of inflation and unemployment as explanatory variables in the probit that are based on a vector autoregression and that do not include the Romer dates as explanatory variables. These results illustrate the importance of allowing the forcing variables to ratchet down after a Romer date. Because inflation and unemployment are persistent, the predictions using these forecasts tend to lag the events. The misspecified model continues to predict disinflations well after they have happened.

But perhaps more importantly, the results in figure 9.9 provide some evidence that the results in the previous figures are not rigged by virtue of including the Romer date dummies as lagged variables in constructing the explanatory variables for the probits. The fitted probabilities indeed do rise in the quarters before the Romer dates with much the same pattern as in figure 9.8. An exception is the 1979 episode, which is better fit by the model reported in figure 9.9. With this model, the cost of the disinflation is not being affected by the response of forecasted unemployment to the 1978 episode.

9.3 Summary

This paper examines the Fed's decision to disinflate. It focuses on the role of pre-existing economic conditions in the decisions. It finds that these deci-

---

16. As a test of the specification and to further evaluate the new Romer date, I estimated the probit using data fit only through 1985 and then estimates the probabilities for the 1986–92 period. They match quite closely those reported in figure 9.8.

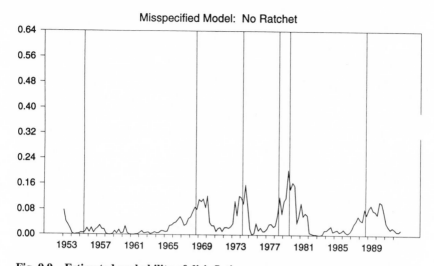

Fig. 9.9   Estimated probability of disinflation

Note: Estimates based on expected present value of inflation and unemployment, but not conditioning on Romer dates. This model is *intentional misspecified* (see text). Vertical lines are Romer dates.

sions are driven both by the prevailing unemployment and inflation rates. Even in periods of high inflation, the Fed will be relatively unwilling to disinflate if the rate of unemployment is otherwise expected to be high. Similarly, especially for the 1969 and 1988 episodes, low unemployment rather than high inflation seems to explain the Fed's action.

In planning this paper, I expected estimating the inflation process to be merely a side issue. But the analysis of the inflation process proves very interesting in itself. While on average the "disinflations" do reduce the rate of inflation subsequently, this average result is driven almost entirely by the 1979 episode. This leads one to ask, what is the Fed accomplishing by putting the economy into a recession? Perhaps it is responding to incipient inflation that is signaled by low unemployment. These could arise through nonlinearities in the Phillips curve not captured in simple specifications. Indeed, perhaps we do not see that region of the Phillips curve because the Fed never lets unemployment get so low. In any case, the economics profession's recent view that the Fed has had great success in reducing the rate of inflation, albeit with a temporary output loss, is largely colored by the achievement of the Volcker disinflation. Over the post–World War II period, the average disinflationary episode has done little to reduce the rate of inflation despite clear evidence that the changes in policy do cause unemployment to rise substantially.

References

Barsky, Robert B. 1987. The fisher effect and the forecastability and persistence of inflation. *Journal of Monetary Economics* 19:3–24.

Dickey, David A., and Wayne A. Fuller. 1981. Likelihood ratio statistics for autoregressive time series with a unit root. *Econometrica* 49:1057–72.

Feldstein, Martin S. 1979. The welfare cost of permanent inflation and optimal short-run economic policy. *Journal of Political Economy* 87:749–68.

Makadok, Richard J. 1988. Can the Federal Reserve affect real output? Senior essay. Yale University.

Romer, Christina D., and Romer, David H. 1989. Does monetary policy matter? A new test in the spirit of Friedman and Schwartz. *NBER Macroeconomics Annual* 4:121–70.

———. 1990. New evidence on the monetary transmission mechanism. *Brookings Papers on Economic Activity,* 149–213.

———. 1992. Monetary policy matters. University of California, Berkeley. Manuscript.

Comment   Bennett T. McCallum

Matthew Shapiro has conducted a careful and interesting re-examination of the effects of U.S. unemployment of the Romer and Romer (1989) dummy variable, which was designed to reflect postwar decisions by the Fed to disinflate. In particular, Shapiro's analysis recognizes the dependence of such decisions on the state of the economy—in other words, of their endogeneity. In the process of conducting his study, he has made a commendable effort to determine whether his results are robust with respect to the sample period utilized and to the maintained hypothesis regarding stationarity of the inflation process. Regarding the former, I would tend a priori to prefer the results based on the sample beginning in 1953, since there were various administrative controls in effect during the Korean War, enough to suggest that market responses would be affected. And as for the stationarity assumption, it is fortunately the case that most of his results are not sensitive to the assumption adopted.

One issue that Shapiro did not consider concerns the effect of including oil price shocks as an additional explanatory variable. This issue has been raised in a pair of recent papers, by Hoover and Perez (1992) and Dotsey and Reid (1992), which suggest that the Romer and Romer (R&R) dummy loses its significance[1] when oil price shocks are included in the regression equation. In a recent working paper, Romer and Romer (1992) responded to the Hoover-Perez contention by demonstrating that their policy dummy retains signifi-

---

Bennett T. McCallum is the H. J. Heinz Professor of Economics at Carnegie Mellon University and a research associate of the National Bureau of Economic Research.

1. In this Comment, all references to "statistical significance" will be understood to apply to a 0.05 significance level.

cance in three out of four specifications considered, although by a small margin when the sample period used in their original study is utilized.[2] This working paper does not respond explicitly to the Dotsey-Reid claim that the dummy's effect is insignificant when oil price shocks are entered with separate coefficients for positive and negative changes. One possible reason for the discrepancy relative to the Romer and Romer (1992) results is that Dotsey and Reid (1992) include only twenty-four lagged values of the policy dummy, rather than thirty-six. A more likely reason, however, is that the Dotsey-Reid test pertains to the joint insignificance of all lagged values of the dummy, whereas Romer and Romer look at the (cumulative) effect as depicted by the impulse response function. In this regard, I would share the Romers' belief that the latter is more appropriate—a point that is relevant to the discussion below.

My main reservation concerning Shapiro's study pertains to its motivation, that is, to his reasons for devoting valuable time, energy, and ingenuity to improving upon existing estimates of the effects of the R&R dummy variable on unemployment—and, in his study, inflation. This reservation might be expressed as follows. In work conducted prior to that of Romer and Romer (1989), it was customary to use variables such as money-growth rates or interest-rate changes to measure monetary policy actions in regressions explaining macroeconomic phenomena such as inflation, output growth, or whatever.[3] Then Romer and Romer suggested the use of their disinflation dummy, with dates for its "on" values based on their reading of the Fed's "Record of Policy Action," and emphasized a motivation expressed largely[4] in terms of the putative exogeneity of this measure. But Shapiro has correctly recognized that this dummy is not plausibly exogenous, so the question that naturally arises is, what *are* its actual differences in comparison with the traditional measures? In response, one has to recognize that the traditional measures are variables that can range over a near-continuum of values, rather than assuming only one of two values, and can therefore distinguish between major and minor policy actions.[5] A second difference is that the R&R dummy recognizes as "nonzero" actions only those in a contractionary direction—decisions to be more expansionary are lumped together with normal policy behavior. And,

2. That period is 1948.2 or 1950.2 through 1987.12; Romer and Romer (1992) also extend the period through 1991.12, in which case an additional disinflation (dated December 1988) is included.

3. This statement does not pertain to studies based on vector autoregression (VAR) systems, in which all fluctuations are attributed to the innovation or "surprise" component of one of the system's variables. Except in cases in which it is presumed that only surprise components are important, which was not the presumption of Romer and Romer (1989), the VAR-type attribution seems less appropriate for answering questions of the type, Does monetary policy matter? A recent study that includes the R&R dummy in a VAR context is Leeper (1993).

4. But not exclusively.

5. In this regard, Shapiro's finding that inflation appears not to respond to disinflation decisions (except in the Volcker case) may be a manifestation of the inadequacy of the 0–1 dummy as compared with a measure reflecting different degrees of intensity. The Volcker disinflation was, I think most observers would agree, a larger and more sustained action than the others in the sample.

third, values of the R&R dummy are based on what it is that the members of the Federal Open Market Committee *say*, not on what it is that the Open-Market desk actually *does*. Since the dummy is not exogenous, these seem to me to be the main differences—that the R&R dummy reflects changes in only one direction, does not reflect the intensity of policy actions, and is based on statements rather than actions. Thus one is led to wonder how use of this dummy, instead of a traditional measure, constitutes an improvement over previous practice. My tentative view would be that it does not.

But use of the disinflation policy dummy was not the only novelty of the Romer and Romer (1989) study. Also unusual was the decision to include many[6] lagged values of the policy variable and to retain them, even when virtually all are individually insignificant in terms of explanatory power, while focusing attention on the impulse response function that measures the cumulative effect of the policy variable. This aspect of the Romers' approach is conceptually distinct from their use of the policy dummy, and strikes this reviewer as the more important contribution. Be that as it may, this part of the Romer and Romer strategy would evidently be just as appropriate in combination with one of the traditional policy measures as it is with the R&R dummy.[7]

Similarly, any reservations that one might have about the merits of the R&R dummy do not negate the value of Shapiro's procedure, which involves construction of an instrumental variable based on predetermined determinants of policy actions. This procedure for taking account of the endogeneity of policy responses should be applicable whether the researcher is using a dummy variable or a more conventional measure of policy actions.

References

Dotsey, Michael, and Milton Reid. 1992. Oil shocks, monetary policy, and economic activity. *Federal Reserve Bank of Richmond Economic Review* 78 (July/August): 14–27.
Hoover, Kevin D., and Stephen J. Perez. 1992. Post hoc ergo propter hoc one more: An evaluation of "Does monetary policy matter?" in the spirit of James Tobin. Working Paper. University of California, Davis.
Romer, Christina D., and David H. Romer. 1989. Does monetary policy matter? A new test in the spirit of Friedman and Schwartz. *NBER Macroeconomics Annual.*
———. 1992. Monetary policy matters. Working Paper. University of California, Berkeley.
Leeper, Eric M. 1993. Are the Romers' monetary disturbances monetary policy shocks? Working Paper. Federal Reserve Bank of Atlanta.

6. Thirty-six, in regressions with monthly data.
7. In addition, the move away from emphasis on VAR innovations seems desirable (as mentioned above).

Contributors

Laurence Ball
Department of Economics
400 Mergenthaler Hall
3400 N. Charles St.
Johns Hopkins University
Baltimore MD 21218

Ben S. Bernanke
Woodrow Wilson School
Princeton University
Princeton, NJ 08544

Olivier Jean Blanchard
Department of Economics
Massachusetts Institute of Technology
50 Memorial Drive
Cambridge, MA 02139

Alan S. Blinder
Department of Economics
105 Fisher Hall
Princeton University
Princeton, NJ 08544

Michael F. Bryan
Research Department
Federal Reserve Bank, Cleveland
P.O. Box 6387
Cleveland, OH 44101

Stephen G. Cecchetti
Ohio State University
1945 N. High St.
Columbus, OH 43210

Martin Eichenbaum
Department of Economics
Northwestern University
2003 Sheridan Rd.
Evanston, IL 60208

Martin Feldstein
NBER
1050 Massachusetts Ave.
Cambridge, MA 02138

Benjamin M. Friedman
Department of Economics
Littauer Center 127
Harvard University
Cambridge, MA 02138-5398

Robert E. Hall
Hoover Institution
Stanford University
Stanford, CA 94305

Anil K. Kashyap
Graduate School of Business
University of Chicago
1101 East 58th Street
Chicago, IL 60637

N. Gregory Mankiw
Department of Economics
Littauer 223
Harvard University
Cambridge, MA 02138

Bennett T. McCallum
Graduate School of Industrial Adminis-
    tration
Carnegie-Mellon University
Pittsburgh, PA 15213

Jeffrey A. Miron
Department of Economics
Boston University
270 Bay State Rd.
Boston, MA 02215

Christina D. Romer
Department of Economics
787 Evans Hall
University of California
Berkeley, CA 94720

Matthew D. Shapiro
Department of Economics
University of Michigan
Ann Arbor, MI 48109

Jeremy C. Stein
Sloan School of Management
E52-448
Massachusetts Institute of Technology
Cambridge, MA 02139

James H. Stock
Kennedy School of Government
Harvard University
Cambridge, MA 02138

John B. Taylor
Department of Economics
Encina Hall, 4th Floor
Stanford University
Stanford, CA 94305

David N. Weil
Department of Economics
Box B
Brown University
Providence, RI 02912

Kenneth D. West
Department of Economics
7458 Social Science Building
1180 Observatory Dr.
University of Wisconsin
Madison, WI 53706

Michael Woodford
Department of Economics
University of Chicago
1126 East 59th St.
Chicago, IL 60637

Stephen P. Zeldes
Department of Finance
The Wharton School
University of Pennsylvania
3620 Locust Walk
Philadelphia, PA 19104

Author Index

Subject Index